EE 1'96			
FE 1 9'96			

The Historical Figure of Jesus

E. P. SANDERS

The Historical Figure of Jesus

**ALLEN LANE
THE PENGUIN PRESS**

ALLEN LANE
THE PENGUIN PRESS

Published by the Penguin Group
Penguin Books Ltd, 27 Wrights Lane, London w8 5tz, England
Penguin Books USA Inc., 375 Hudson Street, New York, New York 10014, USA
Penguin Books Australia Ltd, Ringwood, Victoria, Australia
Penguin Books Canada Ltd, 10 Alcorn Avenue, Toronto, Ontario, Canada m4v 3b2
Penguin Books (NZ) Ltd, 182–190 Wairau Road, Auckland 10, New Zealand

Penguin Books Ltd, Registered Offices: Harmondsworth, Middlesex, England

First published 1993
1 3 5 7 9 10 8 6 4 2
First edition

Filmset in 10/12 pt Monotype Bembo
Typeset by Datix International Limited, Bungay, Suffolk
Printed in England by Clays Ltd, St Ives plc

A CIP catalogue record for this book is available from the British Library

ISBN 0–713–99059–7

For Jack and Susan

CONTENTS

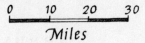

Miles

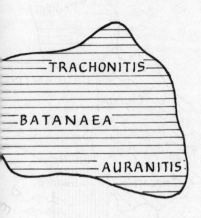

TRACHONITIS

BATANAEA

AURANITIS

D
E
C
A
P
O
L
I
S

Palestine in the time of Jesus

—————— *Border of Herod's realm*

To Archelaus

To Herod Antipas

To Philip

To Province of Syria

Salome's portion

ABBREVIATIONS

—————

Antiq.	Josephus, *Jewish Antiquities*, in Josephus' *Works*, edited and translated by H. St J. Thackeray, Ralph Marcus, Allen Wikgren and Louis Feldman, Loeb Classical Library, 10 vols., London and Cambridge MA, 1926–65
BCE	Before the Common Era (= BC)
CE	Common Era (= AD)
HJP	Emil Schürer, *History of the Jewish People in the Age of Jesus Christ*, revised and edited by Geza Vermes, Fergus Millar and Martin Goodman, 3 vols. in 4 parts, Edinburgh, 1973–87
J&J	E. P. Sanders, *Jesus and Judaism*, London and Philadelphia, 1985
JLJM	E. P. Sanders, *Jewish Law from Jesus to the Mishnah: Five Studies*, London and Philadelphia, 1990
NRSV	New Revised Standard Version of the Bible
P&B	E. P. Sanders, *Judaism: Practice and Belief, 63 BCE–66 CE*, London and Philadelphia, 1992
RSV	Revised Standard Version of the Bible
SSG	E. P. Sanders and Margaret Davies, *Studying the Synoptic Gospels*, London and Philadelphia, 1989
War	Josephus, *The Jewish War*, Josephus' *Works* (as above)
//	Parallel to (Matt. 9.14–17 // Mark 2.18–22 means that the passages are parallel to each other)

CHRONOLOGICAL TABLE

===

597 BCE	Conquest of Jerusalem by Nebuchadnezzar of Babylon; leading Jews taken to exile in Babylonia
559–332	Palestine under Persian rule
538	Beginning of the return to Jerusalem
520–515	Rebuilding of the Temple
333–332	Conquest of Palestine by Alexander the Great
c. 300–198	Palestine under Ptolemies of Egypt
198–142	Palestine under Seleucids of Syria
175–164	Antiochus IV (Epiphanes), king of Syria
167	Profanation of the Temple; beginning of Hasmonean (Maccabean) revolt
166–142	Hasmonean struggle for full autonomy
142–37	The Hasmonean period
63	Conquest of Judaea by Pompey
63–40	Hyrcanus II high priest and ethnarch
40–37	Antigonus high priest and king
37–4	Herod the Great king
31	Battle of Actium: Octavian (later titled Augustus) becomes supreme over the Roman empire
4 BCE–6 CE	Archelaus ethnarch, ruler of Judaea
4 BCE–39 CE	Antipas tetrarch, ruler of Galilee and Peraea
c. 4 BCE	**Birth of Jesus of Nazareth**
6–41 CE	Judaea governed by Roman prefects
14	Tiberius succeeds Augustus as emperor
c. 18–36	Joseph Caiaphas Jewish high priest
26–36	Pontius Pilate prefect of Judaea
c. 30	**Death of Jesus**
37	Gaius (Caligula) succeeds Tiberius as emperor

41	Claudius succeeds Gaius
41–44	Agrippa I king, ruling over Herod's former kingdom
44–66	Judaea, Samaria and part of Galilee ruled by Roman procurators
48–66	Agrippa II given piecemeal parts of his father's kingdom
66–74	Jewish revolt against Rome
70	Fall of Jerusalem, destruction of Temple

PREFACE

Most scholars who write about the ancient world feel obliged to warn their readers that our knowledge can be at best partial and that certainty is seldom attained. A book about a first-century Jew who lived in a rather unimportant part of the Roman empire must be prefaced by such a warning. We know about Jesus from books written a few decades after his death, probably by people who were not among his followers during his lifetime. They quote him in Greek, which was not his primary language, and in any case the differences among our sources show that his words and deeds were not perfectly preserved. We have very little information about him apart from the works written to glorify him. Today we do not have good documentation for such out-of-the-way places as Palestine; nor did the authors of our sources. They had no archives and no official records of any kind. They did not even have access to good maps. These limitations, which were common in the ancient world, result in a good deal of uncertainty.

Recognizing these difficulties and many others, New Testament scholars spent several decades – from about 1910 to 1970 – saying that we know somewhere between very little and virtually nothing about the historical Jesus. Excess leads to reaction, and in recent decades we have grown more confident. Confidence, in fact, has soared, and recent scholarly literature contains what I regard as rash and unfounded assertions about Jesus – hypotheses without evidence to support them.

My own view is that studying the gospels is extremely hard work. I sympathize with the scholars who despaired of recovering much good evidence about Jesus. I also think, however, that the work pays off in the modest ways that are to be expected in the study of ancient history.

The present book gives an account of the difficulties and the fairly modest results, those that I regard as both basic and relatively secure – quite secure in relation to the rest of our knowledge about ancient Palestine in general and Jewish religious figures in particular. We know a lot about Jesus, vastly more than about John the Baptist, Theudas, Judas the Galilean, or any of the other figures whose names we have from approximately his time and place.

While I was writing, I was aware that the pages of introductory material were piling up. Despite my intention to reduce them, they steadily increased in number from draft to draft. I still wish that the reader could get to the heart of the matter more quickly, but I think that the introductory chapters are necessary. Knowledge of the gospels remains very widespread even in our secular age, but understanding of their critical problems is less common. I hate to say that there is a difficulty without explaining what it is: this accounts for a lot of the material. I have also given a more detailed description of the political and religious setting of Jesus' life than is usual, since more often than not these topics are misrepresented in books on Jesus, whether they are written by amateurs or professionals.

I have, however, practised a few economies, especially in giving references. I avoid both debates with other scholars and bibliographical endnotes by citing my own earlier works, where I have discussed both the primary sources and secondary literature more extensively. I have also tried to hold discussion of foreign words and terms to a minimum.

Biblical quotations usually follow the Revised Standard Version, which I continue to think is the most satisfactory English translation overall, but I have occasionally used the New Revised Standard Version. I have sometimes modified the translation in order to bring out more precisely the wording of the Greek text.

Rebecca Gray read and commented on two drafts of the book, for which I am very grateful. I am indebted to Frank Crouch for preparing the index of passages and to Marlena Dare for typing it. I wish also to thank Peter Carson and Miranda McAllister of Penguin Books for very helpful advice and a good deal of patience, and Donna Poppy for her meticulous work on the typescript.

I. INTRODUCTION

On a spring morning in about the year 30 CE, three men were executed by the Roman authorities in Judaea. Two were 'brigands', men who may have been robbers, bandits or highwaymen, interested only in their own profit, but who also may have been insurgents, whose banditry had a political aim. The third was executed as another type of political criminal. He had not robbed, pillaged, murdered or even stored arms. He was convicted, however, of having claimed to be 'king of the Jews' – a political title. Those who looked on, among whom were some of the women who had followed the third man, doubtless thought that their hopes for a successful 'insurgency' had been destroyed and that the world would little note what happened that spring morning. For quite some time the world – as represented by the literary remains of the elite members of the Roman empire – did indeed take very little note. It turned out, of course, that the third man, Jesus of Nazareth, would become one of the most important figures in human history. Our task is to understand who he was and what he did.

I shall not try to explain why, in the centuries since his death, he has been so important. That is another question, one that requires the study of the development of Christian theology during the centuries after Jesus' execution, especially the next four centuries. Jesus became the centre of a new religion, and he became a *theological* figure: not just the historical founder of a religious movement, but someone whose person and work were the subject of philosophical and theological thought. For almost 2,000 years most Christians have regarded Jesus' teaching and other activities in Palestine as less important than his relationship to God the Father and the significance that God attributed to his life and especially to his death: he died as a sacrifice for the sins of the whole world.

I shall say a few more words about the Christ of the Christian creeds in ch. 10, and here I wish only to explain that this book is not a theology. I shall discuss neither what God accomplished or did not accomplish through the life and death of Jesus, nor how Jesus partakes or does not partake of divinity. I shall discuss Jesus the human being, who lived in a particular time and place, and I shall search for evidence and propose explanations just as does any historian when writing about a figure of history.

In another sense, to be sure, theology will be important in this work. Jesus had theological ideas, as did his followers. The people who transmitted and developed the traditions about Jesus, and the authors of the gospels, gave him an important place in their understanding of God's action in the world. I shall occasionally discuss the theology of the earliest Christians because it is necessary to do so in order to analyse what they wrote about Jesus, and I shall discuss more extensively Jesus' own theology because that is very much a part of who he was. I shall not, however, try to square these theologies with later Christian dogma. I believe that there were continuities between what Jesus himself thought and what his disciples thought after his death, and between what they thought and what the Christians of later centuries believed. But there were also changes and developments. We shall not follow this interesting story beyond the date of the last gospel, approximately the year 80.

Jesus' own theology and the theologies of his first followers are historical questions, which are to be explored in the same way as one studies what Jefferson thought about liberty, what Churchill thought about the labour movement and the strikes of 1910 and 1911, what Alexander the Great thought about the union of Greek and Persian in one empire, and what their contemporaries thought about these great men while they still lived.

Since some readers will be unaccustomed to exploring the life and thought of Jesus historically, I wish to set the present work in perspective by saying a few words about the other topics just mentioned. They involve different degrees of difficulty, and they require the use of different types of material. Jefferson on liberty and government is a large topic, one that requires careful study, but one on which the documentation is very good, partly because of Jefferson's large correspondence, which has been carefully preserved.[1] Churchill's actions with regard to a miners' strike in 1910 and a railway strike in 1911, and in particular his orders to the police and the army about the use of force, were widely discussed in the press at the time, and popular views developed that have continued to this day but that are often incorrect. The historian must carefully evaluate the various accounts, including rumours and gossip, in order to establish precisely what Churchill did and what he thought of issues that aroused great passions. It appears that a full study of all the documents, both public and private, largely exonerates him of the accusations against him.[2] What Alexander the Great thought about his unparalleled conquests is a murky question, one that cannot be decisively answered on the basis of present evidence. We know that he conquered the Persian empire, that he married a Persian princess, and that he ordered some of his officers also to marry Persian noblewomen. But just what he thought lies beyond our grasp. We may infer, in general, that he sought some kind of union or harmony between his Macedonian officers and the Persian nobility, but we cannot say precisely what he wanted.[3]

All of these questions are like questions about Jesus in one basic respect: the chief characters are legendary figures. People talked about them and passed on stories about them during their own lifetimes, and the passing of the years has enhanced some aspects of their lives, while causing others to be largely forgotten. In the study of Jefferson or Churchill, the scholar has excellent sources for getting behind legend and hearsay. The biographer of Jefferson has an extremely large amount of source material, while the biographer of Churchill is almost immersed in evidence. Finding out what Jesus thought is much closer to the quest for the historical Alexander. Nothing survives that was written by Jesus himself. The more or less contemporary documents, apart from those in the New Testament, shed virtually no light on Jesus' life or death, though they reveal a lot about the social and political climate. The main sources for our knowledge of Jesus himself, the gospels in the New Testament, are, from the point of view of the historian, tainted by the fact that they were written by people who intended to glorify their hero. The sources for Jesus are better, however, than those that deal with Alexander. The original biographies of Alexander have all been lost, and they are known only because they were used by later – much later – writers.[4] The primary sources for Jesus were written nearer his own lifetime, and people who had known him were still alive. That is one of the reasons for saying that in some ways we know more about Jesus than about Alexander. On the other hand, Alexander so greatly altered the political situation in a large part of the world that the main outline of his public life is very well known indeed. Jesus did not change the social, political and economic circumstances of Palestine. Despite this, as we shall see more fully below, we have a good idea of the external course of his life, especially his public career. The superiority of the evidence for Jesus is seen when we ask what he thought. His followers started a movement that was based in part on what Jesus himself had taught and done. If we can discover which of their ideas they derived from Jesus, we shall know a lot about his thinking. Diligent study of the gospels can often distinguish the deposit of Jesus' own views from the views of his followers, as we shall see more fully below.[5] Our confidence is increased by the fact that some of our sources are independent of one another. Paul gives important evidence that reveals some of Jesus' views and expectations, and Paul's letters were written before the gospels. On the other hand, his letters were collected and published after the gospels were written; thus Paul did not know the gospels, and the authors of the gospels did not know Paul's letters.

Nevertheless, our sources leave a lot to be desired. The gospels report Jesus' sayings and actions in a language that was not his own (he taught in Aramaic, the gospels are in Greek), and they place each piece of information into a setting devised by his followers, usually by followers at one remove. Even if we knew that we have his own words, we would still have to fear that he was quoted out of context.[6]

The historian who studies a great human being, and reports fully on his or her findings, will almost certainly write at least a few things that some admirers would rather not read. People whose image of Jefferson has been created by imagining the character of the author of the Declaration of Independence may be shocked by a study of his love life and his consumption of alcohol. Those who think of Churchill as the man who 'marshalled the English language and sent it off to war' (as John Kennedy said of him) will find a description of Churchill the domestic politician less appealing. This is not a warning that I am going to 'expose' something truly shocking about Jesus, such as sexual promiscuity. I shall stay with the evidence, which is completely silent on such topics. If Jesus had any serious faults, they are beyond retrieval. I shall not, however, write only about how nice he was, nor shall I ignore the aspects of his life and thought that many of his most ardent admirers wish would go away. We have to understand why he stirred up controversy and why he had enemies. The traditional Christian view that other Jews hated him because he was good, and because he favoured love, which they opposed, will not do. I shall try to deal with him and his contemporaries more realistically than that.

The search for the Jesus of history is now over 200 years old. At the end of the eighteenth century a few brave Europeans began to apply literary and historical criticism to the books of the New Testament, which until then had been off-limits: too sacred for the secular scholarship of the Renaissance and the Enlightenment.[7] Reading the accounts of Jesus that have been written by earnest and dedicated scholars during this 200-year period reveals that conclusions have been remarkably diverse, a fact that leads many to the view that we do not really know anything. This is an over-reaction; we know quite a lot. The problem is to reconcile our knowledge with our hopes and aspirations. Because of the subsequent importance of Jesus and the movement that he initiated, we want to know everything about him, especially his inmost thoughts, such as what he thought of himself. As I indicated above, I think that we have good evidence for some of the things that Jesus thought. But inmost thoughts, even those of people whose public lives are well documented, are usually elusive. What did Lincoln really think, deep in his heart, about the emancipation of slaves? This is a difficult question, though we have a lot of material about Lincoln, and we know what he did and what the effects were. Similarly with Jesus, though our documentation is less thorough: we know some of the things he did, a fair amount about what he taught, and a great deal about the effects. We must then try to infer what he thought, deep inside. We should not shy away from such inferences, but we should recognize that they are less certain than are his words and deeds – which are difficult enough to ascertain with certainty.

The aim of this book is to lay out, as clearly as possible, what we can know, using the standard methods of historical research, and to distinguish this from inferences, labelling them clearly as such. The general discussions of Jesus' miracles and teaching will incorporate some passages whose reliability I doubt (as I shall make clear in the appropriate places), but the evidence that I regard as certain will control the topics, the categories and the conclusions.

This aim is modest, but fulfilling it is difficult. Authors often wish to dwell on the complexities of their subjects, so as to elicit the reader's sympathy. Certainly I hope for sympathetic readers, but I also think that books about Jesus actually are harder to write than are books about other people for whom we have comparable documentation. I have already indicated that people who are content with general information about other ancient figures want to know much more about Jesus. There are other special problems. One is that the primary sources, the gospels of the New Testament, have been very widely read and are immediately available to the reading public. This requires the author to explain in some detail how he uses the sources, a task that the biographer of other ancient figures can deal with briefly or even omit altogether. All historians have views of their sources, but usually they have to explain them only to other scholars. Discussion of the problems posed by ancient sources is almost necessarily technical, and this imposes an extra burden on author and reader. A more important problem is that virtually everyone has his or her own view of Jesus, and thus has a preconception of what a book on Jesus should say. With very few exceptions, these views are extremely favourable. People want to agree with Jesus, and this often means that they see him as agreeing with themselves.

Jesus' ethical teaching in particular has drawn praise from almost all quarters. The teaching collected in the Sermon on the Mount (Matt. 5–7), especially the commandments to love one's enemies and to turn the other cheek, along with the parables in Luke, such as the story of the Good Samaritan, have often served as the summary of true religion in the thinking of the great and famous, including those who were out of sympathy with all or much of organized religion. Thomas Jefferson was the enemy of an established church (that is, an official religion of the state), and this view became part of the United States Constitution; but Jefferson went even further. He wrote that he had 'sworn upon the altar of God, eternal hostility against every form of tyranny over the mind of man', including in particular the doctrines of many Christian denominations.[8] Jesus, however, he regarded as a 'master workman', whose 'system of morality was the most benevolent and sublime probably that has been ever taught'. Jesus, Jefferson held, was 'sensible of the incorrectness of his forbears' ideas of the Deity, and of morality', and he had 'endeavored to bring them to the principles of a pure deism, and juster notions of the attributes of God, to reform their moral doctrines to the standard of reason, justice, and philanthropy, and to inculcate the belief of a future state'.[9] Jesus, that is, was very much like Jefferson.

Charles Dickens was scathing about the Victorian church. On an autumn day in Coketown (Dickens' fictional city in which all the social and ecological disasters of the industrial revolution were to be seen), he wrote, 'there were larks singing (though it was Sunday)'.[10] In an extended passage in *Little Dorrit* Dickens dwelt on the horrors of Sunday. One character, Clennam, recalls a legion of past Sundays, 'all days of unserviceable bitterness and mortification'. The novelist contrasted the dreary Victorian sabbaths, however, with 'the beneficent history of the New Testament', of which Clennam had learned nothing during the hours he had spent in church.[11] Near the end of the book, the heroine urges the harsh Mrs Clennam not to cling to her vindictive religion, but to 'be guided only by the healer of the sick, the raiser of the dead, the friend of all who were afflicted and forlorn, the patient Master who shed tears of compassion for our infirmities'. Dickens' dislike of Sunday did not extend to Jesus. Sundays may have been dismal in Coketown, but the real problem was that the men in control, such as Mr Gradgrind, thought 'that the Good Samaritan was a Bad Economist'.[12]

Winston Churchill, though he did not dislike official Christianity, took the same view of Jesus. According to a diarist, during a long talk with Harry Hopkins and others in 1941, Churchill discussed the task of rebuilding the world when the war would finally end. 'We could find nothing better than Christian Ethics on which to build and the more closely we followed the Sermon on the Mount, the more likely we were to succeed in our endeavours.'[13] Eleven years later Churchill still regarded the Sermon on the Mount as 'the last word in ethics'.[14]

The general approval of Jesus shows how well the authors of the gospels did their job. They intended people to turn to him, to admire him, and to believe that he was sent from God and that following him would lead to eternal life. Seldom have hopes been more completely fulfilled. In the view of the authors, admiration of Jesus and belief in him went together. Matthew and Luke (to whom we owe the Sermon on the Mount and the Good Samaritan) would not have appreciated having Jesus' teaching separated from their own theological conviction that God sent him to save the world. Nevertheless, the way in which they composed their books allows the reader to pick and choose, and many readers have done so, admiring Jesus but disagreeing with Christian theology. In such cases, at least some of the evangelists'* aims have been fulfilled.

It falls to the lot of the historian to be the person who subjects the gospels to rough handling. The historian may or may not assent to the theology of the gospels, the view that *God* acted through Jesus. In either case, he or she must be aware that the authors had theological convictions and that they may have revised their accounts to support their theology. The historian must also suspect that the ethical teaching that has so impressed the world has been enhanced by homiletical use and editorial improvements between the time of Jesus and the publication of the gospels. Apart from these suspicions, the scholar has a professional obligation to subject sources to rigorous cross-examination: 'You *say* that "every Jerusalem-ite" went out to hear John the Baptist (Mark 1.5) and that Jesus healed "every disease and every sickness" (Matt. 4.23). I submit to you that you grossly exaggerate.' In these two passages, of course, the historian only observes rhetorical exaggeration. But the questions must go on: 'You *say* that his enemies were full of malice and deceit. I submit to you that some of them were sincere, honest and devout, and that therefore the conflict was not as simple as a Western movie, in which some people wear white hats and others black.' And so on, through the whole account. That is, the historian, unlike the politician, novelist or moralist, cannot pick and choose just those parts of the gospels that are noble and that can be used to inspire others. The historian selects, but on different principles: what can be proved, what disproved, what lies in between?

The plan of what follows is this. In the next five chapters there is

---

* 'Evangelist' in this work means 'author of one of the gospels'. It is not perfect, but I think that it is slightly better than 'gospeller'.

further introductory material: ch. 2 is a preliminary sketch of Jesus' life and times; ch. 3 is a brief account of the political situation in first-century Palestine; ch. 4 contains a few basic points about Judaism as a religion; chs. 5 and 6 discuss some of the difficulties of our sources. The substance of the book will be chapters that attempt an historical reconstruction of Jesus' activities, his teaching, his conflicts with others and his death. An epilogue will offer reflections on the stories of his resurrection.

2. AN OUTLINE OF
JESUS' LIFE

As I have just indicated, there is a lot of introductory material to cover before we can begin the detailed exploration of Jesus' activity and message. We shall have to describe the political and religious world into which he was born and the nature and problems of our sources. It may be useful, however, to begin with a very brief sketch of his life, which will serve partly as a framework and partly as a launching pad for a fuller account. I shall add a paragraph on how the disciples viewed Jesus' life in retrospect, which we need to be aware of, though that is not the subject of the book.

There are no substantial doubts about the general course of Jesus' life: when and where he lived, approximately when and where he died, and the sort of thing that he did during his public activity. When we begin to probe beneath the surface, difficulties and uncertainties arise, but for the present we shall stay on the surface. I shall first offer a list of statements about Jesus that meet two standards: they are almost beyond dispute; and they belong to the framework of his life, and especially of his public career. (A list of everything that we know about Jesus would be appreciably longer.)

Jesus was born *c.* 4 BCE, near the time of the death of
    Herod the Great;
he spent his childhood and early adult years in Nazareth, a
    Galilean village;
he was baptized by John the Baptist;
he called disciples;
he taught in the towns, villages and countryside of Galilee
    (apparently not the cities);
he preached 'the kingdom of God';
about the year 30 he went to Jerusalem for Passover;

he created a disturbance in the Temple area;

he had a final meal with the disciples;

he was arrested and interrogated by Jewish authorities, specifically
the high priest;

he was executed on the orders of the Roman prefect, Pontius
Pilate.

We may add here a short list of equally secure facts about the
aftermath of Jesus' life:

his disciples at first fled;

they saw him (in what sense is not certain) after his death;

as a consequence, they believed that he would return to found
the kingdom;

they formed a community to await his return and sought to win
others to faith in him as God's Messiah.

Most of the items on this list will be the subject of fuller discussion
later in the book. Now I shall supplement the outline with a short
narrative summary.

The year of Jesus' birth is not entirely certain. We shall return to
the birth narratives in Matthew and Luke later, but here I shall say a
few things about the date. Most scholars, I among them, think that
the decisive fact is that Matthew dates Jesus' birth at about the time
Herod the Great died. This was in the year 4 BCE, and so Jesus was
born in that year or shortly before it; some scholars prefer 5, 6 or
even 7 BCE.

That Jesus was born a few years before the beginning of the era
that starts with his birth is one of the minor curiosities of history. In
this work I use the letters BCE and CE to mean 'Before the
Common Era' and 'Common Era'. ('Common' means 'accepted by
all, including non-Christians'.) The traditional abbreviations, however, are BC and AD, 'Before Christ' and 'Anno Domini' ('in the
year of the Lord'). These letters divide history into years before
Jesus was born and after his birth. How, then, could he have been
born 4 BC (or BCE)? In the sixth century a Scythian monk who
was resident in Rome, Dionysius Exiguus, introduced a liturgical
calendar that counted years 'from the incarnation' (the birth of
Jesus) rather than according to the system established by the pagan
Roman emperor Diocletian. Dionysius' information, however, was

limited. He could fix neither the death of Herod (Matt. 2) nor the census of Quirinius (Luke 2) precisely, and he seems to have made an estimate based on other information in Luke: John the Baptist, who preceded Jesus, began preaching in the fifteenth year of Tiberius (Luke 3.1); Jesus was about thirty years old when he began his ministry (Luke 3.23). The fifteenth year of Tiberius was (by modern reckoning) 29 CE; if Dionysius Exiguus allowed one year for John the Baptist's mission, he would have concluded that Jesus began his ministry in 30 CE. If Jesus was precisely thirty years old at the time, he was born in the year 1. This is probably the reasoning that led to our present calendar.[1] Modern scholars note that Jesus' age in Luke 3.23 is a round number, and that Luke as well as Matthew sets the beginning of the story 'in the days of Herod the king' (Luke 1.5). As I just indicated, this seems to be the firmest piece of evidence regarding the time of Jesus' birth. The calendar based on Dionysius' calculation, however, which was not based on the date of Herod's death, gained general support in the sixth and subsequent centuries, with the result that scholars now date Jesus' birth a few years 'Before Christ'.

Jesus lived with his parents in Nazareth, a Galilean village. One of Herod the Great's heirs, Antipas, was the ruler of Galilee for the entirety of Jesus' life (except for the very earliest period, when Herod the Great was still alive). It is a strong possibility that virtually all of Jesus' active ministry, except the last two or three weeks, was carried out in Antipas' Galilee.[2] Jesus was not an urbanite. The cities of Galilee – Sepphoris, Tiberias and Scythopolis (Hebrew, Beth-Shean) – do not figure in the accounts of his activities.[3] He doubtless knew Sepphoris, which was only a few miles from Nazareth, but he nevertheless seems to have regarded his mission as being best directed to the Jews in the villages and small towns of Galilee. Nazareth itself was quite a small village. It was in the hill country, away from the Sea of Galilee, but Jesus taught principally in the villages and towns on the sea. Some of his followers were fishermen. Rural images are fairly frequent in the teaching that is ascribed to him.

When Jesus was a young man, probably in his late twenties, John the Baptist began preaching in or near Galilee. He proclaimed the urgent need to repent in view of the coming judgement. Jesus heard John and felt called to accept his baptism. All four gospels point to this as an event that transformed Jesus' life. According to Mark's account, Jesus 'saw the heavens opened and the Spirit descending upon him like a dove'; he also heard a voice saying, 'You are my beloved son' (Mark 1.9–11).

Antipas arrested John because he had criticized his marriage to Herodias (the gospels) or because he feared that the Baptist's preaching would lead to insurrection (Josephus)[4] – or both. At about that time Jesus began his public ministry. Whereas John had worked outside settled areas, Jesus went from town to town, village to village, usually preaching in synagogues on the sabbath. He called a small number of people to be his disciples, and they joined him in his travels. Unlike John, Jesus not only preached but also healed the sick. He developed a reputation, and people thronged to see him. Soon he too had to preach in open areas because of the crowds.

We do not know just how long this itinerant ministry continued, but apparently it lasted only one or possibly two years. After preaching and healing for this period of time in Galilee, Jesus, with his disciples and some other followers, went to Jerusalem for Passover. Jerusalem was in Judaea, which, unlike Galilee, was a Roman province. Jerusalem itself was governed by the Jewish high priest, who was responsible to a Roman prefect. Jesus rode into the city on an ass, and some people hailed him as 'son of David'.[5] When he went to the Temple, he attacked the money-changers and dove-sellers. The high priest and his advisers determined that Jesus was dangerous and had to die. After the Passover meal with his disciples, Jesus went apart to pray. One of his followers had betrayed him, and the high priest's guards arrested him. He was tried, after a fashion, and turned over to the Roman prefect, with the recommendation that he be executed. After a brief hearing, the prefect ordered his execution. He was crucified as an insurgent, along with two others.

He died after a relatively brief period of suffering. A few of his followers placed him in a tomb. According to some reports, when they returned two days later to anoint his body, they found the tomb empty. Thereafter his followers saw him. These resurrection experiences convinced them that Jesus would return and that in Jesus' life and death God had acted to save humanity. The disciples began to persuade others to put their faith in Jesus. They gave him various titles, including 'Anointed' (which is 'Messiah' in Hebrew and 'Christ' in Greek), 'Lord' and 'Son of God'. These titles reveal that, as the decades passed, Jesus' disciples and their converts developed various views of Jesus' relation to God and of his significance in God's plan for Israel and the world. Their movement finally separated from Judaism and became the Christian church. When the gospels were written, however, Christology (theological explanations of the person and work of Jesus) was at an early stage, and the separation of Christianity from Judaism not yet complete.

To repeat: every sentence of this sketch requires explanation, and we shall examine most of these points in some detail. Now we must set the stage by explaining the political and religious conditions of Palestine at the time, and then by considering the sources of our information about Jesus.

3. POLITICAL SETTING

Jesus was born when Rome was supreme over the eastern Mediterranean. A Roman administrator ordered his execution. For most of his life, however, he had not been subject to direct orders from Roman officials. We shall examine the political environment in which he lived and worked, since we need to know who had authority over various aspects of life in the different parts of Palestine. There was a three-fold division of power during the late twenties and early thirties. Herod Antipas was the tetrarch of Galilee and Peraea; Pontius Pilate was the prefect of Judaea (which at this time included three geographical regions: Samaria, Judaea and Idumaea); Joseph Caiaphas was the high priest in Jerusalem. This division will be easier to understand if we begin with a short survey of the political history that led up to it. First, however, I shall introduce the man whose writings provide most of our information about Palestine in Jesus' day.

Josephus son of Mattathias was born of an aristocratic priestly family in the year 37 CE, a few years after Jesus' execution. Josephus was extremely well educated in biblical law and history, and he had also studied the principal religious parties of his day (the Essenes, the Sadducees and the Pharisees). He showed great promise. While still a young man he was sent to Rome to persuade Nero to release some Jewish hostages. When the revolt against Rome broke out in 66 CE, he was only twenty-nine, but nevertheless he received command of Galilee. His forces were defeated, but by luck and guile he survived. He flattered the conquering general, Vespasian, by predicting that he would become emperor. When this happened, in 69, Josephus' stock went up. Vespasian's son, Titus, who completed the war against the Jews, used Josephus as an interpreter and spokesman to the Jewish defenders of Jerusalem. After the war,

Titus took Josephus to Rome, where he established him with a house and pension, and Josephus wrote the history of the war (*Jewish War*). This was published in the seventies. Later he wrote a vast history of the Jews (*Jewish Antiquities*), published in the nineties. He also wrote a defence of Judaism against its critics (*Against Apion*) and an apologetic autobiography (*Life*). By the standards of the day, he was a very good historian, and for some parts of his historical narratives he had excellent sources. The following history depends heavily on Josephus, who is the only source for much of it.[1]

Rome was the successor of earlier empires: the Persian, that of Alexander the Great, and the various Hellenistic empires that succeeded Alexander.[2] Although empires rose and fell, imperial systems did not change very much. Subject nations paid tribute to the imperial power, and in return they were protected against invasion and allowed to live in peace – if they were willing to do so. Subject states were sometimes governed by 'independent' local rulers, sometimes by an imperial governor who used local leaders for day-to-day governance. There are numerous modern analogies. In the colonial empires of the eighteenth and nineteenth centuries, the imperial nation appointed a governor and garrisoned the country with troops, but utilized natives to some extent in the bureaucracy and the police force; sometimes natives served as middlemen between the government and the populace.[3] The alternative form of imperial government was employed by the Soviet Union after the Second World War. The Soviet Union established 'independent' local governments in the countries of eastern Europe and intervened with its own military forces only when there was a serious insurrection or a substantial threat to its hegemony.

From the sixth to the mid-second century BCE, the Jews in Palestine constituted a very small nation in one of the great empires, a nation whose territory was restricted to the Judaean Hills, with no access to the sea and off the main trade routes. It was ruled by the high priest and his council, who were answerable to the imperial governor or directly to the capital city itself. During this period of approximately 400 years, there were no substantial conflicts between Judaea and the imperial power. The Jews lived peacefully under the Persians and the Hellenistic kings.

In 175 BCE, with the accession of Antiochus IV Epiphanes to the throne of the Seleucid empire, centred in Antioch, this began to change. In Jerusalem, some of the aristocratic priests wanted to adopt a more Hellenistic style of life, including the introduction of a *gymnasion*, one of the primary institutions of Greek civilization. Here boys and youths were educated, and as part of their education they exercised in the nude. This brought into prominence a major difference between Hellenistic and Jewish culture: Jewish males were circumcised, as a sign of the covenant between God and Abraham (Gen. 17), while the Greeks, believing in a sound mind in a sound body, abominated circumcision as mutilation. Some Jews had an operation to disguise their circumcision (I Macc. 1.14f.).

Such extreme steps led to a reaction. Jews had not been opposed to all forms of foreign influence. During the Persian period they had adopted numerous aspects of Persian religion and culture, and by 175 they had also accepted some aspects of Hellenism. The *gymnasion*, however, was too much, since it led to removal of circumcision, the sign of the covenant. We shall not trace subsequent events in detail. The Jewish reaction resulted in direct measures by Antiochus IV to force Hellenization on the Jews. The Temple in Jerusalem was defiled by pagan sacrifice, Jews were forced to sacrifice to pagan gods, and some Jews were forced to eat pork and transgress the law in other ways. This, in turn, led to a revolt, led by the Hasmoneans, a priestly family, often called 'Maccabean' because of a nickname, 'the hammerer', given to Judas, one of the brothers who led the revolt. The Hasmonean movement ultimately succeeded, being greatly aided by dynastic wars in the Seleucid empire after the death of Antiochus IV.[4]

The Hasmoneans established a new dynasty. They ruled Jewish Palestine as high priests and eventually also took the title 'king'. The fully independent Jewish state lasted about a hundred years, during which time Hasmonean priest-kings vastly enlarged the territory, until finally it became approximately the same size as David's kingdom. The end of Jewish independence came as the result of internecine strife between two Hasmonean brothers, Hyrcanus II and Aristobulus II. During their struggle for power, both appealed to the Roman general Pompey for support. He responded by conquering Jerusalem and detaching some of the territory recently won by conquest (63 BCE). He appointed Hyrcanus II high priest and 'ethnarch' ('ruler of the nation', a lesser title than 'king'), and he also installed an Idumaean, Antipater, as a kind of military governor. Antipater subsequently appointed two of his sons, Phasael and Herod (later to be known as Herod the Great), as governors of Judaea and Galilee respectively.

Pompey's invasion changed the status of the Jewish government. It was no longer fully independent, but instead was semi-independent. Hyrcanus II became a 'client' ruler. He paid tribute to Rome and was obliged to support Roman policies and military actions in the eastern Mediterranean. In return, he was allowed autonomy within his borders, and Rome was tacitly committed to protecting him and maintaining him in office. Aristobulus II was not happy with this settlement. He and his son, Antigonus, revolted. Aristobulus was assassinated by friends of Pompey, but his son continued the struggle, allying himself with the Parthians, the principal military threat to Rome at this period. In 40 BCE they overran the Near East, captured Hyrcanus II and Phasael, and established Antigonus as king and high priest. Herod fled and managed to reach Rome. Supported by Mark Antony and Octavian (later titled Augustus), Herod was declared king of Judaea by the Roman Senate, and he also received the support of Roman troops so that he could claim his crown.[5]

Herod was chosen because he was strong, an excellent soldier, and loyal to Rome; but his appointment was also in keeping with Roman imperial policy. Herod had been a supporter of Hyrcanus II, who had been Rome's original choice. In appointing Herod and lending him troops, Rome was protecting its client and opposing the side of Aristobulus II and Antigonus, who had allied himself with Rome's enemy. Herod, with Roman troops, won the civil war. The victorious king sent Antigonus to Mark Antony, who had him executed, and by the year 37 had established Jewish Palestine again as an 'independent' state – that is, a semi-independent client kingdom.

I have wanted to emphasize the relative independence of Jewish Palestine since New Testament scholars in particular often think of Rome as 'ruling' and 'occupying' Palestine in Jesus' day, with soldiers on the street corners. The situation varied from time to time and place to place (as we shall see), but Rome generally governed remotely, being content with the collection of tribute and the maintenance of stable borders; for the most part it left even these matters in the hands of loyal local rulers and leaders.[6]

Herod and his family were Idumaeans, from a region just south of Judaea, which had been conquered by Jewish arms during the Hasmonean period. Many Jews regarded him as only half Jewish, and they resented his reign. Moreover, he had supplanted the Hasmonean family, which, though partially discredited by internecine strife, still commanded the loyalty of much of the populace. Herod married Mariamme, a Hasmonean princess, but he realized that this was not enough to endear him to the nation. He feared a revolt, and over the course of several years he eliminated the remaining Hasmoneans, including Mariamme and his two sons by her.

Once he had conquered Palestine, he ruled it effectively until his death thirty-three years later. The Roman troops who had aided his conquest went elsewhere, and Herod was fully master of his own house. He could not, of course, act against the interests of Rome. On crucial points, Augustus had the last word; but otherwise Herod ran his kingdom as he wished. He engaged in great building schemes, which employed tens of thousands of workers, he increased trade and made crown lands more prosperous, and he ruthlessly suppressed all opposition, even minor protests. By the end of his life, he had executed three of his sons because he suspected them of treason. Augustus, who had approved the trial of the first two sons, remarked that he would rather be Herod's pig than his son;[7] Herod kept the Jewish law fairly carefully, and he did not eat pork.

Herod was, on balance, a good king. I do not mean that we should accord him our moral approbation, but that by the standards of the day his faults were not so bad, and they were partly offset by better qualities. The ideals that motivate modern democracies had not arisen. In comparison to one of his patrons, Augustus, Herod was unnecessarily brutal and short-sighted. Were we to compare Herod to the next four Roman emperors (Tiberius, Caligula, Claudius, and Nero), however, he would appear almost lenient and merciful, and he was more effective as a ruler. He qualifies as a good king on balance because he raised Jewish Palestine to a new prominence throughout the world, he continued his father's policy of obtaining benefits for Jews outside of Palestine, he did not allow civil war – which had marred the Hasmonean period and would flare up again during the revolt against Rome – and, perhaps most important, he kept Jewish citizens and Roman troops apart. As long as Jewish Palestine was stable and strong, Rome left it alone.

When Herod died in 4 BCE, Augustus considered his wills (he left two) and decided to divide the kingdom among three sons. Archelaus received the title 'ethnarch' and was appointed to rule Judaea, Samaria and Idumaea. Antipas and Philip were designated 'tetrarchs', 'rulers of a fourth'; Antipas inherited Galilee and Peraea, while Philip received more remote parts of Herod's kingdom. Antipas proved a good client ruler and governed Galilee for forty-three years, until 39 CE. Archelaus fared less well; his subjects protested against some of his actions, and they were vindicated when Rome deposed and exiled him (6 CE). Augustus then appointed a Roman official to govern Judaea, Samaria and Idumaea.

Herod established a minor dynasty, and it seems that his own name was assumed by (or assigned to) his successors. Just as the successors of Julius Caesar were called 'Caesar', Herod's successors were called 'Herod'. The consequence is that in the New Testament several different people are called Herod. The note identifies the various 'Herods' of the New Testament.[8] I shall always call Herod's sons and grandsons by their own names.

The Government of Galilee at the Time of Jesus

In the Galilee of Jesus' day (about 4 BCE to 30 CE), the political arrangements were the same as they had been before Herod's death. Antipas governed Galilee as his father had governed a much larger state, and on the same terms and conditions: he paid tribute, co-operated with Rome and maintained public order. In return Rome protected him against invasion: not by stationing troops in the country or on the borders, but by the implied threat of retaliation against invaders. Locally, Antipas could do whatever he wished, as long as the main conditions were fulfilled. For example, he minted his own coins – one of the principal signs of 'independence'.

Antipas, like his father, was fairly observant of the Jewish law. He had his palace decorated with figures of animals, which many Jews regarded as a transgression of the commandment prohibiting graven images; probably he regarded his palace as his own business. His coins, however, bore only agricultural designs, which Jews considered acceptable. There is no indication in any of the sources that he tried to impose Graeco-Roman customs and organizations on the Jewish populace. The institutions in the towns and villages in Galilee were thoroughly Jewish. The gospels imply that there were synagogues in all the small towns and villages. Schools were Jewish, and Jewish magistrates judged cases according to Jewish law.[9]

If Herod was a good king, on balance, Antipas was a good tetrarch. He adequately fulfilled the main conditions of successful rule. From Rome's point of view, this meant that he paid tribute, did not allow civil unrest and defended his borders (we shall note an exception to this last point just below). Consequently, Rome did not have to intervene in Galilee, and Antipas kept the Jewish citizenry and Roman troops from coming into conflict.

Josephus records no instance in which Antipas had to resort to force in order to suppress an uprising. The fact that the Jewish populace tolerated their ruler fairly well probably indicates two things. One was that he did not publicly flout the Jewish law. The single instance of semi-public disobedience, the decoration of his palace, however, had repercussions years after Antipas was deposed. At the time of the revolt against Rome, a Jewish mob destroyed the palace because of its decoration.[10] We may assume from this that many of his subjects disapproved of Antipas while he was in power, and thought that he was not a sufficiently devout Jew, but they did not revolt. The lack of uprisings also indicates that Antipas was not excessively oppressive and did not levy exorbitant taxes (that is, they were not exorbitant by the prevailing standard). Moreover, like his father, he undertook large building projects that helped reduce unemployment. Galileans in Jesus' lifetime did not feel that the things most dear to them were seriously threatened: their religion, their national traditions and their livelihoods.

Rulers such as the Herodians had to calculate how best to maintain public order. They did not have to seek popularity, though some did so. What was required, however, was that they prudently estimate what the populace would bear. For example, they wanted as much tax revenue as they could get, but they did not want a revolt because of taxes. All ancient rulers knew that, when a public controversy arose, they should sometimes placate and sometimes discipline the populace. In Judaea, Archelaus could not strike the right balance. Partly because Galilee was less difficult to govern, partly because he was more judicious than Archelaus, the tetrarch of Galilee had a long and peaceful rule.

Antipas, however, committed at least one major blunder. Since the story involves John the Baptist, who baptized Jesus, and since it illustrates Antipas' status as an 'independent' client ruler, we shall consider it. Antipas became entranced with Herodias, his half-niece, who was already married to another of her uncles, one of Antipas' half-brothers. (The Herodians frequently intermarried. Herod had ten wives, there were a good number of children, and they had lots of possibilities of forming half-blood relationships. Marriage between uncle and niece is allowed by the Hebrew Bible.[11]) To accommodate Herodias as his new wife, Antipas planned to send away his former wife. She fled to her father, Aretas, who was an Arab king. Angered, he invaded Antipas' domain and inflicted a severe defeat before withdrawing. Aretas did not come up against Roman troops, but Antipas' own army; Rome later used its troops stationed in Syria to retaliate on behalf of its client ruler.[12] Both the New Testament and Josephus connect these events to John the Baptist. According to Mark 6.17–29, John had openly criticized Antipas for marrying his brother's wife, and this led to his execution. According to Josephus, Antipas was afraid that John, who had a large following, would incite a revolt, and so he executed him. John was widely believed to be a prophet, and the populace saw Aretas' defeat of Antipas as being divine retribution against the tetrarch for executing the Baptist.[13]

In about 39 CE, years after Jesus' death, Herodias' ambition led to Antipas' fall. She was not content with his status as tetrarch and wished him to seek the title of king. He went to Rome to request this elevation, but there were accusations against him. He was found guilty of storing arms and was deposed. He and Herodias went into exile.

Judaea at the Time of Jesus

Judaea – the political entity that during this period consisted of three geographical areas, Samaria, Judaea (including Jerusalem) and Idumaea – had quite a different history in Jesus' day. Herod's successor, Archelaus, had serious difficulties with the populace because of some of his father's actions near the end of his life (Herod had executed two popular teachers and appointed an unpopular

high priest). Archelaus did not handle the matter adroi..
his attempts to placate the crowd were inadequate, while h.
to suppress dissent were not sufficiently ruthless. In any case, p.
protests eventually led to his dismissal by the Romans. To be fair ι
him, we should note that his part of Palestine was more difficult
than Antipas', since it contained both Jerusalem and Samaria. The
Jews were very sensitive about what happened in Jerusalem, and
also the large public gatherings there for religious festivals created
conditions in which riots could easily erupt. There was a good deal
of hostility between Jews and Samaritans, and this also led to
disputes.

When Augustus decided that Archelaus was not a satisfactory
client ruler of Judaea, rather than give the territory to another
member of Herod's family, he chose to appoint a governor (6 CE).
Administration was assigned to a Roman official of the equestrian
order, which we may conveniently think of as a lower aristocracy,
below the consular and praetorian orders.[14] A recently found
inscription indicates that during the period 6 to 41 CE this officer
was a 'prefect', while from 44 to 66 CE he was a 'procurator'.[15] The
prefect (as he was in Jesus' day) lived in Caesarea, on the Mediterranean coast, in one of the luxurious palaces built by Herod the
Great. The prefect had at his disposal perhaps 3,000 troops, which
was not enough to handle serious trouble. There was a small
Roman garrison in the Antonia Fortress in Jerusalem, and other
fortresses in Judaea were also lightly garrisoned, but Rome did not
actually govern Judaea on a day-to-day basis. Towns and villages
were run as they always had been: by a small group of elders, one
or more of whom served as magistrate. Difficulties that might lead
to bloodshed would cause the leading citizens to send a message to
the prefect. Substantial upheavals required the intervention of the
legate of Syria, who was superior to the Judaean prefect, and who
had large forces at his disposal (four legions, totalling appoximately
20,000 infantry, and 5,000 cavalry).[16]

The Roman prefect and additional troops came to Jerusalem
during the major festivals to ensure that the huge crowds did not
get out of hand. Public assemblies were on the whole carefully
watched in the ancient world, and the festivals in Jerusalem were
known to be hazardous. During the 150 or so years before Jesus'
death, we know of at least four substantial upheavals that began

during a festival – this despite the fact that both Jewish and Roman rulers were prepared for trouble and had forces near by.[17]

With one exception, only the prefect had the right to sentence anyone to death. Rome allowed the priests to post warning notices in the Temple, in both Greek and Latin, warning Gentiles to enter no further than a given point. Anyone who transgressed, even a Roman citizen, was subject to immediate execution, without the need to send the culprit to the prefect. Apart from this, the prefect's right to execute was not only exclusive but also absolute; he could execute even a Roman citizen, and he did not have to formulate a charge that would stand up in a court in Rome. In these outposts of empire, the prefect had to be able to do whatever he thought was necessary for the good of Rome, and this included the power to discipline the army.[18] If he had the right to execute a Roman military officer without a full Roman trial, he could treat members of the subject nation more or less any way he wished. Most prefects were judicious and did not wantonly sentence people to death. But if a prefect was unusually harsh, the subjects had only a few means of recourse. They could meet en masse and persuade their leaders to try to get the prefect to be more lenient. If supported by these leaders, they could petition the Roman legate in Syria, who might intervene. The Syrian legate, for example, could send the Palestinian prefect to Rome to answer for his actions. Finally, the subject people might be allowed to send a delegation directly to Rome. For this, they would probably need the legate's permission, and he might protect himself by holding hostages, so that he would not become the delegation's target.[19] Neither Augustus nor his successor Tiberius wanted a riot or revolt. Consequently, Rome was sometimes responsive to requests. During the approximate period of our study, Rome dismissed two native rulers (Archelaus and Antipas) and two Roman administrators, including Pilate.

We have noted that under the prefects local government was in the hands of leading citizens: in Jewish towns and villages, the effective rulers were prominent Jewish priests and laymen; in Samaritan towns and villages, they were prominent Samaritan priests and laymen. Judaea was much more complicated than Galilee, since in some cities there were large numbers of Gentiles, and one of the geographical areas, Samaria, was not Jewish. We may narrow our focus, however, to Jerusalem, since that is the only Judaean city that is important for the life of Jesus.

Jerusalem was governed by the Jewish high priest and his council. This was simply a reversion to the system that had been followed in the Persian and Hellenistic periods, before the Hasmonean revolt. The high priest, often in concert with 'the chief priests', sometimes with 'the powerful' or 'the elders' (influential laymen), was in charge of ordinary police and judicial procedures, and he – alone and in such combinations as just described – figures large in the gospels, in Acts and in Josephus. There is a long-standing custom of attributing too much of a governing role to the council, in Hebrew called the Sanhedrin. I shall not here argue against the traditional view of the Sanhedrin and its supposed legislative and judicial authority, but rather speak generally about the high priest and his council. It is adequate to say that the high priest and his advisers, both formal and informal, governed Jerusalem.[20]

I should offer here a word of explanation about how the high priest was chosen. Priesthood was hereditary; the Jewish priests traced their lineage to Aaron, Moses' brother, who was considered the first priest (e.g., Exod. 28.1). During the Persian and Hellenistic periods, the high priests, who were the rulers of the nation, were (or were thought to be) members of the family of Zadok, the priest who anointed Solomon king (I Kgs 1.28–45). The Hasmoneans were hereditary priests, but they were not Zadokites. When they rose to power as a result of the successful revolt against the Seleucids, however, the natural consequence was that the leading member of the family was declared high priest. When Simon the Hasmonean ascended to the high priesthood (I Macc. 14.41–9), the previously ruling Zadokite family was deposed, though the system of government by the high priest remained the same. About a hundred years later, however, the revolt of Aristobulus II and his son led to Herod's appointment as king, and this changed the system. Herod could not claim descent from a priestly family. While he was king, he simply appointed high priests. When Rome deposed Archelaus and sent a prefect to govern Judaea, it also began to appoint the high priest. Thereafter it sometimes granted the right to name the high priest to a member of Herod's family, but sometimes this right was retained by the prefect or procurator of Palestine, or by the legate of Syria. During the period 6 to 66 CE, the high priests were always chosen from one of four families of aristocratic priests. The high priests as political appointees did not have quite the prestige and authority of the hereditary high priests of earlier periods (the Zadokites, followed by the Hasmoneans), but nevertheless they had some prestige and a lot of authority. For the most part, they governed Jerusalem successfully for sixty years (from 6 to 66 CE).

In Jerusalem, then, even when Judaea was formally under 'direct' Roman rule, Jewish leaders were in day-to-day control. The magistrates were Jewish and ruled according to Jewish law, the schools were Jewish, and the religion was Jewish. The high priest and his council had a wide range of responsibilities. For example, they were required to organize the payment of tribute and to get the money and goods to the right person.[21] Jerusalem was policed by the Temple guards, commanded by the high priest. During the civil war that accompanied the Jewish revolt (66–74 CE), 8,500 guards died defending Ananus, a former high priest.[22] This may give an idea of the maximum police force available. We noted above that during the festivals the prefect and extra Roman troops came to Jerusalem in case of trouble.

The high priest was a suitable ruler for three reasons: government by the high priest was traditional; Jews held his office in reverence; the Roman prefect considered him to be the official spokesman for and to the population of Jerusalem. We have dealt adequately with the traditional character of priestly rule: high priests had governed Jewish Palestine from about 445 to 37 BCE. The other two points require a little further explanation.

The populace disliked some of the individuals who served as high priests during the Roman period; the mob hunted down and killed one former high priest when the revolt against Rome broke out in 66 CE. Other high priests, though, were respected. The first revolutionary government, chosen by public acclamation, was headed by two former high priests: the mob could distinguish the good from the bad. But whether the high priest was personally beloved or not, reverence for the office was deep and genuine. First Herod and then Rome took control of the high priest's vestments and released them only on special occasions. With them on, he wielded too much authority. Cases concerning control of the vestments, and with it the appointment of the high priest, more than once went directly to the Roman emperor for decision. Who controlled the vestments and the office really mattered; it mattered because the man in the office was intermediary not only between Rome and the populace, but also between God and his people. He was the one who, on the Day of Atonement, went into the Holy of Holies, and who made atonement for the sins of the people of Israel.

Presumably there were some people who did not like the system, people who did not want to be governed by the high priest and who would have preferred a ruler who was directly responsible to a council. They nevertheless had to go along. The Romans considered the high priest to be the responsible official in Jerusalem. If people wanted to deal with Rome, they went through the high priest. If Rome wanted to communicate with the people, the prefect summoned the high priest. If things went wrong, the high priest was held accountable.

The high priest at the time of Jesus was Joseph Caiaphas. He was a success: he served seventeen years, longer than any other high priest under Roman rule; and for ten of those years Pilate was prefect. Presumably they co-operated well.

Since so many readers and scholars of the New Testament have imagined Jesus living in a context in which the populace was daily oppressed by Roman soldiers and officials, and some scholars are now claiming that there was a substantial Gentile population in the Jewish cities, I wish to re-emphasize the actual situation.[23] In Galilee there was no official Roman presence at all. Greek-speaking Gentiles lived in the cities that they had long inhabited, which formed a kind of crescent around Galilee: there were Gentile cities to the east, to the north and to the west.[24] In geographical Galilee there was one Gentile city, Scythopolis, but it was independent of political Galilee. In Judaea the official Roman presence was very small. There was one Roman of rank in residence, and he was supported by a handful of troops. This Roman and his small military force lived among a lot of other Gentiles in Caesarea, seldom came to Jerusalem, and did nothing to plant Graeco-Roman laws and customs in the Jewish parts of the country. In Jerusalem there was not a substantial Gentile presence. In place of the image of Roman soldiers patrolling the towns and villages of Palestine, forcing Jews to carry their burdens, and motivating shopkeepers and farmers to cater to their tastes, we should think of a few Roman soldiers, banded together, living in or around one city, with only very small outposts occupying forts in potentially hostile territory. Effective rule was in the hands of local aristocrats and elders.

In terms of culture, the emperor and the Senate of Rome did not intend that the Jews of Judaea should become Romanized. Despite the view of some New Testament scholars, Rome did not 'annex' Palestine – not even Judaea, though it was a Roman province. The prefect did not impose Graeco-Roman educational, civil, religious or legal institutions on the Jewish populace. There was no hope that sometime Judaea would be like Gaul, studded with Roman colonies, some areas enjoying Roman rights, and so forth. Rome's interests were quite limited: a stable region between Syria and Egypt. Rome was not even interested in financial profit. Profit came from Egypt and Asia Minor, and those countries had to be protected against invasion by the Parthians; Palestine lay between them. We do not know enough about taxation and expenses to know whether or not Rome administered Judaea at a financial loss, but it is possible. Prefects and procurators, to one degree or another, lined their own pockets. Such money was regarded as the natural accompaniment to service in a 'barbaric' and hostile environment.

In the late twenties and early thirties Jewish Palestine was not tottering on the brink of revolt. Josephus tried to depict Roman misgovernment and Jewish restiveness as escalating steadily in the decades before revolt broke out in 66. He wrote with the benefit of hindsight, and he wanted the tempo of unrest and violence to increase as the war neared. Many scholars think that it was obvious at the time that full-scale war was coming closer with every passing year, and that crisis succeeded crisis at a quickening pace. If, however, one counts the uprisings and tumults that Josephus himself names, one does not see a steady increase. Rather, uprisings occurred when there were changes in leadership or governmental procedures. There were outbreaks of violence when Herod died, when Archelaus tried to assert himself as Herod's heir, and when Rome deposed Archelaus. Once Rome settled fully into control, things quieted down. The main protests near the lifetime of Jesus were largely non-violent. Pilate had troops march through Jerusalem carrying their standards, and this offended Jewish sensibilities; perhaps the standards were regarded as 'graven images'. In any case a large number of people went to Caesarea to protest. When Pilate ordered his troops to surround them, they bared their necks and professed to be readier to die than to see the law trampled. Pilate backed down.[25] The temper of the times can better be seen by noting a major potential cause of revolt a few years later. In about the year 40 the emperor Gaius (nicknamed Caligula) decided to have a statue of himself – or of Zeus, with Gaius' features – erected in the Temple in Jerusalem. This was truly alarming; writing from Alexandria, the Jewish philosopher and statesman Philo threatened a world-wide revolt. In Palestine, Jewish farmers planned an agricultural strike, which would have led to starvation and enormous upheaval, doubtless including riots; otherwise, the principal response was that a large delegation pleaded with the Roman legate – again professing to prefer death but apparently brandishing no arms. The legate, impressed by the ardour and number of the people who appealed to him and by the threat of a strike, delayed carrying out the order. The situation was ultimately resolved to the satisfaction of all: Gaius was assassinated.[26]

Here, about a decade after Jesus' execution, we have a provocation that would certainly have led to substantial bloodshed had the threat to the Temple been carried out. But there is no indication that the populace was actually ready to go to war.

This is not to say that Jews were happy with the situation in the twenties and thirties, nor that Rome – and, in their respective domains, Antipas and Caiaphas – did not have to exercise wary vigilance. There had been an armed uprising when Rome took direct control of Judaea in 6 CE and conducted a census for tax purposes, and in the fifties at least one group of Jewish enthusiasts would require the procurator to bring heavily armed troops into action (see just below). According to Josephus, Antipas executed John the Baptist because he feared that his preaching would lead to revolt. Thus the potential for war existed, both in Galilee and Judaea. In Judaea there might at any moment be some incident that would result in a Roman soldier drawing his sword, and if that happened other swords might be drawn. All the more reason for Caiaphas to keep control of Jerusalem, and to use his own guards to do so.

Some, perhaps most, of the violence that did occur reveals a hope for divine intervention that is generally (though misleadingly) called 'Messianic expectation' – the hope for an anointed representative of God. It is very likely that Antipas executed John the Baptist in part because he proclaimed the coming judgement.[27] After Jesus' time, prophets arose who gathered followers and promised 'deliverance'. One of these, Theudas, seems to have led a non-violent movement. He promised his adherents that if they followed him to the Jordan River it would part – presumably signalling a second Exodus and the coming time of freedom. The procurator sent lightly armed cavalry, who killed several people and returned with Theudas' head. Later, a man known only as 'the Egyptian' led a movement that posed a more serious threat. According to one account, he promised his followers that if they marched around the walls of Jerusalem they would fall – probably thinking himself to be a second Joshua, who would establish Israel in its own land in peace and freedom. According to the second account, the Egyptian led his followers in a charge against one of the gates of the city and was met with heavily armed troops, who killed many, though the Egyptian himself got away. Josephus adds that other prophets gathered followers in the Judaean Desert and promised them 'tokens of deliverance', that is, the hope of divine intervention. All were put down by Rome.[28]

When the revolt finally broke out in 66, it is almost certain that many joined in because they believed that God was ready to deliver them. There had been enough tumult and bloodshed to force the Syrian legate to march on Jerusalem. Inexplicably, he broke off the siege, turned tail and retreated, and his troops were ambushed. This must have appeared to many as a sign from heaven.[29] Few Jews, if any, thought that they could successfully revolt on their own. God, however, had freed them in the past, and when he was ready he would do so again (e.g., *Life* 290). Many were willing to take up arms when the signs of the time were clear enough. The result would be (they thought) that God would step in and give them the victory.

Such hopes for God's assistance did not require the expectation of a 'Messiah', a descendant of David standing by ready to become king.[30] They did not even require the expectation that God's ultimate, final kingdom was about to be established. Thus we cannot say that Jewish hopes for freedom were necessarily 'Messianic', or even more generally eschatological.[31] The Hasmonean revolt against the Syrian empire in the second century BCE had succeeded by the grace of God, but Jews did not think that the kingdom of God had arrived. We cannot know, of the Jews who joined insurgencies against Rome or followed a prophet, how many thought that the *final* kingdom was about to arrive. It is fair to say, however, that they all looked for God's assistance. Jews thought that God controlled history and that he decided the outcome of all major events. The situation would be decisively changed only if God intervened. Some people, perhaps only a few, thought that in the near future he would establish his own reign on earth.[32]

This chapter has dealt with the political history of Palestine prior to and during Jesus' time, and especially with the different political and judicial arrangements in Galilee and Judaea in the twenties and thirties of the Common Era. We have covered a lot of ground in a small space; as is always the case when brief political summaries are given, the reader has met a lot of dates and names. I shall offer a list of the points that are most relevant to understanding Jesus.

(1) Rome did not actually govern Palestine on a day-to-day basis. It governed Palestine indirectly, either through a client (puppet) king, ethnarch or tetrarch, or through a resident governor who, in turn, utilized local aristocrats, especially the high priest.

(2) In Galilee during Jesus' lifetime, Antipas was a semi-independent client tetrarch. He was as independent as his father, Herod the Great, had been, though he seems to have been milder and less ruthless. The troops were his, the taxes were his (though he paid tribute to Rome), the district governors were his appointees, and local magistrates served at his pleasure.

(3) In the twenties and thirties Judaea was under the alternative imperial system: a Roman governor (the prefect) and a small number of troops were resident in Palestine, though for the most part they stayed away from Jerusalem, the capital city, because the Jews were so sensitive about offences against their religion in the holy city. Day-to-day control was in the hands of the high priest, who had informal councillors and also a small formal council. Most councillors were aristocrats, and many were aristocratic priests.

(4) Jewish Palestine was not on the edge of revolt when Jesus was executed. There had been tension between the Jews, especially the Jerusalemites, and Pilate because he marched Roman standards through the city. On another occasion (not discussed

above), he also appropriated some sacred money to build an aqueduct, which led the crowd to protest, but Roman soldiers interspersed throughout the crowd quickly subdued would-be rioters with cudgels.[33] Nevertheless, there were no major outbreaks of violence during his ten years in office (26–36). A few years later, in 40 or 41, when Gaius wanted to put a pagan statue in the Jerusalem Temple, there would be a serious threat of full-scale war.

(5) Despite the lack of major violence while Pilate was prefect, during the Roman period there was always the possibility of serious insurrection, in both the areas governed by client rulers and those in which a prefect or procurator was resident. Herod himself had been afraid of revolt, and Antipas had similar worries. In Judaea, the high priest and the prefect had to be vigilant to prevent the outbreak of violence, especially when enormous crowds gathered for the festivals. But none of this was new. Large crowds usually had to be watched in the ancient world. Moreover, civil war marked Jewish history during this entire period. There had been very substantial revolts against one of the Hasmonean kings, Alexander Jannaeus.[34] Pompey entered Palestine because of civil war between two Hasmoneans. That is, the Roman imperial system was no more conducive to revolt than the Hasmonean system – a fully independent Jewish priest-king. Palestine was not especially close to revolt in Pilate's day, but the fear of uprisings was present then, as it was throughout the Hasmonean, Herodian and Roman periods.

(6) Many Jews wanted freedom from Rome's suzerainty, and they thought that this could be attained only with God's help. The nature and scope of the longed-for change varied a good deal, as did views about how God would bring the change about. Relatively few people expected a Davidic Messiah who would liberate the Jews by defeating the Roman army. Some people expected a very grand sign that the time of liberation had arrived (such as the collapse of Jerusalem's walls), while others probably expected no more than that God would strengthen the hands of the righteous and strike terror into the hearts of Rome's soldiers.

4. JUDAISM AS A RELIGION[1]

====

In the previous chapter I presupposed a certain amount of knowledge of Judaism. Here I shall lay out some of the basic beliefs and
practices that were common in first-century Jewish Palestine and
give a thumbnail sketch of the main groups and parties.

In the first-century Mediterranean world, Jews and Gentiles
agreed on a lot of things. Most of them believed in supernatural
beings, in worshipping God (or the gods) by sacrificing animals,
and in various kinds of rites and purifications. Ethically, there was
also a lot of common ground: everyone was against murder, theft,
robbery and adultery. In giving a few of the basic elements of
Judaism, I shall emphasize the theological ideas and religious practices that distinguished Jews from others. We start with theology.

Common Judaism

(1) *Monotheism*. Jews believed that there was only one true God. He
    had created the world and still governed it.[2] Many Jews believed
    in other supernatural beings – angels and demons. The apostle
    Paul, who represents common Jewish opinion on these topics,
    considered pagan deities to be demons (I Cor. 10.20). He could
    even call the archdemon, Satan, the 'god of this world' (II Cor.
    4.4; for 'Satan', see II Cor. 11.14). Such beliefs did not, in the
    mind of first-century Jews, constitute a denial of monotheism.
    In the end, all other powers would yield to the one God (I Cor.
    15.24–6; Phil. 2.10f.). In the meantime, only that God was
    worthy of worship. Gentiles (Jews thought) should have been
    able to see this, since the creator can be inferred from the
    creation, as a pot proves the existence of a potter.[3] Jews, in any

33

case, were the recipients of revelation, and they were strictly prohibited from having anything to do with pagan gods.

(2) *The divine election and the law*. Jews believed that God had chosen Israel and created a covenant with the Jewish people, which bound them to obey him and bound him to guide and protect them. The most important three moments in the history of the establishment of this covenant were the call of Abraham (Gen. 17), the exodus from Egypt (Exod. 14), and the revelation of the divine law to Moses on Mount Sinai (Exod. 19.16 to the end of Deut.).

(3) *Repentance, punishment and forgiveness*. People who transgressed the law should make reparations if their misdeeds harmed other people, repent and bring a sacrifice. Transgressions that did not harm other people (such as inadvertently working on the sabbath) required repentance and sacrifice. God would always forgive the repentant sinner. Those who did not repent were subject to divine punishment, which was manifested, for example, in sickness. If they accepted this as God's chastisement for their misdeeds, they were still worthy members of the covenant.[4] In general, the same system applied to the nation as a whole. Its transgressions led to national punishment, such as the Babylonian captivity, and calamities led to humble contrition. God would always redeem his people, and, despite lapses, they would always remain true to him.

The covenant-establishing acts (the call of Abraham, the exodus, the giving of the law) gave Israel its decisive character, but God's revelation to, and action on behalf of, the nation did not end with Moses. God bestowed the land of Palestine on the Israelites. Subsequently he spoke through prophets. The Israelites were God's own people; he had promised to defend them and make them great, and he guaranteed their redemption. This promise was part and parcel of the election.

In the first century the meaning of 'redemption' varied (as we saw above, pp. 29–31). Some Jews hoped for national redemption in a fairly mundane socio-political sense, others expected individual redemption at the time of death, others a great event that would transform the world, exalt Israel above other nations and persuade the Gentiles to convert. While they waited, Jews were to observe the law of God and seek God's forgiveness if they transgressed it.

These beliefs constituted the core of Jewish 'orthodoxy' ('correct opinion'). Inherent in them is the requirement of 'orthopraxy' ('correct practice'). We shall now list some of the main practices that marked observant Jews, especially, again, points that distinguished Jews from Gentiles.

(1) Jews were to *worship* or *serve* God (implied by the second of the ten commandments, which prohibits 'service' of other gods: Exod. 20.4; Deut. 5.8). This meant, above all, worshipping him at the Temple in Jerusalem. The Bible requires Jewish males to attend the Temple three times each year, at the pilgrimage festivals. In the first century the spread of the Jewish population made this impossible; Jews from the more remote areas in Palestine probably came to the Temple once a year, but Jews who lived in other countries (collectively called the Diaspora) made the pilgrimage very rarely. Whether they attended or not, Jews still paid the Temple tax, which supported the sacrifices that were offered on behalf of the whole community.
Jewish worship was not, however, confined to the Temple. Deuteronomy 6.4–6 requires that Jews recall the main commandments twice a day ('when you lie down and when you rise up'). Most Jews probably obeyed the instructions of this passage: first thing in the morning and last thing at night, they repeated the heart of the text in Deuteronomy 6 ('love the Lord your God with all your heart . . .') and a few of the most basic commandments. They also used these morning and evening periods for prayer. Most or all Jewish communities had synagogues, in Greek usually called 'houses of prayer', where people gathered on sabbaths to study the law and pray. Thus, besides occasionally worshipping God at the Temple in Jerusalem, Jews worshipped him daily at home and weekly in the synagogue. (We shall discuss synagogues in more detail in ch. 8.)

(2) Jews *circumcised* their infant sons. This was the requirement laid on the people by the covenant with Abraham (Gen. 17).

(3) Jews did not work on the *sabbath, the seventh day of the week* (the fourth commandment, Exod. 20.8–11; Deut. 5.12–15). The Bible extends the day of rest to include the entire family, servants, foreigners who lived in Jewish towns, and cattle. Moreover, every seventh year Jewish farmers in Palestine sowed no crops, and the land itself rested.

(4) The Jews avoided certain *foods* as being 'impure' and 'abominable' (Lev.11; Deut. 14). Pork and shellfish are the two most famous foods that are prohibited by the Bible, but there are many others, such as birds of prey, rodents and carrion.

(5) Before entering the Temple, Jews had to *purify* themselves. The principal sources of impurity were semen, menstrual blood, other emissions from the genital area (such as those caused by gonorrhoea and miscarriage), childbirth and corpses (Lev. 11; 15; Num. 19). Religious purification before Temple worship was part and parcel of all ancient religion. Jewish law required that the bodily processes connected most intimately with *life and death* be kept away from what was holy and *unchanging*: the presence of God. In the first century some groups extended purity rules beyond the basic biblical requirements. For example, some washed their hands before prayer, some before or after meals.

These are the main aspects of practice that distinguished Jews from the rest of humanity. This does not mean that they were unique in kind. Far from it: they are only particular definitions of general practices that were widespread in the ancient world. All people worshipped their gods by sacrificing animals, and they all supported temples. The Jews were distinctive in having only one temple and in worshipping only one God. Similarly everyone in the Graeco-Roman world observed holy days, but not the seventh day of every week. Greeks and Romans purified themselves when entering temples and before sacrificing; sprinkling and handwashing were common. In Palestine, and possibly in a few places in the Diaspora, Jews immersed their entire bodies, which was (as far as I know) unique. Almost every culture has food laws, though few ascribe these laws to God. Vultures, weasels, rats, mosquitoes and the like are a feature of few menus. Greeks and Romans did not usually eat dogs. The Jewish prohibition of pork and shellfish is almost unique, but Egyptian priests abstained from pork. Circumcision is more complicated. There is again a parallel with Egyptian priests, and other Semites also circumcised males. Despite this, Jews were famous for requiring circumcision, since it had such an important place in their culture.

Because modern New Testament scholars often attack – the word is not too strong – first-century Jews for observing some of these laws (especially the commandments governing sacrifice, food and purity), I wish to emphasize that these criticisms amount only to saying that ancient Jews were not modern Protestant Christians or secular humanists – a point that could be made with less animosity and self-righteousness than such scholars display when they discuss Judaism. Jews were not unique for having laws and customs, or for having laws and customs that covered these topics. More or less everyone did.

Even though Jewish practices had parallels in other ancient religions, Gentiles regarded the Jewish observances as being noteworthy, and some Gentiles ridiculed them. They thought that it was odd to have a temple without an idol and anti-social to refuse to worship the gods of Greece and Rome. They also thought that Jewish food laws were strange, since pork was the favourite meat in the Mediterranean countries. The Jewish refusal to work on the sabbath was the third practice that most attracted Gentile comment. The reason these Jewish observances stood out was that Jews were so devoted to their customs. Those who lived in the Diaspora – and in some areas they were very numerous – would not assimilate to the common culture. This refusal has an obvious explanation, and the explanation also reveals the quality of Judaism that was most distinctive. What truly set Judaism apart was that the Bible includes so many practices under the heading 'divine commandments'. The Jewish 'customs' were commanded in the law that God gave to Moses on Mount Sinai. While everyone had conventional food laws, Jews had divine commandments governing food. *The most striking point about Jewish law is that it brings the entirety of life, including civil and domestic practices, under the authority of God.* Jews were not free to assimilate: they could not keep other peoples' holidays or forgo their own; they could not eat some of the foods that other people ate. In the Jewish view these and many other customs were not merely social conventions, they were decreed by God.

'Religion' in Judaism was not only festivals and sacrifices, as it was in most of the Graeco-Roman world, but rather encompassed all of life. 'Religion governs all our actions and occupations and speech; none of these things did our lawgiver leave unexamined or indeterminate' (Josephus, *Apion* 2.171). All cultures think that tradesmen should use honest scales; Jews attributed the commandment to use just weights and measures to God (Lev. 19.35f.). Everyone favoured charitable practices in theory; in the Hebrew Bible, God requires charity and specifies how it should be carried out (Lev. 19.9f.). What this means is that in Judaism God required morality in public and private life. When Leviticus attributes moral laws to the same God who requires purity, it thereby *elevates* the moral laws. The ancient world really believed in God (or the gods), and all people thought that divine ordinances required them to purify themselves and offer sacrifices. Everything else had a lower status in terms of its source and absoluteness. *Judaism elevated all of life to the same level as worship of God* (see especially Lev. 19). It attributed to God the view that honesty and charity were as important as purifications.

Today, most people who evaluate religions do so in terms of humanism: a good religion is one that inculcates humane values. Some people go further and inquire about a religion's stance towards the entirety of the cosmos. First-century Jewish thinkers were ready to evaluate their own religion and defend it on humanistic grounds, and some pointed out its advantages for the non-human parts of the world. Jews claimed for themselves the widely praised virtue of *philanthropia*, 'love of all humanity'.[5] Jewish teachers could summarize the law by quoting Leviticus 19.18, which commands love of one's neighbour.[6] One of the virtues of the law, Josephus pointed out, was that it required consideration towards enemies in war; for example, it forbade Jewish troops to cut down their enemies' food-bearing trees (Deut. 20.19; *Apion* 2.212). Perhaps the most striking 'humanistic' defence of the law is seen if we look beyond human life to the welfare of animals, plants and the soil. God required rest on the seventh day, and the commandment extends to beasts of labour (*Apion* 2.213). Josephus even calls this *philanthropia*. Why did God decree the sabbath year? He could have forbidden Jews to work in the seventh year, but he did not; he ordained that the land should lie fallow. Had he only prohibited Jewish labour, the land could have been rented to Gentiles. Obviously God (according to Philo) acted 'out of consideration for the land' (*Hypothetica* 7.18).

Philo, after commenting on these and similar points, realized that many readers (who did not know about ecology and animal rights) would find all this trivial, and he replied: 'These things are of nothing worth, you may say, yet great is the law which ordains them and ever watchful is the care which it demands' (*Hypothetica* 7.9). The greatness of the law, in Jewish eyes, lay in part in the very fact that it covers all the trivia of life and of the creation. Josephus also thought that Moses had been correct in leaving 'nothing, however insignificant, to the discretion and caprice of the individual' (*Apion* 2.173). Rabbis remarked on the same point, though not in connection with animals: 'Ben Azzai said: Run to fulfil the lightest duty even as the weightiest, and flee from transgression; for one duty draws another duty in its train, and one transgression draws another transgression in its train' (*Avot* 4.2). Here life is seen as a seamless whole. In every aspect one may either fulfil or transgress God's will, and one thing leads to another. The universe is God's garden; humans are not his only creatures.[7]

Priests and Parties: The Question of Leadership

Since divine law covered all of life, one of the qualifications for being a leader was knowledge of the law. A military man, such as Herod, could take political control of Jewish Palestine without being an expert in Jewish scripture and tradition. But even Herod was careful not to transgress Jewish laws and customs too flagrantly.[8] This shows that he was prudent, but it also implies that he had expert advisers. Almost by definition, experts on religious law want people to follow their views and to accept their interpretations of correct behaviour. Religious experts naturally see themselves as the agents through whom God's will is made known. In first-century Jewish Palestine there was considerable competition among experts who sought to lead the populace. Political and military conditions, to be sure, meant that in some areas of life there could be no competition among would-be leaders. It was pointless for most Jews to have opinions on some large issues, such as foreign policy; a leader who argued that God wanted the Jews to ally with the Parthians (for example) would have had a very short career.

Despite such restrictions, a lot of life was not controlled by Rome, Antipas or Pilate. Individual families had some freedom of choice about how to observe the sabbath, how to keep the festivals, what foods to eat, when to avoid sexual intercourse (because of the woman's menstrual period), and so on. These topics, along with many others of great importance in daily life, were all covered by the Mosaic law, which in turn had to be interpreted. For example, the ten commandments include the prohibition of work on the sabbath (Exod. 20.8–11; Deut. 5.12–15), but the Hebrew Bible gives very few concrete definitions of 'work'. Virtually all Jews wanted to obey their laws, and so, every sabbath, they needed to know what they could and could not do. Similarly the Bible forbids sexual intercourse when the woman is menstruating (Lev. 18.19; 20.18), and it defines the menstrual period as lasting seven days (Lev. 15.19). But precisely how should one count the days? What if, on a supposedly safe day, blood appeared after intercourse? Had the law been transgressed? Individuals did not actually rethink the law and come to new decisions each time a question arose. They observed the law in traditional ways and in ways recommended by experts. Life then as now was very complicated, and new questions constantly arose. For example, a Jewish farmer might have the opportunity to buy land that lay outside the traditional area of Jewish settlement as described in the Hebrew Bible. He would need to know whether or not he owed Temple dues on the proceeds of the land. He would wish to ask an expert.

In Judaism, the definition of expertise was precise knowledge and sound interpretation of the Mosaic law and the various traditions about how to observe it. When the revolutionary council decided to investigate Josephus' conduct of the war in Galilee, they sent a delegation made up of experts – experts not in military science but in Jewish law and tradition. The four-man delegation consisted of two Pharisees who were 'from the lower ranks' of society (that is, who were neither priests nor aristocrats), one Pharisee who was a priest, and one priestly aristocrat (a descendant of high priests). If the Galileans indicated that they were loyal to Josephus because he was an expert in the law, the delegates could reply that so were they; if his leadership resulted from his priestly office, the delegates could point out that two of them were priests (*Life* 197f.). Leadership of the nation – that is, in Jesus' day, the aspects of life that were not decided by Rome, Pilate or Antipas – depended heavily on expertise in Jewish law and lore. We learn from this passage that there were two groups of acknowledged experts – priests and Pharisees.

In Jewish history since at least the return from the Babylonian exile, priests had been the principal experts. It is a widespread view that by the first century they had ceded their authority to lay Pharisees. This is, however, incorrect. Priests had by no means withdrawn from leadership, and much of the populace looked to them when questions arose. I shall not argue this case here, but I shall give a brief account of the priesthood and priestly authority before dealing with the Pharisees and the other parties.[9]

The priests who served in the Temple in Jerusalem did not constitute a party as such. They were, rather, a class, a large and important class. The priests were the only people who could offer sacrifices. They were assisted by a lower order of clergy, the Levites, who served in the Temple in various ways: some sang the Psalms during the public services; some guarded the gates; some cleaned the Temple area; some brought forward the animals and wood for the altar. There appear to have been about 20,000 priests and Levites together (*Apion* 2.108). These sacred offices (which, as we saw above, were hereditary) were not full-time occupations. Any individual priest or Levite performed his sacred offices for only a few weeks each year. Both the priests and the Levites were divided into twenty-four divisions, called 'courses', each of which served in the Temple for one week at a time. During the three annual festivals, all the courses were on duty. Both priests and Levites were partially supported by the tithes and first-fruits that farmers gave the Temple; but when they were not serving in the Temple, they worked at other jobs, except farming, since the Bible forbade them to work the land. Some were professional scribes (who drew up legal documents), but some engaged in manual labour. When Herod rebuilt the temple, he had some priests trained as stone-masons, so that they could build the most sacred areas (*Antiq.* 15.390). There were a few special restrictions on the priests: they could not marry prostitutes or divorced women (Lev. 21.7), and they were forbidden to come into contact with corpses, except the nearest of kin (Lev. 21.1–3).

Most priests and Levites had no party affiliation. We know that some of the aristocratic priests were Sadducees and that some of the ordinary priests were Pharisees,[10] but the priests and Levites for the most part simply belonged to common Judaism. They shared the beliefs and the practices of their compatriots, and in addition they followed the special Mosaic laws that applied only to priests (see Lev. 21; Num. 18).

The scene in the gospels called 'the cleansing of the Temple', in which Jesus calls the Temple a 'den of robbers' (Mark 11.15–19 and parallels), has led many people to think that the priesthood was venal and corrupt. That is not, however, an accurate generalization. Most priests and Levites were dedicated to the worship of God. In any system there will be some dishonesty and abuse, and Josephus gives us the name of one corrupt aristocratic priest (*Antiq.* 20.213). He also cites a few cases in which a chief priest misused his authority. But these cases stand out by contrast to the general rule: the priests believed in God, they served him faithfully in the Temple, and they tried to set a good example by strict adherence to the divine law.

We return now to the point that the priests were traditionally the legal and religious authorities in Judaism. According to the Bible, God gave the law to Moses, but before his death Moses consigned it to the priests and elders (prominent laymen) (Deut. 31.9). Deuteronomy also requires the king, when there was one, to write out for himself a copy of the law that was 'in [the] charge of the Levitical priests' (17.8). Josephus, himself a priest, also regarded the priests as the natural rulers of the nation. In explaining the Jewish constitution, he wrote that God assigned administration to 'the whole body of priests', who exercised 'general supervision' and also tried cases and punished malefactors (*Apion* 2.165). He called this constitution, which was in effect in Judaea in his day (born 27 CE), a 'theocracy', government by God, mediated by his priests. Josephus and many others preferred this form of government. The New Testament makes 'son of David' a substantial category for understanding Jesus, and this sometimes misleads readers into thinking that all Jews hoped for a revival of Davidic kingship. A lot of the Bible, however, is hostile towards a monarchical system, and this hostility was widespread in the first century. Monarchs, in Jewish experience (as well as in the experience of other nations), tended to become tyrannical and dictatorial. Many Jews thought that it was better to be governed by a theocratic aristocracy (members of the leading priestly families), under the distant supervision of a foreign governor.[11]

In the previous chapter we saw that this system was in effect in Judaea, and especially in Jerusalem, during most of Jesus' lifetime. The Roman governor was not as distant as most Jews would have liked, and he could meddle more than they wished, but for the most part it was the high priest who had actual authority in Jerusalem when government was formally in the hands of a Roman prefect. This corresponded to one of the main biblical theories of government, to Josephus' view of the most natural Jewish constitution, and to the preference of a good proportion of the populace: the priests were in charge.

Finally, we note that it was the priests serving in the Temple who finally declared war against Rome in 66 CE. They were persuaded by a priestly aristocrat (Eleazar son of Ananias) 'to accept no gift or sacrifice from a foreigner'. Previously there had been sacrifices on behalf of Rome and Caesar. The serving priests now rejected those sacrifices and allegiance to Rome along with them. They listened neither to the aristocrats nor to Agrippa II (Herod's great-grandson) nor to the leading Pharisees: the sacrifices on behalf of Rome stopped (*War* 2.409–21). This may have been the most decisive single step in leading the nation into war.

There were, however, non-priests who also played a leadership role in Jewish life by virtue of their expertise in the interpretation of scripture. Since the law was written, all literate Jews could read it, and the non-literate heard it read and discussed in the synagogue. The consequence was that, on the whole, Jews knew their law extremely well. Moreover, anyone could become an expert. In other religions, only priests needed to know all the details of how to worship each god, since religion covered little else than temple worship. But since the Jewish religion covered all of life, there was considerable incentive for lay people to learn very carefully the parts that applied to their own lives. We noted above the need to know how to observe the sabbath and when sexual intercourse was permissible. I shall offer another illustration of a law that was relevant to a large percentage of the population. The Bible has several ways of requiring charity, all of which apply to farmers. The hereditary Jewish priesthood was forbidden to farm the land, and so the laws of charity applied only to laypeople.[12] One law is this:

When you reap the harvest of your land, you shall not reap your field to its very border, neither shall you gather the gleanings after your harvest. And you shall not strip your vineyard bare, neither shall you gather the fallen grapes of your vineyard; you shall leave them for the poor and for the sojourner: I am the Lord your God. (Lev. 19.9f.)

The requirement to leave the fallen grain and grapes is perfectly clear. But how many grapes should be left on each grapevine? How close to the border of grain fields should one reap? The conscientious Jewish farmer, who believed in God and the law, wanted to leave the right percentage of the harvest for the poor. But how much was that? Over the centuries, common practices had evolved, and the sons who inherited farms also inherited traditions about the practice of charity. But this law, like most others, is open to study and interpretation by anyone who is learned, intelligent and diligent. This description fitted some laymen, among whom the Pharisees were prominent.

The Pharisaic party, which seems to have originated fairly early in the Hasmonean period (before 135 BCE), consisted largely but not entirely of non-priests.[13] At the time of Herod, there were about 6,000 Pharisees (*Antiq.* 17.42). Theologically, the Pharisees shared common Jewish orthodoxy (they believed in one God, the election of Israel, the divine origin of the law, and repentance and forgiveness). The Pharisees, like most other first-century Jews, also believed in some form of existence after death, an idea that is hard to find in the Hebrew Bible (the only clear reference is Daniel 12.2). Moreover, they developed a substantial body of non-biblical 'traditions' about how to observe the law. Some of these traditions made the law more difficult, but some made it less restrictive. For the most part, the Pharisees made special rules only for themselves and did not try to force them on everybody. (During the Hasmonean period they probably did try to enforce their views, but apparently not during the Herodian and post-Herodian periods.) In either case, the Pharisees were known for the precision with which they interpreted the law and the strictness with which they kept it. According to Josephus, they practised 'the highest ideals both in their way of living and in their discourse' (*Antiq.* 18.15).

Since the Pharisees play an even larger role in the New Testament than does the high priest, I shall give two examples of Pharisaic non-biblical 'traditions' in order to put a little flesh on a very bare-bones description. One has to do with sabbath law. The prophet Jeremiah had forbidden Jews to carry burdens out of their houses on the sabbath (Jer. 17.19–27). This made festive dining very difficult, since the easiest way for friends to dine together was for each family to bring a cooked dish, and sabbaths were the only days when socializing was possible (because the demands of daily work were so heavy). The Pharisees decided that, when several houses were next to each other along an alley or around a court, they could make them all into one 'house' by joining them with a series of doorposts and lintels. They could then carry pots and dishes from one part of the 'house' to another, and thus dine together on the sabbath. The Pharisees knew that this and other symbolic actions that altered the sabbath limits – actions that are technically called 'eruvin – had no support in the Hebrew Bible, but they made it a 'tradition of the elders' and observed it. Some Jews thought that they were transgressing the law, since they carried vessels out of what most people would call a house.

The second example is handwashing. The Mosaic law requires bathing to remove certain impurities before entering the Temple. The Pharisees added a purity rule. They washed their hands before sabbath and festival meals. Probably handwashing before meals on holy days made the day a little more special. Eventually Jews began to wash their hands before all meals.[14]

These small Pharisaic adjustments to the law reveal how carefully people *thought* about the law and about observing the will of God. The law in principle covers all of life. Pious first-century Jews thought through every detail, so as to observe God's will in every possible way.

Because of their devotion and precision, the Pharisees were respected and liked by most other Jews. In the Hasmonean period, the Pharisaic party had been a major political force. It was so no longer. Under Herod, no one else had any political power, and those who sought it were promptly executed. The Pharisees lay low. In Galilee, Herod was succeeded by Antipas, who was no more inclined than his father to give authority to a group of pious religious teachers. And in Jerusalem, after Archelaus was deposed, the high priests were in charge, backed by the awesome power of Rome. The Pharisees continued to lie low. They worked, studied, taught and worshipped. Probably they increased in general popularity, but they had no actual power.

To understand the Pharisees' role in society in Jesus' day, we can best fix our attention on the beginnings of the revolt against Rome a few decades after Jesus died. As relations between the procurator and the Jewish populace deteriorated, the aristocratic priests and laymen continued to plead for calm and moderation – with some success, but not enough. At the last minute, the chief priests called in the leading Pharisees to help. Even they could not calm the Jerusalem mob, and full revolt broke out. In the war itself, Pharisees played a leading part (as did the chief priests). These events show that the Pharisees had no public responsibility during the rule of Rome's governors. The high priest and his advisers were the responsible parties in the eyes of Rome. The Pharisees, however, were still around and they still commanded public attention. Thus in a dire emergency the ruling aristocrats called on them. When conditions were right – when they were no longer held in check by Herod or Rome – the Pharisees stepped forward to play a substantial role in Israel's political and military affairs. But during Jesus' lifetime, they must be regarded as principally *religious* teachers and experts, deservedly popular and respected.

We know the titles of two other parties in first-century Palestine: the Essenes and the Sadducees. The Essenes are described by both Josephus and Philo;[15] most scholars identify them as the group responsible for the Dead Sea Scrolls. If this identification is correct, and I think it is, we know a great deal about the Essenes. The Essenes formed a small party, divided into at least two branches and numbering about 4,000 altogether.[16] The party consisted of both lay people and priests, but the priests were dominant. When the Hasmoneans came to power in 142 BCE, they deposed the previous high-priestly family, the Zadokites. Some of the displaced aristocratic priests joined what became the Essene party, and they seem to have been largely responsible for governing it. Nevertheless, the laymen who were members also studied the Bible and the special rules of the party, and they could become as expert as the priests. The Essenes, as far as we know, played no direct role in Jesus' life and work, and so I shall not offer a description. Those who are interested will find that the Essene literature is now relatively easy to study, thanks to good translations and a reliable body of introductory material.[17]

I do wish, however, to employ the Essenes to make a point about the Pharisees. The Essene literature reveals intense study of the Hebrew Bible and a wealth of community rules in addition to those in the Mosaic law. The Essenes were far stricter than the Pharisees in almost every conceivable way. If the Pharisees were thought the 'strictest' observers of the law (as Josephus says), the word 'strict' bears the connotation of 'most accurate' rather than 'most extreme'.[18]

The Sadducees were the third party for which we have a name. We know little about them, except that most Sadducees were aristocratic, did not believe in any form of life after death, and did not accept the Pharisees' special traditions. Most scholars suppose that a lot of the high priests during the Roman period were Sadducees, but we have direct information from Josephus about only one: Ananus, who was high priest in 62 CE (when he illegally had James the brother of Jesus executed) and who was one of the leaders in the revolt against Rome, was a Sadducee.[19] The reader of the New Testament meets the Sadducees only a few times; it confirms their close association with the aristocratic priesthood and the fact that they did not believe in the resurrection.[20]

We have seen that in Jesus' day certain beliefs and practices were common in Judaism. The motive power was faith in God and devotion to the way of life that he established for the Jewish people through the mouths of his spokesmen: Moses and subsequent prophets and priests. Most people in the ancient world were religious, but even so the piety and dedication of the Jewish people stood out. Moreover, they were committed to a noble religion, one that inculcated an upright life, love, prayer and repentance.

We have also seen that, in the view of many people, the hereditary priesthood constituted the natural leadership of the nation. Nevertheless, the basic character of Judaism meant that lay people could challenge the priesthood and could claim to be the best interpreters of the law. (The law was written, it governed all of life, anyone could study it, and everyone listened to discussion and interpretation in synagogues on the sabbath.) Special groups arose, with their own interpretations and claims to be the true spokesmen on behalf of God. One branch of the Essene party was separatist; members of this group believed that only they had the one true covenant. Otherwise, members of the parties participated in common Judaism. They shared the beliefs and practices that we listed in the first part of this chapter, though they differed in some details. Most important, they all worshipped at the same Temple and accepted its services as mediating between them and God – even when they disliked the high priest and disagreed with the precise way in which priests carried out some of their duties. Even the separatist branch of the Essenes participated in common Judaism in a quite important way: they believed in one God, the divine election, the giving of the law, and repentance and forgiveness. They also observed all the biblical commandments. They were separatist because of their radical definitions: only they were truly in the covenant, only they had the right interpretation of the law, only their priests were acceptable, and so on.

The three main parties did not *constitute* Judaism: most Jews were members of no party. The parties serve us, rather, as examples: Judaism was not entirely in the hands of the leading Jerusalem priests; lay people could come to their own views. All Jews, like the Pharisees, believed that they should understand the divine law and obey it. We need only add that from time to time individuals stood up and claimed to be the truest representatives of God. In general terms, this is where Jesus fits. He was an individual who was convinced that he knew the will of God.

5. EXTERNAL SOURCES

The primary sources for knowledge about Jesus (as we noted above) are the gospels in the New Testament. In this chapter, however, we shall consider 'external' sources; I shall discuss a few examples of information in non-Christian literature that bears on the life of Jesus, and also the use of one scientific discipline, astronomy.

Non-Christian Literature

Jesus became such an important man in world history that it is sometimes hard to believe how unimportant he was during his lifetime, especially outside Palestine. Most of the first-century literature that survives was written by members of the very small elite class of the Roman empire. To them, Jesus (if they heard of him at all) was merely a troublesome rabble-rouser and magician in a small, backward part of the world. Roman sources that mention him are all dependent on Christian reports. Jesus' trial did not make headlines in Rome, and the archives there had no record of it. If archives were kept in Jerusalem, they were destroyed when revolt broke out in 66 CE or during the subsequent war. That war also devastated Galilee. Whatever records there may have been did not survive. When he was executed, Jesus was no more important to the outside world than the two brigands or insurgents executed with him – whose names we do not know.

Within ten or so years of Jesus' death, Romans knew that someone named Chrestus was causing tumult among the Jews in Rome.[1] That is to say, there was conflict in the Jewish community in Rome about whether or not Jesus had been sent by God and was the Messiah. ('Chrestus' is a slight misspelling of 'Christos', the

Greek word that translates the Hebrew 'Messiah'.) In another twenty years Christians in the capital city were prominent enough to be persecuted by the emperor Nero, and people knew about their strange 'superstition' and their devotion to a man who had been crucified.[2] But knowledge of Jesus was limited to knowledge of Christianity; that is, had Jesus' adherents not started a movement that spread to Rome, Jesus would not have made it into Roman histories at all. The consequence is that we do not have what we would very much like, a comment in Tacitus or another Gentile writer that offers independent evidence about Jesus, his life and his death.

Jesus was mentioned in Josephus' *Antiquities of the Jews*. Josephus (as we saw above) was born in 37 CE, just a few years after Jesus' death, and he wrote the *Antiquities* in the nineties. The Jewish historian certainly knew something about Jesus, and there is a paragraph on him in the *Antiquities* (18.63f.). But Josephus' works were preserved by Christian scribes, who could not resist the temptation to revise the text and thus make Josephus proclaim that Jesus 'was the Messiah'; that he taught 'the truth'; and that after his death he was 'restored to life'.[3] Failing a fluke discovery, we shall never know what Josephus actually wrote. He was not a convert to Christianity, and he did not really think that Jesus was the Messiah. But there is good news: the Christian scribes probably only rewrote the text. It is highly likely that Josephus included Jesus in his account of the period. Josephus discussed John the Baptist and other prophetic figures, such as Theudas and the Egyptian. Further, the passage on Jesus is not adjacent to Josephus' account of John the Baptist, which is probably where a Christian scribe would have put it had he invented the entire paragraph. Thus the author of the only surviving history of Palestinian Judaism in the first century thought that Jesus was important enough to merit a paragraph – neither more nor less.

This paragraph, whose precise wording we do not know (see n. 3), is the best objective evidence of the importance of Jesus during his own lifetime. The gospels create the impression that the entire populace was vitally interested in Jesus and what happened to him. Certainly he did attract attention. But if we measure the general impact of prophetic figures by the degree of disturbance they caused, we shall conclude that Jesus was less important in the eyes of most of his contemporaries than

were John the Baptist and the Egyptian. Both John the Baptist and
Jesus alarmed Antipas, but Jesus obviously was less troublesome than
John, since Jesus got out of Galilee alive. Years later, the Egyptian
caused the Romans to bring heavily armed troops into action to
suppress his movement. This would have excited the populace much
more than the stealthy arrest and quick execution of Jesus.

Since the histories written by Roman authors primarily deal with
the history of Rome, and not the outlying provinces, we would
think that such a history might mention the one Roman in the
gospels, Pilate, but not give him a prominent place, since Pilate was
prefect of a minor province. This expectation is met. Tacitus, the
major source of information about Roman history during this
period, mentions Pilate, but incidentally and only in connection
with Nero's persecution of Christians: Nero provided illumination
for a party by burning followers of Christos, a man whom Pilate
had executed.[4] This passing reference shows how unimportant
Palestine was. Yet the major Jewish writers, Josephus and Philo,
who were deeply concerned with Palestinian history, discuss Pilate
extensively and in very unflattering terms.[5] The gospels agree with
Josephus and Philo on Pilate's dates, but they disagree with regard
to his character. We shall briefly discuss Pilate's character below,
pp. 273 f.

Dates and Astronomy

I wish now to explain a little more fully our problems with dates.
It is very difficult to fix ancient dates, for a variety of reasons, one
of which is that the ancient world had no uniform calendar, with
the result that our sources express time periods in diverse ways. I
give two examples, one from Luke and one from Josephus:

In the fifteenth year of the reign of Emperor Tiberius, when Pontius Pilate
was governor of Judaea, and Herod [Antipas] was ruler of Galilee, and his
brother Philip ruler of . . . , and Lysanias ruler of . . . , during the high
priesthood of Annas and Caiaphas, . . . (Luke 3.1)

This calamity [Herod's conquest of Jerusalem in 37 BCE] befell the city of
Jerusalem during the consulship at Rome of Marcus Agrippa and Caninius

Gallus, in the hundred and eighty-fifth Olympiad, in the third month, on the day of the Fast, as if it were a recurrence of the misfortune which came upon the Jews in the time of Pompey, for they were captured by Sossius on the very same day, twenty-seven years later. (*Antiq.* 14.487)

These passages are unusually elaborate, but they illustrate the problem posed by the lack of a common calendar. '29 CE' and '37 BCE' would have been much simpler, but ancient authors who wrote in Greek for an empire-wide audience did not have this kind of date as an option.[6] They had to refer to several markers of time; the event in question happened when several events overlapped. It was difficult to keep all this straight. The lack of a common calendar meant that even ancient historians, who were accustomed to their own ways of dating, had a harder time than we do in recording and remembering dates. They also had few 'fallbacks', such as archives of newspapers, to help them out.

The lack of archives is clear in the quotation from Luke 3.1, which mentions 'the high priesthood of Annas and Caiaphas'. There could be only one high priest at a time. Both these men were, at different times, high priests. Luke does well to know both their names; we should not expect perfection, given the circumstances. The quotation from Josephus is even more problematic, though I shall not go into the difficulties in detail. In Schürer's *History of the Jewish People*, it requires almost two pages of fine print to consider the principal issues and the various ways of resolving them.[7] I shall mention only one problem: a study of all the evidence about the conquests of Jerusalem by Pompey and Herod makes it virtually impossible to believe that Herod's conquest (aided by the Roman general Sossius) took place twenty-seven years to the day after Pompey's. Josephus, rather, liked dating calamities on the same day as some previous disaster.[8] We may simply dismiss this part of his statement, but difficulties remain.

With regard to the dates of Jesus' birth and death, there are basically three sorts of problems. I shall take them in turn.

(1) The references to times, people and events in the gospels are sometimes in conflict. As we saw, both Matthew and Luke place Jesus' birth late in Herod's reign (that is, *c.* 6–4 BCE). Luke, however, offers a conflicting date as well, the year of a

census under Quirinius (6 CE). Quirinius was not the legate of Syria while Herod was alive (despite Luke 1.5, 26; 2.2). When Herod died, Varus was the legate.[9]

(2) It is sometimes difficult to reconcile the gospel accounts with Josephus. For example, in *Antiq.* 18, Josephus mentions both Jesus and John the Baptist. His discussion of Jesus is in the context of various events, most of which took place in the years 15–19 CE. His discussion of John seems to place him in the period 34–7 CE. The gospels, of course, link their careers very closely. According to them, John started his public work before Jesus, was arrested shortly after he baptized Jesus, and was executed while Jesus was still active.

(3) In two instances it is difficult to square the gospels with astronomy. According to Matthew, a star attracted wise men from the east at the time of Jesus' birth. Scholars search for astronomical events that might explain this. The second instance in which astronomy plays a role in assessing the gospels has to do with Jesus' death. According to all four gospels, he was executed on a Friday. According to John, on this particular Friday the Passover lambs were sacrificed: therefore it was Friday, 14 Nisan, in the Jewish calendar. The synoptic gospels (Matthew, Mark and Luke),* however, put the crucifixion on Friday, 15 Nisan, the next day of the month, but the same day of the week. This is partially an internal conflict (category 1), but also partly a problem of reconciling the gospels with our present astronomical knowledge, since it is difficult to find a year in the late twenties or early thirties in which 15 Nisan fell on a Friday; this puts the synoptics in conflict with astronomy. (15 Nisan is like 25 December: it does not always fall on the same day of the week. In some years it falls on Friday, but not in others.)

This situation probably sounds worse than it is. As I wrote in ch. 2, there are no really substantial doubts about when and where Jesus lived. Similarly we know approximately when Herod conquered Jerusalem, even though Josephus' paragraph on the date of the event is full of difficulties. With regard to the dates during which

* Differences between John and the other three gospels, collectively called 'the synoptic gospels', will be described in the next chapter.

Jesus lived, the gospels mention Augustus Caesar (31 BCE-14 CE) at the time of his birth and Tiberius (14–37 CE) later in his life (Luke 2.1; 3.1). When Jesus was executed, Pontius Pilate was prefect of Judaea (26–36 CE) and Caiaphas was high priest (18–36 CE) (Matt. 26–7 and elsewhere). These dates lead to the conclusion that Jesus died between 26 and 36 CE. This broad range is based on 'big' pieces of information. Tiberius, Pilate and Caiaphas: everybody in Palestine knew those three names and during what period of time they held their respective offices. We should trust this information unless we have good reason not to do so; that is, unless the stories in the gospels contain so many anachronisms and anomalies that we come to regard them as fraudulent. That is not the case, and this general time span is beyond reasonable doubt.

It is true, however, that the precise dates of Jesus' birth and death are uncertain. With regard to his birth, there is no information at all about the month and day, and there is conflict with regard to the approximate year (near the time of Herod's death in 4 BCE and at the time of Quirinius' census in 6 CE). Even if we accept the general view that Jesus was born late in Herod's lifetime, we still do not know the precise year (see above, p. 11). The gospels are also in conflict with regard to the day Jesus died. This, in turn, means that we do not know what year it was. Even if we accept the synoptic gospels and agree that Jesus was executed on Friday, 15 Nisan, we do not know the precise year, since modern calculations of the ancient Jewish calendar do not reveal a year in which 15 Nisan fell on Friday (see Appendix I).

These uncertainties do not make Jesus unique or even unusual. Because in the Christianized west we have had standard calendars for so long, we have become accustomed to certitude about dates. From the modern point of view, it is strange that scholars do not know when Jesus was born and when he died. This will not be surprising to those who read academic discussions of ancient history. The uncertain aspects of the chronology of Jesus' life do not lead to the conclusion that no one knows anything, nor do they mean that any conceivable reconstruction of events is possible since there are no absolutes. We know quite a lot about him. We just need to be cautious and judicious rather than hasty and extreme. In all probability Jesus was born in 5 or 4 BCE and died between 29 and 31 CE (though many scholars prefer 33).

Recently there has been a renewed flurry of interest in the date of Jesus' execution, and I have added an appendix on this topic. Here I wish to comment generally on the mistakes (as I perceive them to be) of the scholars who bring forth extreme proposals on such points, such as that Jesus was executed in 26 or 36. Since the evidence is diverse and hard to reconcile precisely, there is a tendency to seize on one point, to say that it is determinative, and then to beat the other pieces of evidence into the necessary shape. That is, there is a danger of sporadic fundamentalism in studying ancient texts – not just the Bible. 'Fundamentalism' refers to the notion that some ancient text – or ancient literature in general – tells the precise and unvarnished truth. Fundamentalism, however, is always sporadic: fundamentalists believe that *some* people never exaggerated, made mistakes or mislaid their notes; or, at least, that some sections of some texts are perfectly reliable. Reading chronological studies on the New Testament reveals a lot of fundamentalism – usually sporadic. A scholar will maintain, for example, that John's chronology is better than Mark's and Matthew's (and thus that theirs is not true). Next, he or she will accept John on the numerous points where that gospel disagrees with the other three:[10] there were three Passovers during Jesus' public career rather than one, he was executed on 14 Nisan rather than 15 Nisan, and during his ministry he was in his forties (he was 'not yet fifty', John 8.57) rather than in his thirties, as Luke has it. Having dismissed the chronology of Matthew, Mark and Luke, some scholars then seize upon Matthew's story of the star that stood over Jesus' birthplace, and they try to match it with the appearance of a comet – apparently not noticing that this particular star, according to our only description of it, did not blaze across the heavens, but rather 'stopped over the place where the child was' (Matt. 2.9). Why take the star of Matthew's story to be a real astral event and ignore what the author says about it? Why pay attention to Matthew's star anyway, since he was wrong about the date of Jesus' death (which John got perfectly right)?

These same scholars are the very ones who decide that some of the paragraphs in Josephus are the literal and complete truth, and that in them he told it just like it was, without shifting a word, but that other paragraphs do not count: since Josephus places his discussion of Jesus in an earlier section of *Antiquities* 18 than the discussion of John, one of these is precisely correct, and the other must be moved. (In fact, these sections of Josephus' work are not in chronological order: see Appendix I.)

Ancient history is difficult. It requires above all common sense and a good feel for sources. Our sources contain information about Jesus, but we cannot get at it by dogmatically deciding that some sentences are completely accurate and some are fiction. The truth will usually lie somewhere in between. As I have already said more than once, and may repeat several more times, we have *very good* knowledge of Jesus at a somewhat general level. With regard to chronology, we know that he was active during some part of the period 26–36 CE. It is wrongheaded to try to turn the gospels – and, for that matter, Josephus – into modern encyclopaedia articles, or to suppose that one sentence is dead right, and the others are completely wrong.

This introduces the next chapter, the particular problems of studying our main sources, the gospels. What kind of works are they? How can we best make use of them?

6. THE PROBLEMS
OF THE PRIMARY SOURCES

═══

We shall now turn to one of our most difficult tasks: exploring the nature of the gospel material. We shall examine a few of the questions that the gospels themselves pose to careful readers. Although my view of the sources is on the whole positive, many of the points in this chapter will be negative, the most general one being that we cannot fill out the brief sketch of Jesus' life (ch. 2 above) by simply combining all the information in the four gospels. In an earlier book Margaret Davies and I gave a fairly full account of how to study the first three gospels.[1] It was not until p. 301 that we began to explain how one derives knowledge of the historical Jesus from these sources. The present description will be much briefer, principally because I shall leave out a lot of issues. Here I wish more to illustrate some of the problems of using the gospels than to lead the reader through solutions and back to the historical Jesus step by step. I shall include only enough topics to substantiate the following points:

(1) The earliest Christians did not write a narrative of Jesus' life, but rather made use of, and thus preserved, individual units – short passages about his words and deeds. These units were later moved and arranged by editors and authors. This means that we can never be sure of the immediate context of Jesus' sayings and actions.

(2) Some material has been revised and some created by early Christians.

(3) The gospels were written anonymously.

(4) The Gospel of John is quite different from the other three gospels, and it is primarily in the latter that we must seek information about Jesus.

(5) The gospels lack many characteristics of biography, and we
    should especially distinguish them from modern biographies.

The History of the Gospel Material

We begin with a general description of how the gospel material
originated and was communicated. This will serve as a kind of road
map through sometimes difficult terrain.

When Jesus was executed, his followers fled or hid, but their
hopes were renewed when they saw him alive again. Here I wish to
say nothing at all about the disciples' resurrection experiences,
which we shall briefly consider in an epilogue, but rather focus on
their subsequent behaviour. They were convinced that the kingdom
that Jesus had predicted would soon arrive, and that he would
return. They settled down in Jerusalem to wait. While waiting,
they tried to convince others that their master was the Messiah of
Israel and that he would soon return to establish the kingdom of
God. They did not sit together, collectively search their memories,
and write a biography of Jesus. They thought that he would soon
be back, and the question of how best to preserve knowledge of his
life for future generations did not arise.

In trying to convince others, they sometimes told stories of things
that Jesus had said and done. In the early years this material was
probably not written, but was simply passed on orally. When the
disciples used incidents from Jesus' life, they wanted to illustrate
points, points that were important at the time. For example, a
disciple might say something like this:

Jesus was extremely compassionate. Those of you who are poor and who
feel downtrodden should follow him as Lord. Once he said, 'Blessed are the
meek, for they shall inherit the earth.' On another occasion, he commanded
us to let children come to him, 'for of such is the kingdom of God'.

Besides winning new adherents, the disciples also instructed one
another and their growing number of converts by recalling incidents
from Jesus' life. Sometimes they debated with Jewish teachers who
rejected Jesus; these disputes provided a third context in which
material from and about Jesus was employed.

Positively, these ways of using material from Jesus' lifetime preserved it. It was preserved, however, in a form that was valuable to Jesus' followers in their various activities. Thus, negatively, Jesus' words and deeds were pulled out of their original context (in his own career) and thrust into another context, the disciples' preaching and teaching.

The years passed, and the Lord did not return. Yet the faith of the followers of Jesus, whose numbers now included many people who had never seen him, remained strong. They were persuaded that he still lived as the heavenly Lord. In their evangelistic and pedagogical work, they began to cite individual incidents from the lifetime of Jesus in set short forms. That is, instead of quoting only the punch line (as in the hypothetical example above), Christian preachers and teachers used a small unit of material, one that included a brief introduction as well as the saying or action that concluded the unit. An example of such a tradition is this:

At that time the disciples came to Jesus, saying, 'Who is the greatest in the kingdom of heaven?' And calling to him a child, he put him in the midst of them, and said, 'Truly, I say to you, unless you turn and become like children, you will never enter the kingdom of heaven. Whoever humbles himself like this child, he is the greatest in the kingdom of heaven.' (Matt. 18.1–4; on 'at that time', see below)

At some point these small units were written down and collected into larger groupings, usually on the basis of subject matter. The results of this process may now be seen in the verses that follow the passage quoted immediately above, where there are further sayings about children and 'little ones' (probably not children, but the meek and lowly).

The years became decades. Some of the original disciples had been martyred, and others may have gone on lengthy missions to distant countries. Some Christians decided that they might after all need connected accounts of Jesus. We do not know how many stages lay between the units used in sermons and our present gospels, but let us say there were two. We shall now also use the best technical name for these small units, many of which survive in our present gospels: pericopes. The word literally means 'cut around'. Each pericope has an obvious beginning and end, and each can be cut out of its present place in one of the gospels and moved to another. It appears that groups of pericopes dealing with similar topics, such as healings or debates with opponents, were written on sheets of papyrus, copied, and circulated among various Christian communities. Next, these groupings were put together to form what we now call proto-gospels – works that told a connected story, but not the whole story. A proto-gospel, for example, might consist of a series of pericopes dealing with conflict between Jesus and other Jews, and conclude with his arrest, trial and execution. Or a proto-gospel might be a large assemblage of sayings relevant to the ongoing life of Christian communities (ethics, questions of rank, sayings about missionary work and the like). Finally, the first gospel as we have it was written. Most scholars think that this was Mark. Subsequent authors used Mark and incorporated other materials, such as proto-gospels or topical collections that the author of Mark had not included. The final gospels as we have them were probably composed between the years 70 and 90, though some scholars put Mark earlier, in the sixties.[2]

I wish to emphasize that we *do not know* that this is precisely how the gospels originated. We infer the process from the finished product. We note that the synoptic gospels (Matthew, Mark and Luke) consist of movable pericopes. We *know* that the final authors moved pericopes, because some units are in one context in one gospel and another in another. We *infer* that this had been the case for some years, and probably for some decades. We *do not know* that there were once 'fly-sheets', brief topical collections. We *infer* their previous existence from the fact that some material is now arranged topically. Similarly some scholars have inferred the existence of proto-gospels by analysing our present gospels, where they find signs of an earlier arrangement that has been altered.

I have offered a sketch of four stages: (1) units used in homiletical or pedagogical contexts; (2) collection of related units into groups of pericopes (perhaps circulated on individual sheets of papyrus); (3) proto-gospels; (4) our gospels. It is not necessary to believe in this four-stage process in order to understand the material. Some scholars, in fact, doubt (2) and some doubt (3). What is necessary is to comprehend the general development of the tradition. Jesus said and did things in a context, the context of his own life; he responded to the people he met and to the circumstances as he perceived them.

But we do not move directly from his life to the gospels. We move, rather, from his life to early Christian use of *individual incidents* as examples to score some point or other. Only gradually were pericopes assembled in books that purport to describe his career. But decades had passed, and the original context that inspired a given saying or action had been lost.

Above I quoted Matthew 18.1–4 as an example of a pericope that could be used to illustrate Jesus' concern for those who were powerless (he called a child, etc.). Its present introduction, however, is 'at that time', which implies a chronological setting. Those words are probably the setting provided by the final author. Matthew puts the passage about being like a child late in the narrative, just three chapters before the entry to Jerusalem. It immediately follows discussion of the Temple tax, a discussion which, he wrote, took place in Capernaum (Matt. 17.24–7). Mark places the same passage late, and also in Capernaum (Mark 9.33–7), but not after the story of the Temple tax, which he does not have. Luke puts the pericope about the child quite early in his gospel, ten chapters before the entry to Jerusalem (9.46–50). There is no reason to think that any of the authors knew precisely when Jesus uttered the statement about being childlike, or the particular circumstances that triggered it. Rather, each of them situated it where he wished. Matthew's phrase 'at that time' sounds like a biographical statement, as if the author knew that the saying about the child took place very late in Jesus' career and immediately after he was asked about the Temple tax. This is simply a narrative convenience. Matthew has taken one passage from an otherwise unknown source (the pericope about the Temple tax) and inserted it before a passage from Mark (the pericope about a child), linking the two with 'at that time' to make the whole read like a connected account. In fact, we do not know the setting of the event in the lifetime of Jesus.

I have been writing as if all the early Christians did to the material was to move it around and write brief introductions such as 'at that time'. But they also revised it. Revision of material that is reused is inevitable. The alternative to introducing minor alterations to make a pericope relevant to a new audience and a new situation would be embalming it. The Christian material was kept alive and fresh, even though it was used over and over again, by being applied to living issues – not all of which were the issues of Galilee between 25 and 30 CE.

Moreover, the early Christians also created new material; they made things up.[3] This sounds like an accusation of fraud or dishonesty, but it is only a sharp way of putting a procedure that they saw quite differently. Christians believed that Jesus had ascended into heaven and that they could address him in prayer. Sometimes he answered. These answers they attributed to 'the Lord'. We now want to know which Lord: Jesus before he was crucified or the risen Lord, resident in heaven? The Christians thought that it was all the same Lord. In the letters of Paul there is one clear instance of hearing the Lord answer prayer, though this must in fact have happened numerous times. Paul suffered from a 'thorn in the flesh', some undefined ailment. Three times in prayer he asked the Lord to remove it. '[The Lord] said to me,' Paul wrote, '"My grace is sufficient for you, for my power is made perfect in weakness"' (II Cor. 12.7–9). Here is a direct quotation of the heavenly Lord. We have Paul's letter, and so we can tell that he heard this in prayer. But some other Christian, or even Paul himself, might have repeated the saying without specifying that it came from the heavenly Lord. The consequence might have been that 'my power is made perfect in weakness' ended up in a gospel, attributed to the historical Jesus. In this case that did not happen, but it could have happened, and we must assume that sometimes such things did happen. Some of the early Christians thought that the heavenly Lord communicated quite freely with them. I cite again Paul, whose letters are the earliest surviving Christian literature:[4] he claimed to 'impart . . . in words' things that were 'not taught by human wisdom but taught by the Spirit' (I Cor. 2.13). As he wrote elsewhere, 'the Lord is the Spirit' (II Cor. 3.17). In other terms the Spirit that freely communicated with Paul and other Christians could be thought of as the Spirit of the risen Lord, who was in some way or other continuous with the historical Jesus.

I am not proposing that the early Christians engaged in wild flights of fancy, in which they created all sorts of things and attributed them to the Spirit = the Lord = Jesus. When we study the sayings in the synoptic gospels, I shall frequently point out how limited was early Christian creativity. I think it quite likely that the major changes in the material were those involved in altering context and making minor adjustments. But we must also accept that some material was created – that is, that Christians heard it in prayer.

A second potential source of newly created material was Jewish scripture (which became the Christian 'Old Testament' after Christians decided that some of their literature was also scripture, which they called the 'New Testament'). Christians thought that Hebrew prophets had spoken about Jesus, and that he fulfilled prophetic expectations. They could therefore read the prophets and find things that Jesus *must* have done. I shall explain this view in detail in the next chapter.

Scholars have developed various devices to try to determine which sayings and actions are 'authentic', that is, to distinguish newly created material from material that actually goes back to the lifetime of Jesus. I shall not describe these here, but some of them will appear in subsequent chapters. I have given a fairly full list of criteria, with examples, in *Studying the Synoptic Gospels* (chs. 20 and 21).

Two views are implicit in our account thus far, which I should now make explicit. One is that the gospels as we have them were not written by eyewitnesses on the basis of first-hand knowledge of Jesus. The other is that there is a major difference between the first three gospels and the fourth.*

Anonymity

We do not know who wrote the gospels. They presently have headings: 'according to Matthew', 'according to Mark', 'according to Luke' and 'according to John'. The Matthew and John who are meant were two of the original disciples of Jesus. Mark was a follower of Paul, and possibly also of Peter; Luke was one of Paul's converts.[5] These men – Matthew, Mark, Luke and John – really lived, but we do not know that they wrote gospels. Present evidence

---

* Such terms as 'First gospel' and 'Fourth gospel', here as elsewhere, refer to the sequence of the gospels in the New Testament, not to the order in which they were written.

indicates that the gospels remained untitled until the second half of the second century. I have summarized this evidence elsewhere,[6] and I shall not repeat it here, except for one point. The gospels as we have them were quoted in the first half of the second century, but always anonymously (as far as we can tell from surviving evidence). Names suddenly appear about the year 180. By then there were a lot of gospels, not just our four, and the Christians had to decide which ones were authoritative. This was a major issue, on which there were very substantial differences of opinion. We know who won: those Christians who thought that four gospels, no more and no fewer, were the authoritative records of Jesus.

Although we now know the outcome, in the late second century it was very uncertain. Some Christians wanted more gospels to be officially recognized, some fewer. I shall comment on only one part of the story: the existence of gospels that, in the end, were not accepted in catholic Christianity. These gospels, which are usually called 'apocryphal' ('hidden') gospels, have fascinated people for a long time. Some of them (such as the Gospel of the Egyptians) are lost and are known only by a few short passages that were quoted by writers whose work has survived. One can now read numerous other apocryphal gospels in English translation, but most of these were written after 180.[7] Two are relatively early and contain interesting material: the Infancy Gospel of James and the Gospel of Thomas. The first of these is a specialist gospel, as the title suggests: it deals only with Jesus' birth and childhood. The Gospel of Thomas is a collection of sayings found among gnostic manuscripts in Egypt. (Gnosticism was a world view that held everything material to be evil; the god who created the world was a bad god, and the creation was wicked. Gnostics who were also Christians held that the good God had sent Jesus to redeem people's souls, not their bodies, and that Jesus was not a real human being. The Christians who objected to these views finally declared them heretical.)

I share the general scholarly view that very, very little in the apocryphal gospels could conceivably go back to the time of Jesus. They are legendary and mythological. Of all the apocryphal material, only some of the sayings in the Gospel of Thomas are worth consideration. This does not mean that we can make a clean division: the historical four gospels versus the legendary apocryphal gospels. There are legendary traits in the four gospels in the New

Testament, and there is also a certain amount of newly created material (as we saw just above). Nevertheless, it is the four canonical gospels that we must search for traces of the historical Jesus.

We now return to the story of naming the gospels. To members of the winning party (those who wanted four and only four gospels), it was important to be able to attribute the 'right' gospels to people who, historically, were closely connected with Jesus or his greatest apostles. Christian scholarly detectives went to work, and from details in the gospels, which they regarded as clues to authorship, they derived views about who wrote each gospel. One example: in the gospel that now stands fourth in the New Testament, an unnamed 'beloved disciple' is prominent. This gospel, however, does not mention John, even though he was one of the main disciples (as we know from the other gospels, Acts and Paul's letter to Galatia). Second-century Christian detectives probably reasoned that the Fourth Gospel was written by John, who preferred to refer to himself as 'the beloved disciple', and accordingly we now call the Fourth Gospel 'the Gospel according to John'. Here the second-century Christians inferred authorship from the non-occurrence of a name.

The second-century academic/detective work was quite shrewd. It is, in fact, precisely on the basis of minor clues that today we try to say things about the authors of anonymous works. Their names may elude us, but surely not their characteristics. The conclusions of second-century Christians about names, however, were a lot firmer than the evidence warrants. In John (that is, the gospel now called John) the author was making *some* point by his frequent references to the unnamed 'beloved disciple'. He also had views about the other disciples' names, which differ from those of Matthew, Mark and Luke in a few respects (below, pp. 120–22). But we cannot be certain that his special treatment of disciples was intended as a clue to his own name. The first readers of the gospel may well have got the point, whatever it was. Why was our gospel not immediately attributed to John? The most probable answer is that the attribution was made quite late and was a guess rather than a well-established tradition.

It is unlikely that Christians knew the names of the authors of the gospels for a period of a hundred years or so, but did not mention them in any of the surviving literature (which is quite substantial).

It is also intrinsically probable that the gospels originally were headed only 'the gospel [good news] about Jesus Christ' or something of the sort, and did not give the names of their authors. The authors probably wanted to eliminate interest in who wrote the story and to focus the reader on the subject. More important, the claim of an anonymous history was higher than that of a named work. In the ancient world an anonymous book, rather like an encyclopaedia article today, implicitly claimed complete knowledge and reliability. It would have reduced the impact of the Gospel of Matthew had the author written 'this is my version' instead of 'this is what Jesus said and did'.

I shall throughout refer to the gospels by the names that are now familiar. For example, I shall call the author of the Gospel of Luke 'Luke', and I shall also call the gospel itself 'Luke', using a descriptive term in the case of ambiguity (for example, 'the evangelist Luke' is the author). I use the names for the sake of convenience only. My judgement is that all the gospels were written anonymously and that the names were assigned after the year 150, on the basis of clues such as the one I proposed for John.

The Synoptics and John

In the previous chapter we noted briefly that John's chronology is different from that of the other three gospels. I wish now to explore this and other differences, which are very substantial.

Matthew, Mark and Luke are collectively called 'the synoptic gospels', since in the eighteenth century scholars began studying them in books with parallel columns, called 'synopses', which means literally 'seeing together'. One can print the texts of Matthew, Mark and Luke side by side and make many close comparisons. The general outline of Jesus' life is the same, and many of the units are also the same. We shall see examples in chs. 11, 12 and 16. John stands apart. The narrative outline is different, and the discourse material bears little similarity to the sayings of the synoptics. We shall consider the narrative outline first.

The synoptic gospels refer to Passover only once, and the entire action seems to have taken place in less than twelve months. In Mark 2.23–8 grain is edible raw, which puts this incident in early summer; in 6.39 it is spring, since the grass is green; that same spring Jesus goes to Jerusalem for Passover (Mark 11; for Passover, see 14.1, 12). If these clues to seasons are accurate and are in the right place, the entire ministry took place between one early summer or late spring and the next spring. In John, however, Jesus goes to Jerusalem for Passover early in his career (2.13), and there is another Passover (6.4) before the final one (11.55; 13.1; 18.28). This makes the public ministry slightly longer than two years. John's narrative also places a good deal of Jesus' ministry in Judaea, whereas the synoptic account puts all but the final week in Galilee. We also noted in the previous chapter that John places Jesus' execution on 14 Nisan, while the synoptics have it on 15 Nisan.

Two other aspects of John's narrative deserve mention. The 'cleansing of the Temple', which in the synoptics is a prime cause of Jesus' execution, in John comes at the very beginning of his ministry, on his first trip to Jerusalem (2.13–22), and it has no serious consequence. The Johannine account of the trial before Jewish officials is substantially different in content from the synoptic versions. In the synoptics there is a formal trial before a Jewish court, the Sanhedrin. Witnesses are called and testify, and finally Jesus is interrogated. The high priest formulates an official charge: guilty of blasphemy. In John, Jesus is interrogated, apparently privately, first by Annas (who formerly had been the high priest, and who was the father of five subsequent high priests) and then by Caiaphas, the serving high priest, who is said to have been the son-in-law of Annas (John 18.12–40). There is no mention either of witnesses or of a formal charge.

In terms of *intrinsic probability* the Johannine trial scene is much more likely than that of the synoptics. The person who reads Josephus will find that John describes a kind of trial that would have been considered adequate in a minor case: the high priest consulted advisers (in this case a former high priest, Annas) and made a recommendation to the prefect, who acted on it. This is more likely than that there was a full trial before a formal court during the festival. On the trial, then, John seems superior. With regard to the placement of the 'cleansing of the Temple', however, the synoptic account, which puts it late, is much likelier than John's. Jesus is said to have attempted to interfere with some of the buying and selling that was necessary for the continuation of the Temple service – a service explicitly commanded by God. This must have been offensive, and a close connection between Jesus' action in the Temple and his execution is highly likely.

With regard to the duration of Jesus' ministry, it is hard to choose. John certainly catches the rhythm of life in Jewish Palestine, which was punctuated by thrice-yearly feasts. Besides the three Passovers, John mentions a feast without further specification (5.1), while John 7 is set during the feast of Booths (or Tabernacles). The following table compares John's references to feasts with the feasts that would have taken place if there were three Passovers during Jesus' ministry:

Passover (spring)	John 2.13
Weeks (Pentecost, early summer)	perhaps John 5.1
Booths (Tabernacles, autumn)	not mentioned
Passover	John 6.4
Weeks	not mentioned
Booths	John 7
Passover	John 11.55

Although there are gaps, John's general outline is perfectly plausible. But so is the synoptic account. It runs as follows. About the time John the Baptist was arrested, another prophet arose – Jesus; he preached and healed for a few months, making a noticeable stir, but not so much commotion that he scared Antipas; he went to Jerusalem at Passover, made a grand gesture in the Temple, said some provocative things about authority and 'the kingdom', and was quickly dispatched. This is perfectly reasonable. Josephus' references to other prophetic figures are compatible with very short careers. They offered 'signs of deliverance' in the desert, crowds followed them, and the Romans quickly sent troops – who did not have to wait for a formal Jewish trial before using their swords. (On these prophets, see pp. 29f. above.) Further clues make the short ministry of the synoptics somewhat more likely than John's. Jesus seems to have been itinerant, and his close followers gave up their normal occupations to be with him. We hear of outside support (Luke 8.1; below, p. 109), but nevertheless none of the material explains how the small group lived, where its members slept, or who paid the bills. (John 13.29 implies that they collected cash in some unspecified way.) It is at least slightly easier to explain this general absence of information on the hypothesis of a short ministry, one that was based on improvising ways and means. A longer ministry implies more organization, and one would expect to find more signs of that in the gospels. (On the itinerant lifestyle, see pp. 107–11 below.) The synoptic framework is at least as plausible as John's, and it may have a slight edge.

This discussion may seem to imply that we must accept one or the other: either John (three Passovers; early cleansing of the Temple; informal trial) or the synoptics (one Passover; late cleansing; semi-formal trial). It is tempting to alternate between them on the basis of plausibility or intrinsic probability, while compromising on the question of duration: a ministry of eleven to twenty-five months (compromise); cleansing of Temple near the end (synoptics); informal trial (John). We must, however, entertain another possibility altogether: perhaps none of the authors knew what took place when (except, of course, the trial and crucifixion). Possibly they had scattered bits of information, from which they constructed believable narratives that contain a fair amount of guesswork. Or perhaps they did not care about chronological sequence and arranged the material according to some other plan (for example, by topic). This would have resulted in chronological clues being scattered at random, and we could not draw good inferences from them. It may be that the summer scene of Mark 2.23–8 should not come before the spring scene of Mark 6.39; perhaps it belongs to the next summer rather than the previous one. In this section of Mark (2.1–3.6) the arrangement is topical, and it is quite possible that Mark put 2.23–8 where it now is only because it suits the theme of the section (minor legal disputes in Galilee).

When we turn from the narrative outline to the contents, we find that John and the synoptics are again very different.

(1) In the synoptics many of Jesus' healings, in fact some of those on which the story turns, are exorcisms. In John there are no exorcisms. (On exorcisms and other miracles, see ch. 10.)

(2) In the synoptics, when asked for a 'sign' of his authority, Jesus refuses to give one (Mark 8.11f). Among the most prominent aspects of John is a series of 'signs' of Jesus' status and authority (John 2.11, 23; 3.2; 4.48, 54; 6.2, 14; 7.31; 9.16; 11.47; 12.8, 37; 20.30).

(3) The synoptic Jesus asks the disciples who people say that he is (Mark 8.27), but he does not explicitly comment on the subject himself. When challenged about his authority, he simply asks about the authority of John the Baptist and refuses to say anything about his own (Mark 11.27–33). In John, on the other hand, the principal subject of Jesus' discourses is himself – his status, his identity and his relation to God and to the disciples. These are not private communications to his followers, they are the substance of his public teaching.

(4) The chief topic of the synoptic sayings material is the kingdom of God. In John this term occurs only in 3.3–5.

(5) Perhaps most striking is the difference in teaching *style*. In the synoptics we find short sayings on diverse topics. The only substantial discourses consist of a series of such sayings. The other main literary form is the parable, in which a simple story serves to make a point about God and his kingdom. The comparison is indicated by the phrase 'is like': the kingdom of God is like the following story. In literary terms the synoptic parables are based on the simile, and many are simply extended similes. In John there are lengthy and involved metaphorical discourses, notably lacking the word 'like', and therefore not similes. Most characteristic of John's metaphorical discourses are the 'I am' sayings, such as 'I am the true vine' (John 15.1). This is a metaphor in which the author identifies Jesus as the reality that is indicated by the symbol. A vine is a symbol of life; Jesus is the real vine; therefore Jesus *is* life. He is not *like* something – in this case, a vine – but rather he is the only *true* vine. Similarly Jesus is bread (John 6.35), that is, the only real bread; everything else called bread is only a paltry imitation. Unlike the synoptic teaching material, in John there are no stories, no actions, that illustrate how God deals with people. Just as there are no synoptic-like similes or parables in John, there are no symbolic metaphors in the synoptics.

It is impossible to think that Jesus spent his short ministry teaching in two such completely different ways, conveying such different contents, and that there were simply two traditions, each going back to Jesus, one transmitting 50 per cent of what he said and another one the other 50 per cent, with almost no overlaps.

Consequently, for the last 150 or so years scholars have had to choose. They have almost unanimously, and I think entirely correctly, concluded that the teaching of the historical Jesus is to be sought in the synoptic gospels and that John represents an advanced theological development, in which meditations on the person and work of Christ are presented in the first person, as if Jesus said them. The author of the Gospel of John would be the first to point out that this does not mean that the discourses that he attributed to Jesus are 'untrue'; he would not have agreed that historical accuracy and truth are synonomous, any more than he thought that a true vine was a vegetable. In John's view, something that is accurate on the surface is by definition not 'true'. Real water quenches thirst for ever, a property that the wet stuff that appears to be water does not have (John 4.13).

The author offers his own view of the teaching material in his gospel perfectly clearly (attributing it, of course, to Jesus):

I have yet many things to say to you, but you cannot bear them now. When the Spirit of truth comes, he will guide you into all the truth; for he will not speak on his own authority, but whatever he hears he will speak, and he will declare to you the things that are to come. (John 16.13)

Similarly, in 14.23 the author of John says that Jesus 'will come' to his followers in the future, and in 14.25 that the Holy Spirit 'will come' and teach them everything. The author reveals that he has been listening to the Spirit of Truth that has come to him; this Spirit may also be called 'Jesus'. John's view of Jesus was strongly trans-historical; the boundaries of ordinary history were inadequate, and Jesus, or the Spirit (not clearly distinguished), continued to teach after the crucifixion.

All Christians would have agreed with this to some degree. The Lord, we saw above, still spoke to them in visions and during prayer. We should assume that some of these messages ended up in the synoptic gospels. But the author of John went further; he wrote a gospel based on this premise. In his own terms his work contains many teachings of the Holy Spirit, or of Jesus, who has 'come' to the author after the crucifixion and resurrection, and who has told him truths that the disciples did not hear.

Once we conclude that we should rely on the synoptics for the teaching of Jesus, what impact does this have on the question of the narrative outline? Is John's sequence of events as strongly determined by the author's own theology as its discourse material? There are two cases where we must answer in the affirmative. Previously we noted that according to John, Jesus died on Friday, 14 Nisan, instead of Friday, 15 Nisan, as the synoptics have it. The reason is that the author wanted to depict Jesus as the Passover lamb, which was sacrificed on the fourteenth. In describing Jesus' death, John wrote that the soldiers did not break Jesus' legs, as they did those of the other two men, since scripture (the Hebrew Bible) had said, 'Not a bone of him shall be broken' (John 19.36). This quotation refers to the Passover lamb (Pss. 34.20; Exod. 12.46; Num. 9.12). In John 1.36 Jesus is called 'the lamb of God', and the equation Jesus = lamb has determined John's dating of the crucifixion. At the very time when the Passover lambs were being sacrificed in the Temple, the *true* lamb of God was dying outside the walls of the city. Once we see that the date in John agrees so strongly with its theology, we are inclined to prefer the synoptics and conclude that Jesus was executed on Friday, 15 Nisan.[8]

John's placement of the cleansing of the Temple is probably also to be attributed to a theological theme. The antagonists of Jesus in John's Gospel are 'the Jews', who are part of 'the world', which is bad and which rejects Jesus and the disciples (John 1.9–13; 15.18f.). It suits this theological conflict to put the incident at the Temple very early in the gospel. The ministry starts with a stark conflict between Jesus and the traditional religion of Judaism.

The consequence of these considerations is that we can say neither that John was creative only with the teaching material, nor that he had a good source for his narrative and that he followed it faithfully. I would like to accept John's account of the Jewish trial because it is so much more believable than the synoptic trial, but it would be arbitrary to choose this part if I cannot show that a good source underlies John 18.12f., 24, and I cannot. Possibly John was just more astute with regard to *realpolitik* than were the other evangelists, and so wrote a story with greater verisimilitude. The Jewish trial in John is *like* the sort of thing that really happened in Judaea and in other Roman provinces that were governed in the same way. Whether it is an accurate account of what happened on that particular night in Jerusalem is another question.

The synoptic gospels are to be preferred as our basic source of information about Jesus. Yet their authors too were theologians and were capable of creativity. Just as we cannot pose an absolute alternative between the legendary and mythological apocryphal gospels and the historical canonical ones (since there are legendary and mythological elements in the gospels of the New Testament), so also we cannot make a clean division between the theological Gospel of John and the historical synoptics, since the synoptics also are the work of theologians. There are no sources that give us the 'unvarnished truth'; the varnish of faith in Jesus covers everything. Yet the synoptic authors did not homogenize their material, as John did. The joints and seams are visible, and the contents are quite diverse. There is nothing like the sameness of the Johannine monologues. The synoptic authors, that is, revised traditional material much less thoroughly than did John.

The Synoptic Gospels as Biographies

We saw above that the synoptic gospels are made up of bits and pieces, easily separable, put together by the authors. We may consider references to relative times as an example of the editorial work. Mark often used 'immediately' as the chronological link between passages:

1.12 the spirit immediately drove him . . .
1.21 they went into Capernaum; and immediately on the sabbath . . .
1.29 immediately he left the synagogue and entered the house of Simon . . .

There are, of course, variations: 'that evening' (1.32); 'in the morning' (1.35). Most often, there is no chronological marker at all:

1.39f. he went throughout all Galilee . . . and a leper came to him
2.13 he went out again beside the sea
3.1 again he entered the synagogue

The use of 'immediately' is a narrative device to give pace and drive to the account, and it works very well. But the impression is overwhelming that Mark had isolated events and sayings, and that he put them together. There is no *biography* in our sense of the word: no development, seldom a concrete setting (such as, 'this was an important issue just then, because . . .'), just short accounts stitched together with an introductory word or phrase. Approximately the same is true of Matthew and Luke, who probably relied on Mark, though their construction is more complicated.

The synoptic gospels lack most of the things that we now expect in the story of someone's life. Looks, personality, character – we know very little. When it comes to the other figures besides Jesus, we are really in the dark. Pilate, curiously, is given touches of personality and character by Matthew and John, but for the most part the other actors are very flat. Peter, we learn, was a little wishy-washy. What was John like? James? We do not know. What about the Pharisees? They appear in a group, denounce Jesus, sometimes are denounced in turn, and disappear. What were they up to? Were they all equally hostile towards Jesus? Where did they go when they disappeared? If they thought that Jesus' disciples were breaking the sabbath law (Mark 2.24), why did they not lay a charge by reporting them to a priest (who might have fined them by requiring that each bring a sin offering, two birds, when next in Jerusalem)?

Many readers today do not realize how episodic the synoptic gospels are, since Christians have had almost 2,000 years to build up a more novelistic view of the events and people in the gospels. Books have been written, movies made, explanations offered. On Sundays numerous priests, pastors and teachers retell some aspect of the gospel account, adding personality and motive. Judas, the disciple who betrayed Jesus, is often depicted as a frustated zealot who wanted Jesus to lead a revolution, who thought of himself as a great man in Jesus' kingdom, and who was bitterly angry when he learned that Jesus wanted another sort of kingdom.[9] This gives the story colour and drama. There is nothing in the gospels about Judas' ambitions at all. Perhaps he realized that Jesus was a marked man and decided to get out when he still could, while also making a profit. One guess is as good as another. Similarly Mary Magdalene has appealed enormously to people who have imagined all sorts of romantic things about her: she had been a prostitute, she was beautiful, she was in love with Jesus, she fled to France carrying his child. For all we know, on the basis of our sources, she was eighty-six, childless, and keen to mother unkempt young men.

At a very early date Christians began improving on the gospels' sparse accounts by making up stories. The apocryphal gospels are full of romantic incidents and all sorts of lovely touches, such as that an ox and ass were in the stable where Jesus was born and that they worshipped him. This is from a gospel written in the eighth or ninth century, now called the Gospel of Pseudo-Matthew. The author had studied the Gospel of Matthew and wrote in the same style. He offered proof of his account by quoting Jewish scripture, while in fact deriving his information from the quotation, just as Matthew did: 'An ox and an ass worshipped him. Then was fulfilled that which was said through the prophet Isaiah: "The ox knows his owner and the ass his master's crib" (Isa. 1.3).' This colourful image has been used in art and music, and is probably as familiar as the stories about Jesus that are actually in the New Testament. The only basis for putting an ox and an ass in the nativity scene is this gospel, whose author discovered a sentence in Isaiah that had not yet been used to provide information about Jesus.

So much romantic imagination has been lavished on the gospels for so many centuries that the modern reader does not at once see how stark they are. We automatically add novelistic details, many of which have reached people who have never entered a church or read the Bible. Apart from the birth narratives in Matthew and Luke, where novelistic interest has already penetrated, there is not much in the rest of the gospels. The individual scenes are brief and to the point. This presumably means that they have been *shaped* precisely in order to make their point, other matter being pruned away. The consequence is that we cannot write a biography of Jesus. We do not have letters in which he reflects on events and offers his own version to a close friend or relative; we do not have diaries written by people who knew him or even who heard about him; we do not have newspapers telling us just what was going on in Capernaum in 29 CE. We have a general outline of his life, plus brief stories, sayings and parables, and from them we can learn quite a lot, but we cannot write 'the life of Jesus' in the modern sense, describing his education, tracing his development, analysing the influence of his parents, showing his response to specific events – and so on.

Therefore a book about Jesus cannot be very much like a book about Jefferson or Churchill (to go back to our earlier examples). Our information is also deficient in comparison to what is available for most of the great men of the Graeco-Roman world. Men like Brutus, Caesar, Pompey, Antony, and so on came from well-known families, lived a lot of their lives in the public spotlight, and associated with men of letters, who sometimes wrote about them, or about the events in which they participated. Plutarch, the biographer of the rich and famous of the time, could in some cases write something very much like a biography in our meaning of the word. But he could not always do so. When his information was too limited to permit a chronological study that included successes, reverses and the like, he produced instead very short passages that were introduced by such informative words as 'again' or 'and'. The reader of Plutarch's study of Phocion who does not know what was going on in fourth century BCE Athens will be puzzled. One reads witty remarks on individual points, but it is hard to see what they add up to. That is the situation in which the synoptic gospels place us – except that people have had a long time to fill in the gaps, and an apparently endless amount of energy and inventiveness to use in the endeavour.

I am an academic, a professional scholar, and a historian by inclination and education. I shall do what I can to fill in the gaps and to make coherent sense of the bits and pieces that we have. This effort (the reader may already have noticed) is somewhat like reconstructive surgery: breaking comes before rebuilding. Unlike the surgeon, however, I do not start out with a picture of what our subject originally looked like. Nor do I have a fixed view of what he *should* look like when the operation is over. I start out with the results of plastic surgery that aimed at glorification and that often did not preserve the original place and significance of the individual bits. I aim at recovering the historical Jesus. But the difficulties will always mean that results are partial at best. A true title of the project would be 'basic information about Jesus: important aspects of what he did, what he thought, and what others thought of him'.

In the reconstruction of history, we must always consider *context* and *content*. The better we can correlate the two, the more we shall understand. The reason politicians and others complain about being quoted out of context is that context matters as much as the words that are quoted. Jesus said, 'Love your enemies' (Matt. 5.44 // Luke 6.27). Who were his hearers' enemies? Often people say that they were the Roman soldiers. Jesus meant, love Roman soldiers, and if they hit you turn the other cheek. But there were not any Roman soldiers in Galilee (unless they were on vacation there). Perhaps the enemy was the village magistrate or the biggest property owner. If this book were a sermon, it would not matter much. 'Love your enemies' can be applied sermonically to a lot of cases, and the original context need not determine the present-day significance of the saying. But if we want to know what Jesus was up to, what he had in mind, what sort of relations he worried about, at what level he addressed other people – national, local or familial – we need to know the context as well as the words. Our task in general is to search for good fits between the units of which the synoptic gospels are composed and a context in Jesus' day and time. If we can do that, we shall know a lot about Jesus.

7. TWO CONTEXTS

Contexts come in all shapes and sizes. We now know that we live in an enormous universe, which seems to keep getting bigger. Meanwhile, our own planet is shrinking; it is harder and harder to find a remote corner in it. Biologically, we humans are mammals. These are our own large contexts: we are life forms, specifically mammals, who inhabit a given corner of a large universe. Knowing them gives us perspective and sometimes very direct information about our behaviour. Scientists often explain behaviour that is common to all humans by putting it in the context of animal behaviour in general: we protect our territory, we huff, puff and turn red when angry, and so on. These and other responses to danger and hostility are explained by referring to a very large context: we are animals. At the level of folk wisdom, people often use a similar explanatory device: 'that's human nature' is brought forward to explain and sometimes excuse individual actions that reveal greed, selfishness and other unlovely traits.

We also live in a given part of the world at a given time in its history. Our home towns, counties, states and countries provide us with a myriad of contexts. And then, close to home, are our families, friends and associates. All of these contexts help make us who we are and help explain what we do. We often explain such characteristics as understatement, bragging and gesticulating by attributing them to the country or state from which the person comes: the British understate points, Texans brag, Italians gesticulate.

The explanatory power of immediate contexts is even greater. We appeal to very recent history, or continuing situations, to understand more or less everything. A very large context explains why my pulse races when I am alarmed, but only a very close context explains why my pulse races at some particular moment. There are also a lot of intermediate contexts. In recent years, for example, western nations have moved from building weapons that could destroy the Soviet Union to giving aid to some of its component parts. Given recent history, this change is easy to understand. If, centuries later, someone were to discover only the facts about weapons and aid, he or she would have to conclude that the context had changed. But did the western democracies move closer politically to the Soviet Union? Or the reverse? Without context, we usually do not know what is going on or what an action means. Some actions, however, suggest their own context or (more usually) give us a choice of two or three different contexts.

Ideals and ideology also provide contexts, contexts that we carry around with us all the time, in our heads. These contexts are much trickier, since they are not places and events, but mental constructs. This makes them and their effects much harder to study, since we cannot read minds. Nevertheless, such contexts exist and exert power over human actions. An example: Americans can justify war to themselves if they can place it in the main ideology of the nation: a desire for freedom and democracy. If a US government wants to engage in military activity, it will ordinarily try to place it in the context of American ideology. Wars to protect economic interests are much harder to sell to the public. That is to say, many Americans have an ideological context in which war has a proper place. If a war does not fit that particular context, they have a hard time finding another context that will justify it. Sometimes, needless to say, people fool themselves, and sometimes leaders deliberately try to mislead the public because of what they regard as overriding national interest. Deception of either sort shows how strong the ideology is. Such ideological contexts are interesting historically: looking back, we can see that people viewed an activity as fitting in, and this explains their behaviour. Ideological outlook is also a context that helps shape actual behaviour in the here and now. If I think that freedom and democracy are threatened, I shall be much readier to march off to war than if I think that what is really at stake are the profits of a few large industries.

We would understand Jesus better if we knew everything about his world and its history, including what people of his day thought, what their ideals were. We need more knowledge of context than the opening chapters of this book provide. It would also help if we could uncover the precise circumstances in which the gospels were written. In this chapter, however, I wish to explain only the two contexts that will be of greatest help in understanding the gospels and Jesus himself. The first is the theological (or ideological) setting in which the synoptic gospels, especially Matthew and Luke, place the story. Most early Christians shared this mental construct, but I shall limit discussion to the synoptic gospels, with only a few references to Paul by way of further example. The second is the context given by our knowledge of what happened immediately before Jesus started his work and soon after it ended: the direct context of his public career.

The Theological Context: The History of Salvation

The gospels present Jesus as the person who fulfils the hopes of Israel and through whom God will save the world. That is, they put him in the context of the 'history of salvation', taken directly from the Hebrew Bible and adapted. This history runs as follows: God called Abraham and his descendants, gave them the law through Moses, established Israel as a kingdom in the time of Saul and David, and punished Israel for disobedience by exile; he will some day raise his people again, if need be defeating their oppressors in war; many Gentiles will turn to worship him.[1] This scheme is a Jewish theological construct, and it is presupposed in the gospels, but they expand and alter it slightly. The gospels were written in full knowledge of the fact that Jesus' own movement was spreading much better among Gentiles than among Jews. Thus in some ways they de-Judaized the scheme by emphasizing Israel's partial rejection of Jesus and his acceptance by a few Gentiles.

The design as such, however, is well known from biblical and other Jewish literature. Parts of Isaiah, for example, predict that eventually Gentiles will turn to the God of Israel and thus be saved (e.g., Isa. 2.2f.). The inclusion of Gentiles, though stressed in Christianity, was not novel. We note that this theological plan is partly past and partly future. In the past, God called Abraham, and so forth; in the future, he will redeem his people and the Gentiles as well. Jews could explain their own history by seeing it in light of this ideology. If they suffered, they could explain that God was punishing them but would later restore them; if they flourished, God was fulfilling his promises; if they flourished a little but not much, God was giving them a foretaste of full redemption. Obviously these explanatory devices, which place events in a larger ideological construction, could be used to explain current events at any time. The theological scheme was there and could be exploited. If something dramatic happened, anyone could stand up and say, 'See here, this is part of God's grand design. It is time for our redemption.'

I doubt that very many Jews construed current events as key points in the history of salvation, except for very major events, such as Rome's destruction of Jerusalem in 70 CE. Some Jews were more inclined to see the things that happened around them as an important part of God's overall plan, some less. Fortunately, we do not need to be able to count noses; we only need to know that an ideological/theological framework existed and allowed people to take account of current events and make sense of them by saying that they fitted a larger divine plan.

The early Christians saw Jesus as having a major place – in fact the ultimate place – in the context of Jewish salvation history. Paul, for example, thought that it was time for the Gentiles to turn to the God of Israel, and that calling them was his own special mission.[2] The authors of the gospels also accepted the scheme. This required them to highlight certain moments in the history of Israel, moments that were centuries apart. Matthew and Luke, in different ways and to different degrees, focus on the great figures of that history as precursors or ancestors of Jesus: Abraham, Moses and David.

According to Matthew, Jesus was descended from Abraham and David (Matt. 1.1). His birth fulfilled a prophecy that the ruler of Israel would be born in Bethlehem, the city of David (2.6). In the earliest scene from the period of Jesus' adulthood, Matthew has John the Baptist warn his hearers not to count on the fact that they are Abraham's descendants (3.9; also Luke 3.8). Matthew identifies the Baptist as Elijah, an Israelite prophet whom some expected to return (17.12f.; cf. Mark 9.13).[3] In the future kingdom, people from east and west will sit down with Abraham, Isaac and Jacob (8.11; cf. Luke 13.28; for the image, see also Luke 16.29, 31). In the Sermon on the Mount, Jesus supplements and corrects the law of Moses

(5.21–42). Some of Jesus' disciples have a vision in which he talks with Moses and Elijah (Matt. 17.1–8; also Mark 9.2–8; Luke 9.28–36). When Jesus enters Jerusalem, some of the people hail him as 'son of David' (21.9). In teaching, Jesus discusses whether or not the Messiah must be a son of David, apparently arguing not (22.41–5; similarly Mark 12.35–7; Luke 20.41–4). People who need help address him as 'son of David' (15.22; 20.30f.; so also Mark 10.47f.; Luke 18.38f.). Even when the relationship between Jesus and Moses, Abraham or David is partially negative, as it is in a few cases (for example, Jesus corrects the law), the context is still the same: Matthew sets Jesus in a framework of Jewish salvation history.

Luke, besides sharing some of these references, has others. When John the Baptist is born, his father remembers the oath that God gave to Abraham, promising to rescue Israel (Luke 1.73f.). An angel predicts that God will give to Jesus 'the throne of his father David' (1.32). Jesus will rule over 'the house of Jacob for ever' (1.33). Luke emphasizes that Jesus' birthplace was the city of David (2.4, 11). In Luke's resurrection account Jesus interprets for the disciples the portions of the law of Moses and the writings of the prophets that concern himself (24.27, 44).

Mark lacks a birth narrative, and consequently there is less opportunity to discuss Jesus' lineage, but this gospel as well is set in the context of Jewish salvation history, as we see from the references to Mark in the paragraph on Matthew. Moreover, all the gospels are heavily marked by words, phrases and themes that are well known in Jewish scripture.[4]

That the New Testament follows the Old Testament is well known to all. One ends and the other begins. That is the way the gospels present the situation. The authors of the gospels did such a good job here as in other cases that we do not notice how striking their view is. The history is extremely selective, the key events come at very great intervals, and people often miss the fact that several centuries intervened between events. Moreover, several centuries drop out entirely; the reader of the Protestant Bible has very little information about the period 400 to 4 BCE; the reader of the Roman Catholic Bible has only a little more.[5] An ordinary historian would expect people who thought of Jesus as 'king' to discuss him in light of more recent kings than David – Herod, for example, or one of the Hasmoneans. In salvation history, the number of centuries does not matter, since God is in charge. According to a traditional biblical chronology (one that dates the creation at the year 4004 BC), God called Abraham in 1921 BC, Moses led the Israelites out of Egypt about 1500 BC, and David flourished about 1030 BC. These were Jesus' main predecessors in salvation history. An approximate parallel today to the gospel's treatment of Jesus would be to describe Elizabeth II by saying that she is heir to the throne of William the Conqueror, that she fulfills the promise of King Arthur, and that she is what her name implies, a second Elizabeth, and is therefore like Elizabeth I – and, moreover, to do this without saying anything about Cromwell's overthrow of Charles I, the restoration of Charles II, the bloodless revolution that brought William of Orange and Mary to the throne of England, the way in which the monarch became subject to an elected government, and so on.

The modern historian wants to know the circumstances in which Jesus worked, why his efforts sometimes succeeded and sometimes failed, why the Christian movement developed as it did, and the like. The gospels answer: God now decided to bring to culmination a process of salvation that he started with the call of Abraham. The plan of God is difficult for a historian to study. To stay with our analogy, let us suppose that today someone, completely convinced that Elizabeth II fulfils the promises of future greatness that are implied in the stories of Arthur, the Conqueror and Elizabeth I, wrote an account of Elizabeth II partly based on stories about her predecessors. Here our analogy starts to break down, since we know so much about Elizabeth II. An author who wrote that she is a virgin (like Elizabeth I), that her sword is named Excalibur (like Arthur's), that French is her first language (like William the Conqueror) would not be believed. Our supposed author could, to be sure, appeal to genuine parallels in order to support his case: there are now troubles with the Irish, as in the days of Elizabeth I; Elizabeth II can speak French. Such parallels, however, would not prove to us that other aspects of the reign of Elizabeth I or William the Conqueror should provide information about Elizabeth II.

The authors of the gospels offer this kind of information about Jesus, information that is based on the assumption that he fulfilled biblical statements. This does not prove that they were dishonest historians. They were not historians at all, except accidentally (though Luke had some of the attributes of a Hellenistic historian). Nor were they dishonest. They believed that Jesus really did fulfil the promises of Hebrew scripture. If he did so in one case, presumably he did so in another. There were some genuine overlaps, and this made it very easy for the early Christians to add new facts derived from Jewish scripture. As late as Pseudo-Matthew, who read in Isaiah that the ox and ass know their master, and who therefore added these animals to the nativity scene, this process was still going on (above, p. 75).

This way of understanding and using the Bible, in technical language, is 'typological'. A person or event in Jewish scripture constitutes a 'type', in the sense of an archetype or prototype. Something or somebody later is the fulfilment of the type, and the prior event gives information about the subsequent one. Paul uses this term: the people who followed Moses out of Egypt, but who then transgressed and were punished by death, are a 'type for us', a 'type' that is intended to warn 'us' not to transgress in the same way (I Cor. 10.1–12).[6] 'These things happened to them as a type, and they were written down for our instruction' (I Cor. 10.11). The gospels' view of promise and fulfilment works very much the same way.

This way of seeing history was of great assistance to the authors of the gospels. It allowed them to fill in a few of the blank spaces in the story of Jesus. They were probably set on this course by genuine parallels between John the Baptist and Jesus, on the one hand, and biblical characters or predictions on the other. That is, first-century Jews sometimes intentionally modelled their own actions on those of biblical figures. It may well be that John the Baptist actually did dress like Elijah. It is likely that Jesus rode into Jerusalem on an ass, thus consciously recalling a prophecy in Zechariah (see Matt. 21.4f., where Zech. is quoted). There is good evidence that, in the decade or so after Jesus, other prophets intentionally acted in ways that recalled biblical stories of events that had taken place centuries before (above, pp. 29f.). It was not only Matthew, Mark and Luke who saw Jesus' true context as being the saving history of Israel, nor was Paul the only first-century Jew who thought in terms of 'types' and fulfilment; others, quite possibly including Jesus, thought in the same way.

The more parallels there were between Jesus and characters or prophecies in Hebrew scripture, the more likely Matthew, Mark and Luke were to invent still more. They may have reasoned that if there were six similarities, there probably had been a seventh. I think that there is no doubt that they did invent some, though the possibility of overlaps, or of Jesus' own conscious imitation of scriptural types, means that we must often be uncertain. The clearest cases of invention are in the birth narratives. Matthew and Luke write that Jesus was born in Bethlehem but grew up in Nazareth. This probably reflects two sorts of 'facts': in ordinary history, Jesus was from Nazareth; according to salvation history, the redeemer of Israel *should* have been born in Bethlehem, David's city. The two gospels have completely different and irreconcilable ways of moving Jesus and his family from one place to the other. I shall put summaries of the passages in columns:

Matthew 1.18 – 2.23	Luke 2.1 – 39
	Joseph and Mary *lived in Nazareth*. Augustus Caesar required all males ('all the world') to register for tax purposes, and to register in the home town of a remote ancestor. Joseph was descended from David,
Joseph and Mary *lived in Bethlehem*.	and so he *went to Bethlehem*, taking Mary along. While there, she bore Jesus.
When Jesus was born, an angel warned them to flee, since Herod who had heard that a new king would be born, intended to kill all male infants.	
They took refuge in Egypt and, when Herod died, returned to their home in Bethlehem. There, however, they found another Herod (Archelaus), and so *moved to Nazareth* in Galilee (where there was a third Herod, Antipas).	When she was able to travel, the family *returned to their home in Nazareth*.

It is not possible for both these stories to be accurate. It is improbable that either is. They agree only on the two sets of 'facts': in real history, Jesus was from Nazareth; in salvation history, he must have been born in Bethlehem. They disagree on which town was originally the family's home, and they also have completely different devices for moving it from one place to another. Luke's device is fantastic. According to Luke's own genealogy (3.23–38), David had lived forty-two generations before Joseph. Why should Joseph have had to register in the town of one of his ancestors forty-two generations earlier? What was Augustus – the most rational of Caesars – thinking of? The entirety of the Roman empire would have been uprooted by such a decree. Besides, how would any given man know where to go? No one could trace his genealogy for forty-two generations, but if he could, he would find that he had *millions* of ancestors (one million is passed at the twentieth generation). Further, David doubtless had tens of thousands of descendants who were alive at the time. Could they all identify themselves? If so, how would they all register in a little village? One can, of course, revise what Luke wrote so that it is less fantastic: Caesar really decreed that select males, those who considered themselves descended from the royal family of each of the kingdoms in the empire, should register in this way. But such a revision would not solve the problem. People resort to such alterations of the text in order to try to save it: the text must be true, and if we revise it we can still claim that it is true. Revision, however, overthrows the principle. Substantively, the proposal that only royal families had to register in their ancestral homes overlooks the fact that there was a royal family in power in Palestine: Herod's. Augustus supported Herod. He would not have asked members of a royal family that had been out of power for over 500 years, and that had been superseded by two successive dynasties (the Hasmonean and the Herodian), to register in some special way. He would not have wanted the social tension that reviving hopes of a Davidic kingdom would have created.

But it is not reasonable to think that there was ever a decree that required people to travel in order to be registered for tax purposes. There are a lot of difficulties with Luke's census. One is that he dates it near Herod's death (4 BCE) and also ten years later, when Quirinius was legate of Syria (6 CE). We know from Josephus, supported by an ancient inscription, that in the year 6 CE, when Quirinius was legate, Rome did take a census of people who lived in Judaea, Samaria and Idumaea – not Galilee, and not by asking them all to travel.[7] Luke's Mary and Joseph, who lived in Galilee, would not have been affected by Quirinius' census, which covered only people who lived in the two Roman provinces, Judaea and Syria. Galilee (we recall from ch. 3) was independent and not a Roman province. Further, ancient census-takers wanted to connect land and landowners for tax purposes. This meant that the census-takers, not those being taxed, would travel. Possibly because there were riots after Herod's death in 4 BCE and also at the time of the census in 6 CE, Luke has conflated the two times. This is a relatively slight historical error for an ancient author who worked without archives, or even a standard calendar, and who wrote about a period some eighty or so years earlier. The most likely explanation of Luke's account is this: he or his source accidently combined 4 BCE (Herod's death) and 6 CE (Quirinius' census); having 'discovered' a census at the time of Herod's death, he then decided to elaborate the event so that it became a reason for Joseph to travel from his home in Nazareth to Bethlehem.[8] In any case, Luke's real source for the view that Jesus was born in Bethlehem was almost certainly the conviction that Jesus fulfilled a hope that someday a descendant of David would arise to save Israel. Zechariah had predicted that God would 'raise up a horn of salvation for us in the house of his servant David' (quoted in Luke 1.69); Jesus was this 'horn of salvation'; therefore Jesus was born in David's city.

Matthew's story has greater verisimilitude. Herod was ruthless, and he did kill people who seemed to pose a threat to his reign, including (as we saw above) his favourite wife and their two sons, plus one of his sons by another wife. Did he slaughter 'all the male children in Bethlehem and in all that region who were two years old or under' (Matt. 2.16)? It is not likely. Josephus narrated a lot of stories about Herod, dwelling on his brutality, but not this one. Matthew probably derived this information from the story in Exodus 1.21f., according to which Moses, when an infant, was threatened by a similar order from the Egyptian Pharaoh. Matthew saw Jesus as a second, superior Moses (as well as son of David), and he cast a good deal of his opening chapters in terms of the stories about Moses. The narrative of the flight into Egypt and the return reminds the reader of the history of Israel and the exodus from Egypt. Matthew cites a statement in Hosea: 'Out of Egypt I have called my son' (Matt. 2.15). This originally referred to Israel as God's (collective) son, led out of Egypt by Moses (note the past tense). Matthew applies the quotation to Jesus, whom he considered *the* Son of God, and the statement in Hosea, which referred to the exodus at the time of Moses, was probably the only source of Matthew's story about Jesus and his family. In Matthew 5, Jesus goes up on to a mountain (as did Moses when he received the law), and while there he comments on some of the ten commandments and other parts of the Mosaic law (Matt. 5.21–48). In one section Matthew places ten miracles (Matt. 8–9), perhaps to recall the miracles of Moses in Exodus 7.8–11.10. All three synoptics say that Jesus was in the desert for forty days, partly to recall the sojourn of forty years in the desert at the time of Moses. These parallels with Moses make it all the more likely that Matthew derived elements of the birth narrative from stories about Moses. Luke, we note, did not agree with Matthew about the importance of Moses as a 'type', a precursor of Jesus. His birth narrative is focused only on David, and he emphasizes that the sayings that Matthew puts in the Sermon on the Mount were said on a plain (Luke 6.17). In Luke, Jesus is not a second Moses. Luke and Matthew agreed that Jesus fits into Jewish salvation history, but they disagreed on details. Luke thought that Jesus fulfilled Jewish prophecy, and was the promised son of David, but he did not view him as a new Moses.

The birth narratives constitute an extreme case. Matthew and Luke used them to place Jesus in salvation history. It seems that they had very little historical information about Jesus' birth (historical in our sense), and so they went to one of their other sources, Jewish scripture. There is no other substantial part of the gospels that depends so heavily on the theory that information about David and Moses may simply be transferred to the story of Jesus. But we note that the early Christians regarded this as perfectly legitimate. By their lights, it was. Their view of God was that he planned it all: the call of Abraham, the life of Moses, the exodus, the reign of David, the life of Jesus. They also thought that God gave indications in advance – signs, portents and prophecies – of what he would do. They were convinced that God sent Jesus to save the world, and so naturally they thought that he had previously signalled what he would do and that his prophets had predicted it. A lot of other first-century Jewish writers thought in the very same way.[9]

But there were limits, both in the composition of the gospels and in other Jewish literature. Echoes of Jewish scripture are everywhere in the gospels, but nevertheless no one would ever mistake the Jesus of the gospels for either Moses or David. Although Matthew's story of Jesus contains a lot of parallels with stories about Moses, there are also striking differences. Jesus did not carry stone tablets down from the mountain; he did not marry, as Moses did; Jesus did not rely on his brother's assistance, as Moses relied on Aaron's; Jesus did not live for 120 years; he did not die out of sight. Similarly the gospels *claim* a connection between Jesus and David, but they do not present Jesus as being in the least like David. There are no real parallels: no equivalent of Saul, Jonathan, Bathsheba or Absalom; nor is Jesus a great warrior.

The gospel material is not unique in modifying Jewish typological expectation to fit changed circumstances. On the contrary, other writers of the time appealed to salvation history by using names and titles from the past, while making substantive changes. I shall give here two examples to which we shall return, since they involve the titles 'Messiah' and 'son of David'. A hymn written approximately 63 BCE, the time of Pompey's conquest of Jerusalem, looks forward to the time when a son of David will purge Jerusalem of evil people. This future son of David, however, 'will not rely on horse and rider and bow, nor will he collect gold and silver for war. Nor will he build up hope in a multitude for a day of war' (*Psalms of Solomon* 17.33). That is, he will be quite unlike the original David. Similarly the sectarians who are known from the Dead Sea Scrolls looked forward to two Messiahs, one a descendant of Aaron the priest, the other a descendant of David. The son of David seems to do nothing at all, and the priestly Messiah has real authority. According to one of the scrolls (*The War of the Sons of Light against the Sons of Darkness*), there will be a great battle, and the Sons of Light will engage the Sons of Darkness. A Davidic Messiah plays no role in the war. Priests do; they blow trumpets and give orders. An army gathered from the twelve tribes of Israel carries banners and marches around. But the real fighting is done by angels, and the final blow is struck by God himself. Thus other Jews who looked forward to a Messiah descended from David did not carry this expectation to the point of describing the future figure in terms derived from the biblical stories about David. The title – 'Messiah' or 'son of David' – was the only connection.

Jews who looked forward to a better future wanted to tie it to their history, the history of God's dealing with Israel, and so they used names and titles that were prominent in the Bible. But times had changed. The Romans were going to be a lot tougher than the Canaanites and Philistines, and Jews knew that they needed angelic hosts to fight on their side. A mere David would not do. Further, many Jews in Jesus' day did not want a monarchy. Some of them, such as the Dead Sea sectarians, might still talk about 'David', but even they seem not to have wanted his kind of kingdom. Kings tended to be dictatorial, and the Dead Sea sectarians preferred a more democratic and theocratic mode of government.[10]

When the authors of the gospels, then, cast the story of Jesus in terms of Jewish salvation history, they used motifs from scripture, especially motifs connected with Abraham, Moses and David, but they did not model their own Messiah on those scriptural characters. Something of the real Jesus was certainly preserved, and the authors also added their *own* ideals, which might be quite different from those of Genesis, Deuteronomy, II Samuel or I Kings. They thought that Jesus had gone beyond Moses and was a different sort of king from David. Thus we do not get a cardboard pop-up depiction of Jesus as a new Moses or David.

There are no absolutely certain signs that tell us when a passage in the gospels has been invented as a parallel to an earlier stage of the history of salvation, when it has been recast to emphasize an actual parallel, and when Jesus himself (or John the Baptist) intentionally created a reminiscence. We have to study the material, examine how close the parallel is, and use common sense. We must always be aware, however, that the authors did not intend to write academic history. It is perfectly reasonable for us to try to get it out of them, but we cannot expect them to give us their full co-operation. They wanted to convince readers that Jesus fulfilled God's promises to Israel. These promises included the redemption of the people of Israel, but also the salvation of the Gentiles. The gospels depict Jesus as saviour of the entire world, but he is a universal saviour who fits into Jewish salvation history.

The authors wanted their readers to believe that Jesus was the

Jewish universal saviour because they believed that it was absolutely true. Nevertheless, we have seen, they disagreed on important points (for example, whether or not Jesus was to be understood as a fulfilment of the Mosaic 'type'). This disagreement is instructive for the historian. It would be folly for a historian to argue whether or not the historical Jesus was reminiscent of Moses, and to hope to settle the issue by comparing Matthew and Luke. Matthew gave law a larger role in religion than Luke did, and consequently his Jesus is more of a legal teacher than Luke's. This is a theological disagreement within a broader theological agreement: Jesus fulfilled scriptural 'types'. It would not be folly, however, for a historian to ask whether or not the individual passages about Jesus' words and deeds that Matthew transmits make it appear that he was a legislator. Does Matthew's detailed evidence subvert Matthew's theological view?

In this particular case the answer will be 'partly yes, partly no'. What we must see is that Matthew and Luke had theological views that are essentially beyond the scope of historical inquiry: we can learn that they had them, and we can study how they worked them out, but we cannot deal with the question of whether or not they are 'true'. Nevertheless, the gospels contain material that the theological views did not create. Moreover, there are three synoptic gospels, with somewhat differing theological views, and these disagreements sometimes allow us to see what parts of the material are *not* explicable as planks in a theological platform. I should repeat that the authors of the gospels – and probably most early Christians – would not at all like this kind of analysis. The authors, in their own views, wrote the truth, and they call on the reader to believe it. The historian replies that he or she wishes to distinguish one kind of truth from another, and to study only the second, mundane kind. I suspect that the authors of the gospels were less interested in the second kind. To the degree that this is true, we should find it easier to uncover and extract some bits of ordinary history within the grand framework of salvation history. If they were not very interested in making all the details fit their theology, they would not have changed the details very much.

The Context of Jesus' Own Career

We shall now consider the second of our two contexts, the context that should immediately attract the attention of the modern historian who wishes information about Jesus: the events that immediately preceded and followed his own ministry and that were closely connected to it. The first of these was the preaching of John the Baptist.

John, we saw above, made a notable impression on Galilean society. I wish to repeat and expand slightly the discussion of John's importance and the reasons for his execution (above, p. 22). Josephus relates that people interpreted Antipas' defeat at the hands of Aretas as punishment for the execution of John. This implies that the populace held John in great esteem. Why did Antipas execute him? In Josephus' version the Baptist preached 'righteousness' and 'piety'. These two terms are fairly uninformative, since they simply summarize the two aspects, or 'two tables', of the Jewish law: treating other people correctly (righteousness) and worshipping God with true devotion (piety). Josephus wrote in Greek, and these two words were used very widely by Greek-speaking Jews to summarize their religion.[11] There is no reason to doubt that John stressed both, but these terms tell us nothing distinctive about the content of his preaching. Despite attributing to John such a bland message, Josephus writes that Antipas executed John because he feared that his preaching might lead to an insurrection. 'Righteousness' and 'piety' were taught every sabbath in the synagogues of Galilee, and Galilee remained at peace. John must have said something more remarkable.

The gospels ascribe to John two sorts of statement: (1) Antipas, in marrying Herodias, had broken the law (Matt. 14.4 // Mark 6.18); (2) the day of judgement was at hand and people should repent (Matt. 3.7–10 // Luke 3.7–9). They attribute John's execution to his personal criticism of Antipas' marriage. This, at least, is plausible. But if we combine our sources and accept them both – an unusual procedure in the present work – we have an even more likely account. John preached righteousness and piety, especially urging repentance of transgressions against other people and God, and warning that in the judgement, *which was near at hand*, those who did not repent would be punished or destroyed. Perhaps he singled out Antipas' marriage as an example of an unrighteous deed that required repentance. The proclamation of the coming judgement was accompanied by the prediction that *God was about to redeem Israel*, as promised by Isaiah (Mark 1.6; also Matthew and Luke). This led people to think that the redemption was at hand. The idea of redemption made some people think that they might lend God a hand and strike the first blow against immoral rulers. Antipas saw the threat and had John executed. That is, if we combine Antipas' fear of insurrection (Josephus) and John's prediction of a dramatic future event that would transform the present order (the gospels), we find a perfectly good reason for the execution. If John also criticized Antipas' marriage, Antipas would have been all the readier to strike, and Herodias may have urged him on. It should be recalled that Antipas was on the whole a good ruler, who did not wantonly execute people just because they favoured righteousness. I think that we should maintain Josephus' view, that the issue concerned the safety of the realm. But for the contents of the Baptist's message we must rely on the gospels, since Josephus' summary tells us nothing and the account in the gospels makes very good sense of the execution. Enthusiasm about a coming new order made rulers very uneasy. Throughout his writings, Josephus systematically deleted information about Jewish hopes for redemption, since such hopes had possible political and military repercussions, and he wished to present his people as not threatening the *pax Romana*.

John, therefore, warned people to repent in view of 'the coming wrath'. 'The axe is already laid at the root of the tree' (Matt. 3.10 // Luke 3.9). This message is usually called eschatological. *Eschatos* in Greek means 'last', and thus eschatology is 'discourse or thought about last things'. The term can be misleading when it is translated literally. Most Jews who thought that judgement and redemption were at hand expected the world to continue. God would do something dramatic; he would transform the order of things; but then he would reign, either directly or through a viceroy, such as the Messiah of Aaron in the Dead Sea Scrolls. We cannot say in detail what the Baptist expected, but evidently it was a dramatic future event that would change the present order.

According to the gospels, Jesus began his active ministry after being baptized by John. That he accepted John's baptism is virtually certain. The gospels and Acts reveal that John had a sizeable following, and the authors were a little embarrassed at having to admit that their hero, Jesus, had been at first a follower of the Baptist. The first and fourth gospels go out of their way to make sure that John himself testifies that Jesus is really greater. According to Matthew 3.14, John protested when Jesus came to be baptized, saying that Jesus should baptize him. The Gospel of John is more emphatic: John (the Baptist) 'confessed, he did not deny, but confessed, "I am not the Christ."' 'The next day he saw Jesus . . . , and said, "Behold the Lamb of God . . ."' 'And John bore witness, "I saw the Spirit descend as a dove from heaven, and it remained on him."'[12] We must doubt that the Baptist recognized Jesus' superiority in this way. According to another tradition, when John was in prison, he sent a message to Jesus and asked him if he could prove himself (Matt. 11.2–6).

I shall introduce here an explanation of one way scholars have of testing material for 'authenticity', that is, historical accuracy. We doubt things that agree too much with the gospels' bias, we credit things that are against their preference. This rule cannot be applied mechanically, since some things that actually happened suited the authors very well, but it will stand us in good stead here. Matthew wants John's subservience to Jesus to be clearly recorded (Matt. 3.14). Yet he transmits a tradition that is opposed to that bias (11.2–6). Therefore we trust the second tradition: John, while in prison, was still not certain of Jesus.

In view of this, it is most unlikely that the gospels or earlier Christians invented the fact that Jesus started out under John. Since they wanted Jesus to stand out as superior to the Baptist, they would not have made up the story that Jesus had been his follower. Therefore, we conclude, John really did baptize Jesus. This, in turn, implies that Jesus agreed with John's message: it was time to repent *in view of the coming wrath and redemption*.

We now move to our surest information about the period shortly after Jesus' execution, which is provided by the letters of Paul and Acts, especially the former. Paul thought that history was about to reach its climax. He was converted to the new movement and began to preach in the mid-thirties, moving from Syria west across Asia Minor and into Greece. The earliest known Christian document is his letter to one of his churches in Macedonia, at Thessalonica.

We learn from this letter that when Paul had founded the church, he had told his converts that Jesus had been raised to heaven and that he would return *soon* to establish his kingdom. Some of the converts died, and the church sent word to ask Paul whether the dead would miss out on the kingdom. Paul answered that when Jesus returned, the dead converts would rise to greet him first, and then the Christians who still lived (I Thess. 4.13–17). This is an extremely informative exchange. Paul so strongly expected Jesus to return immediately that he had not taught the Thessalonians that those who died would be raised.

Paul fiercely disputed some points with other Christians, but not this one. They all believed that Jesus would establish a kingdom in the very near future, in their lifetimes. Sayings to this effect are still found in the gospels (we shall discuss this topic more fully below, pp. 180–84). The only reasonable explanation of this early Christian conviction is that during his lifetime Jesus had led his followers to expect a new kingdom to be established soon. After his death and the resurrection appearances, they became persuaded that Jesus himself would return to establish the kingdom, but they did not make up the whole idea that the kingdom of God would fully arrive in their generation.

At the beginning of Jesus' career, then, we find him accepting the mission of John the Baptist, who said that the climax of history was at hand. Within no more than a decade after Jesus' execution, we have firm proof that his followers expected this dramatic event very soon. *Jesus must fit this context.* We do not yet have precision and nuance. Just what did he think would happen? What was his own role to be? We shall do what we can to answer these questions, though they must be answered tentatively, since we seldom have the immediate context of a particular saying. The intermediate context of which we may be confident – Jesus stands between John the Baptist and the early Christian movement – provides us with a secure basic conclusion: Jesus thought that God would soon bring about a decisive change in the world. This context is historically crucial, since it is the framework of Jesus' overall mission: it includes the man who baptized him, and also his own followers.

The setting of Jesus' mission is more important for understanding his life and work than any other conceivable context. We would like to know to whom Jesus referred when he said 'love your enemies', and knowing the precise circumstances in which he said this would help us a great deal. Although we cannot know the actual occasion of individual sayings (because people reapplied them and moved them around), we do know the context that is most vital for understanding Jesus as a historical figure.

We have now considered two different kinds of context: the gospels' view that Jesus was the fulfilment of Jewish salvation history; the view of Jesus' predecessor and successors that the climax of history was at hand. We have also seen that this second view must be attributed to Jesus himself. It is thus far a *general* conception within which Jesus' own teaching will have a particular place. These two contexts overlap: both are Jewish, both are orientated towards the future, and both assume that God will do something in *history* that agrees with other things he has done. At a very basic level everyone we have mentioned agrees: John the Baptist, Jesus, Paul, the authors of the synoptic gospels, Jesus' other followers. What was really going on, they thought, was that God was up to something very special. The God they believed in was the God of Israel, the God who called Abraham, gave the law to Moses and elevated David to kingship. That God would now bring his work to fruition.

In one sense, then, Matthew, Mark and Luke were right on target when they set Jesus in the framework of Jewish salvation history. That is how he himself saw the world. This does not mean that every single passage in the gospels that has a reminiscence or echo of Hebrew scripture really took place. Nor does it mean that Jesus tried to imitate David and Moses. We shall see evidence that he was critical of some of his own tradition, though he accepted its central premise (the God of Israel would redeem his people). Nor does it mean that we do not need to know the social and political climate of Galilee and Judaea in the twenties and thirties. I wish the gospels had told us more about that and less about supposed parallels between figures in the Hebrew Bible and Jesus. But now we can see the authors of the gospels and their work more clearly. They were theological idealists. But this book is about a theological idealist. Lots of first-century Jews and Christians were theological idealists.

In the previous section of this chapter, we saw that Matthew and Luke place their story in the context of Jewish salvation history, and

I suggested that we could examine the gospels and extract from them material that does not owe its existence to their own particular views. Now we see that we cannot pare the gospel material down to a non-theological core, and then proclaim that we have found Jesus, since Jesus himself was a theologian. But just as Matthew and Luke did not entirely agree with each other, we may also assume that Jesus' views may be distinctive, or partly distinctive, and that the evangelists have sometimes superimposed their theology on his. We can hope to find *his* theology within the gospels.

Sorting all this out is obviously a difficult task, and results will often be tentative. I shall repeat the aim of the book: I shall try to lay out what we can know about Jesus with great confidence, and to separate it from less certain inferences.

8. THE SETTING AND METHOD OF JESUS' MINISTRY

===

The centre of Jesus' work seems to have been a small Galilean town called Capernaum. It was near there that he called his chief disciples, two pairs of brothers: Peter and Andrew, and James and John.[1] Peter had a house in Capernaum, and there Jesus healed Peter's mother-in-law. In its synagogue he healed a paralytic (Mark 2.1–12 & parr.[2]). And it was in Capernaum that he shared a meal with the tax collector Levi. The meal took place 'in his house', probably meaning 'in Levi's house', though 'in Jesus' house' is not impossible (2.13–17). According to Mark 2.1, Jesus was 'at home' in Capernaum. After preaching elsewhere he would return there. Mark sets the discussion of true greatness in Capernaum (Mark 9.33–7), and Matthew the debate about the payment of the half-shekel Temple tax (Matt. 17.24–7).

It will help us visualize Jesus' life if we consider the physical settings in which these and other activities took place. We shall consider synagogues (where, according to the gospels, Jesus first taught) and then a few points about Galilee. Since some scholars have proposed that there were no synagogues in first-century Palestine (which would mean that the several references to synagogues in the gospels reflect the time and place of composition, not the lifetime of Jesus), I shall treat the question of their existence in a little more detail than would otherwise be necessary. The principal issue, however, is to understand in what circumstances Jesus began to tell other people his views of the kingdom of God. How was it that he could enter a new town and teach in the synagogue? Did he stand up in the back of a large hall and interrupt the sermon? Was it socially unacceptable behaviour for a stranger to insist on speaking in a synagogue? We shall ask what synagogues were like and what people did in them.[3]

All the evidence indicates that, by the first century, synagogues were common wherever Jews lived, though we do not know when or where they originated. A synagogue was not a temple. In the ancient world, a temple was a place where people worshipped God by sacrificing animals. A temple was regarded as sacred; the deity in some sense dwelt there, and there were laws and rituals governing approach to him or her (many of the most prominent pagan temples were dedicated to the worship of a goddess). As we saw above, Judaism was in these respects similar to other ancient religions, though there were also substantial differences. There was only one Jewish Temple, which was in Jerusalem, and its innermost chamber was empty, dedicated to the worship of the unseen God, rather than being the residence of an idol representing the god. Despite these differences, anyone in the ancient world would have found the Jerusalem Temple and its worship services generally familiar. Synagogues, on the other hand, were not sacred, and access was not limited to those who were ritually pure. Animals were not sacrificed in synagogues. Jews could do in these buildings the normal things that people do when they gather: eat, sing, pray, lecture one another, argue, share information and gossip. Synagogue buildings functioned in part as town halls.

Synagogues are unknown in the Hebrew Bible, and consequently there were no firm laws about them, though of course customs developed. Their main purpose was to serve as a place where Jews could gather on the sabbath to listen to a reading from their scriptures, which was followed by discussion. Some synagogues were probably more democratic than others; that is, in some cases one or two leaders would teach while most people listened and learned, but in some discussion was freer. In Greek, synagogues were often called 'houses of prayer', which leads us to suppose that prayer (and possibly songs) were included in the service.[4] There was, however, a lot of variety, since there were no biblical laws. It is likely that synagogues in or near Jerusalem did fewer things than those that were remote. People who could attend the Temple fairly often probably had fewer religious needs than did those who lived some distance away. Distance from the Temple, in fact, probably explains the origin of synagogues. Some scholars think that they originated during the Babylonian captivity, as a substitute for worship in the Temple. Others propose that the first synagogues appeared in the Greek-speaking Diaspora. In any case, in first-century Palestine there were synagogues, even in Jerusalem, as a supplement to worship in the Temple.

Synagogues had some sort of organization. Someone was 'head of the synagogue', and in some synagogues there may have been other offices. Priests could and sometimes did serve as heads of synagogues, and priests sometimes read the scripture or commented on it. But lay people could take all these roles, if they were equipped to do so: they had to be literate, learned and respected. Synagogue leaders and speakers could be quite ordinary people, provided that they had studied the Bible.

Archaeology can tell us only a little about Palestinian synagogues in Jesus' day. A total of three have been found that can be dated to the period before the destruction of Jerusalem in 70 CE. An inscription describing improvements in a synagogue in Jerusalem has also been found; thus there is physical evidence of a total of four. There are three explanations of why so few pre-70 synagogues have come to light.

(1) Archaeologists are not free to dig up cities that are now inhabited (such as Tiberias). All three pre-70 synagogues that have been definitely identified were found at sites that have been uninhabited since the revolt against Rome and can therefore be excavated.

(2) In many places archaeologists have found large synagogues from the third and fourth centuries, which was a period when synagogue-building flourished. Many of these were probably built on the sites of earlier synagogues, which were destroyed.

(3) In small towns and villages, synagogues were probably only converted houses, which would make them harder to identify now. The slight physical evidence can be supplemented by references to synagogues in ancient literature. Josephus, for example, mentions synagogues in Tiberias and Caesarea on the Sea. More important, however, his discussions assume the existence of synagogues, which leads to the conclusion that they were common.

In the three surviving first-century Palestinian synagogues, seating was on benches that went all the way around the walls, except for the windows and doors. Leaders probably spoke from the middle of the room, but this seating plan also encourages brief comments or questions from the congregation. This point is of considerable importance. The evidence thus far is that first-century Palestinian synagogues were not like most synagogues, churches and theatres now. They were not large halls with seats facing a raised stage at the front. In the pre-70 synagogues thus far uncovered, those in attendance could look at one another and (at least sometimes) talk to one another. In this sort of physical setting, someone with something to say could say it. We do not know precisely what the customs were. Possibly the scriptures were read, a leader offered comments, and then the floor was open for discussion. Or possibly someone with an important message might speak to the leader in advance and ask to be recognized. In a small town the first of these seems to be more likely. It is reasonable to think that visitors were welcomed, just as they are now and for the same reasons (curiosity; happiness to see a fresh face; general goodwill induced by the sabbath rest, prayer and study of scripture). A visitor might even be singled out and asked if he had something to say.[5]

I am now speculating. We do not know that the floor plans of the three surviving synagogues represent all synagogues in Galilee. Nor do we know what the rules were about addressing a synagogue audience. I find the presentation of Jesus' early ministry in the gospels, however, to be entirely plausible. All towns and villages had synagogues; visitors were welcome; they could even speak. Mark's first pericope on Jesus' teaching begins in this way: 'And they went into Capernaum; and immediately on the sabbath he entered the synagogue and taught' (Mark 1.21). There would have been more to it than that (for example, he waited until the leader had finished his comments), but Mark's sentence is quite believable.

Galilee

The people who gathered in the synagogues of Galilean towns and villages, for the most part, worked the land or fished the Sea of Galilee for food. There were the other normal occupations of small-town rural life. Boats sailed around the coast of the small inland sea, providing the opportunity of trade with other Galilean villages and also with the cities of the Decapolis to the east of the sea (on these, see below). Trade with non-Galilean cities meant that there were customs officers at the harbours. The production of food, however, was the main occupation. Galilee was very fertile, and its climate made it an ideal agricultural area. Around the Sea of Galilee grew

the walnut, a tree which delights in the most wintry climate . . . , palm-trees, which thrive on heat, and figs and olives, which require a milder atmosphere . . . Not only has the country this surprising merit of producing such diverse fruits, but it also preserves them: for ten months without intermission it supplies those kings of fruits, the grape and the fig [both of which can be dried and preserved]. (*War* 3.517–19)

The character of Capernaum, however, was probably determined by the fact that it was on the sea. The Sea of Galilee, also called Gennesaret, is a very small sea, and some ancient authors (Luke, Josephus and Pliny the Elder) called it a 'lake'. It is fed by the Jordan River from the north, and to the south the Jordan continues towards the Dead Sea. The Sea of Galilee is about thirteen miles long and eight miles wide at the broadest point. The fish population differs from that of other lakes and rivers, and many of the fish found in the Jordan and the Sea of Galilee are otherwise unknown. Boats were probably quite small. Josephus describes a naval battle on the sea during the Jewish revolt against Rome (66–74 CE). The Jews had small skiffs, holding a handful of men. The Romans felled trees and built large rafts, carrying many soldiers each; and they easily won the engagement, slaughtering the Jews to the last man, leaving the sea red with blood.

According to Josephus, the skiffs had been used for 'piracy' or 'brigandage'. This may mean that they were used in smuggling, as it is hard to imagine a whole fleet of pirate ships on such a small sea. The skiffs may also have been converted fishing boats, in which case we learn that such boats could hold 'a handful' of men (*War* 3.522–31). The gospel accounts suppose that fishing boats were operated by two or three men (Mark 1.16–20 & parr.).[6]

Most fishing was by drag-net, a weighted and buoyed net drawn behind a boat. In a parable Jesus refers to this type of net (a 'seine'): the kingdom of heaven is like a drag-net cast into the sea, which gathers in both good and bad fish, which need to be sorted (Matt. 13.47–50). A second kind of net was used, a casting-net, which could be cast out and drawn in either from a boat or from the shore. This kind of net seems to be in view in Mark's story of Simon and Andrew (Mark 1.16). They are casting their nets into the sea, and they leave them to follow Jesus; there is no mention of a boat. James and John, however, were in their boat mending their nets (Mark 1.19). There may have been a social differentiation between those who could afford boats and the larger drag-nets and those who had to cast from the shore. Fishing by drag-net was almost certainly more profitable.

Most of the settled areas around the sea were quite small. Mark 1.33 calls Capernaum, Jesus' home base, a 'city', but that is too grand a designation. Here and elsewhere in the gospels the term is used loosely. Josephus referred to Capernaum as a 'village' (*Life* 403), but 'small town' would probably be the best description. The ruins of the ancient settlement lie in a narrow strip of land along the seashore, about 500 metres long and 350 wide (*c.* 550 x 380 yards). One of the excavators estimates that, after space for streets and public buildings is subtracted, this area would provide living space for about 1,500 to 2,000 people.[7] One can now see there the ruins of a very fine synagogue. It was sixty-five feet long and two storeys high. This synagogue, however, dates from the third century, the period of many large synagogues in the region. It is likely that the synagogue of Jesus' day was on the same spot, but was less grand.

Jesus also preached and healed in the other towns and villages of Galilee. We hear of Mary Magdalene, presumably from Magdala, also close to the sea. Other nearby villages mentioned in the gospels are Chorazin, about two miles north of Capernaum, and Bethsaida, probably a small settlement on the sea.[8] In Matt. 11.20–24 // Luke 10.13–15 there is a formidable 'Woe' on Chorazin, Bethsaida and Capernaum for not repenting when Jesus did his 'mighty works' there: 'It shall be more tolerable on the day of judgement for Tyre and Sidon than for you.' This is an instructive passage, since it points to greater tension between Jesus and the seaside towns than the gospels otherwise lead us to expect. Mark and the other synoptics depict Jesus as extremely popular in and around these small towns. Moreover, Jesus drew his followers from them. Yet obviously he did not see the sort of response for which he had hoped.

The same is true of his home, Nazareth, where his message was rejected: 'he could do no mighty work there, except that he laid his hands upon a few sick people and healed them. And he marvelled because of their unbelief' (Mark 6.1–6). We know even less about ancient Nazareth than about Capernaum. It must have been a minor village, since it is not mentioned in the Hebrew Bible, Josephus or rabbinic literature. It was not on a major road, but it was only a few miles south-east of Sepphoris, a substantial city (see below) in the interior of Galilee. A few scholars now wish to see Nazareth's proximity to Sepphoris as an important factor in the village's life. In Nazareth, it is imagined, people benefited from the supposedly Graeco-Roman culture of Sepphoris: they could attend Greek plays, listen to Greek philosophers, and generally acquire cosmopolitan polish. This is exceptionally improbable. Village life was dominated by work. People worked six days a week, and on the sabbath travel was limited to 1,000 yards or so (about 900 metres).[9] It is not likely that many residents of Nazareth spent much time in Sepphoris. When they took holidays, during one or more of the pilgrimage festivals, they travelled away from Sepphoris, south to Jerusalem. Villagers, of course, may have taken food or other products to Sepphoris to sell in the market. In this case, they would have had to rise before dawn, grind grain and prepare food, eat, load the donkey, walk with it to Sepphoris (one to two hours) and sell their goods. When the trading day was over, they would have packed up and gone home. They could not have taken a donkey back to the village after dark, since they could not risk an injury to it. They did not earn enough to allow them to enjoy the theatre and stay overnight. In short, villagers then, like villagers ever since, up to the present day, lived in their village and made relatively few trips, except to sell or barter their goods.[10]

To the east of the Sea of Galilee and the Jordan River lay the Decapolis, 'Ten Cities' of Macedonian and Greek foundation that were politically independent.[11] In the third century BCE the successors of Alexander the Great founded numerous new cities (or refounded old ones), giving them Greek constitutions and political freedom (under only the general supervision of the ruling power). Such cities were very important to empires, whose troops served for years in remote lands: conquerers gave land to retired soldiers, and the promise of land of their own was a major factor in the recruitment of troops. The men settled down, and each found a wife, possibly a woman who had followed the army on its campaigns. They became farmers, craftsmen and the like: good, solid citizens who were loyal to the empire. The cities of the Decapolis served the Hellenistic kingdoms as a defensive shield against raids from the desert. The Hasmonean kings, especially Alexander Jannaeus, conquered many of these cities. Rome gained control over them when Pompey conquered Palestine. In the view of the Hellenistic cities, he had liberated them from Jewish government, and their coins reveal that they regarded Pompey as establishing a new era. The descendants of the Macedonian and Hellenistic armies transferred their loyalty to the Roman empire.

According to Mark, Jesus twice went into the region of the Decapolis, but apparently not into any of the cities themselves.[12] Similarly, he once went 'to the region of Tyre and Sidon', two major non-Jewish cities on the Phoenician coast, but again not to the cities (Mark 7.24).

We shall gain a better feel for Jesus' Galilee, and perhaps understand him a little better, if we say a few words about the principal cities of Galilee, which are to be contrasted with the areas where he worked. Sepphoris was for many years the major city of Galilee. It was destroyed (or partially destroyed) in 4 BCE, during the uprisings after Herod the Great's death. According to Josephus, the Syrian legate, Varus, burned the city and sold the populace into slavery – though most of them had no connection with the rebels and did not support them (*War* 2.56, 68).[13] Antipas promptly rebuilt and resettled Sepphoris, making it the 'ornament of all Galilee' (*Antiq.* 18.27). It was for a time his capital city, and it was the home of the Galilean aristocracy. The population was solidly Jewish, though there were some Gentiles as well. At the time of the Jewish revolt (66 CE), the city remained loyal to the Romans, and the civic leaders asked for and received a Roman garrison (*War* 3.30–34; cf. 2.511). The Galileans who joined the revolt naturally hated Sepphoris passionately, but it is likely that the animosity had deeper roots: the rich and aristocratic city would not have been popular even before the war, and Sepphoris' loyalty to Rome at the time of the war reflects its basic orientation, which was resented by many Galileans.

Antipas built Tiberias in 25 CE as a new capital city. The city is on the shores of the Sea of Galilee, which provided better access than did Sepphoris to the various parts of Antipas' tetrarchy. The population of Tiberias was mixed, though Jews were in a clear majority. Tiberias was built partly on a graveyard, and pious Jews were reluctant to live there, since walking over a grave resulted in corpse impurity. Corpse impurity, according to biblical law, is not wrong: survivors are supposed to care for the dead, and thus to become impure. Purification was achieved by a rite lasting seven days. The impurity prevented only entrance into the Temple and sharing the Passover meal, and thus in Galilee it had no practical effect; nevertheless many pious Jews did not wish always to be impure. The consequence was that Antipas' capital attracted Gentiles and relatively impious Jews; some were persuaded to live there only by the offer of free houses and land. Tiberias, like Sepphoris, was probably looked on with suspicion by many Galilean Jews.[14]

A third city, Scythopolis, was founded as a Greek city on the site of ancient Beth Shean. As we noted above, Scythopolis was in geographical Galilee, but was politically independent; it was not governed by Antipas, and it had never been governed by Herod. It was the only city of the Decapolis on the west bank of the Jordan. Despite the Hellenistic foundation, in Jesus' day the population of Scythopolis was mixed. When the revolt broke out in 66, the Jewish citizens (numbering about 13,000) were forced to help the Gentiles defend the city against the Jewish rebels. Despite this, the Gentile population of the city massacred the Jews (*Life* 26).

As far as we can tell, on the basis of the gospels, Jesus knew only one real city, Jerusalem, though he must have visited Sepphoris at least occasionally. He was not a cosmopolitan, but rather based his work in the towns and villages of Galilee, especially those on the coast of the sea. Although Jesus was disappointed at his reception in the villages of Galilee, against some of which he uttered a 'Woe' (as we saw), Sepphoris, Tiberias and Scythopolis did not get even that.

It is difficult to know just how much to make of Jesus' avoidance (as it appears to be) of the urban centres. We shall see below that he offered the kingdom to outcasts and sinners, including tax collectors and prostitutes. One would think that such a mission would have taken him to Tiberias, the capital city. He might have gone to Sepphoris to protest against the wealth of the aristocracy. A desire to summon all Israel might have sent him to the major population centres. Yet Jesus worked among his own: the residents of villages, people who were minor artisans, tradesmen, farmers and fishermen.

He may have done this simply because they were his own. He identified with the meek and lowly, and they were the natural focus of his mission. Further, he, like many prophets and visionaries, did not calculate in our terms. The implied questions of the last paragraph – if you want to call sinners, why not go to Tiberias? – would not have posed themselves to him in this way. When he thought about 'all Israel', he did not count noses and ask, 'How can I reach the greatest number of my people most efficiently?' He certainly thought in symbolic terms and probably in representative terms – the twelve disciples symbolize all Israel, and they also represent it (below, pp. 120, 184f.). A few years later, we learn, Paul, Peter, James and John thought in similar ways. They divided up the mission to the world – Peter to the Jews, Paul to the Gentiles (Gal. 2.9) – but no one went to Alexandria. When Paul had founded churches in perhaps a dozen cities in Asia Minor and Greece, he said that he had 'completed' the gospel and had no more room for work in that area, and so had to go on to Spain (Rom. 15.19, 23). The 'completion' was only symbolic and representative.

Jesus, then, a man from a village in Galilee, worked in other villages and small towns there, and in the surrounding countryside – and yet he saw his ministry to be significant for all Israel.

An Itinerant Movement

We have seen that the gospels depict Jesus and his disciples as itinerant. Some or all of them had homes and families, but they spent a lot of time on the road, and there is no mention of their working during Jesus' active career. In part they were busy proclaiming the kingdom; in part the condition of the call of the close disciples was that they give up everything. Yet they had to have some financial support. Birds of the air eat for free (Matt. 6.26) but not people. In Matthew 10 there is a mission charge to the disciples. In its present form the passage reflects knowledge of the post-resurrection church, but it may nevertheless provide information about how Jesus' followers were expected to live:

Take no gold, nor silver, nor copper in your belts, no bag for your journey, nor two tunics, nor sandals, nor a staff; for the labourer deserves his food. And whatever town or village you enter, find out who is worthy in it, and stay with him until you depart. (Matt. 10.9–11)

Paul's letters show that these conditions were observed by some of the Christian missionaries after Jesus' death. Paul cites a 'word of the Lord' to the effect that 'those who proclaim the gospel should get their living by the gospel' (I Cor. 9.14), which makes the same point as the quotation from Matt. 10.9–11. Although he and Barnabas did not accept money, Paul wrote, and although he himself worked with his own hands, this was not the case with the other apostles. They lived and travelled, taking along their wives, at the expense of the churches (I Cor. 9.3–7). It turns out, however, that Paul did not entirely refrain from this apostolic right: he took money from other churches while working in Corinth (II Cor. 11.8f.), and in Philippians 4.14–16 we learn that the church there supported him while he was in Macedonia. Finally, in Romans 16.2 he names Phoebe as the patroness of himself and others.[15] Thus Paul often lived according to the saying of the Lord, 'the labourer deserves his food' – that is, charitable contributions.

According to John 21.1–3, Jesus' disciples returned to fishing after his execution. According to Acts, however, they were immediately active in Jerusalem, where they had no visible means of support. The movement attracted followers who had possessions, such as Barnabas (Acts 4.36f.), who put their money and goods into a common treasury. From the beginning of their work the apostles relied on financial support from others.

Thus the evidence from the earliest days of the church indicates that Jesus' followers expected to be supported by others while they conducted their mission. This expectation was probably derived from their practice while following Jesus during his lifetime. The gospels occasionally depict Jesus, and sometimes the disciples, as dining at someone's house. This is the case in Mark 2.15–17.[16] In Luke 7.36–50 Jesus eats with Simon, a Pharisee; in 11.37–44 with another Pharisee; and in 19.1–10 he stays with Zacchaeus the tax collector. We do not know that these details are accurate, but we should accept the general thrust of the passages: as Jesus and his followers moved from village to village, they found one or more individuals willing to provide a meal and simple lodging. According to Luke, they had ampler means of support: while Jesus and the Twelve went through Galilee, they were accompanied by women, including 'Mary, called Magdalene, from whom seven demons had gone out, and Joanna, the wife of Chuza, Herod's steward, and Susanna, and many others, who provided for them out of their means' (Luke 8.1–3).

The author of Luke, who also wrote Acts, liked to call attention to the prominent women who supported first Jesus and then his apostles: in Thessalonica 'some . . . were persuaded, and joined Paul and Silas; as did a great many of the devout Greeks and not a few of the leading women' (Acts 17.4). Luke had a special interest in the piety of women and their role in religion generally, and he also wished to show that Christianity appealed to the higher classes. Thus it is possible that in Luke 8.1–3 the author is exaggerating the degree to which Jesus and his band were supported by women, including one of some rank (the wife of Antipas' steward).

It is clear, however, that in early Christianity there really were such women. We noted above Phoebe, who was a patroness of Paul and others. From Corinth we know of Chloe, prosperous enough to send her slaves or freedmen to Paul with a message (1 Cor. 1.11). Further, there are analogies: women were sometimes the chief supporters of other religious movements. This was so at a fairly early stage of Pharisaism. Despite the opposition of Herod the Great to the Pharisees, they were partially protected and provided for by women of the court. Herod's court historian, Nicolaus of Damascus, took this as discrediting the Pharisees: they attracted only women.[17] In emphasizing women, therefore, Luke was not necessarily presenting Jesus and his movement in a light which contemporary readers would regard as favourable.

It seems, then, that we can accept Luke's statement as generally probable: Jesus and the others were partly supported by prosperous women, some of whom also 'followed' him. In what sense were they *followers*?

In Luke 8.1–3 women accompanied Jesus and his male disciples while they travelled 'through towns and villages'. Further, women were in the group of people who accompanied Jesus from Galilee to Jerusalem. According to Matthew 27.55f., there were 'many women', including Mary Magdalene, Mary the mother of James and Joseph, and the mother of the sons of Zebedee. Luke does not at this point mention names, but refers only to 'the women who had followed him from Galilee' (22.49). Mark names Mary Magdalene, Mary the mother of James the younger and of Joses, and Salome, adding that they had followed him in Galilee and 'served him'. He adds that there were 'also many other women who came up with him to Jerusalem' (15.40–41). The word 'served' is *diakoneo*, the same word used in Luke 8.3. It probably means 'supported'. I think it likely that women physically *followed* Jesus only on rare occasions, such as pilgrimages to Jerusalem, when it was generally acceptable for men and women to travel together in groups. If women had actually travelled with Jesus and his disciples on other occasions, and spent the night on the road, there would probably be some echo of criticism of this scandalous behaviour in the gospels. Female supporters probably played their more traditional role by providing lodging and food.

Jesus said that 'foxes have holes, and birds of the air have nests; but the Son of Man has nowhere to lay his head' (Matt. 8.20). Did he and his closest disciples sometimes do without lodging for the night? Was his ministry seasonal? There are no certain answers. The mean temperature of Tiberias in January is now 65° maximum, 50° minimum, and it rains between thirty and fifty days each year, most of the rain falling from early December to early March.[18] Many days, however, are harsher than these temperate figures indicate. Further, Jesus and his followers for part of the time would have been away from the Sea of Galilee, and therefore in a slightly more rigorous climate. The group could not always have returned to Capernaum on bad days. He probably led an impoverished and homeless life during his active career; but sometimes he and the others must have had shelter and beds, and this is especially true if he travelled during the winter.

These considerations bring us back to the issue of the length of Jesus' ministry (above, pp. 66–9), but they do not settle the question. Had his ministry lasted only a few months, ending with Passover in the spring, he would still have had one winter to get through, and for that he and the others needed a certain degree of support. On the basis of a few clues, we must guess what his life was like: he was essentially homeless; he travelled in the company of his disciples, including more than just 'the Twelve' at least some of the time; the group had minimal financial reserves; he was sometimes able to eat and sleep in comfort, thanks to the fact that he found at least some supporters of means, especially women.

9. THE BEGINNING OF JESUS' MINISTRY

=====

After narrating Jesus' baptism, which we discussed in ch. 7, the synoptic gospels have further introductory material: the temptation, the call of disciples, and the healing and teaching that first brought him to the notice of others.

Fasting and Temptation (Mark 1.12f.; Matt. 4.1–11; Luke 4.1–13).

After Jesus was baptized, he went into the desert to fast, and there (according to the gospels) he was tempted by Satan (Mark) or the devil (Matthew and Luke). In the view of all three gospels, Jesus was following the guidance of the Spirit of God. Mark's story of the temptation is extremely brief: 'The Spirit immediately drove him out into the wilderness. And he was in the wilderness forty days, tempted by Satan; and he was with the wild beasts; and the angels ministered to him.' Matthew and Luke, however, offer much more circumstantial accounts; they especially elaborate on the temptations. We shall briefly consider the historicity and significance of these passages.

The statement that Jesus' fast lasted forty days recalls the forty years during which Israel wandered in the desert after escaping from Egypt. Once we note the parallel between Israel's forty years in the desert and Jesus' forty days, we face the common difficulty of not knowing whether it was Jesus or the early Christians who created the correlation. It is intrinsically likely that from time to time Jesus sought solitude for prayer and meditation, that he sometimes felt tempted, and that he fasted before beginning his public activity. Even the number 'forty days' may also go back to Jesus. As we shall see below, he used at least one number symbolically (twelve), and it is possible that he himself later spoke to his disciples about a fast of forty days. Although no one can live for forty days without food and water, in Jewish usage the word 'fast' does not necessarily mean that one abstains completely from all sustenance. Even Luke, who writes that Jesus 'ate nothing' during the forty days (4.2), does not say that he drank no water. It is reasonable to think that Jesus fasted and prayed for several days, with only minimal sustenance.

Although later in his public ministry Jesus withdrew for prayer and meditation, the gospels indicate that he did not fast, a fact that brought some criticism (Mark 2.18–22). I assume that Jesus fasted on the Day of Atonement, since this is a biblical commandment and he seems in general to have observed the biblical law. But he and his disciples did not observe other fasts that may have become customary.[1]

The physical setting of the fast and temptation deserves comment. The desert or wilderness of Judaea is an awesome place. It is very hilly, rocky and arid. Lying between the Judaean Hills and the Jordan Valley, it extends for approximately 75 miles north and south, and for about 10 miles east and west. Travelling east from Jerusalem towards the Jordan Valley and the Dead Sea, one very soon runs into the desert, as one begins the sharp descent from the hills to the valley, a drop of 3,800 feet (c. 1150 metres) in about twelve miles (from c. 2,500 feet, or 760 metres, above sea level to c. 1,300 feet, or 390 metres, below sea level). It is dangerous for a solitary traveller to leave the road and to walk into the desert. There are steep cliffs, and the terrain is extremely rugged. It is easy to sprain or break an ankle, and to be unable to return. Some, to be sure, learn their way around the desert, and it has served as a haven for the persecuted and also for thieves (as in the Parable of the Good Samaritan). For food and water, however, one must walk down to the Jordan Valley, where there are springs and areas of fertility. Jericho, one of the oldest continuously inhabited cities in the world, is an oasis on the eastern edge of the desert, made green and fertile by an abundant spring. The Dead Sea sect lived near another spring, somewhat south of Jericho.

The story of Jesus' temptation in the desert is both symbolic (forty days) and mythological. A myth is a story in which a supernatural being acts on the human level. In the present case Satan (or the devil) is the supernatural being. Mark gives him no more than a bare mention, but in the longer accounts in Matthew and Luke the devil talks to Jesus, takes him from the desert to the Temple mount, and shows him a vision of 'all the kingdoms of the world', offering him dominion over them. These features are 'mythological'. A myth is not the same as a lie; a myth may be true in some sense. Some ancient readers, like some modern ones, believed that there was a precise correspondence between a mythological story and what actually happened. Others regarded myth as being poetic and imaginative, not literally true. I borrow an example from H. J. Rose's discussion of mythology in the *Oxford Classical Dictionary*.

It was commonly said ... that the gorge of Peneus had been created by Poseidon [the Greek god of the sea] ... To Herodotus himself this was merely a picturesque way of saying that the gorge had been formed by an earthquake ... But it seems far more probable that the originator of the story had a vivid mental picture of the gorge, which to his eye suggested a great cut, being hewn out by a gigantic and powerful being, and that, finding the picture satisfactory to his imagination, he was not troubled with any question as to its probability.[2]

I think it quite likely that Matthew and Luke, who believed in angels, demons and the Spirit of God, thought that the devil actually carried Jesus to the pinnacle of the Temple and showed him visions. But we can seldom be sure when ancient authors regarded their narratives as merely picturesque and when they believed them to be literally true. We shall return to a related question in the next chapter, where we shall discuss miracles.

In Mark's account Jesus was tempted by 'Satan'. Though writing in Greek, Mark used this Hebrew term, while Matthew and Luke used the usual Greek equivalent, 'devil' (Matt. 4.12; Mark 1.12; Luke 4.2). The word *satan* in Hebrew means 'adversary', and in the Hebrew Bible 'the adversary' is not necessarily an enemy of God. The word is used in Numbers 22.22 for one of God's own angels. Satan becomes prominent in the Book of Job, where he is one of God's counsellors, but one who doubts the firmness of Job's piety and who is allowed by God to make Job suffer in order to see if his faith would break.

It appears to have been during the Babylonian captivity (597 to 537 BCE) that Satan grew in malevolent stature to be virtually a wicked, second god. By the time of the New Testament, Satan, under one or another name, was assigned his own sphere, as the chief spiritual power that opposed God. His realm was one of fire, to which guilty souls were sent (Matt. 25.41). He could enter the heart and create evil (Matt. 13.19), and it was he who caused Judas to betray Jesus (Luke 22.3; John 13.2). Finally, he had his own angels, just as God had his (Matt. 25.41).

Why did Satan grow to such prominence during this period? It was apparently during the Babylonian exile that Jews began to be complete monotheists. Previously, they had thought that their god was the best god, but they had not denied the complete existence of other gods. A religion that believes that there is only one god has a difficult time explaining evil. Did the one good God create it? Why does he permit it? Faced with the actual existence of both good and evil, some religious traditions have posited the existence of two opposing gods. This is the most distinctive theological belief in Zoroastrianism, which began in Persia in the sixth or fifth century BCE and which influenced Mediterranean thought in several ways. Judaism probably owes to Zoroastrianism the idea that an evil power opposes God. (Christianity, in turn, inherited the idea from Judaism.) Judaism remained true to monotheism and did not grant that there was an opposing *god*, but it accepted some aspects of Persian dualism, such as the conflict between God and the forces of evil. The expectation, of course, was that the good God would ultimately triumph over the evil power, though in this world it often seemed that evil was winning – as it still does.

Jesus' conflict with evil, in the form first of Satan and then of demons, is one of the major themes of the gospels. We shall return to the conflict with demons in the next chapter, when we discuss exorcisms. Here we note that the gospels put at the outset a major conflict with the chief of the powers of evil, Satan himself.

Matthew and Luke recount three temptations. The devil urged Jesus to turn stones into bread; to cast himself down from the pinnacle of the Temple, trusting that he would be saved by angels; and to accept 'all the kingdoms of the world and the glory of them'. These offers had a condition: 'All these I will give you if you will fall down and worship me' (following Matthew's order: Matt.

4.1-11; cf. Luke 4.1–13). To each temptation Jesus replied by quoting scripture. He answered the temptation about stone and bread by responding, 'Humans shall not live by bread alone, but by every word that proceeds from the mouth of God' (quoting Deut. 8.3). He declined the temptation to tempt God and attract attention by throwing himself from the top of the Temple wall by quoting Deuteronomy 6.16, 'You shall not tempt the Lord your God.' With regard to the temptation to become king of the world by worshipping Satan, he could quote one of the best-known passages in the Bible: 'You shall worship the Lord your God, and him only shall you serve' (Deut. 6.13). This is from the passage called in Hebrew the *Shema'*, 'Hear', from the opening word of the commandment: 'Hear, O Israel, the Lord your God is one Lord, and you shall serve the Lord your God with all your heart, soul, mind and strength.' This passage, recited twice daily by devout Jews, Jesus would subsequently quote when asked about the greatest commandment.

Two of the answers attributed to Jesus are of a piece with major aspects of his later career. In the first place he hesitated to make a show and was reluctant to 'prove' himself by 'signs'. Secondly, his conception of himself was that he was a servant of God. He worked within the general framework of the ideas about God and Israel provided by the Jewish scripture, and accordingly he pointed not to himself but rather to God. It is noteworthy that, in answering the tempter, he did not speak in the first person. He did not say, 'That is not the way I do things', but rather, in effect, 'That is not according to God's will as revealed in the scripture.'

The temptation to be a worldly king is the most interesting of the three. We shall see that Jesus looked forward to the coming of the kingdom of God, but that it is difficult to say just what sort of kingdom he expected. He was executed as would-be 'king of the Jews', and after his death and resurrection his disciples considered him the Messiah, the 'anointed' leader of Israel. Other aspects of his teaching and actions show that he did think of himself as in some sense a king. This temptation is the beginning of a large and rich theme in the gospels: God's kingdom would come, but it would not be based on showy miracles, and it would not be a kingdom in the ordinary sense of the word. Jesus may well have had to wrestle with himself about what kind of kingdom he wanted, and the story of this temptation puts that inner debate in graphic form.

The question of changing stone into bread also has echoes in the later stories of the gospels, since twice Jesus is said to have multiplied loaves and fishes, and according to John he changed water into wine at a marriage feast in Cana. The refusal to change a stone into bread does not begin a series of similar refusals. The point may be only that Jesus was fasting: hunger would not lead him to ask for special favours from God. We shall see throughout the gospels a tension between performing miracles and not appealing to them for proof of who he was. The refusal in this case is not a refusal to give a sign to others, since Jesus was alone. It seems only to be a story of his moral courage and dedication, as he began a life in which he did not spare himself, but would give up anything for his cause – including his life.

The refusal to cast himself down from the Temple, so as to be saved by angels, is the hardest to explain, since this kind of dramatic display does not enter the later stories in the gospels. It is in agreement, however, with the subsequent refusal to give a 'sign' when his enemies challenged him to do so.

The temptation account, even in Mark's short form, plays an important role in the story of Jesus. The authors of the synoptic gospels put first and foremost his intense dedication, his withdrawal into solitude so that he could think about his mission, and his refusal to follow the easy path, to make grand displays, and to be the kind of king which most people would expect. They also signal that Jesus could be tempted, that he had to wrestle with himself. Luke concludes his account not by saying that the angels ministered to Jesus (as do Matthew and Mark), but by indicating that Satan would be back: 'he departed from him until an opportune time' (Luke 4.13). Luke was probably thinking ahead. Self-doubt reappears at a crucial point near the end of the story: when Jesus, alone, prays that 'this cup' – his looming execution – would pass from him (Mark 14.36 & parr.).

I suspect that the close interplay of themes between the temptation accounts and stories later in the gospels reveals literary art. Yet it is also reasonable to think that Jesus really did fast and pray before beginning his active ministry and that he was subject to temptation. The safest conclusion is that the synoptic gospels, especially Matthew and Luke, are 'mythological' elaborations based on fact.

The Call of Disciples

After his period of fasting, Jesus returned to Galilee to begin his active career. The synoptic gospels agree that Jesus was rejected at Nazareth, that he went to Capernaum, and that he called disciples in and near Capernaum; but they do not agree on the precise sequence of these events. For convenience, we shall start with Nazareth, where the gospels report only failure. He was too well known, and the crowd asked, 'Is not this the carpenter (Matthew, 'carpenter's son'), the son of Mary and brother of James and Joses and Judas and Simon, and are not his sisters here with him?', and they refused to listen. He withdrew, commenting, 'A prophet is not without honour, except in his own country, and among his own kin, and in his own house' (Mark 6.1–6; Matt. 4.12f.; 13.53–8; Luke 4.16–30).

Whether before or after this disappointment, Jesus found a more receptive audience in Capernaum, on the coast of the Sea of Galilee. There he called his first disciples. He saw Simon (later called Peter) and his brother Andrew casting their nets into the sea, and he charged them, 'Follow me, and I will make you fishers of men.' They immediately followed him. Jesus also called another pair of brothers who were fishermen: James and John, the sons of Zebedee. They were with their father, mending their nets, and they left both boat and father when Jesus called them (Matt. 4.18–22//Mark 1.16–20).

The story of the call of the first four disciples in Matthew and Mark emphasizes Jesus' commanding presence and the disciples' readiness to give up everything to follow him. Subsequent stories support this general point. Peter once asked what they would receive as a reward for surrendering everything. Jesus replied that in the new age his disciples would be judges of the twelve tribes of Israel and that others who left 'houses or brothers or sisters or father or mother or children or lands, for my name's sake, will receive a hundredfold, and inherit eternal life' (Matt. 19.27–9). But for the present, self-sacrifice was required.

Luke's account of the call of the first disciples is strikingly different. Jesus was teaching by the sea, and the crowd pressed close around him. He got into one of the fishing boats, which belonged to Simon, and taught from the boat. Then he told Simon to put down his nets, and Simon protested that they had fished all night in vain. Nevertheless, he put down the nets and trapped a shoal of fish, so many that other fishermen too filled their nets. Simon recognized Jesus as spokesman of God and urged him to leave, saying, 'Depart from me, for I am a sinful man.' He and his partners – James and John – were amazed at the event. They returned to shore, and all three became followers of Jesus (Luke 5.1–11). We note that Luke includes Peter, James and John in the same scene, making them already partners, but leaves out Andrew.[3]

Although for the most part we shall ignore John, in this case we should make an exception. There we find a completely different story (John 1.29–51). Two disciples of John the Baptist heard John say of Jesus, 'Behold the lamb of God', and they followed him. One of them was Andrew, who brought Peter, and they joined Jesus then – before John's arrest, and apparently in Bethany, not Capernaum (Bethany: John 1.28). In Galilee, Jesus found Philip and called him, and Philip in turn enlisted Nathanael. (Nathanael is not mentioned in the synoptics.) The Gospel of John wishes to stress the Baptist's subordination to Jesus, and it is part of this scheme to have Jesus take one of John's disciples away from him. The story in the synoptic gospels (Matthew, Mark and Luke), that Jesus called his first disciples while they were fishing, seems more likely. Even so, we must suppose it to be abbreviated and idealized, and to leave out details in emphasizing the immediacy of the response. We see in Luke the need of additional circumstances to explain why the disciples followed Jesus: Peter, James and John saw a miracle, the great catch of fish, and this persuaded them to become his followers. It may be supposed that Jesus' fame and his message had already reached the fishermen, and that they knew something about the man who called them from their work. I regard the basic story as historically reliable: the earliest disciples were Galilean fishermen; among them were Peter, Andrew, James and John; they left their nets to follow Jesus.

The synoptic stories of the call of the disciples allow us to illustrate the way in which the tradition developed (above, ch. 6). The future disciples already knew something about Jesus, so that when he called them they had some idea of who he was. In Mark and Matthew, we see that all the original details have been pruned away. All that is left is the main point: Jesus called; the disciples obeyed his summons. Luke then *reintroduces* a narrative context that provides an explanation: Jesus won the trust of the fishermen by telling them where to catch fish. They at first resisted but finally became disciples. It is doubtful that Luke had an ancient tradition that went back to the real event. He felt the lack of an explanation, and so he supplied one; that is, he made up a story.

The traditions about the number and identity of Jesus' closest followers are both important and interesting, and so we shall look at them in greater detail. We note, first, that although all four gospels, Acts and Paul agree that there were twelve special disciples (often referred to collectively as 'the Twelve'), they do not agree precisely on their names. The most probable explanation is that Jesus himself used the term symbolically, and that it was remembered as a symbolic number, even though the precise number of close disciples may have varied. The symbolic meaning of the number would have been obvious to everyone: it represented the twelve tribes of Israel. In calling disciples, and in speaking of them as 'the Twelve', Jesus intended to show that he had in view the full restoration of the people of Israel. The symbolic value of the number is especially clear in Matthew 19.28: the twelve disciples will judge the twelve tribes of Israel. Ten of the tribes had disappeared centuries before, when Assyria conquered the northern kingdom. Many Jews continued to hope, however, that God would someday restore the lost ten tribes: 'twelve' therefore points to the expectation of an eschatological miracle, a decisive act by God to redeem his people.

Paul's letters were written earlier than the gospels, and so his reference to the Twelve is the earliest evidence. It comes in a passage that he repeats as 'tradition', and is thus to be traced back to the earliest days of the movement. In I Corinthians 15 he gives the list of resurrection appearances that had been handed down to him: Jesus appeared to Cephas (Peter), then to the Twelve, then to 500, then to James, then to 'all the apostles', then to Paul himself (I Cor. 15.5–8). We note that in Paul's list the symbolic number twelve is still used, even though Judas was by then dead.

Matthew, Mark and Luke give full lists of the Twelve, and Luke's is repeated in Acts (Matt. 10.1–4; Mark 3.13–19; Luke 6.12–16; Acts 1.13). The Gospel of John refers to the Twelve (John 6.67–

71; 20.24), but does not give a list, though some individuals are named. Some interesting things can be learned from the lists and general discussions of the Twelve. (The following analysis of evidence about the twelve disciples is summarized in a list in Appendix II.)

There were three disciples in the inner circle: Simon (later called by Jesus 'Peter') and the two sons of Zebedee, James and John. In the gospels these are often singled out, and they became leaders of the Christian movement after Jesus' death and resurrection. These three are prominent in Matthew, Mark and Luke, and the leadership of Peter and John is evident in Acts and the Pauline letters. Curiously, the Gospel of John does not name James and John, though it does mention 'the sons of Zebedee' (John 21.2). Some people think that the unnamed 'beloved disciple' in the Fourth Gospel is the disciple John.

All four gospels and Acts mention Andrew as Peter's brother, and Philip and Thomas as two of the Twelve, but only John gives them distinctive roles. If we did not have the Gospel of John, these three disciples would only be names on a list.

Mark, Luke and Acts list Matthew among the disciples. The Gospel of Matthew identifies him with the tax collector whom Jesus called, but who is named Levi in Mark and Luke.

All four gospels and Acts name Judas as the disciple who betrayed Jesus.

There was a second Simon, called in Matthew and Mark 'the Cananaean' but in Luke and Acts 'the Zealot'.

James the son of Alphaeus is in the lists in Matthew, Mark, Luke and Acts. His mother Mary is named as being present at Jesus' execution (Matt. 27.56; Mark 15.40, where he is called 'James the younger' or 'the lesser'; Mark 16.1; Luke 24.10). Nothing else is known of him.

The name Bartholomew appears in the lists in Matthew, Mark, Luke and Acts, but there is no more information about him.

According to Matthew and Mark, the twelfth disciple was named Thaddaeus, while according to Luke and Acts he was named Judas the son of James. The Gospel of John gives a small speaking role to 'Judas, not Iscariot' (14.22).

Finally, John gives a special place to Nathanael, who is not otherwise mentioned in the New Testament. In John 1.45–59 Philip brings Nathanael to Jesus, and Jesus' knowledge of what he had just been doing (sitting under a fig tree) leads him to exclaim, 'Rabbi, you are the Son of God! You are the King of Israel!' Jesus points out that his feat was quite minor, but he promises, 'You shall see greater things than these.' This prophecy is fulfilled too, and John subsequently names Nathanael as one of the seven disciples to whom Jesus appears by the Sea of Galilee (John 21.2).

It is clear that we have more than twelve names, and it is also clear that John has a special list and otherwise unattested stories. The Fourth Gospel emphasizes otherwise minor disciples (Andrew, Philip and Thomas) and also gives a substantial role to an otherwise unknown disciple (Nathanael). Further, John supports Luke and Acts in naming a second Judas as within the close circle.

Some of these discrepencies traditionally have been solved by assuming that some disciples had two names. Thus Thaddaeus (Matthew and Mark) is often thought to be the same person as Judas the son of James (Luke and Acts) and as Judas (not Iscariot) (John). Similarly it is often thought that Levi was simply an alternative name for Matthew. These equations are based on the desire to make the names add up to precisely twelve, as if the number were not only symbolic but also literally precise and should be mechanically applied. It is far more likely that the number twelve possesses a different kind of historicity: Jesus' own use of the number as symbolic. It is not the case that Jesus had just twelve disciples. It appears that he had somewhat more, but he spoke of the Twelve in order to indicate that his mission was to all Israel as well as his expectation that Israel would be *fully* restored in the coming kingdom.

In reality Jesus had a group of followers, at any one time numbering more or less twelve. Some of the minor followers fell away, so that later the early Christians did not agree precisely on who counted as among the Twelve. He himself, however, used the number as a symbol of his mission and his hope. The gospels set the story of Jesus in the context of Jewish salvation history: God called the people of Israel and would ultimately redeem them. Jesus saw his own work in the same context. His message was, in part, that in the coming kingdom the twelve tribes would have a place.

Disciples, Followers and Supporters

Now that we have examined the traditions about the Twelve, we can profitably return to the 'followers' and 'sympathizers', and make finer distinctions (see ch. 8, 'an itinerant movement'). We want to see what roles they play in the gospels as we have them, and also where they stood in Jesus' mission historically. I shall make the most general point in advance. Jesus proclaimed the kingdom of God to far more people than he 'called' to 'follow' him. He had: (1) close disciples; (2) slightly more remote followers; and (3) still more remote sympathizers or supporters. He would have liked everyone to be a supporter, but apparently he intentionally called only a few to *follow* him in the strict sense of the word.

(1) The close disciples (the Twelve) do very little in Mark's account. In many ways they play a negative role. Others respond to Jesus with complete faith, but the disciples remain puzzled and doubtful. When, after the feeding of the 5,000, they saw Jesus walking on the water, 'they were utterly astounded'. Mark comments that 'they did not understand about the loaves, but their hearts were hardened' (Mark 6.47–52). Mark's disciples serve as a foil to others (the Syro-Phoenician woman, the centurion at the crucifixion) and to Jesus himself, and the portrayal of their dimness and lack of response is exaggerated.

In Matthew and Luke the disciples fare slightly better, but the general impression is still that they were imperceptive and not very helpful to their master. There is, however, one passage in all three synoptics that gives them a positive role in the proclamation of the kingdom, as an extension of Jesus' own activity. Jesus called the Twelve and sent them out, telling them to 'go nowhere among the Gentiles, and enter no town of the Samaritans, but go rather to the lost sheep of the house of Israel'. On their mission they were to proclaim that 'the kingdom of heaven is at hand', and to heal and exorcize (Matt. 10.5–15; compare the somewhat different mission charge in Mark 6.7–13; Luke 9.1–6).

Disciples who did not understand Jesus or his mission could not have carried out the assignment of Matt. 10.5–15 & parr. My guess is that during Jesus' lifetime they were neither as uncomprehending as Mark usually depicts them, nor as lacking in faith. I equally doubt, however, that the disciples conducted a fully independent mission prior to the crucifixion. Their lack of comprehension and faith serves as a contrast with others, and the independent mission serves as a guide to later Christian missionaries. The historical truth probably lies somewhere in between: they understood Jesus better than Mark would have the reader think, but they were not yet able to strike out on their own.

It is interesting to speculate on why Jesus wanted disciples. I assume that part of the answer is simply that people who feel called to teach and lead need students and followers. Despite Mark's portrait, the disciples really did learn things from Jesus, and after he was no longer with them (except in spirit) they put what they learned to good use. They also had a lot of symbolic value. Jesus spoke of the Twelve in order to symbolize the coming restoration of Israel, and his close followers also symbolized his belief that the kingdom of God would especially embrace the poor, the meek and the lowly. Having disciples whose superiority was obvious to one and all would have conveyed the wrong message. Finally, I suspect that Jesus thought that his followers would play a very concrete role in the coming kingdom, but this is a topic that we shall take up in ch. 11.

(2) We have already met some other 'followers'. According to Mark and Luke, a tax collector named Levi followed Jesus but was not one of the Twelve. (Matthew, however, equates the tax collector with the disciple Matthew). Women also followed Jesus (above, pp. 109–11). Two of these were the mothers of disciples (the mother of the sons of Zebedee and Mary the mother of James and Joses – presumably this is James the son of Alphaeus). Luke, we saw, mentions the wife of Chuza, Antipas' treasurer, and Susanna (8.3). Mark also names Salome (15.40), and all the synoptics refer to other women. The best-attested woman, however, is Mary Magdalene, who is prominent in all four gospels.

The women followers play an absolutely essential role in the gospel accounts. When Jesus was arrested, the male disciples fled (Mark 15.40f. & parr.). It was the women who saw Jesus' death, who saw which tomb he was laid in, who saw that the tomb was empty, and who saw the resurrected Lord. That is, the identity of Jesus' tomb with the empty tomb depends on their testimony. The authors of the gospels were interested in the women because they played this crucial role. It is hard to be sure of their importance to Jesus during his lifetime, but I think that their support was significant (as suggested above, pp. 110f.).

It was presumably these women who joined with the disciples in prayer in the upper room, before Peter's first sermon (Acts 1.14). We do not know anything else about them: history was then, as for centuries before and after, the history of males, and for the most part women play only supporting roles. For this one brief period, crucial to Christianity, Jesus' women followers are in the limelight.

According to Luke, Jesus had a large group of other followers: after the mission of the Twelve (Luke 9.1–11) Jesus commissioned seventy to go before him on his way to Jerusalem, two by two (10.1–16). Luke puts here some of the material that is in Matthew's mission charge to the Twelve (Matt. 10.5–15). The seventy returned, reporting success at exorcism (Luke 10.17). It is difficult to know what to make of this. On the one hand, the story accurately reflects the fact that Jesus had more than twelve followers. On the other hand, Luke's account is dependent on the mission of the Twelve in Matthew: he seems to have had no fresh information about the mission of the seventy. It may be that Luke, recognizing that there were more followers, wished to give them a concrete role in Jesus' lifetime.

One other passage seems to shed some light on the number of Jesus' followers. In a tradition quoted by Paul, after Jesus' death he appeared to 'more than 500 brothers and sisters at one time' (I Cor. 15.6). This points to a large number of people who trusted and believed in Jesus' mission while he was still alive. Possibly these 500 should go below, under 'sympathizers'.

It is noteworthy that Jesus' family were not followers. Joseph does not appear after the birth narratives, but most of the material in the gospels about Jesus' mother and brothers is negative. At one point Jesus' family tried to seize him, saying that 'he is beside himself' (Mark 3.21). According to Mark 3.31–5, Jesus' mother and brothers stood outside where he was and sent a message to him. He replied, 'Who are my mother and my brothers?' and, looking around at his followers, added, 'Here are my mother and my brothers! Whoever does the will of God is my brother, and sister and mother.' Other sayings attributed to Jesus reflect this critical attitude towards family. Thus Matthew 10.35–7: 'I have come to set a man against his father ... He who loves father or mother more than me is not worthy of me.' Yet after the resurrection Jesus' mother and brothers joined the disciples and the women followers in prayer (Acts 1.14), and some of Jesus' brothers, notably James, became leaders of the early church.[4] Their wonder at the behaviour of Jesus and his claim to be God's spokesman was at last overcome.

(3) Finally, we note the 'sympathizers'. Jesus and his disciples, we showed above, attracted some support from people who did not follow him. Only occasionally do the gospels give them names. One is Simon the Pharisee, with whom he dined, another Zacchaeus the tax collector (Luke 7.36–50; 19.1–10). Joseph of Arimathea, a member of the council, obviously dissenting from the view that Jesus should be executed, donated a tomb and buried his body (Mark 15.42–7). Noteworthy, again, are women. There is an interesting complex of passages that reveals them partly as followers who helped support Jesus (as above, pp. 110f.) but more as *sympathizers*.

We shall start with the story of Mary and Martha of Bethany in John 12.1–8 and work back from this story to the probable historical basis. John's narrative runs as follows: Jesus visited the home of Mary and Martha in Bethany of Judaea, where previously he had raised Lazarus their brother. At dinner Martha served, while Lazarus and others reclined at table. Mary entered, carrying a jar of nard, an expensive perfume. She poured it on Jesus' feet and wiped them with her hair. Judas Iscariot protested that the money would have been of more use if it had been given to the poor. But Jesus replied that the anointment was for his burial, and he added, 'The poor you will always have with you, but you will not always have me.'

This appears to be a composite account, drawn from three separate stories in the synoptics.[5] One is the story of Jesus' dining with Simon the Pharisee. A woman who was a 'sinner' entered, wet Jesus' feet with her tears, dried them with her hair, and kissed and anointed them with oil (Luke 7.36–50). In a second story (Luke 10.39–42) Jesus was in a house with Mary and Martha, on his way to Judaea, but still either in Galilee or Samaria. Mary sat and listened to the master, while Martha was occupied with preparing the meal. When Martha grumbled about her sister's behaviour, Jesus supported Mary, replying that she had chosen the better thing to do.

The third story, in both Matthew 26.6–13 and Mark 14.3–9, is very similar to John's, but it takes place in a different household. Jesus was in Bethany at the house of Simon the Leper when a woman came to him carrying an alabaster jar of expensive perfume, which she poured on his head. As in John's story, the disciples were indignant, protesting that the perfume could have been sold and the money given to the poor. Jesus' reply was also as it is reported in the Gospel of John, but went on, 'Wherever this gospel is preached throughout the world, what she has done will also be told, in memory of her.'

If we analyse the component parts of John's story of Mary and Martha of Bethany, and number the other stories 1 to 3, we shall see these agreements:

John	Synoptics
	(*story no.*)
Names: Mary and Martha	2
Place: Bethany	3
Martha served	2
Mary anointed	cf. 2: Mary listened
Jesus' feet anointed with oil	cf. 3: his head
Feet wiped with woman's hair	1
Protest at extravagance	3
Poor you have always with you	3

These stories probably rest on memories, though details have been exchanged and possibly confused. It is nevertheless evident that Jesus attracted women who were not 'followers', but who admired him, heard him with pleasure and wished to serve him. We cannot know how many others there were, but we see behind the stories great human appeal. For the most part the gospels depict Jesus out of doors, either travelling from one place to another or talking to a crowd. These stories show him inside, a gracious guest and an appealing man.

Mark's Summary of the Early Ministry

We shall now follow Mark for the story of Jesus' early activity in Galilee after the call of the first disciples. The pace is fast, as one brief narrative follows another, and the focus is largely on Jesus' miracles, with less attention paid to his teaching.

Jesus and his disciples went to Capernaum, on the shore of the sea, where he taught in the synagogue. Mark does not tell us *what* Jesus taught, and this is typical of his gospel. He often says that Jesus taught, but he gives relatively little of the contents. In the present instance he describes only the reaction: 'They were astonished at his teaching, for he taught them as one who had authority, and not as the scribes' (Mark 1.22). While Jesus was still in the synagogue, a man who was possessed by an evil spirit cried out, 'What have you to do with us, Jesus of Nazareth? Have you come to destroy us? I know who you are, the Holy One of God.' Jesus rebuked the spirit, commanding it to leave the man. The exorcism was effective. The spirit departed, convulsing the man and crying out. Jesus' fame quickly spread (Mark 1.23–8).

Jesus then went to the house of Simon and Andrew, where Simon's mother-in-law was ill with fever. Jesus took her hand and lifted her up, and she was cured (Mark 1.29–31). The day ended when, at sundown, the people brought him many who were ill. He healed them, especially by exorcism (Mark 1.23–4).

In the morning Jesus withdrew. Simon and the others found him and told him that 'everyone' was searching for him. He decided to go on to the next towns, 'that I may preach there also; for that is why I came out' (Mark 1.35–8). We then have another summary: he went throughout Galilee, preaching in the synagogues and casting out demons. He was followed by a great crowd (Mark 1.39).

Next a leper came to him and was healed, which led to even greater crowds: he 'could no longer openly enter a town, but was out in the country, and people came to him from every quarter' (Mark 1.40–45).

The story of the leper bears on one of the most important questions about Jesus, namely his stance towards 'official' Judaism: the nation of Israel as a political entity; the Temple; the priesthood;

the law; the feasts and fasts; the synagogues. We have seen that some of Jesus' early teaching and healing took place in synagogues. The story of the leper sheds some light on his view of the Temple and its sacrifices. The leper asked Jesus to be 'made clean'. Jesus touched him, said, 'Be clean', and charged him to tell no one, but rather to go to the priest and to take an offering as specified in Leviticus (two birds, one of which is sacrificed, one set free, Lev. 14.2–9, followed by further sacrifices).[6] The case of the leper is the clearest instance in which Jesus is represented as affirming the Temple, the priests and the purity laws, but it is unambiguous. Here Jesus shows himself in agreement with and obedient to the sacrificial and purity laws.

Mark next gives a series of conflict stories, some of which involve healings. While he was 'at home' in Capernaum a large crowd gathered. Four men, bearing a litter with a paralytic on it, could not get through the crowd, and so they climbed the roof, removed some of the tiles, and let down the litter with the paralytic. Jesus healed him by saying, 'My son, your sins are forgiven.' Some scribes there asked themselves what he was doing, forgiving sins on his own authority (Mark 2.1–12).

Further conflicts follow: Jesus ate with tax collectors and was criticized (Mark 2.13–17); he was the target of more criticism because his disciples did not fast when the disciples of John the Baptist and the Pharisees were fasting (Mark 2.18–22); his disciples plucked ears of grain on the sabbath, which led to an attack by the Pharisees (Mark 2.23–8). Finally, he healed a man with a withered hand on the sabbath, by saying 'stretch forth your hand'. This (according to Mark) led the Pharisees and the Herodians to plot how to kill him (Mark 3.1–6).

This rapid sequence seems to have taken place over only a few days, during which Jesus' fame spread far and wide, and the Pharisees and others decided that he should die. The author has compressed events to achieve dramatic effect. Each story is exceedingly brief. Jesus says or does something and there is an immediate reaction: either of fame and adulation or of hostility. In Mark 2.1–3.6, which is a collection of stories of opposition, scribes and Pharisees seem to materialize out of nowhere in order to confront Jesus. He does something, they say something, he replies, and the passage ends. In real life things moved more slowly, exchanges lasted more than a few lines, there was fuller discussion of what he was up to and who he was, opposition only gradually developed, and the spread of his fame required more than a day or two. The opening sections of Mark are dramatized summaries, in which Jesus' life is made to consist only of quick challenges and brief and telling replies. We are not reading a circumstantial diary, one that would give us access to an average day in the life of Jesus.

For the sake of emphasis and clarity, I wish to comment once more on the nature of the material that the gospels incorporated and also on how the authors utilized it. When Mark wrote his gospel, he had before him a lot of individual pericopes, and he put them together in a narrative without, however, destroying the basic pericope form. We saw above his brief links: 'immediately', 'again' and similar vague indications (pp. 73f.). The quick stringing together of the pericopes allowed Mark to open his gospel in a dramatically forceful way, by racing through brief accounts of healings and conflicts, up to the conclusion that some people plotted Jesus' death. Matthew and Luke did not always keep Mark's sequence, and they moved some of the stories to other places in their gospels. Thus, for example, Matthew did not put the story of the healing of the paralytic where it would go if he had been following Mark's order, in his ch. 4, but rather with other miracle stories in ch. 9. The pericopes could be moved to suit the interests of each author. This reminds us once again that the gospels are not biographies in the modern sense of the word.

Mark may not have been the first to put pericopes together to make a story. Many scholars think that the series of conflict scenes in 2.1–3.6 came to him ready-made. It is noteworthy that the conclusion (the Pharisees and Herodians plotted Jesus' death) comes too early for the structure of the gospel as a whole. The Pharisees and Herodians are reintroduced nine chapters later (Mark 12.13), where they are said to be trying to entrap Jesus. Historically it is not likely that the fairly minor conflicts in Mark 2.1–3.5 actually led to a plot to put Jesus to death (3.6), and editorially it is not likely that Mark himself created the plot where it now stands in 3.6, only to reintroduce a weaker version of opposition from these two parties in 12.13. The most likely explanation of 3.6 is that the conflict stories of 2.1–3.5 had already been put together and that they immediately preceded a story of Jesus' arrest, trial and execution. That is, a previous collection – a proto-gospel – may have consisted of conflict stories, a plot against Jesus, and the successful execution of the plot.[7]

For the moment it is important to see that, in reading the first chapters of Mark, we are not reading a first-hand diary of 'life with Jesus in Galilee', but an edited collection of individual events that may originally have had another context.

In this chapter and the previous one we have considered the physical and social environments in which Jesus worked (villages, towns and open areas, not cities), how he at first used synagogues in order to gain a hearing, who the people were who looked favourably on his mission (disciples, followers and sympathizers), and the first groups of passages in the gospels. This has enabled us to see how to move from the gospels back to the historical Jesus. I have proposed, for example, that the temptation narratives are partly legendary and mythological, but that it is reasonable to think that Jesus actually did withdraw to pray and fast before beginning his public ministry. We have seen that the stories of how he called disciples are compressed and dramatized, but that he did in fact call disciples from the villages and small towns around the Sea of Galilee. Study of the number of close disciples and their names enabled us to see that Jesus himself used the number twelve symbolically. We searched for the history behind the apparently contradictory statements that the disciples did not understand Jesus and that they conducted an independent mission during his lifetime. Similarly the diverse stories about women in the gospels (including John) rest on a substratum of fact. Consideration of Mark 1.21–3.6 and parallels made clear how the authors of the gospels, and possibly previous authors or editors, arranged pericopes and linked them in order to produce a narrative.

We are now ready to take up the most substantive aspects of Jesus' ministry: miracles and his message about the kingdom of God.

10. MIRACLES

The emphasis of the early part of Mark is on miracles. We noted above that the gospel states that Jesus taught, but it gives little teaching material, while narrating the miracle stories in some detail. The large bodies of teaching material in Matthew and Luke, and especially Matthew's Sermon on the Mount (chs. 5–7), have led most people to think of Jesus primarily as a teacher. He certainly was a teacher, and what he taught is both important and gripping. But his contemporaries also attached great significance to what he did, and especially to his miracles. In one of the earliest Christian sermons, Peter describes Jesus as a man whose miracles ('mighty acts', 'wonders' and 'signs') showed that he was 'attested by God' (Acts 2.22).

In the modern world Jesus' miracles have played a substantial role in the evaluation of Christianity. Some have viewed the miracles as obviously fictional and have concluded that Christianity is based on a fraud, while others find in them proof that Jesus was more than merely human, the incarnate Son of God. We shall see that both of these extreme views miss the ancient perspective, which saw miracles as striking and significant, but not as indicating that the miracle-worker was anything other than fully human.

Though today somewhere between many and most people in the industrialized countries think that there are no true miracles, in the ancient world most people believed in miracles, or at least in their possibility. Jesus was by no means the only one to whom miracles were attributed. The early Christians thought that Jesus was the Messiah, the Son of God, *and* a miracle-worker. This has led many modern Christians to think that first-century Jews looked for a Messiah who performed miracles, and that Jesus' contemporaries would conclude that a miracle-worker was the Messiah. This view is incorrect. The few references to a coming Messiah in Jewish literature do not depict him as a miracle-worker. There was no expectation of a coming Son of God at all. Like other ancient people, Jews believed in miracles but did not think that the ability to perform them proved exalted status.[1] The combination of the titles 'Messiah' and 'Son of God' with the ability to perform miracles is a Christian one, the result of assigning both titles to Jesus, who was known in his day as a miracle-worker.

Discussion of this topic is tricky because there are a lot of issues that overlap, and the strictly historical questions become intertwined with what people today think and believe even more than is usually the case. In the previous three paragraphs I referred to several different topics, and things will be simpler if I enumerate them. In studying Jesus' miracles, we must bear in mind numerous points of view, some ancient and some modern:

(1) Ancient:
    (a) what ancient people thought about miracles in general;
    (b) what Jews who did not accept Jesus thought about his miracles;
    (c) what Jews who did accept him thought;
(2) Modern:
    (d) what modern people think about miracles in general;
    (e) what they think about Jesus' miracles (i. if they are Christian; ii. if they are non-Christian);
    (f) what importance they think Jesus' followers attached to his miracles;
    (g) what they think Christians are *supposed* to believe about Jesus' miracles.

The concern in this chapter is limited to the topics under (1) – what people thought then. It is difficult to discuss Jesus' miracles historically, however, because convictions about what Christians believe or should believe interfere very strongly. I shall spend a page on the topics under (2). This is only a ground-clearing exercise, an attempt to show that Jesus' miracles are to be studied in the light of other miracles of his day, not in the context of the subsequent Christian doctrine that he was both human and divine.

A lot of Christians, and possibly even more non-Christians, think that central to Christianity is the view that Jesus could perform miracles because he was more than a mere human being. We shall take walking on water as an example. A vast majority of people today think that it is impossible to walk on water. Some Christians, though by no means all, think that they are required to believe that Jesus could do so; this ability was limited to him, since he was more than human. Many non-Christians also think that Christians must believe this. Moreover, a lot of Christians and non-Christians think that the faith of the first Christians depended on Jesus' miracles.

Historically, none of this is accurate. In the substantive part of this chapter, we shall see that in the first century Jesus' miracles were not decisive in deciding whether or not to accept his message and also that they did not 'prove' to his contemporaries that he was superhuman. The idea that he was not a real human being arose in the second century, and it continued for some time, but it was eventually condemned as heresy. Ever since the fifth century (when the issue was officially settled), orthodox Christians have believed that Jesus was 'true man of true man' and that his divinity (which they also affirm) neither combined with nor interfered with his humanity: he was not an odd mixture. It is heretical to say that his divinity buoyed him up while his human feet lightly grazed the water. The definitive statement on this issue is that he is 'of one substance with us as regards his manhood; like us in all respects, apart from sin' – not, 'apart from the ability to walk on water'.

It lies beyond my meagre abilities as an interpreter of dogmatic theology to explain how it is possible for one person to be 100 per cent human and 100 per cent divine, without either interfering with the other. The Chalcedonian Definition (451 CE), from which I have quoted, is mostly defensive, not constructive. The orthodox believer learns more about what not to say than about how to talk about Jesus meaningfully. The church fathers believed that it was detrimental to deny that Jesus was human, and so they affirmed it; it was detrimental to deny that he was divine, and so they affirmed that too. Study of why they regarded both denials to be wrong is quite interesting, though the exposition of it lies well beyond the scope of this book. I shall allow myself only two sentences: denial of Jesus' true and full humanity would have resulted in a downgrading of the value of the physical world, and fortunately the orthodox Christians clung to the view of Genesis: God declared that the creation is good. They defended that view against quite serious attack, and part of the defence was the affirmation that Jesus was a real human being. His divinity, they maintained, did not in any way interfere with his humanity, or give to him non-human powers.

I intend this brief discussion of topics (*e*) through (*g*) above to be negative in the spirit of Chalcedon, though my view is historical rather than dogmatic. Historically, it is an error to think that Christians must believe that Jesus was superhuman, and also an error to think that in Jesus' own day his miracles were taken as proving partial or full divinity. I shall now turn to topics (*a*) through (*c*), though I shall occasionally mention modern perceptions of miracles (*d*).

Miracles and Magic in the Ancient World

As today, people then especially hoped for miracles in the case of illness and other physical maladies. They often sought healings from elsewhere than the medical profession. There were physicians, but in general their reputation was not good. The gospels tell the story of a woman who 'had suffered much under many physicians, and had spent all that she had, and was no better but rather grew worse' (Mark 5.26). Those who needed help, but who wished to stay out of the hands of physicians, could turn to three sources.

(1) They could ask God directly, or, in the pagan world, one of the gods. It would be surprising to learn that in the case of illness neither the sufferer nor family and friends prayed. Prayer is extremely inexpensive, and those who regularly prayed found that it was sometimes efficacious: some illnesses were cured, and if people always prayed for cures when sick, their prayers would sometimes be answered. Divine help was often sought privately, but sometimes publically. The Greek god Asclepius, who specialized in healing, had shrines throughout the Mediterranean world. Dozens of brief accounts of his healings have survived. The priests at his principal cult site, Epidaurus in Greece, copied inscriptions from wooden votive offerings on to large stone stelae, which have survived. A modern physician would regard many of these healings as quite believable. A woman who had been unable to become pregnant went to his shrine and slept overnight in the dormitory. During the

night she dreamed that one of Asclepius' sacred snakes entered her. She arose, went home, and immediately became pregnant. The modern medical explanation would be that her inability to become pregnant was psychosomatic and that the vision overcame the mental block, so that her body would function in the normal way. Sigmund Freud, of course, would have a lot to say about the sexual symbolism of the serpent. Other reports of healings, however, are completely incredible by modern scientific standards. A man who had lost his eyes and had only empty sockets dreamed that the god poured ointment into his eye sockets; and when he awoke he had eyes and could see.[2]

The interesting thing is that these stories stand side by side, the priests apparently not seeing that some of the healings are not only more believable than others, but that some are completely imposs-ible. That is, they did not draw boundary lines between credible and incredible where medical science today would draw them. If the god could produce one kind of miracle, he could produce another. The modern reader is inclined to make distinctions: stories that we find credible are regarded as possibly 'true', while those that are incredible are 'fiction'. 'Fiction' usually implies a moral judgement: dishonest. Although ancient people knew about fraud and dishonesty in religious claims, and were often suspicious of fantastic stories, they did not draw the line between truth and fiction precisely where we would. They did not regard it as *impossible* for spiritual forces to influence the physical world in tangible ways, and this view meant that tales of miracles could develop in the circles of sincere and honest people. Today a lot of people regard spiritual forces and miracles in the very same way and do not accept the standards of medical science. Consequently there are still stories of miraculous cures, many of which emanate from Lourdes and other places of religious pilgrimage. My own assumption about such stories is that many of the 'incredible' ones are based on wishful thinking, others on exaggeration, and only a very few on the conscious wish to deceive. I take the same view of the stories told by the pious devotees of Asclepius. The most important points for the reader of this book to bear in mind are that miraculous stories were common in the ancient world and that we should hesitate before assigning them to either 'truth' or 'deliberate falsehood'.

First-century Jews, perhaps needless to say, also prayed to their

God for healing. Very few individual prayers survive, but the naturalness with which Jews turned to God for cures is seen in II Corinthians 12.7–9, where Paul reports that he suffered from a 'thorn in the flesh' – some sort of physical malady that he does not describe – and that he sought relief from it by praying to God. We may assume that Jews routinely sought divine help when in all sorts of difficulties, and especially when suffering from disease or injury.

(2) There were other miracle-workers besides God or the gods. From the Greek world there is a substantial account of Apollonius of Tyana, a travelling philosopher, cult reformer and healer. He was widely thought to have the power to heal and especially to exorcize demons. Once when Apollonius was discoursing on libations – offerings of wine poured out to gods – he attracted the ridicule of a young man, a 'dandy who bore so evil a reputation for licentiousness, that his conduct had long been the subject of coarse street-corner songs'. When Apollonius urged that libations be poured over the handle of the cup, since that part was least likely to have been put to mortal use, 'the youth burst out into loud and coarse laughter, and quite drowned his voice'. Apollonius recognized his behaviour as revealing demon possession.

And in fact the youth was, without knowing it, possessed by a devil; for he would laugh at things that no one else laughed at, and then he would fall to weeping for no reason at all, and he would talk and sing to himself. Now most people thought that it was the boisterous humour of youth which led him into such excesses; but he was really the mouthpiece of a devil, though it only seemed a drunken frolic in which on that occasion he was indulging.

That is to say, some onlookers took a rationalist view of the youth's behaviour. The story continues: Apollonius addressed the demon as a master does a servant, and ordered him to come out and to show it by a sign. The demon promised to throw down a statue, and did so. The youth

rubbed his eyes as if he had just woke up ... and assumed a modest aspect ... For he no longer showed himself licentious, nor did he stare madly about, but he returned to his own self ... ; and he gave up his dainty dress and summery garments and the rest of his sybaritic way of life, and he fell in love with the austerity of philosophers, and donned their cloak, and stripping off his old self modelled his life in future upon that of Apollonius. (Philostratus, *Life of Apollonius*, 4.20)

Jews were especially well known as miracle-workers. Josephus claimed that they inherited the wisdom of Solomon and so knew how to perform healings, especially exorcisms (for an example, see p. 141 below). Illness and irrational behaviour were often attributed to demon possession, and those who could exorcize demons were much in demand. In a population in which the mentally unstable lived with relatives, not in asylums, many people would follow exorcists. And, such is the power of belief, or of mind over body, that cures were actually performed.[3]

Jesus, as we shall see more fully below, granted that some other Jews of his day could perform miracles like his own. We do not know the names of any Jewish miracle-workers who were active during Jesus' lifetime, but we do learn of some who preceded or followed him.[4] Hanina ben Dosa, a famous healer, lived in Galilee about one generation after Jesus. The most famous cure attributed to him closely parallels Jesus' healing of the centurion's servant (Matt. 8.5–13). The son of the great Pharisee, Gamaliel, was ill with fever. He sent two of his disciples from Jerusalem to Hanina in Galilee to ask him to come and heal the boy. Hanina instead went upstairs and prayed. He came down and told the disciples to go home, for the fever had left. The young men asked, perhaps sarcastically, 'Are you a prophet?' Hanina replied, 'I am no prophet, nor am I a prophet's son, but this is how I am favoured. If my prayer is fluent in my mouth, I know that he [the sick man] is favoured; if not, I know that it [the disease] is fatal.' The disciples wrote down the day and hour of Hanina's prayer, returned to Jerusalem, and discovered that from that hour the boy was healed.[5]

Earlier than Jesus was the famed 'Honi the Circledrawer', who lived in the middle of the first century BCE. Honi was especially known for successfully praying for rain. Palestine is subject to drought, and prayers for rain were a feature of normal piety. Such prayers were often accompanied by fasting, which was intended to call God's attention to human suffering and persuade him to relieve it by sending rain. The community's prayers and fasting were often effective; that is, the rains eventually came.[6] Although the entire community would pray and fast, some individuals, such as Honi, had especially good success in appealing to God. On one occasion Honi prayed for rain, but at first without effect. Then he drew a circle, stood inside it, and prayed: 'O Lord of the world, your children have turned their faces to me, because I am like a son of the house before thee. I swear by your great name that I will not stir hence until you have pity on your children.' It began to sprinkle, but Honi was not satisfied: 'Not for such rain have I prayed, but for rain of goodwill, blessing and graciousness.' Then it began to rain steadily, and it continued so long that some of the inhabitants of Jerusalem went to the higher ground of the Temple mount. The leading Pharisee of his day was of two minds about Honi and his achievement: 'Were you not Honi I would have pronounced a ban against you! But what shall I do to you – you importune God and he performs your will, like a son who importunes his father and he performs his will.'⁷ Honi's behaviour, which was so impertinent as to be almost blasphemous, was forgiven because of his intimacy with God.

We also learn about Honi from Josephus. He writes that Honi (Onias in Greek) was well known as the man who, in a drought, had prayed for rain and whose prayer had been answered by God. His reputation was such that, during a period of civil war between Hyrcanus II and Aristobulus II, the supporters of Hyrcanus captured him and ordered him to place a curse on Aristobulus and his faction. Honi instead offered a prayer asking that this not be done: 'O God, king of the universe, since these men standing beside me are your people, and those who are besieged are your priests, I beseech you not to hearken to them against these men nor to bring to pass what these men ask you to do to those others.' The followers of Hyrcanus, Josephus writes, stoned Honi to death (*Antiq.* 14.22–4). Individuals who had the ear of God were not necessarily popular.

Some prophetic figures promised miracles, though we do not hear of their accomplishing them. Not long after Jesus' death and resurrection, in the early forties, Theudas gathered followers in the desert and promised them that they would march to the Jordan River and that the waters would part – making him a kind of second Moses. Later a prophet from Egypt, known simply as 'the Egyptian', promised his followers that they would walk around the wall of Jerusalem and that it would fall – making him a second

Joshua. Neither plan was tested, for the Romans both times sent troops to stop the crowd. Theudas and several followers were killed, as were many followers of the Egyptian, though he himself escaped.[8]

We should especially note that some of the miracles discussed in this section are not healings but 'nature' miracles. Honi (like many others) prayed for rain, while Theudas and the Egyptian promised supernatural events affecting water (the Jordan) or stone (the walls of Jerusalem). Since Theudas and the Egyptian had followers, it is evident that people regarded their promises as credible. It seems to have been generally agreed that Honi could successfully pray for rain. The Jewish assumption in all these cases was that an individual could influence God, who could of course do anything he wished.

(3) We have seen that people could seek miracles from God (or, in the Graeco-Roman world, one of the gods) directly, or from an especially pious or gifted individual. These individuals are usually called 'charismatic': they had a special spiritual power, or a special ability to influence God. Perhaps we should also refer to them as 'autonomous', self-governing, since they related directly to God and were not employees of a ruler or temple. There was also, however, a third potential source of miracles, magicians, who may be thought of as constituting a guild of miracle-workers. Magicians were not charismatic and autonomous; that is, they did not perform miracles because of their special relationship to a god, and their techniques were usually not of their own invention. Hanina, we saw above, knew that if his prayer was fluent in his mouth, God would answer it positively. That was his own test, based on his experience in praying to God. Magicians were different: they followed rules.

Magic was based on a particular application of a widespread view: that there is a Great Chain of Being, in which everything is linked to something else, both above and below it. The manipulation of certain common elements (e.g., garlic, goat's urine and grass) would influence the Beings next higher on the Chain, and so up the entire Chain to the deity. The correct manipulation of the lower elements, together with the right incantations and the use of the right names, would make the higher deity perform one's desires. Magicians were for hire. A man might wish to hire a magician to persuade Venus to send a certain nubile young maiden to his bed-chamber.

A lot of the magic practised on behalf of individuals was negative: it was 'black magic'. Magicians cursed enemies on behalf of their clients, for example. They had an unsavoury reputation, and rulers from time to time tried to repress them. Being a magician was not a career that good families coveted on behalf of their children, though it was based on a world view that was widely held.

Our present interest, however, is in 'white magic'; magicians were a potential source of healing. They could mix various sub-stances, put them on the parts of the body to be healed, say the right incantations, and perform healing miracles. That these magical practices were known in first-century Palestinian Judaism is clear from a story in Josephus. In the course of praising Solomon, Josephus explains that the Israelite king left behind incantations and techniques of exorcism that some Jews still used. Eleazar, according to Josephus, performed one exorcism in the presence of the Roman general Vespasian, his sons, tribunes and others:

He put to the nose of the possessed man a ring which had under its seal one of the roots prescribed by Solomon, and then, as the man smelled it, drew out the demon through his nostrils ... Then, wishing to convince the bystanders and prove to them that he had this power, Eleazar placed a cup or foot-basin full of water a little way off and commanded the demon, as it went out of the man, to overturn it and make known to the spectators that he had left the man.

The demon duly performed, and the wisdom of Solomon was thus clearly revealed (Josephus, *Antiq.* 8.46–9).

The demon in this story, like the one expelled by Apollonius, gave a sign that it had been expelled. But the exorcism was quite different. Apollonius simply commanded the spirit to depart; Eleazar used a secret passed down from the time of Solomon. Apollonius was autonomous: he made up his own rules and exerted his own spiritual, 'charismatic' power. Eleazar had learned which roots should be used in exorcism.

From all these stories (healing by God or a god, miracles per-formed by charismatic individuals and by magicians) we see that most ancient people did not have the hard division between the 'natural world' and the 'supernatural' that is common (though not universal) today. In their view *the cosmos was populated by good and evil spirits, who could at will enter the world of sense perception.* Some people could control these spirits. The general belief in a world populated by spiritual powers can be easily illustrated by quoting Paul: 'at the name of Jesus every knee will bow in heaven and on earth and under the earth, and every tongue confess that Jesus Christ is Lord' (Phil. 2.10–11). There were beings with knees both above and below the earth, as well as on it. The overlap between 'supernatural' and 'natural' is seen especially clearly if we consider the words *ru'ah* and *pneuma*. *Ru'ah* is a Hebrew word meaning either 'wind' or 'spirit' (depending on context), while *pneuma* is the corresponding term in Greek. We now think of 'wind' as natural and of 'spirit' as supernatural. The fact that the same word could serve in both senses in either the Greek-speaking or the Hebrew- and Aramaic-speaking world, however, shows that the ancients did not see reality in the way we do. Both 'spirit' and 'wind' were unseen forces, and, in the view of the majority, a spirit was just as 'natural' as the wind. In John 3 there is a play on the double meaning of *pneuma*: 'the *pneuma* blows where it wills . . . ; so it is with every one who is born of the *pneuma*' (3.8). The translation is this: 'the wind blows where it wills . . . ; so it is with every one who is born of the Spirit'. In the first century neither Greek-speakers nor Hebrew- or Aramaic-speakers thought that wind was the same as spirit. The play on *pneuma* shows that they could distinguish meanings according to context. Nevertheless, the lack of a verbal distinction shows that early in the formation of each language the spirit was as natural as the wind. This view of 'nature' continued in the first century, partly because of the continued use of ancient vocabulary, but partly because the motion of the wind was mysterious and was not seen as emanating from *physical* conditions.

The passage just quoted from Philippians 2 ('every knee will bow'), besides giving evidence of the common belief in spiritual powers, also reveals the assumption that some *names* had power ('every tongue confess that Jesus Christ is Lord'). The question of the name in which something was done was an important one. We see this clearly in the gospels and in many other places. John the son of Zebedee said to Jesus that he and the other disciples had seen a man 'casting out demons in your name', and that they had forbidden him. Jesus replied, 'Do not forbid him; for no one who does a miracle in my name will be able soon after to speak evil of me'

(Mark 9.38–41). On another occasion some of Jesus' opponents accused him of casting out demons by using the name 'Beelzebul', the prince of demons. Jesus denied it and turned the point against his critics: 'If I cast out demons by Beelzebul, by whom do your sons cast them out?' He went on to claim that he exorcized by the Spirit of God (Matt. 12.27–9). Thus he granted that others could exorcize. The question was, by what power? In whose name?

Although belief in spirits and demons was widespread, and although most people, whether Jew or Gentile, believed that human agents could encourage spiritual powers to intervene in the normal course of events, there were rationalist protests. Cicero (106–43 BCE) put it this way:

For nothing can happen without cause; nothing happens that cannot happen, and when what was capable of happening has happened, it may not be interpreted as a miracle. Consequently there are no miracles . . . We therefore draw this conclusion: what was incapable of happening never happened, and what was capable of happening is not a miracle. (*De Divinatione* 2.28)

The view espoused by Cicero has become dominant in the modern world, and I fully share it. Some reports of 'miracles' are fanciful or exaggerated; the 'miracles' that actually happen are things that we cannot yet explain, because of ignorance of the range of natural causes. In Cicero's own day, however, very few accepted this stringent rationalism.[9] The vast majority of people believed in spiritual forces, and they thought that specially selected humans could contest their power, control them or manipulate them. Jesus himself held this view.

In studying Jesus' own miracles, I shall not repeatedly raise the question of whether or not the reported incident could really have happened. On the contrary, I wish temporarily to assume the viewpoint of most of Jesus' contemporaries and of the first readers of the gospels, so that we can see how miracles are presented in our sources and what their significance was in a context in which people in general believed in the possibility of miracles. We shall return, however, to the question of modern responses to the miracle stories.

According to the gospels, Jesus performed two types of miracles: healing miracles and 'nature' miracles (involving food and the sea). Exorcisms are such a large subcategory of healings that I shall give them a separate section.

Healing Miracles (apart from Exorcisms)

In the healing miracles the emphasis is often placed on faith. In the case of the paralytic who was let down through the roof, Mark writes that Jesus healed the man 'when [he] saw their faith' – that is, the faith of those who carried him. We also see this motif in one of the most interesting healing narratives, Mark 5.21–43, where one miracle story is sandwiched inside another. A ruler of the synagogue, Jairus, told Jesus that his daughter was about to die and urged him to come and lay his hands on her. As he went, a crowd pressed around him, including a woman who had suffered a flow of blood for twelve years; this is the woman 'who had suffered much under many physicians' but had become worse rather than better. She touched Jesus' garment and the haemorrhage ceased. Jesus, realizing that something had happened, turned and asked who had touched him. The woman came up, fearful, and explained to him what she had done. Jesus replied, 'Daughter, your faith has made you well.' This seems to be an anti-magic statement: his robe did not possess magical power; rather the miracle was the result of the woman's faith.

Jesus continued towards Jairus' house, but some met him, saying that the girl had already died. Jesus urged Jairus, 'Do not fear, only have faith.' When they reached the house he asked the mourners, 'Why do you make a tumult and weep? The child is not dead but sleeping.' They laughed, but he went in, took the girl by the hand, said to her '*talitha qûmi*', and raised her. She stood and walked.

There are two interesting questions about the story of Jairus' daughter. One is whether or not the narrator intended the reader to think that the girl was really dead. Is one to take at face value Jesus' statement, that she was not dead but only unconscious? There is no clear answer to the question, but the author of Mark does seem to draw back from saying that the girl was dead.

The second question is the function of the address *talitha qûmi*. This is simply the Aramaic for 'girl, rise'. Has it been preserved only because that is what Jesus actually said? Or has the author of Mark put it into his Greek gospel as a foreign word of power, somewhat like a magician's incantation? Again, there is no clear answer. Jesus did speak Aramaic, but that does not explain why

Aramaic appears in the Greek gospels in a very few cases but not in many others. Thus the author did want to make some kind of point, but we cannot be certain what it was. The foreign words focus attention on the speaker and thus on his power, but we cannot go much beyond this.

There are two instances in Mark in which Jesus performs a physical action in addition to addressing and touching the person. A deaf man who also had a speech impediment was brought to Jesus. He took him aside, put his fingers into his ears, spat and touched his tongue. He then looked up to heaven and said *ephphatha*, 'be opened' in Aramaic, and the man was cured (Mark 7.31–7). In Bethsaida a blind man was brought to him. He took him outside the village, spat on his eyes, and laid his hands on him. The man's sight was partially restored: he could see people, but they looked 'like trees walking'. Jesus again put his hands over his eyes, and his sight was fully restored (Mark 8.22–6).

Here we do have some techniques that call to mind 'magic'. The Aramaic word in Mark 7.34 is in a context of physical manipulation, which makes it sound like an incantation. It is noteworthy that neither of these stories is in either Matthew or Luke, though they contain most of Mark's miracle stories. It may be that the later authors saw that Mark's accounts were tending towards magic, and so omitted them. We shall consider in a little more detail the ways in which the various gospels use stories of healing.

In Mark there are two almost contradictory themes with regard to the impact of Jesus' healings. The first is that they drew crowds and accounted for his fame. The result of healing a demoniac in the synagogue in Capernaum was that Jesus' 'fame spread everywhere throughout all the surrounding region of Galilee' (Mark 1.28). Later 'the whole city' gathered, and Jesus healed many (1.33–4). The result of his healing the leper was that he 'could no longer openly enter a town, but was out in the country; and people came to him from every quarter' (1.45). This pattern continues until finally the author writes that Jesus drew crowds not only from Galilee, but also from Judaea and Jerusalem and Idumaea (south of Judaea), from beyond the Jordan, and from Tyre and Sidon (in Syria) (3.7f.).

In counterpoint to this Mark insists that Jesus tried not to attract attention by his miracles, but commanded those cured not to tell. He told the leper, 'See that you say nothing to anyone' (1.44). He told the blind man of Bethsaida to go straight home, not to re-enter the village, apparently to keep the cure secret (8.26). Jesus charged those who saw him heal the deaf mute to 'tell no one' (7.36). Yet the author adds that, despite the admonition to silence, the cured people told their stories, so that Jesus' fame continued to spread (e.g., 1.45; 7.36).

It seems that Mark wants the reader to think that Jesus could have continued his very popular career as healer, but that he preferred not to seek fame. He wished, instead, to be a different kind of religious leader: healing could have brought Jesus great fame and a good deal of money, but he 'came not to be served but to serve, and to give his life as a ransom for many' (Mark 10.45). In Mark's view popularity with the crowd was not the aim of Jesus' career.

Matthew's handling of the miracle stories is somewhat different from Mark's. In general the author de-emphasizes miracles. In Matthew, Jesus' career does not open with a series of rapid events in which miracles play a prominent role, but rather with three chapters of ethical teaching: the Sermon on the Mount. Miracles come later. As we saw above, Matthew viewed Jesus in part as a second and greater Moses. (His birth narrative relies on the stories of Moses' birth, and the Sermon on the Mount is the counterpart to the giving of the law to Moses on Mount Sinai.) It is, then, not surprising that Matthew groups ten miracle stories together in chs. 8 and 9, perhaps recalling the ten signs of Moses (the plagues: Exod. 7.14–12.50). The individual miracles, to be sure, are not parallel to those performed by Moses, but the number may nevertheless be a pointer to the influence of stories about Moses.

Matthew often indicates to the reader that Jesus has fulfilled a prophecy. Several quotations of the Jewish scripture are prefaced by the words 'This was to fulfil what was spoken by the prophet . . .' (1.22; 2.5; 2.15; 2.17; 4.14; etc.). With regard to Jesus' healings, Matthew quotes Isaiah 53.4: 'This was to fulfil what was spoken by the prophet Isaiah, "He took our infirmities and bore our diseases"' (Matt. 8.17). Other Christians would turn to this verse to explain Jesus' death: he took upon himself human weakness and suffering. But Matthew understands it to mean 'he took away sickness', and thus he sees Jesus' miracles as fulfilling the prophecy.

We have already noted that Matthew omits the two miracle stories that might smack of magic (the deaf and dumb man, Mark

7.31–7; the blind man at Bethsaida, Mark 8.22–6). He deletes other miracles, such as the exorcism in Capernaum (Mark 1.23–8), and he regularly shortens Mark's stories, especially by eliminating details. A good example is his treatment of the story of the paralytic who was brought to Jesus on a pallet. Mark wrote that he was carried by four men, that they could not reach Jesus because of the crowd, and that they had to let him down through the roof. All this is missing from Matthew. He wrote only that people brought a paralytic to Jesus and that he healed him by saying, 'Your sins are forgiven.' Matthew retains the controversy with those who object to his apparent claim to be able to forgive sins, but Mark's colourful touches are gone (Matt. 9.1–8).

However, Matthew has some healings that are not in Mark. One of these will introduce us to a substantial theme in Matthew and a crucial aspect of early Christianity: the admission of Gentiles. Did Jesus seek Gentile followers? We shall take up this question in the next chapter and here note only Matthew's story of the servant of a Gentile centurion.[10] The centurion came up to Jesus and begged him to heal his servant. Jesus offered to go to him, but the centurion stopped him: 'Lord, I am not worthy to have you come under my roof; but only say the word, and my servant will be healed. For I am a man under authority, with soldiers under me; and I say to one "Go" and he goes . . .' Jesus answered, 'Truly I say to you, not even in Israel have I found such faith.' He sent the centurion home, where he found that his servant had been healed (Matt. 8.5–13; also in Luke 7.1–10). Matthew, Mark and Luke all favour the Christian mission to Gentiles, but Matthew especially emphasizes it. Naturally he wished to have Jesus speak favourably about Gentiles, and so Jesus' comment on the faith of the centurion, and the lack of faith in Israel, was very important.

Luke's principal contribution to the healing miracles was to increase the number that illustrate some of the main themes that are already found in Mark. Luke added two instances of healing on the sabbath, one of healing lepers, and one of resuscitation. The resuscitation story is especially interesting. In Nain, Jesus saw a dead man being carried out of the city. The man was his mother's only son, and she was also a widow; thus she was left bereft. Jesus, moved with compassion, stopped the procession. He commanded the man to arise, and he did so. The people glorified God and exclaimed, 'A great prophet has arisen among us!'; 'God has visited his people' (Luke 7.11–17). The acclamation of Jesus as 'a great prophet' is quite appropriate. The story is reminiscent of one of Elijah's miracles: he too raised a widow's son (I Kgs 17.9, 17–24). As we have seen, all the gospel writers saw Jesus as fulfilling prophecy, and here we see an instance in Luke.

The story also illustrates Luke's tendency to tell stories that are full of human interest. The social status of people interested him, and he often noted whether a person was rich or poor. Zacchaeus, for example, was 'a chief tax collector and rich' (Luke 19.2). In part 2 of his work, Acts, Luke sometimes mentions converts who were socially prominent. Yet his special concern was for the poor. Where Matthew has 'blessed are the poor in spirit', Luke has 'blessed are the poor', and he adds, 'woe to you that are rich' (6.20, 24). He also has in his gospel several stories cautioning against the dangers of wealth and praising the poor: the Rich Fool (Luke 12.13–21); the Rich Man and Lazarus (16.19–31); the Widow's Mite (21.1–4). Women also play a larger role in Luke than in the other gospels. Luke tells the story of a woman who was a sinner ministering to Jesus (7.36–50). As we saw above, Luke also says that Jesus had several women followers who had supported him and his disciples financially (8.1–3). The plight of widows especially concerned him. Luke tells a parable of a widow who had to make a nuisance of herself in order to be given justice (18.1–8). The story of the raising of a widow's son allowed Luke to enlarge the theme that Jesus could raise the dead, while also working in a story of human interest in which Jesus returns to a poor widow her sole means of support.

Another of the healing miracles found only in Luke focuses on a woman. While Jesus was teaching in a synagogue on the sabbath, he saw a woman who had been unable to straighten her back for eighteen years. Jesus laid his hands on her and healed her. The ruler of the synagogue rebuked him for healing on the sabbath, but he successfully defended his right to do good (Luke 13.10–17). This story is closely related to Mark's story of the healing of a man with a withered hand, which Luke had already included (Luke 6.6–11; Mark 3.1–6). His second story enables him to stress the theme of healing on the sabbath, while also telling a story of human sympathy for an afflicted woman. Other elements of Mark 3.1–6 are repeated in yet another story of healing on the sabbath in Luke: the case of a man who had dropsy. Before healing him Jesus asks, 'Is it lawful to heal on the sabbath, or not?', virtually the same question as the one in the story of a man with a withered hand.

Whereas Matthew collected his material in blocks, a procedure that allowed him to give emphasis by putting related material together, Luke aimed for faster alternation of teaching and healing material. He achieved emphasis by repeating themes in different sections of his gospel. Matthew and Mark each has one instance of healing on the sabbath, but Luke has three: the Man with the Withered Hand (Luke 6.6–11); the Woman Bent Over (13.10–17); the Man with Dropsy (14.1–6). The repetition, as we have seen, not only put emphasis on the question of sabbath observance, but also gave Luke opportunity for added narratives full of human interest, and this is one of the main features of his gospel.

As a final example of Luke's tendency, we may add the healing of ten lepers (17.11–14), which partly repeats the healing of one leper (5.12–16) and which also adds an interesting note: only one of the ten returned to say thanks.

Exorcisms

Exorcisms, which are a significant subcategory of healings, deserve fuller discussion. They were very important in Jesus' culture and also in his own career. Demonology had grown in importance in Jewish thought since the days of the Hebrew Bible, which attributes numerous miracles to prophets (such as Elijah and Elisha), but which does not contain stories of exorcism. Exorcism, however, is the most prominent type of cure in the synoptic gospels. The sheer volume of evidence makes it extremely likely that Jesus actually had a reputation as an exorcist. I shall give a full catalogue of stories of demon possession in the synoptics (for John, see note 11):

(1) Exorcisms by Jesus	
(a) Mark 1.23–8//Luke 4.31–7	Jesus heals a man in a synagogue in Capernaum
(b) Mark 1.32–4//Matt. 8.16// Luke 4.41	summary: he cast out many demons

(c)	Mark 1.39	summary (also in Matt. and Luke, but they do not mention demons)
(d)	Mark 3.11//Luke 6.18	summary
(e)	Mark 3.20–30//Matt. 12.22–37//Luke 11.14–23 and other passages	Beelzebul controversy
(f)	Mark 5.1–20//Matt. 8.28–34//Luke 8.26–39	Gerasene demoniac
(g)	Mark 7.24–30//Matt. 15.21–8	Syro-Phoenician woman
(h)	Mark 9.25//Matt. 17.18//Luke 9.42	epileptic child
(i)	Matt. 4.24	summary; 'demoniacs' not in Mark and Luke
(j)	Matt. 9.32–4	dumb demoniac
(k)	Luke 8.2	Jesus exorcized seven demons from Mary Magdalene
(l)	Luke 13.32	tell Antipas 'I cast out demons'

(2) Exorcisms attributed to others

(m)	Mark 3.15; 6.7, 13; Matt. 10.1, 8; Luke 9.1	disciples given authority to cast out demons (or unclean spirits)
(n)	Mark 9.38//Luke 9.49	the strange exorcist
(o)	Matt. 7.22	hypocrites will point out that they cast out demons in Jesus' name
(e)	Matt. 12.27//Luke 11.19 (Beelzebul controversy; cf. above)	'by whom do your sons cast them out?'
(p)	Luke 10.17	the seventy [-two] report that demons were subject to them 'in [Jesus'] name'

3. Other passages revealing the theory of demon possession

(q)	Matt. 11.18//Luke 7.33	some people say that John the Baptist had demon
(r)	Matt. 12.43//Luke 11.24	description of the movement of an unclean spirit

These passages give rise to numerous comments. In the first place they show that demon possession and exorcism were well-known phenomena and that there were many exorcists in addition to Jesus. In 'the Beelzebul controversy' (e) Jesus himself grants that some Pharisees can exorcize. The gospel tradition indicates that the disciples could exorcize (m and p), that a man who did not follow Jesus exorcized in his name (n), and that later 'hypocrites' would be able to claim that they also exorcized in Jesus' name (o). In this connection we should recall the stories about Apollonius and Eleazar (above, pp. 137f., 141).

In the second place, these passages indicate that the sign of demonic possession was usually erratic behaviour. The Gerasene demoniac (f) had formerly been bound with chains, but had burst them and lived among tombs. The spirit that possessed the epileptic child (h) 'often cast him into the fire and into the water' (Mark 9.22). In Mark's form of the Beelzebul controversy (e) the accusation that Jesus cast out demons by invoking the name of the prince of demons comes immediately after Jesus' family tried to seize him, saying, 'He is beside himself' (RSV), which the NRSV reasonably translates, 'He has gone out of his mind' (Mark 3.21). We shall return to this below, here noting only that Jesus himself may have displayed erratic behaviour.

Thirdly, the authors of the gospels, and probably the early Christian tradition prior to our gospels, expanded on Jesus' reputation as an exorcist. The generalizing summaries have this effect: 'they brought to him *all* who were sick or possessed with demons ... And he ... cast out many demons' (b). The two clearest cases of expansion, however, are (j) and (p) above. The first of these passages, Matthew 9.32–4, is probably a creation of Matthew. It illustrates the healing of the dumb demoniac. The question of invention is an important one, and Matthew 9.32–4 is a good case to examine.

This passage is probably an instance in which Matthew has created an additional correspondence between prophecy and the deeds of Jesus. In 11.5 Matthew quotes Jesus' response to John the Baptist: 'the blind receive their sight and the lame walk, lepers are cleansed and the deaf hear, and the dead are raised up, and the poor have good news preached to them'. This depends on Isaiah 35.5f., and Matthew was probably concerned to illustrate all the points of the scriptural proof text. He already had stories of the healing of a leper (8.1–4), the healing of a lame man (9.1–8) and the raising of the dead (9.18–26), and he needed only cures of the blind and the dumb. Apparently he wanted to illustrate both in this section of his gospel, chs. 8–9. He may also have wanted to round the number of healings up to ten. Whatever his reason, he probably wrote the last two miracles in this section. The healing of the blind he took from a passage that comes later (Mark 10.46 // Matt. 20.29–34), thus creating a duplication; he composed the present passage (the dumb demoniac) by making use of standard motifs. The dumb man was cured by casting out a demon (a common motif); the crowd exlaimed, 'Never was anything like this seen in Israel' (cf. 8.10, 'not even in Israel have I found such faith'); and the Pharisees say that 'He casts out demons by the prince of demons' (taken from 12.24, where this charge follows the cure of a blind and dumb demoniac).

The present story, then, shows that new miracle stories could be created on the basis of others. We also see, however, a lack of real creative ability. For his two new miracles Matthew simply raided others. He seems to have had a small stock of traditional healing stories, and when he needed new ones he drew on it, rather than coming up with entirely new accounts.

Luke 10.17 is a very similar case. We noted above that Jesus probably had more adherents than just the twelve disciples, and that Luke made this explicit by adding a mission of seventy (or seventy-two)[12] of Jesus' followers (p. 125). He had no new material, but rather reused the tradition of Jesus' mission charge to the Twelve, with minor alterations. 'The demons are subject to us in your name' (Luke 10.17) is derived from Mark 6.7 // Luke 9.1.

This analysis, which leads to the conclusion that early Christians sometimes created passages about exorcism, simultaneously makes it unlikely that they invented the entire theme. The reader will recall that, when we find a motif in the gospels that parallels a passage in the Hebrew Bible very precisely, we must always ask whether or not the earlier passage has led to the creation of the later one. Isaiah predicted that lepers would be healed, that the deaf would hear and that the dumb would speak; Matthew, we suspect, created a story about a man who could not speak in order to have Jesus fulfil that prediction. Exorcism, however, is not a theme of the Hebrew Bible. It must, therefore, have a different source. Exorcism was well known in the first century. Is it the case, then, that *any* first-century religious leader would be credited with exorcisms? Apparently not. John the Baptist seems not to have been an exorcist. After Jesus' day, Theudas and the Egyptian promised miracles, but Josephus does not say that they exorcized. Honi and Hanina were not famed as exorcists. Exorcism, then, was a specialization: some religious leaders were exorcists, but not all. I think it strongly probable that Jesus was regarded as an exorcist.

People like neat categories, and a good deal of attention has been focused on the question of what sort of figure Jesus was: into what category should he be placed? Morton Smith, for example, thought that Jesus should be considered more a magician than a prophet.[13] I continue to regard 'prophet' as the best single category. Jesus was *also*, however, an exorcist. An exorcist might imitate the behaviour of the person whom he intended to cure. This might include thrashing about, rolling on the floor, and the like. The only actions that the synoptic gospels directly attribute to Jesus are speaking, touching and spitting; but the passages that mention spitting (Mark 7.31–7; 8.22–6; above, p. 145) are not exorcisms. It is, however, possible that the tradition has been purged of material that attributed strange behaviour to Jesus. We noted that, according to Mark 3.21, Jesus' family tried to seize him because he was 'beside himself'. Conceivably this is a remnant of a once larger body of material that depicted Jesus as engaging in erratic behaviour. If he had sometimes behaved in unconventional ways, people would not necessarily have thought that he was a magician, but they would have looked at him a little strangely.

We have now entered the realm of speculation, and it is time to clarify the point of this investigation. In order to see Jesus as he really was, we must recognize that the ethical teaching of the Sermon on the Mount does not tell the whole story. He was not just a teacher or a moralist. According to Mark, his fame derived from healing, and especially from exorcisms. This, in turn, raises the question of Jesus and magic and erratic behaviour. People who chanted incantations and who mixed strange substances were not among the religious elite in Jesus' day. Many of them sold their services for a price, practised black magic, and were generally unsavoury. Matthew deleted Mark's references to Jesus' use of spittle, and it is possible that other magical or semi-magical elements have vanished from sight. I think that we may be fairly certain that initially Jesus' *fame* came as the result of healing, especially exorcism. This is an important corrective to the common view, that Jesus was essentially a teacher. He was also, and for some people primarily, a miracle-worker. We cannot, however, say that his healing activities put him on the level of magicians. It is a *speculative possibility* that he sometimes used one or more of their devices, including spitting and imitative physical behaviour. He seems principally to have healed by speech and touch.

Nature Miracles

The gospels attribute to Jesus other types of miracles besides healings. These are generally called 'nature miracles', although the title is not always precisely appropriate.

One of the most striking, and also puzzling, is an elaborate exorcism story (*f* above). Jesus and his followers crossed the Sea of Galilee and went either to Gerasa (Mark and Luke) or to Gadara (Matthew). They met a demoniac who was uncontrollable.[14] The citizens had tried binding him with chains, but he pulled them apart. 'Night and day among the tombs and on the mountains he was always crying out, and bruising himself with stones.' He saw Jesus, ran to him and knelt down. He – or rather the demon in him – cried out, 'What have you to do with me, Jesus, Son of the Most High God? I adjure you by God, do not torment me.' Jesus asked his name. He replied, 'My name is Legion; for we are many.' There was a herd of swine near by, and the demons begged Jesus to send them into the swine. Jesus did so, 'and the herd, numbering about two thousand, rushed down the steep bank into the sea, and were drowned'. The herdsman told the tale, and many came to see what had happened. The former demoniac was sitting, 'clothed and in his right mind'. The people urged Jesus to leave. He got into the boat and the healed man begged to go with him. Jesus refused, saying that he should stay and tell the story of how God had had mercy on him. He did stay, preaching about what Jesus had done for him throughout the Decapolis (Mark 5.1–20). According to Matthew, however, the story ends with the request of the populace for Jesus to leave (Matt. 8.28–34).

The story is strange on all counts. It is by far the most dramatic exorcism attributed to Jesus, and it combines exorcism with 'nature' – the swine. One of its details renders it unlikely. Gerasa is about thirty miles south-east of the Sea of Galilee, and there is no other large body of water around. Matthew shifts the scene to Gadara, six miles from the sea, perhaps thinking that this reduces the problem – though a six-mile leap is just as impossible as one of thirty miles. I am at a loss to explain the story in the sense of finding a historical kernel. The apocryphal gospels of later centuries sometimes depict Jesus as performing equally fantastic and grotesque miracles, some of which are even crueller than the destruction of swine, such as killing his childhood playmates and then restoring them to life, or turning them into goats. That is, sometimes Christian authors wished so strongly to present Jesus as a being able to employ supernatural power that they depicted him as being no better than a god of Greek mythology in a bad mood.[15] For the most part the canonical gospels are free of this tendency. Here, however, Jesus' spiritual power over demons is so emphasized that it has resulted in an unattractive story. The intended emphasis, of course, is on the healing of a hopelessly possessed man.[16]

The most famous of the nature miracles concerns a storm on the sea (Matt. 14.22–33 // Mark 6.45–52). Jesus had been teaching. He dismissed the crowd to whom he was teaching and went into the hills to pray, while the disciples crossed the sea in a boat. A storm arose and the boat was in difficulty. Suddenly the disciples saw Jesus walking to them. They were scared, thinking, 'It is a ghost.' Jesus reassured them, but Simon Peter asked for proof that it was he, saying that Jesus should have him, Peter, also walk on the water. Peter left the boat and began walking to Jesus. The wind came up again, and Peter became afraid and began to sink. Jesus caught his hand, asking, 'O man of little faith, why did you doubt?' They got back into the boat and the wind ceased. The disciples were convinced that Jesus was the Son of God. This, at least, is Matthew's version. Mark 6.45–52 lacks the part about Peter, as well as the strong conclusion that the disciples believed Jesus to be the Son of God. According to Mark, they did not understand.

There is another story about a storm on the sea (Mark 4.35–41 & parr.). The disciples and Jesus were in a boat when a storm arose, and the boat was about to capsize. Jesus was asleep. The disciples woke him, saying, 'Teacher, do you not care if we perish?' Jesus awoke, rebuked the wind, said to the sea, 'Peace! Be still!', and the sea became calm.

Just as there are two miracles on the sea, there are two feeding miracles. According to the first (Mark 6.30–44 // Matt. 14.13–21), Jesus and his disciples were attempting to escape the crowd, which gave them no time even to eat. They got into their boat and went to 'a lonely place', which was not lonely for long; for people 'ran there on foot from all the towns, and got there ahead of them'. Jesus taught the crowd, and it became late. The disciples urged him to dismiss his hearers so that they could find food. He replied, 'You give them something to eat.' This did not seem reasonable, since they did not have enough money to buy food for the multitude. Jesus then asked how many loaves of bread they had with them. They found five, and two fish. The crowd sat down, Jesus said a prayer of thanksgiving, and he broke the bread. The fish were divided as well. Despite the small initial amount of food, 'they all ate and were satisfied', and there was food left over. According to Mark, there were 5,000 men; Matthew specifies 'besides women and children'. In a second instance (Matt. 15.32–9 // Mark 8.1–10), seven loaves (so Mark; Matthew adds 'and a few small fish') sufficed to feed 4,000.

The most curious aspect of the nature miracles is the lack of impact that, according to the gospels, these events had. Of the crowd's reaction to the first feeding, the gospel writers say only, 'They all ate and were satisfied' (Mark 6.42 & parr.). The comment after the second feeding is almost identical (Mark 8.8 //Matt. 15.37). Even the disciples make no comment. In between the two feedings in both Matthew and Mark comes the story of Jesus' walking on water. Here Mark writes that the disciples 'were utterly astounded, for they did not understand about the loaves, but their hearts were hardened' (Mark 6.51f.). Matthew, we noted, has a more reverential ending: 'And those in the boat worshipped him, saying, "Truly you are the Son of God"' (Matt. 14.33). The stilling of the storm, the first nature miracle in Matthew and Mark, provoked only wonder: 'What sort of man is this, that even winds and sea obey him?' (Mark 4.41; Matt. 8.27).

When we recall that Mark attributed great impact to a relatively minor miracle, a singular exorcism (Mark 1.28, 'his fame spread everywhere'), it is difficult to explain why the authors of the gospels have so little to say about the public import of such grand miracles as feeding a multitude. We cannot solve the puzzle entirely, but part of the answer is that the early Christians had to take into account a serious historical fact: not many people believed in Jesus as God's final and most important spokesman. It appears from I Corinthians 15.6 that Jesus had a few hundred followers and supporters (above, p. 125). Yet the gospel writers believed that he was the Son of God and that he performed dramatic signs that demonstrated his close relationship with the deity. But if he really performed miracles, and if miracles were proof, then more people should have believed. The authors did not doubt that Jesus performed miracles, but they had to grant that not many people believed in him. This left them with a dilemma. Mark in particular tried to meet it by having Jesus command silence: perhaps not many believed because Jesus had restricted the spread of the news. Yet Mark also says that those commanded to silence did not observe it, but proclaimed Jesus openly, and that he was mobbed by crowds. When these same crowds saw a miracle (the multiplication of loaves and fish), however, they made virtually no response. The modern reader is inclined to think that this curious situation arises in part from a tension between actual history and the evangelists' reporting of it. Perhaps Jesus did not really perform many dramatic miracles, and so naturally not many people were convinced by miracles to follow him. From this it would follow that the Christian tradition augmented and enhanced the miracle stories in order to make them very striking. Thus it could be reasoned that historically there was little response because there were few major miracles, while in the gospels there are great miracles but inexplicably little response. Possibly Jesus' actual miracles were relatively minor and excited the public only temporarily. This is a speculative, though I think reasonable solution. We shall, however, consider possible public responses to Jesus' miracles more fully in the next section.

The Significance of Jesus' Miracles

It will help us achieve clarity if we return to modern explanations of miracles before drawing final conclusions about the evangelists' view and Jesus' probable view. When people today look back on miracles in the ancient world (not just those in the Bible), they naturally wish to explain them rationally, since Cicero's view that nothing unnatural can happen, and that whatever happens is natural, has become the dominant opinion, even though a lot of people do not share it. The principal rational explanations are these:

(1) More or less all the healings are explicable as psychosomatic cures or victories of mind over matter. Instances of illness that are 'hysterical' or psychosomatic are well known and documented. This explanation, if applied to miracles in the gospels, covers exorcism and the healings of the blind, the deaf and dumb, the paralysed, and possibly the woman with a haemorrhage.

Some have attempted to extend this explanation to the story of the Gerasene demoniac and the swine: by mental suggestion Jesus really did cure a 'demoniac', that is, he brought him back to his right mind. The man went into convulsions, which alarmed and panicked the swine, who charged over a cliff. I find this explanation unconvincing, and I doubt that those who have offered it have ever tried to panic a herd of swine by throwing a fit. The story is not subject to rational explanation.

(2) It may be thought that some miracles were only coincidences. The stilling of the storm, for example, may have been an instance in which the storm died out on its own at about the time that Jesus said, 'Peace, be still.'

(3) It has been suggested that some miracles were only apparent. When Jesus was seen walking on the water, perhaps he was on the land but the surface was obscured by a low mist that looked like the sea; or perhaps he knew where there were submerged rocks.

(4) Group psychology has often been used to explain the feeding miracles. Actually, everyone had brought food but was afraid to take it out for fear of having to share it. When Jesus and the disciples started sharing their food, however, everyone in the crowd was encouraged to do the same, and there was sufficient and to spare.

(5) Some miracle stories may be historicizing legends. It is really true, for example, that Peter wavered in faith. He did so first

when Jesus was arrested. He followed from afar and denied that he was one of Jesus' followers when he was asked (Mark 14.66–72). Later he also wavered on the question of whether or not Gentile converts to the Christian movement should be required to observe the Jewish food laws, and Paul claimed that he acted hypocritically (Gal. 2.11–24). Peter's inability to walk on water, according to this explanation, is only a pictorial representation of a character failing. It describes his weakness by narrating a brief legend.

The need for rational explanations is a modern one. The numerous efforts have a conservative aim: if Jesus' miracles can be explained rationally, it is easier for modern people to continue to believe that the Bible is true. That is, true in the modern sense: historically accurate and scientifically sound. I think that some rationalist explanations are so far-fetched that they damage the overall effort, but that the principle is partly right. Ancient people attributed to supernatural powers (good or evil spirits) what modern people explain in other ways. It is perfectly reasonable for us to explain ancient events in our own terms. In my opinion, it is plausible to explain an exorcism as a psychosomatic cure. It is, however, an error to think that rational explanations of the miracles can establish that the gospels are entirely factual. Some of the miracle stories cannot be explained on the basis of today's scientific knowledge.

The more important task for the purpose of this book, however, is to make clear how Jesus' contemporaries and near-contemporaries viewed miracles. We also wish to know more particularly what Jesus' followers thought of his miracles, and as much about what he himself thought as is possible. The evidence on which we can draw – stories of miracles in the gospels and other ancient literature – has given us excellent information about the general view of miracles in Jesus' day (above, pp. 135–43). By studying the gospels, we have also discovered how different Christians – the evangelists – understood the miracles one or two generations after Jesus' lifetime (pp. 145–9). We have to probe behind the gospels, however, to discover what significance Jesus and his followers attached to his miracles, and our conclusions must be somewhat tentative. We now turn to this attempt.

The people who came to Jesus hoping for miracles would have viewed him in light of their own past and present. Our survey of the miracle stories in the gospels confirmed the conclusions of the earlier discussion of miracles in the ancient world generally and in Palestine in particular: most people had no difficulty believing in miracles. Jews read and believed the Hebrew Bible, where they found that Moses, Elijah, Elisha and others had performed miracles. Josephus thought that Eleazar could really exorcize. During a civil war many Jews assumed that Honi's curse would be effective, and it was generally believed that God had once answered his prayer for rain. The common people of Palestine saw no difficulty in thinking that God could and did act in history, sometimes by using a righteous and holy person who worked miracles.

The question that Jesus' contempories asked about his actions was whether or not it was God who acted through him. Jesus' enemies did not suspect him of fraud, but of healing by calling on a demonic power. Those who thought that he cast out demons by the Spirit of God naturally thought that he was God's agent in some sense or other. Can we be more specific about *the range of positive views*? We recall that Jesus had a few disciples, more followers and supporters, and many more sympathizers. Crowds flocked to him, hoping to see or benefit from healings. What would they have thought of him? Were Jesus' miracles like those of Honi and Hanina, signs that the miracle-worker was especially devout and was heard by God? Or were they like the signs promised by Theudas, which indicated that God was about to repeat his mighty deeds on behalf of his people? Or did they prove that Jesus was in some sense the Son of God? I shall take the last question first, since this is the topic that most often misleads modern readers when they read the gospels or other ancient literature.

The synoptic gospels do not depict the people who sought and obtained healings from Jesus as calling him 'Son of God', though they do attribute this view to demons. When Jesus exorcized them, the demons sometimes cried 'Son of God'.[17] Matthew's version of Jesus' walking on water is the only passage in which any humans respond to a miracle by saying that Jesus is the Son of God: we saw above that in Matthew the conclusion of the story is that the disciples make this confession (Matt. 14.33). Mark, however, states that 'their hearts were hardened' (Mark 6.51). This story is not in Luke at all. Those readers today who think that Christianity is based on the view that Jesus was more than human, and that Jesus' miracles gave substance to this belief, naturally find confirmation in this verse in Matthew. A strict construal of the evidence would be that nothing at all points to the view that Jesus' contemporaries found in his miracles proof that he was the Son of God. Historians cannot explain the meanings of demonic cries, but in any case the cries of demons cannot be taken as reflecting a general view that was held by sympathetic onlookers. Matthew 14.33 does not refer to the opinion of the many people who came to Jesus for healings. The sentence is actually evidence only of Matthew's own view, since it is simply a revision of Mark.

Despite the complete lack of evidence that the sympathetic onlookers, or people who came to Jesus hoping to be healed, thought that his miracles proved that he was Son of God, I shall discuss the possibility in general terms. I hope to make the issue of 'Son of God' and miracles a little clearer. We begin by asking what 'Son of God' might mean.

In a Jewish context 'Son of God' does not mean 'more than human'. All Jews were 'Sons of God' or even the (collective) Son of God, as in Hosea 11.1 or Exodus 4.22 ('Israel is my first-born son').[18] Psalm 2.7 refers to the king of Israel as Son of God; Luke applied this verse to Jesus (Luke 3.21), but there is no reason to say that when he did so he redefined 'Son of God' to mean 'more than human'.

In the Greek world there was less of a distinction between human and divine than there was in the Jewish world. Greek mythology depicted gods as consorting with humans and producing joint offspring.[19] The Greeks occasionally declared that a human was divine. Though the Romans were originally not inclined to think of humans as gods, the Greek practice tended to spread throughout the Roman empire.

In the first century, then, the term 'Son of God' in such a passage as Matthew 14.33 might have a range of meaning. Conceivably the meaning is the one that was possible in Greek culture: 'the disciples perceived that Jesus was more than merely human'. I think this unlikely. It is probable that 'Son of God' in this passage and elsewhere in the gospels is closer to the meaning that we saw above in connection with Honi: he importuned God the way a son importunes a father (above, p. 139). An important rabbi thought that he was impertinent and took God's favour too much for granted, but no one thought that Honi attributed to himself a supernatural birth and supernatural powers. On the contrary, he claimed only that God answered his prayers. It is very important to note that in another passage Matthew attributes precisely this view to Jesus. At the time of his arrest, Jesus stopped the disciples' attempt to defend him by asking, 'Do you think that I cannot appeal to my Father, and he will at once send me more than twelve legions of angels?' (Matt. 26.53). This sort of statement of intimate sonship – confidence that if one appeals to God he will do what is asked – is rarely attested in Jewish literature, but it is a possible meaning of 'Son of God' in first-century Judaism.

While it is conceivable that, in the one verse in the synoptic gospels that says that Jesus' miracles provoked the acclamation 'Son of God', the phrase means 'more than human', I doubt that this was Matthew's meaning. In any case there is no reason whatsoever to attribute such an idea to the sympathizers and supporters of Jesus. If Jesus' followers in Galilee, or those who saw his miracles, ever said that he was Son of God, they would have meant what Matthew probably meant: he could rely on his heavenly Father to answer his prayers. There is, to repeat, no evidence for such a response, but the culture would permit it. This title, given for such a reason, would not make Jesus absolutely unique, as we learn both from the story of Honi and from Matthew 7.11, where Jesus tells his hearers that *their Father in heaven* will give *them* what they ask.

If Jesus' contemporaries did not think that his miracles proved that he was more than human, did they see them as proving something else – that he was like Honi, or that he was the final messenger before the coming of the kingdom? The first possibility is likely. We should recall another aspect of the gospels' portrayals of how the populace responded to Jesus' miracles. The evangelists had to accept that Jesus' miracles did not prove to all and sundry that he was God's agent in any sense. Thus they ascribe to those who saw Jesus' miracles various reactions, ranging from calm acceptance (the feedings), to public acclaim (the early exorcisms and healings), to puzzlement (Mark 6.51f.), to accusations of black magic. The gospels have no neat solution to the problem of why some people believed and some did not. One of the striking features of the gospels is that they present some strangers as having faith in Jesus – that is, trust in him and confidence that he can help; examples are the woman with a haemorrhage, the Gentile woman in Syria, the centurion in Capernaum and Jairus. Often, however, those closer to Jesus are simply surprised or else uncomprehending (the disciples in Mark after the second stilling of a storm). This contrast is probably exaggerated for dramatic reasons, and I also suggested above that Jesus' miracles themselves have been exaggerated. A third explanation of the lack of widespread commitment to Jesus is that even people who saw him perform miracles regarded him as they did Honi, who had God's ear and who could therefore accomplish beneficial deeds, but who was not someone to whom people committed their lives.[20]

Our study of non-Christian literature indicated that the miracles attributed to Jesus are not greatly different from those attributed to other Jews in the same general period. The people who saw Honi and Hanina perform miracles concluded only that their prayers were effective. Those who saw Eleazar exorcize by using a herb and a ring concluded only that he had access to the wisdom of Solomon. Overall, the evidence of the gospels about public response to Jesus' miracles points in the same direction. People did not doubt that he was a miracle-worker, but this did not move them to become followers or to conclude that he was God's final spokesman. Some trusted in him and some did not. Some accepted his miracles as having taken place, were grateful, and then went on their way. Jesus' miracles as such proved nothing to most Galileans beyond the fact that he was on intimate terms with God. His enemies, we recall, thought that he was on intimate terms with the devil.

Did Jesus' contemporaries think that his miracles proved that the kingdom was at hand? Later, the followers of Theudas hoped that he would perform a miracle that recalled Moses' parting of the sea.[21] They therefore, I assume, were prepared to think of him as the last great prophet before God brought in his kingdom. That is, some people probably thought that the great new age, the kingdom of God, would be inaugurated with the sort of dramatic signs that marked some of the foundational moments of Jewish history, such as the exodus and the conquest of Canaan. Thus it was possible for a prophet to promise an eschatological miracle and to attract followers. If he then actually produced the miracle, he would have had a much greater following. Although after Jesus' day there were such (unfulfilled) promises, it seems that Jesus did not offer a great eschatological miracle to the public. We must conclude, then, that his miracles as such did not prove to the populace in general, even those sections of it friendly towards him, that he was the end-time prophet. This leaves us with Honi as providing the category into which Jesus fitted in most people's minds.

To conclude this topic: there appear to be two explanations of the relative lack of support for Jesus among the general populace. One is that the gospels exaggerate Jesus' miracles; the other is that miracles in any case did not lead most people to make an important commitment to the miracle-worker. Probably most Galileans heard of a few miracles – exorcisms and other healings – and regarded Jesus as a holy man, on intimate terms with God.

What can we learn about the responses of Jesus' disciples and close followers to his miracles? We have seen that Mark especially depicts the disciples as having less confidence in Jesus than did some strangers, and as being unimpressed with the miracles. Matthew and Luke give the disciples a little more credit, but nevertheless we can hardly doubt such things as that they fled when he was arrested and that Peter followed far off and denied that he was Jesus' follower when asked (Mark 14.54, 66–72 & parr.). Later some of the disciples would be willing to die because of their devotion to Jesus and his message. The explanation of the change is that they saw the resurrected Lord, and these experiences gave them absolute confidence. Jesus' miracles did not do so. That is, *the effect of Jesus' miracles on his disciples was probably no greater, or not much greater, than their effect on other Galileans.* We may assume that the disciples all granted that Jesus was on extremely good terms with God. He told them that God was their Father (Matt. 5.45; cf. 5.9) and that they could rely on him even more than children rely on their earthly fathers. Presumably this applied all the more to Jesus, and the disciples saw that he was a man of God. But they did not think that Jesus' few miracles proved that he was going to change the world. Miracles of the sort that Jesus performed simply could not prove anything that dramatic.

Let us look at this from another point of view. Miracles in the ancient world were often seen as accrediting a spokesman for God. That is surely why Theudas and the Egyptian promised miracles. Jesus' disciples, then, would have been willing to follow Jesus' own lead with regard to the significance of his miracles. Let us suppose that he said this: 'I shall now perform a miracle. I intend this to prove that Joseph was not really my father.' We may further suppose that he performed the miracle and that the disciples all saw it. Presumably they would then have thought that Joseph was not Jesus' father. If, on the other hand, he said that a miracle would prove that God was about to defeat the forces of evil once and for all, his disciples would have seen his miracles in this light. It is possible, however, that Jesus viewed his miracles as signs of the coming kingdom of God, and that he taught the disciples to see them in the same way, *but that they were not fully convinced*. To repeat, it was the resurrection that persuaded them.

In the hopes of clarifying this topic – whether or not Jesus told his disciples that his miracles were signs of the coming age – let us return to the way in which the gospels evaluate the miracles. The disciples originated the stories about Jesus, and it is reasonable to think that the overall treatment of miracles in the gospels reflects something of the disciples' view. The most important single interpretative category in the gospels is that the miracles show that, in Jesus, God was beginning the conquest of evil and its consequences – suffering and death. The healing miracles reflect the view that suffering was the result of sin and evil, and the gospels depict Jesus as locked in pitched battle with the forces of Satan. The exorcisms in particular show him as victorious, but that is true as well of the other healing miracles. The relationship between healing and the defeat of sin and evil is explicit in the story of the healing of the paralytic, to whom Jesus said 'Your sins are forgiven' when he healed him (Mark 2.5).

The gospels also present the nature miracles as further demonstrations of conquest. Nature is tamed and brought to submission by Jesus. An ancient motif in Middle Eastern religions was the conquest of 'the deep' by God (or one of the gods). 'The deep', that is, the primeval ocean, was seen as a dangerous enemy. God subdued and controlled it as one of the first acts of creation (Gen. 1.2, 6). The Psalms also depict God as controlling the sea:

> He spoke and raised a gale,
>   lashing up towering waves.
> Flung to the sky, then plunged to the depths . . .
> Then they called to the Lord in their trouble
>   and he rescued them from their sufferings,
>   reducing the storm to a whisper
>   until the waves grew quiet,
>   bringing them, glad at the calm,
>   safe to the port they were bound for. (Pss. 107.25–30)

This is the passage that the story of Jesus' stilling the storm calls to mind, and the authors of the gospels intended to show him to some degree as exercising the sovereignty over nature that was characteristic of God. If this is correct, they thought that he could call on the power of God, rather than that he was himself a supernatural being.

We may assume that no little amount of the confidence in victory over evil that we see in the gospels springs from Christian assurance that God raised Jesus. In Jesus' lifetime the disciples' faith was not this secure – as we saw above. Nevertheless, this material probably gives us one of the right *categories* for understanding the disciples' evaluation of Jesus' miracles during his ministry: in addition to seeing him as a holy man, intimate with God, they also thought that in his work the forces of good were defeating the forces of evil that afflict humanity. Did they, while they worked with Jesus in Galilee, think that his victory of sin and evil would be *final*? Probably they hoped it, but did not fully believe it.

Finally, we ask how Jesus himself viewed his healings and exorcisms. There are four versions of an instance in which Jesus, when asked, refused to give a sign (Matt. 12.38–42; 16.1–4; Mark 8.11–12; Luke 11.29–32). Mark's account, presumably the earliest, is this: 'The Pharisees came and began to argue with him, seeking from him a sign from heaven, to test him. And he sighed deeply in his spirit, and said, "Why does this generation seek a sign? Truly, I say to you, no sign shall be given to this generation."' According to Luke, Jesus said that he ('the Son of Man') would be a sign to the present generation just as Jonah became a sign to the people of Nineveh. 'The people of Nineveh will arise at the judgement with this generation and condemn it; for they repented at the preaching of

Jonah, and behold, something greater than Jonah is here.' In one of Matthew's two versions (16.1–4) Jesus refers to 'the sign of Jonah' but does not explain it. In the other (12.38–42) 'the sign of Jonah' is a prediction of Jesus' own death and resurrection. 'As Jonah was three days and three nights in the belly of the whale, so will the Son of Man be three days and nights in the heart of the earth.'

Thus we have these versions of Jesus' response to those who asked for a sign: (1) no sign will be given (Mark); (2) the sign is that Jesus calls on his generation to repent (Luke); (3) no sign but the sign of Jonah, but what that is remains unspecified (Matt. 16.1–4); (4) the sign will be the resurrection (Matt. 12.38–42).

It is not difficult to see that the last interpretation agrees fully with later Christian conviction and has the least chance of being Jesus' own. Jesus probably refused to give a sign when challenged to do so (Mark), or he referred vaguely to the sign of Jonah (Matt. 16.1–4). The original significance of Jesus' statement that he offered 'the sign of Jonah' is probably the contrast with Jonah's generation: they repented, the present generation did not. The interpretation of this 'sign' as Jesus' own prediction of his death and resurrection probably originated after the resurrection had in fact taken place; it is most likely the work of Matthew himself. Thus far it appears that Jesus did not wish to rest his case on his miracles. He regarded himself as God's true messenger, but he did not wish to prove it in that way. Or, perhaps, he knew that his opponents would not be impressed by miracles, since miracles in and of themselves prove nothing.

There is, however, another passage about the healing stories that indicates that Jesus viewed them as proving that he was the true spokesman for God. When John the Baptist was in prison, probably shortly after Jesus began his active ministry, he sent some of his disciples to Jesus to ask, 'Are you he who is to come, or shall we look for another?' Jesus answered them,

Go and tell John what you hear and see: the blind receive their sight and the lame walk, lepers are cleansed and the deaf hear, and the dead are raised up, and the poor have good news preached to them. And blessed is he who takes no offence at me. (Matt. 11.2–6)

In this reply Jesus is recalling Isaiah 35, where there is a similar list of miracles, and he is apparently claiming that the prophecy is fulfilled in his own work, which leads to the conclusion that he really was 'the one who is to come'. Why did he offer miracles as 'signs' to John the Baptist, but not to others? Perhaps he hoped that John would see his healings in the way that he himself and some of his followers saw them: evidence that he was the agent of the Spirit of God. The difference in his replies to requests for signs, that is, may show the difference in audience: to his enemies he offered no signs, but those who had eyes to see would perceive that God was active in his ministry.

More fully, he probably saw his miracles as indications that the new age was at hand. *He shared the evangelists' view that he fulfilled the hopes of the prophets* – or at least that these hopes were about to be fulfilled. A new time would come in which pain, suffering and death would be overcome, and the miracles pointed towards it. In response to the charge that he exorcized by using the name of Beelzebul, he answered, 'If it is by the Spirit of God that I cast out demons, the kingdom of God has come upon you' (Matt. 12.28). We should note both the proclamation and the 'if'. We see the recognition that the miracles as such did not establish the presence or impending arrival of the kingdom, but did so only if Jesus acted with the power of the Spirit. There can be no doubt that he thought that he did.

There is one further passage that indicates that Jesus saw his ministry in this light, which Luke puts in his story of the mission of the seventy. When these disciples returned, they told Jesus that 'even the demons are subject to us in your name'. He replied, 'I saw Satan fall like lightning from heaven' (Luke 10.17f.). Jesus, it seems, partially agreed with the view of the authors of the gospels: his miracles were signs of the beginning of God's final victory over evil. We attributed this view to the gospels and the disciples, and now we can attribute it to their source: Jesus.

Jesus did not try to prove this in big and showy ways, and probably the crowds who flocked to him did not know, or at least did not fully understand, the eschatological context in which he himself saw his work. Miracles, as such, would not convey eschatological hope. They did so only to those who understood – who were close enough to him to put his miracles into the context of his teaching, and even they remained uncertain of the significance of Jesus' deeds.

II. THE COMING OF
THE KINGDOM

By word no less than deed Jesus intended to proclaim the power of God. He referred to it as 'the kingdom of God' (Mark and Luke) or 'the kingdom of heaven' (Matthew).[1] Mark summarizes Jesus' message thus: 'The time is fulfilled, and the kingdom of God is at hand; repent and believe in the gospel' (Mark 1.15).

'Kingdom of God' is in some ways clear and precise, but in others ambiguous. What is clearest is the negative connotation: it points to the reign of God as distinct from humans and thus to a radical reorientation of values and power. God, almost any Jew would agree, would not govern his kingdom by appointing Tiberius, Antipas, Pilate and Caiaphas, nor would his prime consideration be the security of the Roman empire. 'God's kingdom', in first-century Palestine, was definitely not the present kingdom.

It is harder to say positively what Jesus meant by 'kingdom of God'. Intensive efforts over the last hundred years to define the phrase have left the issue more confused rather than clearer. There are, however, two meanings that would have been more or less self-evident given standard Jewish views. One is that God reigns in heaven; the 'kingdom of God' or 'kingdom of heaven' exists eternally there. God occasionally acts in history, but he completely and consistently governs only heaven. The second is that in the future God will rule the earth. He has chosen to allow human history to run on with relatively little interference, but someday he will bring normal history to an end and govern the world perfectly. Briefly put: the kingdom of God always exists *there*; in the *future* it will exist *here*. These two meanings are perfectly compatible with each other. Anyone could maintain both at the same time, and in fact millions still do.

What can humans do about the kingdom? Most people who held

one or both of these views would think that they could only prepare and wait for one of three eventualities. At death their souls will enter the kingdom of heaven; or they will die and await the resurrection of the body; or possibly God will bring his kingdom to earth before they die. It would have been reasonable to hold a combination of these views: when individuals die, their souls go to heaven; in the future God will bring his kingdom to earth, at which time he will judge the living and the dead (whose bodies will be raised). Immortality of the soul and resurrection of the body were originally separate ideas: resurrection entered Judaism from Persia, immortality from Greece. But by the first century they were often combined (as we shall see below).

'Kingdom' is a social concept, but the previous paragraph describes only individual preparation for it and participation in it – until God decides to bring the kingdom to earth. One can say, of course, that the individuals who were preparing for the kingdom of God did influence society. Such people lived upright lives, and so they made the world a better place. But thus far 'kingdom' refers only to a supernatural society, one governed by God himself. Humans can get ready for it, but otherwise they cannot do anything about it: the kingdom is like the weather.

Perhaps needless to say, many people have found this unsatisfactory as an interpretation of the teaching of Jesus about the kingdom of God. In his society there was poverty and injustice. Surely he wanted a better society, surely he thought that people could help bring one about, surely this is what he meant when he spoke of the kingdom of God. When we add to these expectations, which are perfectly reasonable, the fact that the word 'kingdom' is used in a diversity of ways in the gospels, we see why the topic 'the kingdom of God in the teaching of Jesus' is one of the most discussed issues in New Testament scholarship. Scholars often propose that Jesus thought that the kingdom was in some way or other present and active in the world, especially in his ministry. People did not have to wait for it, they could participate in it.

It may help if we think of Jesus – or any other first-century Jew who wished to talk about God's rule – as having the option to combine in various ways *here*, *there*, *now* and *later*. The kingdom is either here, in heaven or both. It is either now, future or both.[2] The question is what Jesus primarily meant. In advance, it would be

perfectly reasonable to guess that he would have chosen the both/
both option: the kingdom of God is both there and here, both now
and for ever. Why limit the sphere of God's power? Of course, the
both/both option requires some change in the precise meaning of
'kingdom': *here and now*, the kingdom cannot be quite what it will
be where there are no humans to interfere. The *present* kingdom of
God *on earth* would have to be invisible and non-coercive. Individuals or groups of people might see themselves as living in God's
kingdom if they tried to live in the way that (in their view) God
desired. But they would have to grant that God's will did not
generally prevail and that God did not force humanity in general to
live in one way rather than another.

In another sense almost any first-century Jew could have agreed
that God rules here and now, since he exercises providence[3] and
controls the ultimate outcome. Jews in general thought both that
God was Lord of heaven and that in the end he would govern
everything perfectly. I assume that Jesus shared these views. In
general terms they were completely non-controversial. It seems,
however, that he wanted to say something more particular about
God's kingdom. The kingdom of God in the teaching of Jesus is not
merely God's *ability* ultimately to determine the course of history,
nor is it only God's reign in heaven. Something special was happening, or was about to happen. When Jesus spoke of the kingdom, he
was not offering merely the standard theological views of his day.
Thus we must try to say more precisely what he meant.

Our first step will be to canvass sayings on the kingdom. I shall
divide them into six categories, three of which are simply subdivi-
sions of the future meaning of 'kingdom of God'.

(1) The kingdom of God is in heaven: it is a transcendent realm,
to which people may look for inspiration and into which they will
individually enter at death or at the great judgement: the kingdom
is *there*, both *now* and in the *future*. There are several passages in the
gospels that refer to entering the kingdom (= heaven) at the time
of death or the judgement. An example is Mark 9.47: 'if your eye
causes you to sin, pluck it out; it is better for you to enter the
kingdom of God with one eye than with two eyes to be thrown
into hell' (similarly Matt. 18.9: better to enter life). Here 'kingdom
of God' is opposite hell, and one 'enters' it after death. Similarly
when a rich man asked what he should do to inherit eternal life,

Jesus told him that he should sell all that he had, give it to the poor (so that he would have treasure in heaven), and become a follower (Mark 10.17–22 & parr.). Although this passage does not contain the word 'kingdom', it lends general support to this definition: individuals gain eternal life at the time of death.

The meaning of 'kingdom' is basically the same in some other passages, such as Mark 10.15 // Luke 18.17; cf. Matt. 18.3 (whoever does not receive the kingdom as a child shall not enter it) and Matt. 7.21f. (only those who do the will of God will enter the kingdom 'on that day': i.e., at the last judgement). If we made a more detailed outline of meanings of the word 'kingdom', sayings about the last judgement could be a subcategory. In these, the assumption is either that people die and await judgement, or that the world ends and God (or his viceroy) conducts the judgement then – presumably including those who had previously died. The net effect is the same. People enter the kingdom after death, provided that their lives on earth had met the judge's requirements. God does not create the kingdom then, and so it always exists. This is one of the simple definitions with which we began the chapter, and we see that it is present in the gospels.

(2) The kingdom of God is a transcendent realm now in heaven, but in the future it will come to earth. God will transform the world so that the basic structures of society (physical, social and economic) are maintained but remoulded. All people will live as God wills, and there will be justice, peace and plenty. The kingdom is *there now* and in the future will also be *here*. This is the second simple definition, and it can also be found in the gospels. One of the petitions of the Lord's Prayer implies this view: 'Your kingdom come, your will be done, on earth as it is in heaven' (Matt. 6.10; cf. Luke 11.2). A few passages refer to *ranks* in the kingdom, thereby implying a social structure, which indicates that the future kingdom will be *here*: according to Mark 10.35–40 // Matthew 20.20–23, James and John (Matthew: their mother) asked Jesus if they could sit on either side of him in his glory (Mark) or kingdom (Matthew). Jesus answered that he did not have authority to grant the request. There is also a discussion of 'who is greatest' in the kingdom in Matthew 18.1, 4, and of the 'least in the kingdom' in Matthew 5.19. At his last supper Jesus stated that he would not drink wine again until he could drink it in the kingdom (Mark 14.25 & parr.).

Luke places here the dispute about rank in the future kingdom. Jesus concludes the discussion thus: 'I assign to you, as my Father assigned to me, a kingdom, that you may eat and drink at my table in my kingdom, and sit on thrones judging the twelve tribes of Israel' (Luke 22.29). The prediction that the twelve disciples would judge the twelve tribes of Israel also appears in Matthew 19.28. There it is connected with a more general saying that also implies a social order and material possessions: 'Everyone who has left houses or brothers . . . or lands, for my name's sake will receive a hundred-fold, and inherit eternal life' (Matt. 19.29; similarly Mark 10.29f.; Luke 18.29f.). Here the material reward comes *prior* to eternal life; that is, society will be reorganized so that Jesus' followers are leaders and have substantial possessions, but 'eternal life' lies still further in the future. There will be a kingdom of God on earth, presumably while Jesus' followers are still alive. All these passages depict the kingdom in terms of a greatly transformed human society on earth. We saw above that categories (1) and (2) may be combined: people who die enter the kingdom of God in heaven, but some day God will come to earth to reign there as well.

(3) A special subcategory of sayings looks forward to a future realm that will be introduced by a cosmic event. What sets these passages apart is that they indicate *how* the kingdom will come to earth. The arrival of the kingdom will be accompanied by cosmic signs. I hasten to add that in these passages the word 'kingdom' seldom occurs; nevertheless, the subject is the establishment of God's rule, usually under the suzerainty of the 'Son of Man'. This title has more than one meaning in the gospels (pp. 246ff.); in the passages under consideration it refers to a heavenly figure who descends in order to establish a new order. The principal passage is Mark 13 and its parallels in Matthew and Luke. I shall quote only a few verses:

But in those days, after that tribulation, the sun will be darkened, and the moon will not give its light, and the stars will be falling from heaven . . . And then they will see the Son of Man coming in clouds with great power and glory. And then he will send out the angels, and gather his elect from the four winds, from the ends of the earth to the ends of heaven. (Mark 13.24–7)

The parallel passages are Matthew 24; 10.16–23; 16.27f.; Luke 17.22–37; 21.5–19.

Scholars usually assume that Mark 13 implies the end of the world. We now know that if the stars fell from heaven, the physical universe would be in very serious trouble. To ancient people, however, the stars looked fairly close and quite small (as they do to children today until they are taught the basic facts about astronomy). Thus the predictions of cosmic disturbance do not necessarily imply that the universe is about to be destroyed. It is more likely that these sayings simply describe *how* the kingdom will come to an earth that will remain in existence: the Son of Man and angels will come, accompanied by heavenly signs. The issue cannot be settled with full certainty, but I shall return to it briefly below.

(4) In many passages the kingdom is future, but it is not otherwise defined. The passages generally support the view that Jesus spoke of the kingdom as future, but they are less specific than categories (2) and (3). In Mark 1.15 & parr. there is a summary of Jesus' message: the time is fulfilled and the kingdom has drawn near. The same wording appears also in Jesus' charge to his disciples in Matthew 10.7 and Luke 10.9: they are to preach to others that the kingdom 'has drawn near'. According to Mark 9.1 & parr., some of Jesus' followers 'will not taste death' until they see that the kingdom has come (Matt. 16.28: before they see the Son of Man coming in his kingdom; Luke 9.27: before they see the kingdom of God). Mark 15.43 notes that Joseph of Arimathea was *also* waiting for (or expecting) the kingdom of God (cf. Luke 23.51). Other references to the kingdom as future are Luke 21.31; Matthew 25.34; possibly Matthew 21.31.

(5) It is possible in some passages that the kingdom is a special 'realm' on earth, one that consists of people who are dedicated to living according to God's will and that exists both in and side by side with normal human society. In the centuries after Jesus' death, this is the way Christians have often seen themselves: they simultaneously live in two realms, the temporal and the eccesiastical. There are no passages in the gospels with precisely this meaning, but some come close: the kingdom is like leaven, which cannot be seen but which leavens the whole loaf (Matt. 13.33 // Luke 13.20f.). In Luke 17.20f. the kingdom is 'among you'. This saying includes a line that opposes one form of the idea that the kingdom is future: 'The kingdom of God is not coming with signs to be observed.'

(6) Many scholars have found in two passages the view that Jesus

regarded the kingdom as being somehow present in his own words and deeds: present *here* and *now*, but only in his own ministry. I shall quote the two passages but defer discussion; we shall move immediately into considering what conclusions we may draw concerning the kingdom of God in the teaching of Jesus.

If it is by the Spirit of God [Luke: finger of God] that I cast out demons, then the kingdom of God has come upon you. (Matt. 12.28 // Luke 11.20)

When John heard in prison what the Christ was doing, he sent word by his disciples and said to him, 'Are you the one who is to come, or are we to wait for another?' Jesus answered them, 'Go and tell John what you hear and see: the blind receive their sight, the lame walk, the lepers are cleansed, the deaf hear, the dead are raised, and the poor have good news brought to them. And blessed is anyone who takes no offence at me. (Matt. 11.2–6)

For several decades scholars have contemplated the various categories of kingdom sayings, and they have tried to sort out just what Jesus thought. Johannes Weiss (1892) and Albert Schweitzer (1906) fixed especially on the passages in category (3) above (a cosmic event) and concluded that Jesus expected a great cataclysm within the very near future – during his own lifetime.[4] This was, of course, a very uncomfortable conclusion for Christian scholars, since it meant that Jesus' principal message was in error. Rudolf Bultmann (1926) accepted that Jesus thought of the kingdom as being future, but he was nevertheless able to make this relevant to Christian believers: 'the Kingdom of God is . . . a power which, although it is entirely future, wholly determines the present'.[5] Any great impending event influences present action, and Bultmann thought that Jesus' view of the kingdom worked in that way. Christians should *always* view the kingdom as imminent; then they will live appropriately.

Bultmann's contemporary, C. H. Dodd, argued that, in Jesus' view, the *eschaton* – the decisive moment in history – had already arrived in his own ministry. He proposed, for example, that 'the kingdom has drawn near' (Mark 1.15) should be translated 'the kingdom has come'.[6] Very few people were persuaded by Dodd's arguments in detail, but many thought that he had a point. There *was* a sense in which Jesus thought that what was really important was already happening. This led to a consensus that lasted for a few decades: Jesus thought both that the kingdom was future and that it was 'in some sense' – never specified – present in his own words and deeds. Norman Perrin offered the classic formulation of this view (1963).[7]

In very recent years a few American scholars have decided that Jesus did not expect the kingdom to come in the future at all. Luke 17.20f. – the kingdom of God is among you – is the only passage that really counts when one defines the kingdom. Jesus was actually a political, social and economic reformer, and he did not expect God to do anything dramatic or miraculous in the future.[8]

It is my own view that we cannot recover Jesus' view merely by picking and choosing among the sayings. In particular, I think it impossible to reject any of the major categories completely. I shall soon indicate where my own doubts lie, but I do not think that a historical reconstruction should depend on the notion that we can definitely establish what Jesus did *not* say. If we calmly survey all of the kingdom sayings, we shall see that most of them place the kingdom *up there*, in heaven, where people will enter after death, and *in the future*, when God brings the kingdom to earth and separates the sheep from the goats. We have noted one saying that opposes or partially opposes this view: Luke 17.20f.: the kingdom does not come with signs to be observed, but is among you. This saying, however, is Luke's preface to 17.22–37, which is parallel to Mark 13. After Luke's anti-future preface, we read such verses as these: 'For as the lightning flashes and lights up the sky from one side to the other, so will the Son of Man be in his day.' 'There will be two women grinding meal together; one will be taken and the other left' (Luke 17.24, 35). It seems to me impossible to cite Luke 17.20f. as Jesus' only meaningful saying on the kingdom and as indicating what he really thought. Of the three gospels, Luke is most concerned to minimize and de-emphasize Jesus' future expectation. This concern surfaces, for example, in the author's preface to a parable, in which the readers are cautioned not to expect the kingdom immediately (Luke 19.11). Even 19.11, however, does not deny that the kingdom will come.[9] Both passages (17.20f. and 19.11) are Luke's own modifications of previously existing material. Luke 17.20f. does not appear in Luke's source (here Mark), while 19.11 is the author's comment on the point of a parable. The saying in 17.20f. is the author's own attempt to reduce the significance of the dramatic verses that follow, which discuss the arrival of the Son of Man and the impending judgement. But even if Jesus actually uttered the sentences of Luke 17.20f., they cannot be used to prove that he said nothing about a future cosmic event. I believe that Luke wrote these two verses all by himself, unaided by a transmitted saying of Jesus. In defining what Jesus thought, however, I do not rely on proving that they are unauthentic, and I certainly do not think it impossible that Jesus thought that the kingdom was 'in some sense' present. I am arguing, rather, that one cannot take Luke 17.20f. as cancelling the large number of sayings about the future kingdom – including those that immediately follow in Luke.

I am also unpersuaded by the general interpretation of Matthew 12.28 and 11.2–6 (category 6 above). I have never been able to see in these passages what others do: the claim that, in Jesus' own view, the kingdom was *fully present* in his actions. The statement that the kingdom 'has come upon' Jesus' critics (the first passage) most likely means 'is now bearing down upon you'.[10] Further, in the passage in which Matthew 12.28 occurs, the Beelzebul controversy, Jesus grants that others cast out demons, thus indicating that his own activities are not unique. Did he nevertheless think that in his exorcisms the kingdom was fully present, while other exorcisms proved nothing? We cannot know this, and the passage does not say it. Had Jesus thought that the kingdom was present in his own actions, one would expect him to have said to the people he healed, especially those who had faith in him, that *they* had participated in, or been the beneficiaries of, the power of the kingdom of God. Saying that the kingdom 'has come upon' his *critics*, it seems to me, is a kind of warning: it has come upon you, and if you maintain your present stance you will regret it – in the immediate future.

In the second passage in category (6), Jesus' reply to John (Matt. 11.2–6), Jesus says only that he is fulfilling the promises of Isaiah – not that the kingdom of God is present in his ministry. He could be fulfilling the promises, and the kingdom could still lie in the future. On the basis of this passage, one cannot tell.

In view of my strong doubts about the common interpretation of these two passages, I wish to repeat that my position on the meaning of 'kingdom of God' does not depend on disproving this or any other category. Jesus might have thought that the kingdom was 'somehow' present in his own words and deeds; I cannot prove that he did not think this. I only note that no passage clearly says so. Jesus doubtless thought that the power of God was present, both in his own life and elsewhere; but in view of the lack of good evidence, it is unlikely that he meant that the kingdom was fully present wherever he happened to be.

The simplest and in some ways the best view to take of the complicated question of the kingdom in the teaching of Jesus is that he said *all* the things listed above – or things like them. There is no difficulty in thinking that Jesus thought that the kingdom was in heaven, that people would enter it in the future, and that it was also present in some sense in his own work. Paul's letters very conveniently reveal that one person could mean different things by the word 'kingdom'. He sometimes discussed who would inherit the kingdom (e.g., I Cor. 6.9f.), which implies that it was future. Yet he also wrote that 'the kingdom of God is not food and drink but righteousness and peace and joy in the Holy Spirit' (Rom. 14.17). The full revelation of the kingdom of God may lie in the future, but in the present people can experience some of its benefits.

The passages listed in category (3) above – which predict that the Son of Man will come on clouds while some of Jesus' hearers are still alive – require further discussion. These are the passages that many Christian scholars would like to see vanish. First, they are lurid and, to many modern readers, distasteful. Secondly, the events they predict did not come to pass, which means that Jesus was wrong. Thirdly, and most importantly, if Jesus expected *God* to change history in a decisive way in the immediate future, it seems unlikely that he was a social reformer.

I shall not discuss a matter of taste, but I shall make a few comments on the second and third problems, taking the last first. We noted above that a striking conception of *how* the kingdom comes is the distinguishing mark of the sayings about the Son of Man coming on clouds. But in a very important way this understanding of how the kingdom comes was typical of first-century Jewish thought. God was always the main actor. That is certainly the case in the gospels: the only thing that Jesus ever asks people to do is to live right. In none of the material does he urge them to build an alternative society that will be the kingdom of God. There are few passages that can possibly fit into category (5) above, and even those that I listed there do not urge the creation of an alternate social entity. Jesus said that the kingdom is like leaven; this refers to its invisibility. It is also like a tiny grain of mustard. People who later created a social structure that consisted of small cells in each town or city could of course say that they were the leaven in the dough; they were trying to make society better. But the people who heard these similes in Galilee would have been motivated to look around for clues to the invisible kingdom that would one day erupt as a full loaf or a large tree; the passages do not say 'create small groups of reformers'. Jesus thought that people should and could commit themselves to his way; they were not to be merely passive. But we must note what he urged. He said that by living right, people can *enter* the kingdom (category 1 above). According to the evidence, he thought that there was nothing that anyone could do to *bring* the kingdom, and even he himself could not assign places in it (category 2). It is drawing near, and people await it, but they cannot make it come (category 4). Like leaven, it grows on its own (category 5). In every single case it is God who does whatever has to be done, except that individuals who live right will enter the kingdom. There is no evidence at all for the view that individuals can get together with others and *create* the kingdom by reforming social, religious and political institutions.

The second of the problems mentioned above – if Jesus expected God to change the world, he was wrong – is by no means novel. It arose very early in Christianity. This is the most substantial issue in the earliest surviving Christian document, Paul's letter to the Thessalonians. There, we learn, Paul's converts were shaken by the fact that some members of the congregation had died; they expected the Lord to return while they were all still alive. Paul assured them that the (few) dead Christians would be raised so that they could participate in the coming kingdom along with those who were still alive when the Lord returned. The question of just how soon the great event would occur appears in other books of the New Testament. A saying in the synoptics (discussed more fully below) promises that 'some standing here' will still be alive when the Son of Man comes. In the appendix to the Gospel of John (ch. 21), however, Jesus is depicted as discussing an anonymous disciple, called 'the disciple whom Jesus loved', with Peter: 'If it is my will that he remain until I come, what is that to you?' The author then explains, 'So, the rumour spread in the community that this disciple would not die. Yet Jesus did not say to him that he would not die, but "If it is my will that he remain until I come, what is that to you?"' (John 21.21–3).

The history of these adjustments to the view that God would do something dramatic while Jesus' contemporaries were still alive is fairly easy to reconstruct. Jesus originally said that the Son of Man would come in the immediate future, while his hearers were alive. After his death and resurrection, his followers preached that he would return immediately – that is, they simply interpreted 'the Son of Man' as referring to Jesus himself. Then, when people started dying, they said that some would still be alive. When almost the entire first generation was dead, they maintained that one disciple would still be alive. Then he died, and it became necessary to claim that Jesus had not actually promised even this one disciple that he would live to see the great day. By the time we reach one of the latest books of the New Testament, II Peter, the return of the Lord has been postponed even further: some people scoff and say, 'Where is the promise of his coming?' But remember, 'with the Lord one day is as a thousand years, and a thousand years as one day' (II Peter 3.3–8). The Lord is not really slow, but rather keeps time by a different calendar.

In the decades after Jesus' death, then, the Christians had to revise their first expectation again and again. This makes it very probable that the expectation originated with Jesus. We make sense of these pieces of evidence if we think that Jesus himself told his followers that the Son of Man would come while they still lived. The fact that this expectation was difficult for Christians in the first century helps prove that Jesus held it himself. We also note that Christianity survived this early discovery that Jesus had made a mistake very well.

We shall now look in greater detail at what appears to be the core saying behind this early Christian belief. We just noted that the Thessalonians feared that those who died would miss out on the return of the Lord: therefore Paul had first said that the Lord would return immediately. He responded to their concern by quoting what he called 'a word of the Lord' – a saying that he attributed to Jesus. The saying as he quotes it is very close to sayings ascribed to Jesus in the gospels. I shall now print three versions of the saying in parallel columns.

I Thess. 4.15–17	Matt. 24.27f.	Matt. 16.27f.
We who are alive, who are left until the *appearance of the Lord*, will not precede those who have fallen asleep. For *the Lord* himself will *come down* from *heaven* with a command, with the voice of an *archangel*, and *with a trumpet* of God; and the dead in Christ will rise first, then *we who are alive* . . . at the very same time will be *snatched up* with them in the clouds to greet the Lord in the air.	The sign of the *Son of Man will appear* in heaven, and then all the tribes of earth will mourn, and they shall see the *Son of Man coming* on clouds of *heaven* with power and great glory. And he will send his *angels with a trumpet* of great voice, and they will *gather* his elect from the four winds, from one side of heaven to the other.	*The Son of Man* is about to come in the glory of his father with his *angels*, and then he will repay to each according to his or her deeds. Truly I say unto you, there are some of those standing here who *will not taste death*, until they see the Son of Man coming in his kingdom.

Paul and Matthew have essentially the same component parts. If we delete from Paul's version of the saying his new concern about the dead in Christ, if we delete from the synoptic saying the apparent modification that only *some* will still be alive, and if we equate 'the Son of Man' in the synoptics with 'the Lord' in Paul, we have the same saying. This saying probably does not anticipate 'the end of the world', but rather a decisive divine act that will put 'the Lord' or 'the Son of Man' in charge and gather around him 'the elect'. It is most probable that, in Paul's view, after both the living and the dead Christians 'greet' the Lord in the air, they accompany him to his kingdom on earth. In another passage Paul predicted that Christ would reign for a while until he defeated all enemies, the last of whom was death (I Cor. 15.25f.). This means that humans would still die while the Lord reigned. Only after the defeat of death would the Lord hand over the kingdom to God (15.24), at which time God would be 'all in all' (15.28). Paul may have understood this last stage, *after* the successful reign of Christ, to involve the dissolution of the physical universe.[11]

Scholars who try to 'test' sayings of Jesus for authenticity will see that this tradition passes with flying colours. First, the predicted event did not actually happen; therefore the prophecy is not a fake. An unfulfilled prophecy is much more likely to be authentic than one that corresponds precisely to what actually happened, since few people would make up something that did not happen and then attribute it to Jesus. Secondly, the tradition is attested in more than one source. Paul wrote I Thessalonians before the gospels were composed, and so he could not have been dependent on Matthew or Mark. The synoptic authors did not copy Paul, since they wrote before his letters were published.[12] Moreover, they show no knowledge of the points that distinguished Paul's thought from common Christianity. Therefore, Paul and the authors of the synoptics had *independent* knowledge of this saying. Even though it was a little embarrassing for the synoptic authors, it was so firmly embedded in the tradition about Jesus that they kept it.

The only actual problem in understanding what Jesus and his followers expected is the meaning of 'the Son of Man'. After Jesus' death and resurrection, the early Christians concluded that his references to the coming of the Son of Man were a cryptic way of saying that he himself would return, and accordingly they changed 'the Son of Man will come' to 'the Lord will come (or return)'. We cannot recover precisely what Jesus meant, but we shall discuss 'Son of Man' and other titles in ch. 15. For the present, it is enough to know that Jesus expected something dramatic to happen.

If, then, we were to decide what Jesus *really* thought by picking and choosing among sayings, we would conclude that he thought that in the very near future God would dramatically intervene in history by sending the Son of Man. This is the most securely attested tradition. He probably also thought what we find in the majority of the passages: that individuals who died would enter the kingdom, and that when God sent the Son of Man there would be a great judgement, with some people being assigned to heaven and some to Gehenna (hell). In addition, he thought that the power of God was especially manifest in his own ministry. He could conceivably have called this present power 'the kingdom' (see the discussions above of Luke 17.20f.; Matt. 12.28; Matt. 11.2–6).

I do not think, however, that the issue is settled entirely by studying the individual sayings. Only they can give us any of the nuances of Jesus' thought, but the best evidence in favour of the view that Jesus expected that God would very soon intervene in history is the context of the movement that began with John the Baptist (ch. 7 above). John expected the judgement to come soon. Jesus started his career by being baptized by John. After Jesus' death and resurrection, his followers thought that within their lifetimes he would return to establish his kingdom. After his conversion, Paul was of the very same view. The Christians very soon, as early as I Thessalonians (c. 50 CE), had to start coping with the troublesome fact that the kingdom had not yet come. It is almost impossible to explain these historical facts on the assumption that Jesus himself did not expect the imminent end or transformation of the present world order. He thought that in the new age God (or his viceroy) would reign supreme, without opposition.

As a desperate measure, people whom this makes uncomfortable can say that everybody misunderstood Jesus completely. He really wanted economic and social reform. The disciples dropped that part of his teaching and made up sayings about the future kingdom of God – which they then had to start retracting, since the kingdom did not arrive. This assumes that we can 'know' things for which there is no evidence, while simultaneously 'knowing' that the evidence we have is based on total incomprehension. Such views merely show the triumph of wishful thinking.

We may be quite confident that Jesus had an *eschatological* message. Since this word is very important in discussions of both early Christianity and Judaism, I shall repeat an explanation given above (p. 93). Etymologically, 'eschatology' means the discussion or thought about 'the end'. The term 'eschatology' is so common and has such a long history in biblical scholarship that we cannot discard it. We must, however, stress that it can be misleading when used to describe Jesus' message, as it is when used to describe the future expectations of other Jews. Jesus did not expect the end of the world in the sense of destruction of the cosmos. He expected a divine, transforming miracle. As a devout Jew, he thought that God had previously intervened in the world in order to save and protect Israel. For example, God had parted the sea so that Israel could escape the pursuing Egyptian army, he had fed the people with manna in the desert, and he had brought them into the land of Palestine. In the future, Jesus thought that God would act even more decisively: he would create an ideal world. He would restore the twelve tribes of Israel, and peace and justice would prevail. Life would be like a banquet.

In general terms a lot of Jews thought the same. Jesus' hope for the future will be more comprehensible if we can see it in context, and so I shall say a few words about the restoration of the twelve tribes and the symbolic value of banqueting in the Judaism of Jesus' day. This is not a complete account of what Jews thought about the future; studying these two themes, however, will help us see that Jesus' future hope was shared by many other Jews of his time, but that it nevertheless had distinctive features.[13]

According to Jewish history and legend, Israel consisted of twelve tribes, each descended from one of Jacob's sons. The twelve tribes had divided into two kingdoms in the tenth century BCE, with ten tribes in the northern kingdom and two in the southern. In the eighth century BCE the Assyrians conquered the northern kingdom. Their policy was to scatter conquered peoples in order to reduce the chance of revolt, and the execution of that policy meant the loss of the ten northern tribes. The southern kingdom was subsequently conquered by the Babylonians, who did not scatter the populace, but rather took leaders of the conquered nation back to Babylon (sixth century BCE). The Persians under Cyrus conquered Babylonia and released the exiled Jews. When they returned to Palestine, these Jews, who belonged to the two southern tribes (Judah and Benjamin), re-established a Jewish state, called 'Judah'.

Despite exile and the passing of centuries, Jews remembered the lost ten tribes, and many hoped that they could be recovered. About 200 BCE the sage Ben Sira had looked forward to the time when God would 'gather all the tribes of Jacob' and 'give them their inheritance, as at the beginning' (Ben Sira 36.11). Around the year 63 BCE, at the time of Pompey's conquest of Jerusalem, a devout poet predicted that God would again gather his people and 'divide them according to their tribes upon the land' (*Psalms of Solomon* 17.28–31). The members of the Dead Sea sect expected the armies of Israel, marshalled in twelve groups by tribe, to defeat the armies of the Gentiles and again to worship God in the Temple.[14]

Those who looked for the restoration of the twelve tribes expected a miracle, since human census-taking would never trace the lost ten tribes. God himself would have to intervene directly in history and reconstitute or re-create the lost tribes. This miracle would result in an earthly kingdom, one in which the land would be divided among the tribes, as it had been centuries before. The future was depicted, as in many other cultures, as a return to the beginning, or to an idealized 'golden age' – not the dissolution of the cosmos.

Jesus seems to have shared this hope: the hope for a miracle that would re-create Israel. The twelve disciples would judge the twelve tribes, and his followers even debated questions of their future rank (see the passages in category 2 above). Unlike the Dead Sea sectarians, however, Jesus did not think in terms of a military miracle, one in which the reconstituted tribes fought the armies of the Gentiles. He seems to have expected the Son of Man to descend and God's angels to separate the elect from the wicked. If the sayings about the Son of Man are later Christian additions to the tradition, we would not know how Jesus expected the kingdom to be established, but from the other passages we would still know that he looked for a better age.

Jesus told his disciples that he would drink wine with them in the kingdom (the last supper, Mark 14.25 & parr.). This raises the question of whether or not Jews in general expected the new age to be like a banquet. Was 'banquet', like 'twelve', a standard symbol pointing to God's intervention? I think that it was not. The importance of the last supper in Christian thought and practice has led to the overvaluation of meals in Judaism. One passage in Isaiah looks forward to the time when the Lord 'will make for all peoples a feast of fat things, a feast of wine'. At that time 'he will swallow up death for ever' and 'wipe away tears from all faces' (Isa. 25.6–8).[15] The existence of this passage meant that anyone who spoke about a new age could utilize the image of a banquet. The surviving literature, however, indicates that not many people did so. The Dead Sea sectarians thought that in the future the two Messiahs would join in a banquet with the rest of the elect, but we cannot say that they saw their own daily meals as prefiguring the joys of the coming age.[16] Jesus spoke of a future banquet, not just at the last supper, but also in the prediction that many would come from east

and west and sit at table with the Patriarchs of Israel (Matt. 8.11f. //
Luke 13.28f.). In parables he compared the coming kingdom to a
banquet (Matt. 22.1–14; Luke 14.15–24), and his eating with sinners
and tax collectors (discussed in the next chapter) may have symbolized their inclusion in the kingdom. His enemies accused him of
being a wine-bibber and a glutton. This may indicate that when he
had the opportunity he banqueted; if so, he probably attached
symbolic value to these meals.

This most definitely does not mean that whenever Jews feasted
they were proclaiming the coming kingdom of God. Jewish feasts
celebrated the past with thanksgiving. At Passover, the story of the
exodus from Egypt was central. When recalling God's past acts of
redemption, it would be quite natural to look forward to a future
redemption: if God saved us from the Egyptians, he will eventually
save us from the Romans too. Yet the festival did not symbolize the
future kingdom of God. It appears, however, that *Jesus* saw banqueting in this way: in the coming kingdom 'many' would sit at table
with Abraham, Isaac and Jacob; his disciples would judge the
twelve tribes; the sinners with whom Jesus sometimes ate would
share the kingdom; he would drink wine with his disciples in the
new age.

Jesus, then, used at least two symbols to depict the coming
kingdom of God: twelve disciples representing the twelve tribes and
the banquet. As far as we can tell from the surviving evidence,
however, he did not speak as graphically as did some other visionaries. He left behind nothing as detailed and explicit as the most
eschatological of the Dead Sea Scrolls (the *War Scroll* and the
Temple Scroll), where weapons, banners and the architectural details
of the ideal temple are described. The banquet and the twelve tribes
in Jesus' sayings are very vague in comparison. Nevertheless, his
followers thought it reasonable to discuss who would sit at his right
and left hands when he came into his kingdom.

When dealing with this sort of material, we can never be sure
how literally to take it. Do modern people who believe in heaven,
for example, actually think that angels with wings and harps dwell
'up there'? Or are wings and harps metaphors for indescribable
bliss? Usually, I expect, the latter. When it comes to analysing what
ancient Jews thought, we must remain uncertain about this point.
According to one passage, Jesus held it to be an error to think that,

in the resurrection, people would marry (Mark 12.25 & parr.). This constitutes a salutary warning not to attribute to him the crassest and most literal view of the new age. Although he spoke of drinking wine in the kingdom, he did not (as far as we know) describe how many gallons of wine each vine would produce (as did some early Christians).[17] Paul provides a partial analogy to Jesus. The most explicit statements that Paul makes about the kingdom are that Christ would 'reign until he has put all his enemies', including death itself, 'under his feet', and only then turn the kingdom over to God (I Cor. 15.25–8), and that 'the saints' (Christians) would judge the world (I Cor. 6.2). Paul also thought that people who participated in the new world would have 'spiritual bodies'; they would not be 'flesh and blood', but they would nevertheless be bodies (I Cor. 15.44, 50). I do not mean to say that Paul and Jesus agreed precisely, but they both spoke of a world that would not be precisely like the present world, but that would none the less be recognizable as a world. Even if (in Jesus' view) after the resurrection people will not marry, they will still be recognizable as people.

These partial overlaps between Jesus and other Jews of his time who thought about a new age (twelve tribes), and between Jesus and Paul (people who do not have the same needs as people have now; judgment will be in the hands of Jesus' followers) help us understand Jesus. He did not want to give precise descriptions of the world to come, but he did not think that there would be nothing except incorporeal spirits. Instead, there would be a new and better age in which his disciples – and, it follows, he himself – would play the leading role.

As we noted at the beginning of this chapter, it is possible for any individual to use the word 'kingdom' in more than one sense. Moreover, when thinking of the future, it is possible to hold diverse thoughts simultaneously. Logically, the idea of personal immortality (the soul of each individual departs at death) and the idea of resurrection (people die and await the general resurrection) are contradictory. Yet millions of Christians, including Paul, have held both views. What about Jesus? Did he hold contradictory views of the future, or did one idea dominate? He could have thought both that God would send the Son of Man, who would gather the elect and condemn the rest, and that individuals were judged at the time of death. Jesus' particular brand of eschatology, however, does make some reconstructions of his life and work less probable than others. If he thought that in the immediate future God was going to change human society, it is unlikely that the main thrust of his career was social reform. If he looked for a new and better age, one would expect him to say things about what it would be like, and in that sense to urge people to start living appropriately, but one would not expect him to try to get his hands on the machinery of government, or to plot to overthrow the high priest and to persuade Pilate to appoint his (that is, Jesus') own candidate. It is a question of emphasis. Jesus doubtless had views about the social, political and economic conditions of his people, but his mission was to prepare them to receive the coming kingdom of God.

12. THE KINGDOM: ISRAEL, GENTILES AND INDIVIDUALS

Jesus thought that God was about to bring the kingdom, and that his will would be done on earth as in heaven. I wish now to explore more carefully some of the evidence that this is what he thought, the nature of this coming kingdom, and its relationship to existing groups and individuals. We begin by discussing in greater detail two of the passages listed above (category 2 on pp. 172f.). The first is Mark 10.35–40, which indicates that the disciples understood Jesus to be talking about a 'real' kingdom, one in which rank would count. One day James and John, two of the inner three (Peter was the third), asked Jesus if he would grant them to sit, 'one at your right hand and one at your left, in your glory'. Jesus asked, 'Are you able to drink the cup that I drink, or to be baptized with the baptism with which I am baptized?' They affirmed that they were able. Jesus accepted this, but still said that it was not within his power to decide who would be at his right and left hand: 'it is for those for whom it has been prepared'. This cannot be a late invention. Later everyone recognized that Peter was the leading disciple, and the possible primacy of James and John would not have arisen.[1] The story is also somewhat discreditable to them, which makes it even less likely that it is a Christian creation. Mark continues by saying that the other disciples were indignant, and Jesus emphasized that they should think not of greatness but of service (10.41–5). The entire discussion presupposes the hope for a real kingdom, one in which places and prominence would be ascertainable.

On another occasion Peter pointed out to Jesus that he and the others had left everything in order to follow him, and he asked, 'What then shall we have?' Jesus answered,

Truly, I say to you, in the new world, when the Son of Man shall sit on his glorious throne, you who have followed me will also sit on twelve thrones, judging the twelve tribes of Israel. And every one who has left houses or brothers or sisters or father or mother or children or lands, for my name's sake, will receive a hundredfold, and inherit eternal life. (Matt. 19.27–9)

This saying gives Judas, one of the Twelve, a place among the other disciples, and it could hardly have arisen after Jesus' death, when Judas was known as his betrayer. All the disciples are promised places of authority. We noted above that they will both 'receive a hundredfold' and 'inherit eternal life'. It appears that the promise of hundredfold reward refers to an earthly kingdom, distinct from and prior to eternal life. We also saw in ch. 11 that a kingdom that included the twelve tribes implies a divine miracle, and that other Jews of Jesus' day hoped for that miraculous occurrence (pp. 183–5).

In order to gain perspective, I wish now to contrast with this widespread view, shared by Jesus, the more mundane hopes of some others. One of the greatest Jewish teachers of all time, Rabbi Akiba, who lived in the late first and early second century CE, thought that a Jewish military leader, Bar Kokhba, was the Messiah. This Bar Kokhba led a great revolt two generations after the first one. It was crushed in 135. Akiba and other Jewish teachers were executed. Akiba did not expect the lost ten tribes to be restored,[2] but rather something more realistic: he expected a truly military victory, followed by Jewish independence and freedom, which would be a kind of miracle, but not a miracle of the sort required to re-create the ten lost tribes. The realistic nature of his hope excluded the possibility that the scattered and no longer identifiable ten tribes would be reconstituted.

In Jesus' own day some Jews looked for an entirely realistic kingdom. The Zealot party, known from the period of the first revolt against Rome, did not yet exist, but there were already some who thought in terms of a real war, fought with the resources of men and arms that could be seen and counted. This attitude resulted in acts that were more like brigandage than revolution: caravans would occasionally be ambushed, and the like. Barabbas, who was released by Pilate at the time of Jesus' crucifixion (Matt. 27.15–26), was possibly such a man: a pre-revolutionary brigand rather than a common robber. Barabbas and his kind, like later Bar Kokhba and

Akiba, emphasize by contrast that Jesus and many others expected God to intervene and establish the kingdom miraculously.

The Gentiles and the Future Kingdom

If Israel were to become great again, obviously Gentile nations had to diminish or be weakened. Consequently, some hopes for the restoration of Israel were tied up with the belief that God would defeat the Gentiles who governed the kingdoms of this world. Many Jews, however, hoped that the Gentiles would be converted: that they would turn to the God of Israel and come to Mount Zion, bringing offerings to the Temple. I shall give only one example of numerous available.[3] Shortly after 200 BCE the author of Tobit voiced this hope, which was also one of the major themes of the later biblical prophets:

> Your light shall shine brightly to all the ends of the earth.
> Many nations shall come to you from afar,
> from all the corners of the earth to your holy name;
> they shall bring gifts in their hands for the King of Heaven.
> (Tobit 13.11)

Did Jesus share the hope that in the new age Gentiles would worship the God of Israel? His own mission was to the 'lost sheep of the house of Israel' (Matt. 15.24; see further below), but the gospels do describe some positive contacts with Gentiles. There is one story of the healing of a Gentile in Mark; more precisely, there is one story in which it is important that the healed person is a Gentile.[4] When Jesus was in Syria, near Tyre or Sidon, a Gentile woman begged him to cast a demon out of her daughter. He replied, 'Let the children first be fed, for it is not right to take the children's bread and throw it to the dogs.' She, however, persisted: 'Yes, Lord; yet even the dogs under the table eat the children's crumbs.' Jesus yielded and cured her daughter (Mark 7.24–30). Matthew elaborates the story in three ways. In his account the disciples beg Jesus to send the woman away; Jesus said not only 'Let the children first be fed' (as in Mark), but also that he 'was sent only to the lost sheep of the house of Israel'; and Jesus remarked that the woman's faith was great when he finally acceded to her request (Matt. 15.21–8). Matthew notes the resistance to Gentiles both on the part of the disciples and of Jesus himself, and this heightens the impact of the story: the Gentile woman had very great faith. We recall from above that Matthew has the story of a centurion whose servant Jesus healed, which includes the statement that 'not even in Israel have I found such faith' (8.10). Matthew thus underlines the view that Gentiles who have faith can participate in the kingdom proclaimed by Jesus.

All the authors of the gospels favoured the mission to Gentiles, and they would have included all the pro-Gentile material that they could. Matthew especially wished to emphasize that Gentiles could have great faith, greater than that of Israelites. It is then not surprising that, according to Matthew, Jesus said, 'many will come from east and west and sit at table with Abraham, Isaac and Jacob in the kingdom of heaven, while the sons of the kingdom will be thrown into the outer darkness' (Matt. 8. 11f.).[5] In the context in which Matthew wrote, this accurately reflects the outcome: Jews had for the most part decided not to accept Jesus, while the mission to the Gentiles was fairly successful. What is striking is that the evangelists had so few passages that pointed towards success in winning Gentiles to faith. They could cite only a few stories about Jesus' contacts with Gentiles, and even these do not depict him as being especially warm towards them. We note that Matthew must grant the limitation observed by Jesus himself in telling what he intends to be a story in favour of the Gentile mission: Jesus' own mission was to Israel, and especially to the 'lost sheep' of Israel. He made no effort to seek and win Gentiles. We must suspect that the most favourable statements about Gentiles (Matt. 8.10 and 15.28, on the greatness of the faith of two individual Gentiles) are Matthew's creation. Consequently, we cannot be absolutely sure what Jesus' own view about Gentiles was. On general grounds, I am inclined to think that he expected at least some Gentiles to turn to the God of Israel and to participate in the coming kingdom. The general grounds are these: a good number of Jews expected this to happen; Jesus was a kind and generous man. That is, the alternative to thinking that Jesus looked forward to the conversion of Gentiles would be that he expected them all to be destroyed. This is un-likely.

This discussion provides another opportunity to comment on Christian creativity. The gospel writers did not wildly invent material. They developed it, shaped it and directed it in the ways they wished. But even Matthew did not create a sizeable body of material in favour of the Gentile mission, though he seems to have enhanced what he had.

Jesus' hope for the kingdom fits into long-standing and deeply held hopes among the Jews, who continued to look for God to redeem his people and constitute a new kingdom, one in which Israel would be secure and peaceful, and one in which Gentiles would serve the God of Israel.

The Little Flock

Jesus harboured traditional thoughts about God and Israel: God had chosen all Israel, and he would someday redeem the nation. This aspect of Jesus' view is often lost sight of because of the power and preponderance of the teaching that addresses individuals. One of the most striking things about Jesus is that, despite his expectation that the end would soon arrive, and despite the fact that he thought about the coming kingdom on a large scale, he nevertheless left behind a rich body of teaching that stresses the relationship between individuals and God in the here and now. The future orientation might have led him to be indifferent to individuals: eschatologists often thought of whole blocks of people who would be saved or destroyed at the end, without providing much in the way of spiritual nourishment for the diverse individuals who made up each block.

Jesus could warn and threaten whole cities at a time:

Woe to you, Chorazin! woe to you, Bethsaida! for if the mighty works done in you had been done in Tyre and Sidon, they would have repented long ago in sackcloth and ashes. But I tell you, it shall be more tolerable on the day of judgement for Tyre and Sidon than for you. (Matt. 11.20–22)

This is a traditional black and white judgement of the sort that one might expect of an eschatologist. But this is not what dominates Jesus' message and his view of God's attitude towards humans. Jesus did not regard God as just a judge, waiting to condemn the imperfect, ready to wipe out whole cities, but as a loving father who cared for and sought the welfare of each person.

Look at the birds of the air: they neither sow nor reap nor gather into barns, and yet your heavenly Father feeds them. Are you not of more value than they? (Matt. 6.26)

Are not two sparrows sold for a penny? And not one of them will fall to the ground without your Father's will. But even the hairs of your head are all numbered. Fear not, therefore; you are of more value than many sparrows. (Matt. 10.29–31)

Fear not, little flock, for it is your Father's good pleasure to give you the kingdom. (Luke 12.32)

An appreciable part of Jesus' teaching consists of assurance that God loves each individual, no matter what the person's shortcomings, and that he wishes the return of even the worst. God's love of the outcast, even those not generally obedient to his will, is the theme of some of Jesus' greatest parables. We shall look at these in greater detail in the next chapter, and here I shall mention only two of them: God is like a shepherd who goes in search of one lost sheep; God is like a good father, who accepts his prodigal son back with rejoicing.

On the human side, Jesus urged people to look to God as a perfectly reliable father, to accept his love and to respond in trust. Since God cares even for the lilies of the field and sparrows, all the more will he provide for his children.

Therefore do not be anxious, saying, 'What shall we eat?' or 'What shall we drink?' or 'What shall we wear?' For the Gentiles seek all these things; and your heavenly Father knows that you need them all. But seek first his kingdom and his righteousness, and all these things shall be yours as well. (Matt. 6.31–3)

Ask, and it will be given you; seek, and you will find; knock, and it will be opened to you . . . Or what man of you, if his son asks him for bread, will give him a stone? Or if he asks for a fish, will give him a serpent? If you then, who are evil, know how to give good gifts to your children, how much more will your Father who is in heaven give good things to those who ask him! (Matt. 7.7–11)

Much of Jesus' teaching – his hope for a coming new age; his confidence that God will provide for and save his children; his call for people to trust and obey God – is summed up in the most repeated part of his teaching: the Lord's Prayer. I shall quote it in both the existing versions:

Our Father in heaven,
hallowed be your name.
Your kingdom come.
Your will be done,
   on earth as it is in heaven.
Give us this day our daily bread.
And forgive us our debts,
   as we also have forgiven our
     debtors.
And do not bring us to the time of
   trial,
but rescue us from the evil one.
(Matt. 6.9–13, NRSV)

Father,
hallowed be your name.
Your kingdom come.

Give us each day our daily bread.
And forgive us our sins,
   for we ourselves forgive everyone indebted to us.
And do not bring us to the time of
   trial. (Luke 11.2–4, NRSV)

The slight variations mean that we cannot be absolutely sure of the wording, but we may assume that we have here a prayer that Jesus used and taught his disciples. It is a prayer that can be prayed by anyone at any time. It does not mention the twelve tribes of Israel, or describe the Gentiles as 'dogs', or elevate Jesus and his disciples. The Jesus of this prayer is the Jesus who has been and is universally admired. If, however, we want to understand him as a historical figure, we must see all sides of him. If all that Jesus had done had been to create such words, he would have made no enemies; but he had enemies. For the moment, we note that in this last section we have seen one of the aspects of Jesus that earns him the adjective 'great' from non-believers as much as from believers.

13 . THE KINGDOM:
REVERSAL OF VALUES AND
ETHICAL PERFECTIONISM

At the beginning of ch. 11 we noted that the kingdom could be defined negatively: it would not be governed by Tiberius, Antipas, Pilate and Caiaphas, and its values would be quite different from those that prevailed. Readers of the gospels have long noted that much of Jesus' teaching points to a reversal of values. One sentence, which appears several times in the gospels, sums up this view: 'the last will be first and the first will be last' (Matt. 19.30 // Mark 10.31; Matt. 20.16; Luke 13.30; cf. Mark 9.35, 'If any one would be first, he or she must be last of all and servant of all'). The admonition to be like a child (Matt. 18.1–4 // Mark 10.13–16 // Luke 18.15–17) belongs here, as does the parable of Lazarus and the Rich Man: Lazarus, who had an exceptionally hard life, prospered in the world to come, while the fortunes of the rich man were reversed (Luke 16.19–31).

The fullest expression of this reversal comes in two parables in Matthew and one in Luke. In the first the kingdom of heaven is like a farmer[1] who hired day labourers at various times during the course of a single day. When it was time to pay their wages, he paid them all the same. Those who had worked the longest protested, but the farmer replied that he could do as he liked with his money. The parable concludes with the moral: the last will be first (Matt. 20.1–16). According to the second parable, the kingdom of heaven is like a king who invited people to a feast celebrating his son's wedding. The invited guests did not come. Finally, the 'servants went out into the streets and gathered all whom they found, both bad and good; so the wedding hall was filled with guests' (Matt. 22.1–10).

Many of Jesus' parables, like these two, are susceptible to more than one interpretation. Pressing each detail will often result in overinterpretation, and one should focus on the main thrust. In these two parables the chief point seems to be that the behaviour of the major figure (the farmer or the king) is surprising. One expects wages to be proportional to labour. Normally, a king would take steps to ensure the attendance of the guests whom he first invited; in extreme circumstances he would call off the banquet. What king would soil his hall with riff-raff? Jesus describes a topsy-turvy world. He seems to be saying,

Do not assume that God will act in ways you can predict. God can be surprisingly generous (the first parable), and also surprisingly undiscriminating (the second). You do not know whom he will count 'in' and whom not. Just because you are a person of rank and long service, you should not suppose that he values you alone; nor should you suppose that his kingdom will not come if you say you are not ready. It is coming, and God will include whom he will, 'both bad and good' (the quoted phrase is from Matt. 22.10).

The third parable in this category is usually called the parable of the Prodigal Son, though parable of a Father and Two Sons would be more accurate. A man had two sons. The younger demanded his inheritance and went away. He wasted his money on fast living and was eventually reduced to feeding swine and eating their food – not a good occupation for a nice Jewish boy. He decided to ask his father to take him back; and when he returned, his father, rejoicing, gave orders to kill the fatted calf and to prepare a feast. The elder brother was resentful, but the father admonished him: 'Son, you are always with me, and all that is mine is yours. It was fitting to make merry and be glad, for this your brother was dead, and is alive; he was lost, and is found' (Luke 15.11–32). This parable is more successful than the two in Matthew, I think, because the characters are not employer and wage-earners, or king and subjects, but father and sons. Probably most of us think that strict equity *should* govern employer–worker relationships, but not that parents should be similarly bound. A lot of parents endlessly forgive and indulge their wayward children. Jesus' audience would have stressed the duty of child to parent more than we would, and would have seen these three relationships as being closer to one another than most of us think today. Nevertheless, the ancient world knew about parental leniency, and comparing God to an extremely indulgent parent was doubtless very effective in Jesus' day. That is, the audience got the point.

They did not all necessarily approve. Such parables as these are morally disquieting. Later, Paul's enemies would accuse him of urging people to sin so that God's grace would abound (Rom. 6.1, 15). That, of course, was not his view: he also urged his converts to be morally perfect (e.g., I Thess. 5.23). But an extreme emphasis on God's grace is subject to misunderstanding, and this is especially so if it comes in the context of stories that say, in effect, that God will actually favour those who forsake their duty and subsequently return, or those who begin productive work only very late in the day. We shall return to the question of Jesus' view of the acceptability of sinners in ch. 14, but now we shall look at the other side of the coin, Jesus' own perfectionist ethics.

Perfectionism and the New Age

The parable of the Marriage Feast, as we now have it, does not end when both the bad and good are gathered. The king then enters and examines the clothing of his guests. He finds that one man did not wear a festive garment. The king commands, 'Bind him hand and foot, and cast him into the outer darkness; there people will weep and gnash their teeth. For many are called, but few are chosen' (Matt. 22.11–14). Most scholars view this second stage as a later creation, designed precisely to remove the moral shock of the main parable and to assert that people must behave correctly if they are to remain in good favour. I agree entirely with this view. Nevertheless, I also agree with the author of the appended portion of the parable: Jesus required high moral standards of his followers. We shall examine Jesus' ethical teaching more closely.

We begin with the best-attested tradition in the gospels: the pericope on divorce. The best-attested tradition is not necessarily the most important, but in the present case it will serve us well. The prohibition of divorce appears a total of four times in the synoptics and once in Paul: Matt. 5.31f.; 19.3–9; Mark 10.2–12; Luke 16.18; I Cor. 7.10f. Two forms of the saying appear in the gospels, a long form (Mark 10.2–12 and Matt. 19.3–9) and a short form (Matt.

5.31f. and Luke 16.18). Paul is closer to the short form. In order to illustrate the editorial freedom with which early Christians used the teaching of Jesus, I shall print three of the five versions of this, the best-attested saying of Jesus: Paul's version, the short form in Luke (which has a parallel in Matthew), and the long form in Mark (also paralleled in Matthew):

I Corinthians 7.10–11
To the married I give charge, not I but the Lord, that the wife should not separate from her husband (but if she does, let her remain single or else be reconciled to her husband) – and that the husband should not divorce his wife.

Luke 16.18
Every one who divorces his wife and marries another commits adultery, and he who marries a woman divorced from her husband commits adultery.

Mark 10.2–12
And Pharisees came up and in order to test him asked, 'Is it lawful for a man to divorce his wife?' He answered them, 'What did Moses command you?' They said, 'Moses allowed a man to write a certificate of divorce, and put her away.' But Jesus said to them, 'For your hardness of heart he wrote you this commandment. But from the beginning of creation, "God made them male and female" [quoting Gen. 1.27]. For this reason "a man shall leave his father and mother and be joined to his wife, and the two shall become one" [quoting Gen. 2.24]. So they are no longer two but one. What therefore God has joined together, let no man put asunder.'

The long form and the short form are so substantially different that it is probable that they were transmitted independently for some time. The existence of independent traditions enhances the probability that the passage is essentially authentic. Moreover, from a very early stage the prohibition constituted a problem for the Christian communities. Paul explicitly attributes the passage to the Lord, distinguishing it from his own opinion (I Cor. 7.12). His discussion, however, reveals that he did not entirely agree with the prohibition of divorce: he preferred that there be no divorce, but permitted it in the case of a believer who was married to a non-believer (I Cor. 7.15: if divorce were desired by the non-believing partner it should be accepted by the Christian partner). The commandment seemed so difficult to Matthew that he has Jesus' disciples say that 'If such is the case of a man with his wife [that he cannot divorce her], it is better not to marry' (Matt. 19.10). It is also probable that Matthew's exception to the prohibition – divorce is permitted if the spouse has already committed adultery (Matt. 5.32; 19.9) – is the author's own attempt to make Jesus' view more suitable for a continuing community. We can hardly think that the early Christians invented the prohibition: they found it very difficult and had to modify it.

It is typical of the material about Jesus that his precise meaning is uncertain even on this topic. The short form of the saying (Matt. 5 and Luke 16; implied also by Paul) is fundamentally a prohibition of remarriage, which is regarded as adultery. As Matthew puts it, 'Every one who divorces his wife . . . makes her an adulteress; and whoever marries a divorced woman commits adultery.' The assumption of this statement is that a divorced woman could not support herself and would therefore have to remarry or become a prostitute; both are adultery. The long form (Matt. 19 and Mark 10) is more absolute. 'In the beginning' God 'made them male and female' and ordained that the two 'become one flesh' (referring to Gen. 1.27 and 2.24). Here Jesus argues that divorce is against the intention of the creator; Moses had permitted divorce only because of the hardness of human hearts (Mark 10.5 // Matt. 19.8). At the conclusion of the passage the condemnation of remarriage is repeated (Mark 10.11f. // Matt. 19.9).

We may be certain that the prohibition of divorce on the grounds that remarriage is adultery goes back to Jesus (both the longer and the shorter traditions). I think it highly likely that Jesus also appealed to the order of creation in order to criticize divorce (the longer tradition). Divorce shows human weakness. An ideal world or society will be like paradise before the sin of Adam: the two become one flesh. This second argument against divorce is known also from the Dead Sea Scrolls.[2] Did Jesus intend his view of divorce to constitute a new law, one that was binding on his followers? That is certainly the implication of the prohibition of remarriage: it is adultery, and adultery is against the law. What about the longer tradition, that divorce is contrary to the intention of the creator? The passage begins with a question posed by the

Pharisees: 'Is it lawful for a man to divorce his wife?' Jesus grants that it is: Moses wrote his commandment governing divorce (Deut. 24.1–4 requires the exchange of a legal document) because of human weakness, but Jesus does not say that the Mosaic regulation should be repealed and a more stringent law adopted. Jesus' view of the Mosaic law will concern us in ch. 14. Here we simply note that he alters the law by defining a term (remarriage is adultery) – a frequently used legal device in his day, as in ours – but does not propose that the written law should be revoked. Besides interpreting the law in such a way as to change it, he also criticizes it. It is not strict enough. Jesus wishes to point his followers to a higher morality, one that corresponds to the ideal world, when Adam and Eve lived in a state of innocence.

Idealistic perfectionism marks substantial portions of the Sermon on the Mount (Matt. 5–7). In Matthew 5, where Matthew's short form of the divorce pericope appears, there are other sayings that are similar in structure and thrust. Jesus cites the law and then says, in effect, that it is not good enough. The section is usually, but not accurately, called 'the antitheses' (see pp. 210–12 below). In addition to the statement on divorce, the section contains other admonitions to live by a higher standard than the law requires. Not only should people not kill, they should not be angry (5.21–6). Not only should they avoid adultery, they should not look at others with lust in their hearts (5.27–30). Not only should they not swear falsely, they should not take oaths at all (5.33–7). Far from retaliating when injured, they should 'turn the other cheek' (5.38–42). Finally, they should love not only their neighbours but also their enemies (5.43–7). Then they will be perfect, as God is perfect (5.48). Scholars generally think that some of these passages have been created by Matthew or an earlier Christian author. Once one has the form of the sayings and the general thrust, it is perfectly easy to produce more examples of going beyond the law.

For our purposes, however, we do not need to decide which of the 'antitheses' go back to Jesus. Let us say that they all do. The more urgent question is the place of ideal perfectionism in his overall mission. I suspect that it was less important in Jesus' own thought than it is in the Gospel of Matthew. At the beginning of this book we noted that the common picture of Jesus depends very heavily on the rigorous ethics of the Sermon on the Mount. I do not at all wish to deny to Jesus such sayings as 'turn the other cheek' and 'love your enemy'. On the contrary: I do not doubt that he said these things. But a few points will help put the perfectionism of Matthew 5 in context.

We note, first, that the reader of Mark and Luke would not know that Jesus prohibited anger and lustful thoughts. Admonition to eliminate feelings that are common to humanity is not a characteristic of Jesus' teaching generally, but occurs only in this section of Matthew. Otherwise, Jesus was concerned with how people treated others, not with what thoughts lurked in their hearts. Like any other good Jewish teacher, Jesus thought that people should examine themselves and their relations with others, doing whatever was necessary to put these relations on a good footing. The continuation of the saying about anger is helpful: 'If you are offering your gift at the altar, and there remember that your brother has something against you, leave your gift there before the altar and go; first be reconciled to your brother, and then come and offer your gift' (Matt. 5.23f.). Any Jewish teacher would agree. The 'gift' here is probably a guilt offering, brought in order to complete the process of atonement for harming another person. The sacrifice did not count if the wrong was not put right first. This is clear in the biblical legislation itself (e.g., Lev. 6.1–7), and later generations got the point. Approximately 200 years before Jesus, Ben Sira had said the same thing, and one reads this also in the writings of Philo of Alexandria and elsewhere.[3] There can be no doubt that Jesus would have encouraged this kind of self-examination, and the most obvious times would be when praying and when attending the Temple. But the passage does *not* say, 'Before worshipping in the temple you must probe your conscience, discover every time you became irritated at someone else and repent.' Jesus may well have warned against harbouring anger in one's heart, but most of his ethical teaching corresponds to Matthew 5.23f.: treat other people right. Examples are Matthew 7.21–3: you will enter the kingdom if you *do* the will of God, and Matthew 25.21–46: at the judgement the Son of Man will reward you if you clothed the naked, visited the sick and comforted the imprisoned; but he will punish you if you did not.

Secondly, the overall tenor of Jesus' teaching is compassion towards human frailty. He seems not to have gone around condemning people for their minor lapses. He worked not among the powerful, but among the lowly, and he did not want to be a stern taskmaster or a censorious judge, who would only add to their burdens:

Come to me, all who labour and are heavy laden, and I will give you rest. Take my yoke upon you, and learn from me; for I am gentle and lowly in heart, and you will find rest for your souls. For my yoke is easy and my burden is light. (Matt. 11.28–30)

To be sure, his closest followers would find discipleship harder than this implies, and Jesus was aware of this: they had to be prepared to give up everything. But when they did that, the gospels represent him as being very patient with their weaknesses and doubts. The beatitudes (Matt. 5.3–12; slightly different in Luke 6.20–26) bless the downtrodden, the poor and the meek, as well as those who hunger and thirst for righteousness, the merciful, the pure in heart and the peacemakers. These sayings imply demands, but the clearest note is sympathy and promise for those who needed them most. The tone of Jesus' ministry was compassionate and not judgemental. People should be perfect, but God was lenient – and so was Jesus, acting on his behalf.

Thirdly, Jesus himself did not live a stern and strict life. For most of us the word 'perfection' calls up images of severe Puritanism: lots of rules, plenty of punishment for error and not much room for fun. This sort of Puritanism, according to Jesus, was all right; an austere life had been fine for John the Baptist, but it was not his own style. He quoted his critics:

John came neither eating nor drinking, and they say, 'He has a demon'; the Son of Man came eating and drinking, and they say, 'Behold, a glutton and a drunkard, a friend of tax collectors and sinners!' (Matt. 11.18f. // Luke 7.33f.)

Moreover, some people criticized Jesus because his disciples did not fast when followers of John the Baptist and Pharisees were fasting, and he responded by asking a rhetorical question: 'Can the wedding guests fast as long as the bridegroom is with them?' (Mark 2.18–22 & parr.). Jesus was no Puritan.

Finally, we must note one of the most interesting aspects of Jesus' ministry: he called 'sinners', and apparently he associated with them and befriended them while they were still sinners. In Matthew 11.18f., quoted just above, Jesus' critics accused him of this behaviour. Jesus' perfectionism did not make him shun the company of even the worst elements of society. On the contrary, he courted it.

Jesus was not given to censure but to encouragement; he was not judgemental but compassionate and lenient; he was not puritanical but joyous and celebratory. Yet he was also a perfectionist. 'Perfection' in the gospels must be carefully defined. The only direct admonition to perfection urges people to be perfect as God is perfect, which in context means to be merciful as God is merciful: 'he makes his sun rise on the evil and on the good, and sends rain on the just and on the unjust' (Matt. 5.43–8). That is the sort of perfection that Jesus urged on all his hearers. The only other use of 'perfect' in the gospels is in the passage on the rich man: 'If you would be perfect, go, sell what you possess and give to the poor . . . ; and come, follow me' (Matt. 19.21; the word 'perfect' is not in the parallels in Mark and Luke). Jesus did not expect many people to be perfect in this second sense. He brought his message of comfort and joy to many whom he did not call to be his followers; he asked only a few to give up all they had.

Jesus' particular kind of perfectionism goes very well with his view that in the kingdom many human values would be reversed. The kind of perfection he had in mind was suitable for the poor and the poor in spirit: the perfection of mercy and humility. Jesus also, of course, wanted his hearers to be moral in the normal sense of the word (honest and upright), but the main aspect of God-like perfection was mercy. He displayed this by being gentle and loving towards others, including sinners.

14. CONTENTION AND OPPOSITION IN GALILEE

Jesus died on a Roman cross, executed as would-be 'king of the Jews'. When we consider his message – God's all-embracing love, the need for commitment to him, love shown to everyone, even enemies – it is hard to understand how he came to this end.

We shall return to this general problem in ch. 16, and consider there the events in Jerusalem that immediately led to Jesus' death. The gospels also offer us, however, a series of conflicts in the midst of his ministry in Galilee. He was already becoming a controversial figure. Antipas heard about Jesus and thought that perhaps John the Baptist had been raised (Mark 6.14 & parr.). Luke adds that at one point some Pharisees warned Jesus that Antipas wanted to kill him (Luke 13.31f.). Despite these hints, Jesus seems to have been in no substantial danger in Galilee. He probably attracted less public attention than John the Baptist, and he seems not to have attacked Antipas or his government. The disputes of the gospels have to do with the Jewish law, and Jesus' critics are usually scribes or Pharisees or both.

Disputes over the law were part and parcel of Jewish life. In Judaism, as I noted above (pp. 37f.), divine law covered every aspect of life. Since God gave the law, and since it covered so many topics, disagreements were potentially quite serious: each side could claim to be obeying the will of God. Therefore it is plausible that Jesus had major conflicts about what seem to most people today to be minor matters. This is not to say that in the first century disputants invariably regarded their opponents as following Satan rather than God and therefore thought that they should be executed. On the contrary, there was quite a lot of tolerance. In order to evaluate the passages in the gospels, we need information about tolerable levels of disagreement in first-century Judaism. Which topics led to most dispute? How serious could disagreement be and still remain within the bounds of reasonable discussion and debate? I have elsewhere reported on debates among the various Jewish parties about the legal topics that are mentioned in the gospels.[1] Here I wish to define possible levels of dispute over the law and exemplify each level. This will give us comparative material in fairly brief compass. The following list of various degrees of disagreement is in descending order of seriousness:

(a) One may argue that a written law is wrong, should be repealed and should be disobeyed. This is a very radical step. Civil disobedience in modern western democracies, a tactic followed by a few protest groups, is very controversial and, when there is a major case, sends something of a shudder through society. Taking this attitude towards part of the Jewish law would be especially shocking, since this would mean saying that God had made a mistake, or that the story of the divine origin of the law was in error.

(b) One may argue that a written law is wrong and should be repealed, but nevertheless obey it as long as it is on the statute books. This is now a very common attitude towards ordinary legislation passed by a parliament. Constitutional change is quite rare, however, and offers a better analogy to the Jewish law than does parliamentary legislation. Because of the view that God gave the law, the proposal to revoke part of this basic constitution would be approximately as heinous as arguing that it should be disobeyed.

(c) Without actually opposing the law, one may claim mitigating circumstances in order to justify transgression on some particular occasion.

(d) One may interpret the law in such a way as to change it. In the United States, the Supreme Court, which is responsible for interpreting the constitution, has been the instrument of a good deal of legal change. In many states blacks and whites used to attend separate schools, despite the constitutional requirement of equality, because the prevailing interpretation was that it was possible for schools to be separate but equal. The Supreme Court decided, in effect, that the word 'equal' was not compatible with 'separate', and as a result schools were required to become racially integrated. Although interpretation is usually less dramatic, judges routinely interpret the law, and sometimes the effect is the same as passing new legislation. Legal interpretation of this sort was alive and well in first-century Judaism.

(e) It is possible to avoid or evade some laws without repealing them. Today some people, especially the rich, can legally avoid income tax by arranging their finances so that they have no net taxable income. It is illegal evasion if they fail to disclose income. In dealing with ancient law, we may not always be able to distinguish avoidance from evasion, and in the examples below I shall not try to do so.

(f) One may propose that the law be extended, and criticize it for not going far enough. Today a lot of people think that speed limits are not strict enough, or that laws limiting pollution are too lenient. They may criticize legislatures severely, but they do not favour breaking the laws that exist.

(g) A society or one of its subgroups may create a lot of supplementary rules and practices that govern precisely how laws are to be fulfilled. People who do not follow a particular practice might think that those who do are transgressing; people who do follow some such practice may think that those who do not are transgressing.

Because first-century Jews thought that God had given the law to Moses, possibilities (a) and (b) above almost never arose. A conscientious person who thought that a commandment in one of the books attributed to Moses was *wrong* should have apostatized – should have renounced Judaism – and a few people did so. Rabbinic literature contains a story of a rabbi who deliberately and flagrantly transgressed, and this allows us to see what such transgression would have looked like. Elisha ben Avuyah rode his horse in front of the Temple mount on a Day of Atonement that fell on a sabbath. Since work is forbidden on both the Day of Atonement and the sabbath, and riding is work, Elisha ben Avuyah deliberately and heinously transgressed. According to the story, a voice came forth from the Temple, saying, '"Return, O faithless children" [quoting Jer. 3.14], except for Elisha ben Avuyah, who knew my strength and rebelled against me.'[2] The story is presumably legendary, but it nevertheless describes the kind of transgression that represents loss of faith in God and his law.

The other categories (*c–f*) can be richly exemplified. I shall offer enough examples to give the reader a feeling for the range of disagreement over the law.

One example will illustrate both (*c*) and one aspect of (*d*). The Bible forbids work on the seventh day of the week – from sunset Friday to sunset Saturday (Exod. 20.8–11 // Deut. 5.12–15). Various passages specify some of the things that count as work, such as lighting a fire, gathering wood or preparing food (Exod. 16; 35.2f.; Num. 15.32–6). There is, however, no systematic definition of 'work'. Work, consequently, was defined by common consent or by direct argument – both forms of interpretation (*d*). The sabbath law is not mentioned in connection with war in the Bible, but an event in the second century BCE reveals that, *by common consent*, fighting had come to be regarded as work. During the Hasmonean revolt against the Seleucid empire, a group of Jews refused to defend themselves on the sabbath, and they were killed. Thereafter, Jews all agreed that on the sabbath they could defend themselves against direct attack. They would allow enemies to bring their catapults into range on the sabbath, but they would not fight back unless they were fired upon. That is, direct military attack was a commonly agreed mitigating circumstance (*c*). In general all Jews agreed that transgression of the sabbath was permitted if human life was at stake.

What about helping people on the sabbath whose lives were not threatened? Here there were various competing interpretations. The pietist groups (the Pharisees and the Essenes) forbade the work involved in the treatment of minor ailments, but rabbinic literature discusses so many possibilities that it is evident that a lot of people were willing to bandage cut fingers (and the like) on the sabbath. The rabbis even offered ways of achieving a beneficial result without actually working: on the sabbath one could not treat toothache by applying vinegar, but one could put vinegar on food and eat it, which would achieve the same result.[3] If rabbis resorted to getting around the law in such ways, we may well imagine that some people thought that they could legally put vinegar on a sore tooth. This example allows us to compare (*d*), interpretation, and (*e*), avoidance. Some people thought that nursing was prohibited work, but that it was possible to achieve the results of nursing without technically working (e). It is likely that some people disagreed with the basic interpretation and held that nursing was not prohibited (d). This is also a topic where there would be various opinions about mitigating circumstances: how serious must an illness be to justify treatment on the sabbath (c)?

Category (f), the extension of the law, was a large one. The written law is very incomplete; in theory it covers all of life, but it often lacks details. Consequently, it had to be extended and applied in all kinds of ways. I shall mention just one case, on which there was disagreement. One of the Dead Sea Scrolls, the *Covenant of Damascus*, criticizes other Jews for allowing men to marry their nieces. Moses, the document correctly points out, forbade marriages between aunt and nephew (Lev. 18.12f.). The laws of incest were written with regard to males, and therefore explicitly command men not to have sexual relations with their aunts, but (the authors of the *Covenant* held) these commandments should be applied equally the other way around: nieces and uncles should not marry (*Covenant of Damascus* 5.7–11). Josephus regarded such a marriage as at least mildly discreditable though not illegal.[4] It is doubtful that there were many uncle–niece marriages, but here we have a very straightforward legal argument: the law should be extended to cover analogous cases, or it should not be. The *Covenant of Damascus* does not directly criticize Moses, but only other Jews for not understanding that Moses intended the law to apply to uncle–niece marriages. Direct criticism of Moses was not only impolitic, it was irreverent; most Jews would almost as soon criticize God. Nevertheless, there is an implied criticism of the law as written.

Our final category (g), supplementary rules, was also a large one. The Pharisees were famous for their 'traditions', interpretations inherited from earlier Pharisees that were not in the written law. In ch. 4 above (p. 45) I gave an example of one of the Pharisees' traditions: using doorposts and lintels to make contiguous houses into one large 'house', so that several families could combine their resources and enjoy a festive meal on the sabbath, without transgressing Jeremiah's prohibition of carrying burdens out of the house on the sabbath day. That is, the Pharisees evolved a 'tradition' (g) that avoided (e) Jeremiah's restriction. A rabbinic story indicates that the

Sadducees objected to the Pharisaic use of '*eruvin*.[5] They probably thought that the Pharisees were transgressing the law, but they seem not to have done anything to force them to follow their own stricter view. The Pharisees, of course, did not criticize the Sadducees for eating in their individual houses. Doing so was not against the law or even against Pharisaic tradition, which in this case was permissive rather than prescriptive.

New Testament scholars have often said that Jesus opposed the law, or that he opposed parts of it. The most common suggestion is that he opposed the ritual law but favoured the moral law. The people who make such suggestions seldom clarify in what sense Jesus opposed the law. That is, they seldom deal with the distinctions that are necessary if one is to discuss the law at all. Do they mean to say that, in Jesus' view, God did not give the law to Moses? That Jesus disagreed with a particular interpretation? That he sometimes avoided individual laws? With such questions in mind, we shall now look at three sections of the gospels: the 'antitheses' in the Sermon on the Mount; a collection of conflict stories in Mark 2.1–3.6; and debates about traditions in Mark 7.

The 'Antitheses' (Matt. 5.21–48)

We discussed this material briefly above, in considering Jesus' perfectionism. Here we ask only if in these passages Jesus opposes the law. The short answer is that he does not: rather, he requires a stricter code of practice. No one who observed the admonitions of Matthew 5 would transgress the law, and Jesus does not propose that any part of the Mosaic code should be repealed. I shall repeat a summary of the sayings in this section of Matthew with brief comments that show that they are not against the law:

> Not only do not kill, do not be angry. (The prohibition of
> killing is still binding.)
> Not only do not commit adultery, do not look on someone else
> with lust. (The commandment against adultery still stands.)
> Do not divorce, despite Moses' permission. (Moses' definition of
> a legal divorce becomes unnecessary, but the follower of Jesus
> will not break the commandment requiring a legal document.)

Do not swear at all. (Obviously one will never swear falsely.)

The law says, 'an eye for an eye . . . But I say to you, do not resist one who is evil. But if any one strikes you on the right cheek, turn to him the other also.' (The commandment 'an eye for an eye' limits retaliation, it does not require it. The person who turns the other cheek will not exceed the legal limit.)

Love your enemies as well as your neighbours. (The commandment to love your neighbour will be observed.)

The editor who brought the various parts of Matthew 5 together understood the antitheses perfectly well. This statement, attributed to Jesus, prefaces them:

Think not that I have come to abolish the law and the prophets; I have come not to abolish them but to fulfil them. For truly, I say to you, till heaven and earth pass away, not an iota, not a dot, will pass from the law . . . Whoever then relaxes one of the least of these commandments and teaches people so, shall be called least in the kingdom of heaven; but he who does them and teaches them shall be called great in the kingdom of heaven. For I tell you, unless your righteousness exceeds that of the scribes and Pharisees, you will never enter the kingdom of heaven. (Matt. 5.17–20)

While this section of Matthew's Sermon on the Mount is not against the law, criticism is implicit: the law does not go far enough. But we should note the way this is put in the passage that comes closest to explicit criticism: the long form of the prohibition of divorce. Moses allowed divorce 'because of the hardness of your hearts' (Matt. 19.8 // Mark 10.5). That is, Moses was too lenient, but it is 'your' fault, not really his.

As it is presently worded, the last antithesis sounds as if it is against the law: 'You have heard that it was said, "You shall love your neighbour and hate your enemy." But I say to you, Love your enemies . . .' (Matt. 5.43f.). This would be against the law if the law actually commanded hatred of enemies, but it does not. The Qumran community taught that members should hate their enemies, and other people may have held this view. One could reasonably maintain, perhaps, that the Romans were the enemies of God and of his people, and that they should be hated. But the best Jewish teachers taught that even in war enemies should be treated decently, and it is not true that Judaism in general taught hatred of enemies.[6] We cannot say that in this passage Jesus opposed either the official or the common Jewish view of enemies.

This section of Matthew has often been cited as showing Jesus' 'opposition' to the law. But heightening the law is not opposing it, though (as we just saw) it implies a kind of criticism. If intensification were against the law, then the main pious groups of Judaism, the Pharisees and the Essenes, were systematic breakers of the law. But in fact no ancient Jew thought that being super-strict was illegal, nor did the author of Matthew. Only modern New Testament scholars have thought that part of the Sermon on the Mount expresses opposition to the Mosaic law, but that is because they have not considered the numerous levels of legal agreement and disagreement.

A Group of Conflict Stories (Mark 2.1–3.6)

I shall again summarize the individual pericopes.

Jesus cured a paralytic by saying 'your sins are forgiven', and some scribes murmured among themselves that he arrogated to himself the authority to forgive sins, terming it 'blasphemy'. Jesus divined their complaint but proceeded with the cure. (2.1–12)

Jesus called a tax collector to follow him; subsequently he dined with many tax collectors. The scribes of the Pharisees complained to his disciples, and Jesus defended his right to call sinners. (2.13–17)

People asked Jesus why his disciples did not fast, at a time when the disciples of John the Baptist and the Pharisees were fasting. Jesus defended his disciples by saying that as long as the bridegroom was with them, the wedding guests should not fast (2.18–22).

On a sabbath Jesus and his disciples were going through a grain field. The disciples became hungry and began to pick the grain. Pharisees emerged and criticized them. Jesus defended his disciples by appealing to a partial precedent, when David and his men were hungry and ate sacred bread, and by two sayings: 'the sabbath was made for humans, not humans for the sabbath' and 'the Son of Man is lord even of the sabbath'. (2.23–8)

On another sabbath he went into a synagogue and healed a man with a withered hand. He directly addressed the audience before anyone said anything to him: 'Is it lawful on the sabbath to do good or to do harm, to save life or to kill?' He performed the cure, and the Pharisees and the Herodians held a council to decide how to kill him. (3.1–6)

There are several interesting points about this collection. We begin by observing that the conflict escalates in severity through these five successive stories. In the first, Jesus' opponents murmur only among themselves, addressing neither Jesus, nor his disciples, nor the crowd. Next they complain to the disciples about Jesus. In the third and fourth stories they object directly to Jesus about his disciples. In the fifth they move past complaint and objection, and decide to kill him.

Secondly, the focus narrows to the Pharisees. Initially the opponents are simply 'scribes' – legal experts. Next they are 'scribes of the Pharisees' – legal experts belonging to the Pharisaic party. Then they are 'people', but apparently followers of either John the Baptist or the Pharisees. In the fourth story they are Pharisees, and in the fifth also Pharisees, though they take counsel with the Herodians.

In this section, then, there is a double escalation – of intensity and of opponents. The escalation is not completely uniform, but the general tendency is clear.

Thirdly, we note that the accounts in and of themselves are implausible. Either the circumstances are improbable or the negative reaction to Jesus is disproportionate to his behaviour. In the first story the offence is said to be that Jesus announces the man's forgiveness, which leads to a charge of blasphemy (Mark 2.7). But such a pronouncement would not be regarded as blasphemy by any known Jewish law or by any known interpretation. The text does not have Jesus say, 'I forgive your sins' but 'your sins are forgiven', in the passive voice. In Jesus' culture the passive voice was used as a circumlocution for God: 'your sins are forgiven' means 'they are forgiven by God'. Jesus only announces the fact, he does not take the place of God. He might have sounded too sure of knowing what God did or would do, and conceivably he appeared arrogant.

But such a claim – to know the mind of God – would not be unique or especially offensive. We may refer back to Honi the Circle-drawer (p. 139). He was very confident about his relationship with God, but he was not a blasphemer, nor was he considered one. The charge of blasphemy in the passage in Mark 2 looks like a retrojection into the early ministry of Jesus of a charge that in fact was made later (on retrojection, see below, pp. 217, 222f.). That is, the charge in this context is unlikely; if scribes actually objected to the healing, the charge would have been less serious. It is striking that even according to the passage, the scribes spoke only 'in their hearts'. We may be confident that this was not a public accusation at the opening of Jesus' career.

The story of picking grain on a sabbath stands out as being improbable. Jesus' disciples are picking grain, when suddenly Pharisees appear. But what were they doing in the midst of a grain field on the sabbath? Waiting on the off-chance that someone might pick grain? We have here, again, retrojection. Some aspects of Jesus' ministry or of the activities of his followers did, at some point, raise the question of the sabbath law. This is not a chronicle of an actual event.

But let us suppose that the incident really did take place. How serious was it? Not very serious, since Jesus argues that there were mitigating circumstances, and he cites biblical precedent as well as general principles in defence of his disciples. David had broken a purity law when he and his men were hungry (Mark 2.25f.). Moreover, the general principle is that the sabbath should be beneficial to humanity (2.27). The Pharisees apparently retired, and no action was taken. Jesus' biblical argument in favour of mitigating circumstances is not really up to the Pharisaic standard, since David did not break the sabbath law. Legally, Jesus would have needed a better analogy. Moreover, in the story of the grain field human life was not at stake. Everyone accepted that 'the sabbath was made for humans', but it would be a pretty weak legal argument to cite this principle in order to justify light snacking. The sabbath, however, was not a fast day, and Jews were supposed to eat a sabbath meal.[7] Thus the argument that there were mitigating circumstances would have gained strength if the disciples had gone a long time without a meal. In any case the story as we now have it shows Jesus as accepting the law and defending a single transgression of it. It is also noteworthy that the disciples are accused, not Jesus. He himself did not break the sabbath – even if the story is completely accurate.

The action that (according to Mark 3.6) leads to the resolution to seek Jesus' death is the most unlikely of all. Jesus heals the man with the withered hand simply by saying 'stretch out your hand'. There was no interpretation of the sabbath law that made speaking unlawful. We would expect someone to object had Jesus massaged and bandaged the hand, but talking is not work. Here we should note that we have the sabbath code of a much stricter party than the Pharisees: the Dead Sea sect. There is nothing in it that approaches the severity of Mark 3.1–6. It is doubtful that anyone would have considered this healing to be a deliberate transgression of the sabbath law. They all agreed with the basic principle that Jesus states, that it is lawful to save life, though they would have noted that the man's life was not at risk. Pharisees might have returned to their studies with the conclusion that Jesus was not a good legal debater, since he stretched 'save life' to cover a minor cure. But, in view of the general level of sabbath disputes in the first century, nothing in the gospel account would have led them to seek Jesus' life.

Some of the stories, then, are improbable. But even if all these stories are precise records of events, there is not a single case of obvious or serious transgression. In comparison with other legal disputes in first-century Judaism, those described in Mark 2.1–3.6 are quite trivial. The only candidate to be a substantial transgression is plucking grain on the sabbath. Plucking is an intentional act, and someone who wanted to demonstrate that the sabbath law should be broken might have harvested food on that day. This, however, is the very case that Jesus defends as being justified by unusual circumstances. A defence based on mitigating circumstances grants that the law is valid, and it reveals that the action was not an instance of opposition to the law. Let us imagine that the Pharisees of the story, who disappear as fast as they appear, had brought Jesus and his disciples before a magistrate, and Jesus had repeated his argument: David did something similar; besides, the sabbath was made for humans, and we were hungry. The magistrate might have fined Jesus and his disciples by requiring each of them to take a sin offering to the temple for the unintentional offence – an offence because the argument was not good enough to prove mitigating circumstances, unintentional because Jesus thought that it was.

In Jesus' day and age the arguments and disagreements of Mark 2.1–3.6 – even if they all took place just as recorded – would not have led to execution. Pharisees disagreed among themselves over more serious issues, and Pharisees and Sadducees disagreed more sharply yet. They were not always killing one another because of these disagreements. There was, to be sure, contention over legal matters among Jews in first-century Palestine, and there was also some civil unrest from time to time. If one looks at the years from the Hasmonean revolution to the end of the first revolt against Rome (about 167 BCE–74 CE), one will find several examples of fairly serious civil war. But people did not kill one another over the sorts of issues that figure in Mark 2.1–3.6. The level of disagreement and argument falls well inside the parameters of debate that were accepted in Jesus' time.

If all this is true, how can we understand the existence of these passages? Because of the principle that 'where there is smoke there is fire', we must explain their origin: the depiction of escalating hostility on the part of the Pharisees over the law must come from somewhere. The question is, where. There are really three separate questions. (1) Where does the collection (Mark 2.1–3.6) come from? (2) Where do its component parts (the five pericopes) come from? (3) Are the individual pericopes integral, or are they themselves composite? That is, do the component parts of each passage belong together?

(1) It is the collection itself, as it now appears in Mark, that makes it seem that the Pharisees were out to get Jesus from a very early date and pursued him relentlessly. The collection, however, is the work either of Mark or a previous author. The sequence of stories, where one confrontation follows another with no intervening narrative or discussion, and where the level of attack is steadily escalated, is dramatic but artificial. Somebody culled stories from here and there, and put them together in such a way as to lead up to an early decision to execute Jesus. If the passages are separated (as they are in Matthew and Luke), they do not give the same impression of unremitting enmity. The underlying events were probably farther apart.

(2) That is not to say that they all really took place. I have suggested that they reveal the signs of retrojection: later disputes have been thrust back into the lifetime of Jesus. The later Christian church, or at least sections of it, did disagree with the Pharisees and their successors, the rabbis, about the law. It is noteworthy that twice in this collection it is the followers who are accused, not Jesus himself (plucking of grain; fasting). These 'disciples' could represent the post-resurrection church, with the dispute retrojected into the lifetime of Jesus. The disputes may have taken place, but not necessarily between Jesus and the scribes and Pharisees.

(3) I think it likely that most of the passages above are not 'integral'; that is, an event or saying has been used to serve a later need by being put into a new setting. We recall that we can never be confident of the immediate context of a pericope. We also cannot be confident that the settings of individual sayings were transmitted without alteration. For example: Jesus may well have said that the sabbath should serve humans, rather than humans the sabbath. This is not necessarily against sabbath law. It could have had a place in a homily praising the creator, who ordained the sabbath not for his own benefit but for the sake of his creation. Other Jews had noted that not only humans, but also animals and the land enjoyed and benefited from the sabbath rest.[8] Possibly, however, Jesus did encounter a less humanistic treatment of the sabbath, some interpretation that seemed to require people to endure hardship. This could have triggered the saying. It appears to be anti-sabbath only when it occurs in a story in which Jesus' disciples are accused of breaking the sabbath.

It would have been very easy to alter the immediate context of one of Jesus' healings so that it became a challenge to the sabbath law. All one has to do is insert 'on the sabbath' and then a negative reaction. Luke adds two more cases to the tradition (Luke 13.10–17; 14.1–6).[9]

The overall impression is that Mark and probably the pre-Markan tradition wanted stories in which Jesus criticized the law and was in turn criticized by Jews who were conscientious in keeping it. There is an analogy with the Christian desire to depict Jesus as having positive relations with Gentiles. The Gentile Christians did not keep parts of the law, and (of course) they thought very highly of Gentiles. They wanted Jesus to agree with them. Yet they could muster strikingly little evidence. They could not cite many traditions favourable to Gentiles, nor could they find any really serious disputes about the Jewish law between Jesus and the scribes or Pharisees. A few passages have been worked on so that they become disputes over the law, though quite minor ones, and at the end there is a decision to kill Jesus. But this is a redactional or authorial construction. When we look at the disputes themselves, we do not find much conflict. The reader of Mark is invited to believe that a series of good deeds by Jesus led the Pharisees to want to kill him. This is intrinsically improbable, and it is disproved by the subsequent history: when the crunch actually came, the Pharisees had nothing whatever to do with his death.

We again see, however, that the Christian tradition was not terribly creative. A saying is taken from here, a setting from there, and a conclusion added. These modifications, at least in Mark, result in a depiction of serious legal disputes between Jesus and other interpreters.

Disagreements about Traditions (Mark 7 || Matt. 15)

We now turn to the third section of the gospels that depicts legal conflict between Jesus and others in Galilee. According to Mark 7, the Pharisees criticized Jesus because his disciples ate with unwashed hands. He replied by attacking one of their other traditions, according to which a person could declare property or money *korban* (dedicated to the Temple), but not surrender it. They could use this, Jesus charged, to deprive their parents of needed help. (We do not know of such a tradition from any other source, but it is intrinsically likely that the Pharisees had traditions about things dedicated to the Temple.) The passage continues: Jesus then called the people together and said, 'There is nothing outside a person which by going into him or her can defile; but the things that come out are what defile' (Mark 7.14f.). He later explained privately to the disciples that food enters a person but is evacuated. The author here comments in the third person: 'he thus declared all foods clean' (Mark 7.15).

Jesus' explanation continues: thoughts that lead to bad actions, such as sexual immorality and theft, are truly defiling (Mark 7.17–23).

To analyse this section, we shall return to the opening setting: the Pharisees criticize Jesus' disciples (not Jesus himself) for not washing their hands before meals. Handwashing was a Pharisaic tradition, not a law. In Jesus' day, it was not even a uniform tradition. Most Jews did not purify their hands before meals. Among the Pharisees, some regarded handwashing as optional; many of them washed their hands only before the sabbath meal; they disagreed with one another with regard to whether or not hands should be washed before or after mixing the sabbath cup. Deadly enmity over handwashing is, I think, historically impossible.[10] Mark 7 moves from handwashing to Jesus' attack on the Pharisees' view of *korban*: they declared their property or money to be dedicated to the Temple so that they would not have to help their needy parents. But this is an attack on what everyone, especially the Pharisees, would have regarded as an abuse. No Pharisee would justify using a semi-legal device to deprive his parents. Some Pharisee, of course, may have done this at some time or other. If so, and if Jesus accused him, decent, God-fearing, parent-respecting Pharisees – 99.8 per cent of the party – would have agreed.

The third section of Mark 7 is the question of what goes in and what comes out. Outside of its present context, the saying in Mark 7.14f. ('nothing that enters from the outside can defile, but rather what comes out') could mean several different things. In Jewish usage the construction '*not*' . . . '*but*' often means 'not only this, but much more that'. When the author of the *Letter of Aristeas* wrote that Jews honour God '*not* with gifts or sacrifices, *but* with purity of heart and devout disposition', he did not oppose sacrifices. On the contrary, he favoured them.[11] The sentence means 'not only with sacrifices, but even more with purity of heart'. Thus Jesus' saying, in and of itself, is not against the law. In the private interpretation, to the disciples alone, Jesus does, however, deny that the Jewish food laws were valid. 'Whatever goes in *cannot* defile' (Mark 7.18). If those are Jesus' precise words, Mark's interpretation would be correct: 'he declared all foods clean'. But Matthew does not agree with Mark. In Matthew's version there is no negative statement about the food laws. Jesus explains that what goes into a person is evacuated, but he does not say that 'what goes in cannot defile'. Matthew also lacks Mark's comment, that Jesus declared all foods clean (Matt. 15.10–20).

Did Jesus transgress the law deliberately? Did he teach his followers that transgression was acceptable or that some parts of the law were abrogated? Not according to Matthew or any of the traditions in Matthew. The Matthean antitheses, as we saw, make the law stricter, but they would never lead anyone to transgress. The Matthean versions of conflicts over food and sabbath also contain no instance of transgression.

Mark, however, did think that Jesus told his followers that they did not have to keep the food laws, and he may have had the same view of the sabbath law. Luke may have agreed with Mark on the sabbath law, but he did not include the debate about 'what goes in'. The author of Luke, as we shall see below, when discussing Acts 10.11–17, attributed the rejection of the food laws to a later period, not to the lifetime of Jesus.

The authors of the gospels disagreed. Can we come to a conclusion? I think that we can: Jesus did not teach his disciples that they could break either the sabbath or the food laws. Had he gone around Galilee, teaching people that it was all right to work on the sabbath and to eat pork, there would have been an enormous outcry. A man who claimed to speak for God, but who taught that significant parts of God's law were not valid? Horrendous! Nowadays, non-Jewish readers may not see how terrible this would have been. Since sometime in the last half of the first century, most Christians have been Gentile. The mostly Gentile Christian church has been accepting parts of the Jewish law but not other parts for more than 1,900 years. Consequently, people today do not feel the shock that this position first occasioned when it surfaced, probably in the fifties, in Paul's debates with other Jewish Christians. Paul thought that Gentiles could become 'children of Abraham' without being circumcised. The fight over this was bitter. Pious Jews – and most Jews were pious – thought that there really was a God, that he had given his law to Moses, that it was recorded in the scriptures, and that it should be obeyed. How in the world could anyone say that *parts* of it were invalid? Either all or nothing. If God gave it, it should be kept. If he did not, or if there was no God, then there was no point in keeping any of it. The difference between Paul's letters to the Galatians and the Romans, on the one hand, and Mark, on the other, is enormous. Mark calmly tosses in the sentence, 'He declared all foods clean.' Paul's letters crackle with the rage and hostility that *his* position on circumcision and food laws occasioned. Paul experienced the debate about the law firsthand. Mark (a second-generation Christian) did not, since it was largely over, nor did Jesus, since it had not yet arisen. The gospels do not contain the kind of material that would have been generated had Jesus taught his followers that they could disregard part of God's law.

Moreover, Jesus' followers observed the sabbath rest, as can be seen from the story of his burial. Jesus died shortly before sunset on a Friday, and Joseph of Arimathea immediately buried him. The women waited until Sunday morning, when the sabbath was over, before they came to anoint the body (Mark 15.42–16.2 & parr.). That is, they did not work on Saturday. The Book of Acts describes persecution of the Christians after Jesus' death and resurrection. They are charged with various offences, but never with breaking the sabbath.

The case of the food laws is even clearer. According to Acts (written by the author of Luke), some time after Jesus' death and resurrection Peter had a vision:

He saw the heaven opened and something like a large sheet coming down, being lowered to the ground by its four corners. In it were all kinds of four-footed creatures and reptiles and birds of the air. Then he heard a voice saying, 'Get up, Peter, kill and eat.' (Acts 10.11–14)

Peter refused, and the voice repeated the commandment twice more. Then the sheet and its contents were taken up to heaven, and Peter was left 'greatly puzzled about what to make of the vision he had seen' (Acts 10.15–17). He eventually concluded that Gentiles could be admitted to the new movement, no matter what they ate. But the story shows that, in Luke's view, Jesus had not taught his disciples that all foods were clean.

The letters of Paul also indicate indirectly that the disciples did not think that Jesus opposed food and sabbath laws. At one point Paul criticized Peter severely because he stopped eating with Gentiles

(Gal. 2.11–14). We do not know what Peter's objection was – whether the food or the company – but if Paul had known that Jesus himself had told Peter that all foods were clean, he could have worked this into his argument. Paul also objected to the fact that his Galatian Gentile converts had begun to observe the sabbath (Gal. 4.10), but he did not argue that Jesus himself had transgressed it.

In short, neither the women who anointed Jesus' body, nor Peter and the other Jerusalem apostles, nor Paul, nor Paul's opponents in Galatia thought that Jesus had told his disciples that they did not need to keep the sabbath and the food laws. I conclude from this that Jesus had himself observed these and the other parts of the Mosaic law, and that he had never recommended transgression as a general practice (though on some particular occasions he may have felt that transgression was justified).

The stories indicating that Jesus broke the law himself, and authorized his followers to do so, are (I proposed above) retrojected from the situation of the early church into the lifetime of Jesus. I wish to explain retrojection a little more fully. There were three principal points of contention over the law within the early church, and between it and the Jewish synagogue: circumcision, sabbath and food. These are *the* legal topics that lead to disagreement in Paul's letters and also in Acts. These three topics have a common denominator: they distinguish Jew from Gentile socially. Therefore they were the main areas that had to be settled whenever Jew and Gentile came together in a community or a common cause. Two of them virtually never arose as problems *within* a Jewish community. In a village occupied almost entirely by Jews, for example, the question of eating pork simply would not arise. There were not any pigs. Similarly, sons would be circumcised as a matter of routine. Sabbath is more complicated, because the Bible is less clear and specific about what counts as work than it is about what foods are forbidden.[12] Therefore on the sabbath it was possible to disagree even in places where there were no Gentiles. There was, however, no disagreement about whether or not one should keep the sabbath, but only about details, such as how far one could walk from one's property. No one farmed or opened a shop or cooked on the sabbath, since everyone agreed that these were forms of work. Debates over such things as minor cures, therefore, were possible, but these were only debates about interpretation, and lots of Jews disagreed over interpretation without deciding to kill one another. There would have been some variation in sabbath practice within nearly any Jewish community.

Of these three issues that we know were crucial in early Christianity after the death of Jesus, two – sabbath and food – dominate the disputes between Jesus and the scribes and Pharisees in the gospels. To return to the question of smoke and fire: we are certain that Gentile or partially Gentile Christian churches became greatly exercised about food and sabbath laws, while these would have been much less controversial in Galilean villages during Jesus' lifetime. Very likely the smoke (the passages in the gospels) arose from the real fire (disputes in Christian churches after Jesus' lifetime). I regard it as almost certain that the *prominence* of sabbath disputes and the verses on the food laws (Mark 7) reflects the situation of Christian churches after Gentiles started to be admitted to the movement. I believe that Mark's interpretation of the saying 'not what goes in' is retrojection, intended to reassure his Gentile readers that they can ignore the food laws. The story about plucking grain is also retrojection (though Jesus may have said, on some occasion or other, that the sabbath was intended to benefit humans). Further, the prominence of sabbath disputes in Mark 2.1–3.6 is the result of Mark's own interests (or those of a previous editor).

I do not wish to deny that Jesus at sometime or other debated sabbath practice. He may well have done so. But he did not act in such a way as to cause people – whether his Palestinian contemporaries or the first Christians – to believe that he had denied the validity of the sabbath law, which would mean denying its divine origin. Jesus lived, on the whole, as a good Jew, and one cannot find any trace of the attitude attributed to Elisha ben Avuyah (above, p. 207).

Positive Traditions

Numerous passages depict Jesus as supporting various aspects of the law. When he was asked what were the greatest commandments, he replied,

'You shall love the Lord your God with all your heart, and with all your soul, and with all your mind.' This is the great and first commandment. And a second is like it, 'You shall love your neighbour as yourself.' On these two commandments depend all the law and the prophets. (Matt. 22.37–40)

The commandment to love God is a quotation of Deuteronomy 6.4f., a passage that all observant Jews repeated twice each day. The commandment to love the neighbour is quoted from Leviticus 19.18. Many Jews of Jesus' day recognized these two commandments as summarizing the two 'tables' of the Jewish law: the commandments governing relations with God (headed by 'love God') and the commandments governing relations with other humans (summarized by 'love your neighbour').[13] Jesus' answer is not merely academically correct; he cites these laws with approval. In another passage he advises his followers, 'whatever you wish that people would do to you, do so to them', characterizing this statement as 'the law and the prophets' (Matt. 7.12). This is an epigrammatic way of saying 'love your neighbour as yourself'. The epigram is very similar to one well known to other Jewish teachers, which they also regarded as summarizing the law.[14]

Besides these indications of whole-hearted approval of the law and its basic commandments, there are other passages indicating agreement. We discussed above the fact that, after healing a leper, Jesus told him to show himself to a priest and to sacrifice, as Moses commanded (Mark 1.40–45, above, pp. 128f.). Jesus told his followers that, when they went to the Temple, they should be sure that they were reconciled to people whom they may have harmed before they sacrificed (Matt. 5.23f.) – again, standard Jewish advice, which reflects endorsement of the sacrificial system. Jesus obviously believed that Isaiah and the other prophets were truly prophets of God, since he quoted them with approval (for example, Matt. 11.2–6). In view of the indisputable fact that Jesus thought that the Jewish scripture contained the revealed word of God, and that Moses had issued commandments that should be followed, we should be very hesitant to accept the common view of New Testament scholars that he had actually opposed the Jewish law. This is all the more true, of course, since the passages in which there are disagreements about the law reveal no direct opposition to it.

Other Legal Topics and Possible Points of Conflict

I have just proposed that Jesus agreed with, and approved of, the entirety of Jewish scripture ('the law and the prophets'). The passages where some people find opposition to the law do not actually reveal it. Even if we ignored retrojection and doubts about authenticity, we would find only one passage in which Jesus permits transgression: Mark 7.15–18 ('he declared all food clean', 'what goes in cannot defile'). Consideration of Acts, Paul's letters and the other synoptic gospels shows that Jesus did not actually tell his disciples that they need not observe the food laws.

If we return to our list of possible levels of disagreement above (pp. 206f.), we will see that Jesus' view of the law does not fall into category (a) or (b). That is, Jesus did not think that the written law was wrong and should be repealed, nor did he say to his followers that they should disobey aspects of it. This gives the overall context in which we must consider strife in Galilee. Jesus was not locked in mortal combat with upholders of the law as a matter of principle. Everyone, including Jesus and his followers, believed that God gave the law to Moses and that he had inspired the other scriptures as well. If Jesus disagreed with other interpreters over details, the disputes were no more substantial than were disputes between the Jewish parties and even within each party.

There are, however, two points where Jesus asserted his own authority in ways that were objectionable or potentially objection-able. These two topics are probably semi-legal rather than strictly legal. The first is Jesus' commandment to 'let the dead bury the dead'. The second is his call of 'sinners'.

A would-be disciple said that he would follow Jesus, but wished first to bury his dead father. Jesus replied, 'Follow me, and leave the dead to bury their own dead' (Matt. 8.21–2). Many readers take this reply to be an aphorism: let the (spiritually) dead bury the (spiritu-ally) dead. But such an aphorism is so offensive that it is unlikely. The idea of not burying the dead was even more repugnant to ancient morality than to ours. The reality was so offensive that a metaphor based on it would not appeal. Jews shared the Greek abhorrence of leaving a body unburied.[15] According to the rabbis, even a priest – normally forbidden to bury the dead or even to enter a graveyard, so as not to contract corpse impurity and be unfit for serving in the Temple – should bury a corpse if there was no one else to do it. The order to 'let the dead bury the dead' was not only contrary to normal human sensitivity, it was also against any reasonable interpretation of the Jewish law, which commands honour of father and mother. The offensiveness of the saying makes it unlikely that 'bury the dead' is a metaphor. The would-be follower probably had a dead father, and Jesus said to him, 'Let the (spiritually) dead bury the (physically) dead.' If so, Jesus thought that following him should override everything else.

We have here a case somewhat analogous to that of the rich man who wished to be 'perfect' and was told to sell everything to follow Jesus. Jesus did not lay this sort of requirement on everyone, but from some he did require complete self-denial. The difference in the case of the man with a dead father is that self-denial would involve a breach of the commandment to honour one's parents. Jesus here commands an exception to the rule, which legally should probably be seen as an appeal to a mitigating circumstance: the need to follow him was so great that it should override the normal obligations of piety.

This appears, however, to have been a one-time-only incident that does not represent Jesus' general practice. If Pharisees or others dedicated to the law had heard it, they would have been scandalized. But nothing seems to have resulted. We learn from the passage not that Jesus opposed honouring father and mother, but that he had an attitude towards his own mission that would lead to ignoring the law if that were necessary. His call was more important than burying the dead. Something of this attitude may have been communicated to the public, and many would have been deeply offended. If this particular incident led nowhere, Jesus' attitude did, as we shall now see.

Jesus' view that his mission took precedence over everything is more fully expressed in the passages about the 'sinners'. Jesus called as one of his followers a tax collector (Levi in Mark and Luke, Matthew in Matthew), and the man accepted the call. Jesus was subsequently accused of eating with tax collectors and sinners (Mark 2.14–17 & parr.). This seems to have been a genuine offence: something he actually did that really offended people. The most reliable passages about the sinners are those in which Jesus discusses the Baptist and contrasts himself to him. John came 'in the way of righteousness' (Matt. 21.32), and he was an ascetic, 'neither eating nor drinking' (Matt. 11.18). Jesus ('the Son of Man', here used of himself) came 'eating and drinking'; yet he too was rejected: 'A glutton and a drunkard, a friend of tax collectors and sinners!' (Matt. 11.19).

Why was his association with tax collectors and sinners a reason for rejecting Jesus? 'Sinners' in the Hebrew Bible, when used generically to refer to a class of people, refers not to those who occasionally transgress, but to those who are outside the law in some fundamental way. To understand the significance of the term 'sinners', we should consider the description of the 'wicked' in the Psalms. They are contrasted with the 'poor'. The wicked prey on the poor, and they say in their hearts that there is no God, or if there is he will not call them to account (Pss. 10.4, 8–13). Modern English translations of the Hebrew Psalms quite rightly use the word 'wicked' in these passages, which is the best translation of the Hebrew word *resha'im*. The Jews who translated the Hebrew Bible into Greek, however, used the word 'sinners' (*hamartoloi*),[16] and this became the term that Greek-speaking Jews used for people who were fundamentally outside the covenant because they did not observe God's law. The word 'sinners' in Jewish Greek could refer to Gentiles (who by definition did not observe the Jewish law) or to truly wicked Jews. The force of the term is seen in Paul's rebuke to Peter: 'We ourselves, who are Jews by birth and not Gentile sinners . . .' (Gal. 2.15); that is, 'not Gentiles, who are completely wicked in that they live totally outside the law'. In the gospels the Greek word *hamartoloi* refers to Jews who systematically or flagrantly transgressed, and who were, therefore, like Gentiles, except that they were even more culpable. Like Elisha ben Avuyah, they knew God but chose to disobey him. I shall refer to them as the 'wicked', since that is almost certainly the word that was used by Jesus and his critics. (They spoke Aramaic rather than Hebrew, but the word is the same.)

The significance of the fact that Jesus was a friend of the wicked was this: he counted within his fellowship people who were generally regarded as living outside the law in a blatant manner.

The phrase 'tax collectors and wicked people' appears frequently in the gospels with no explanation, and it is not immediately clear why the two groups should be linked. The probable explanation is that tax collectors were regarded as dishonest. If so, they were wicked, since their dishonesty was systematic. Anyone who used his office to line his own pocket was doing almost precisely what the wicked do in the Psalms: preying on other people and living as if there were no God, or as if God would not mete out justice. This is Philo's description of the man who, around the year 40 CE, was in charge of tax collection in the province of Judaea: 'Capito is the tax collector for Judaea and cherishes a spite against the population. When he came there he was a poor man but by his rapacity and peculation he has amassed much wealth in various forms' (*Embassy* 199). The word translated as 'tax' here is more literally 'tribute'; Capito was responsible for sending Judaea's tribute to Rome or to the Roman base in Syria. He collected more than he had to remit, and he became rich.

In Josephus there is a more favourable reference to another kind of tax collector: a customs officer. The Caesarean Jews were being bothered by construction work that blocked or hampered their access to a synagogue. John, the customs officer, bribed the Roman procurator, Florus, to settle the dispute in favour of the Jews. The procurator took the money and then left town, leaving the two parties to fight it out (*War* 2.285–8). This customs officer was Jewish, and he acted in concert with the prominent Jews of the city. He was, unlike them, rich enough to come up with a large sum of money for the bribe: eight talents of silver. A talent weighed about 75 lbs (*c.* 35 kgs), though scholarly estimates vary widely. If this figure is approximately correct, we can calculate the value of eight talents of silver in contemporary currencies. Silver trades at about US $4.30 per ounce; this puts the value of eight talents at approximately $41,280, or £26,300. In this story Florus is the villain. If an honest politician is one who stays bribed, Florus was dishonest, and the results were catastrophic. The conflict over access to the synagogue in Caesarea was the first in a chain of events that led to the great Jewish revolt against Rome.

But our interest is in John the customs officer. Of all the Jews in Caesarea, he was the one who was able to offer a large bribe. The customs officer who controlled the port of Caesarea (assuming that this was John's post) was in a very good position. The port's exports were much more valuable than its imports, since it was one of the possible routes by which luxury items from the east reached Asia Minor, Greece and Italy. Duty was probably charged on exports as well as imports, and so most of the cost was passed on to the consumers in other countries. John could charge too much, or skim some off the top, and not hurt the Caesareans.

The tax collectors in the gospels are, like John, customs officers, not collectors of tribute. The small towns around the Sea of Galilee were less prosperous than Caesarea, and both exports and imports were more basic than the luxury goods that passed through the port at Caesarea. Galilee produced a lot of foodstuff, but had to import many manufactured goods. Galilean toll collectors charged duty on things that were used by ordinary Galilean peasants. Presumably the toll collectors became relatively rich – not as rich as a collector of tribute or a customs officer in a large city like Caesarea, but richer than most Galilean farmers and fishermen. Galileans probably considered customs officials 'wicked': they were routinely dishonest.

A lot of scholars, including myself, have thought that tax collectors in Galilee were regarded as collaborators, locals who acted on behalf of an imperial power. They collected taxes in the service of Antipas, but he paid tribute to Rome; thus indirectly they assisted Rome. I am no longer confident of this view. It is quite enough to say that they were suspected of charging too much, and thus of preying on the populace as a matter of course. They therefore lived as if there were no God, or as if he would not avenge; they were 'wicked'.

The only other people whom the gospels mention as belonging to the wicked were the prostitutes. According to Matt. 21.31f., the customs officers and the prostitutes will go into the kingdom before 'you' – apparently the chief priests and elders (see 21.23) – because they believed John the Baptist and repented. Jesus himself is never said to have associated closely with prostitutes. Luke tells a story about a woman who was a 'sinner' anointing his feet, but this was in the presence of a Pharisee, and so there could be no question of improper behaviour (Luke 7.36–50). If we want to ask about Jesus and the wicked, we must confine ourselves to tax collectors.

We noted above the general criticism that Jesus was a friend of tax collectors and wicked people (Matt. 11.19). There are two concrete stories, of which we have already mentioned one: Jesus called a tax collector to follow him, and subsequently he dined with tax collectors. 'Scribes of the Pharisees' asked him why he did so, and he replied, 'those who are well have no need of a physician, but those who are sick' (Mark 2.14–17). This supposes that he wanted to heal them; that is, to get them to stop being dishonest. Successful moral reform is also the point of the other story. When Jesus was going through Jericho, the chief customs officer, Zacchaeus, climbed a tree in order to see him. Jesus looked up and told Zacchaeus that he would stay with him. This led the crowd to grumble that Jesus would stay with someone who was wicked. Zacchaeus promptly promised to give half of his goods to the poor and to repay everyone whom he had defrauded fourfold. Jesus commented that salvation had come to Zacchaeus' house, and he added that 'the Son of Man came to seek and to save the lost' (Luke 19.1–10).

Zacchaeus offered a lot more than the law requires, which is that a person who defrauds another should repay him, add 20 per cent as a fine, and then sacrifice a ram as a guilt offering (Lev. 6.1–7). A person who did this, and who did not return to his former life, was no longer wicked. If Jesus had managed to persuade other customs officers to do what Zacchaeus did, he would have been a local hero. But it seems that he was criticized. How can we understand this? In view of this and other points, which I shall explain just below, I suggested in an earlier work that, in spite of the story of Zacchaeus' marvellous conversion, Jesus was not a preacher of repentance: he was not primarily a reformer, and in his association with tax collectors he was not trying to persuade them to do what Zacchaeus did.[17]

As I foresaw, this suggestion has been unpopular. I shall try again to explain the point. The story of Levi and the other tax collectors (Mark 2.14–17) does not say that they repented, repaid the money, added 20 per cent, and took a sacrifice to the Temple. Moreover, the words 'repent' and 'repentance' are very rare in Matthew and Mark. If Jesus' aim was to bring dishonest people to repentance, we would expect the word 'repent' to be a prominent one in his teaching. I shall briefly review the occurrence of these words (both the verb and the noun) in the synoptic gospels. Mark summarizes Jesus' preaching as including a call to repentance (Mark 1.15) but gives no specific example. Otherwise Mark attributes a message of repentance only to John the Baptist and the twelve disciples (1.4; 6.12). Matthew has the same summary of Jesus' message (Matt.

4.17) and an expanded description of John's, which stresses repentance (3.2, 8, 11). In Matt. 11.20f. Jesus criticizes Chorazin, Bethsaida and Capernaum for not repenting. Matt. 12.41 praises Nineveh for repenting at the preaching of Jonah. Matt. 21.32 (as we saw above) criticizes the chief priests and elders for not repenting at the preaching of John. Luke has parallels to the verses on John the Baptist (Luke 3.3, 8), the Galilean cities (10.13) and Nineveh (11.32). Whereas in Matthew and Mark, when Jesus defends dining with tax collectors, he says that he came to call sinners, in Luke he says that he came to call sinners *to repentance* (Luke 5.32). According to Luke, Jesus concluded the parable about the lost sheep by saying 'there will be more joy in heaven over one wicked person who repents than over ninety-nine righteous people who need no repentance', a conclusion that is lacking in Matthew's version (Luke 15.7; Matt. 18.14). The Lukan parable of the lost coin has a similar ending (Luke 15.10). There are further sayings in Luke that recommend repentance (16.30 and 17.3f.), and the story of Zacchaeus, which we discussed just above, is about repentance.

As this review demonstrates, repentance has a prominence in Luke that it does not have in Matthew and Mark. We then note that repentance has a prominence in Acts, written by the author of Luke, that it does not have in the rest of the New Testament, except the Book of Revelation. The principal Greek words for 'repent' and 'repentance' occur 62 times in the New Testament, of which 14 occurrences are in Luke, 11 in Acts, and 12 in Revelation. The figures for the other gospels are 10 in Matthew, 3 in Mark and 0 in John. If we ask about the use of repent/repentance in the teaching attributed to Jesus, leaving out discussions of the Baptist and others, the numbers fall: 6 in Matthew, 1 in Mark (Mark's own summary) and 11 in Luke. If, instead of the occurrences of words, we count the number of passages that contain those words, the totals are these:

Matthew: 1 John the Baptist; 4 Jesus; 1 Judas
Mark: 1 John the Baptist; 1 Jesus; 1 the disciples
Luke: 1 John the Baptist; 8 Jesus

One of the four Matthean passages in which the word 'repent' is attributed to Jesus is actually about John the Baptist: the chief priests and elders did not repent at the preaching of John (Matt. 21.22).

This reduces still further the passages indicating that Jesus called people to repentance.

For the sake of comparison, we may consider the noun used in Jesus' main proclamation, 'kingdom'. It appears 55 times in Matthew, 20 in Mark, 46 in Luke, 5 in John, 162 in the entire New Testament. 'Kingdom' is statistically a major word in all three of the synoptics, while 'repent/repentance' is significant in Luke, Acts and Revelation. The most reasonable explanation is that the author of Luke/Acts especially liked to emphasize repentance, and that it was not one of the major themes of Jesus' own message.

I realize that this strikes the reader as odd, since everyone, whether religious or not, thinks of repentance as a major and fundamental element of religion. And so it is. Repentance was a main theme in Judaism and later in early Christianity. It has continued as a dominant feature of both religions. It is, therefore, striking that repentance plays so small a part in the teaching of Jesus according to Matthew and Mark. Its small role in these two gospels becomes all the more remarkable when we note that both use the word in their summaries of Jesus' teaching (Mark 1.15; Matt. 4.15). They had no interest themselves in downplaying it; yet it is a minor theme. What is the explanation?

It is not that Jesus disliked repentance and thought that people should never feel remorse and pray for forgiveness. He favoured all this. He thought that the prostitutes who repented at the preaching of John the Baptist, like the Ninevites who repented at the preaching of Jonah, did the right thing (Matt. 21.31f.; 12.41) and that the towns of Galilee should have repented (Matt. 11.20f.). The parable of the Unforgiving Servant (Matt. 18.23–35) discusses appeals for leniency and forgiveness in such a way as to leave no doubt that the speaker valued them. That is not the issue. There are two questions. The first is, what was it about Jesus' association with wicked people that offended his critics? If other wicked people responded as did Zacchaeus, who repented and distributed his wealth generously, what would be the complaint? None, I think.

This leads to the second question: what was Jesus' own mission? What did he think he was up to? Was his goal in life to persuade bad people that they should start being honest, or to persuade the prosperous to share their money? To answer these questions, we must ask just what it is that the gospels say about Jesus' association with the wicked. This examination reveals that only Luke gives concrete stories about Jesus' calling on people to repent, and that only Luke thought that Jesus persuaded the wicked to repent and pay back their ill-gotten gains. That is, Luke's Jesus, who got tax collectors to repent and repay, would not have irritated anyone, at least not on this point. But, since Jesus did run into opposition for his behaviour with sinners, I am inclined to think that Jesus is not to be *defined* as a preacher of repentance. Jesus favoured repentance, but, if we classify him as a type, and describe how he saw his mission, we shall conclude that he was not a repentance-minded reformer.

In the New Testament that title clearly belongs to the Baptist. Jesus was conscious of his differences from John, and he commented on them more than once. The prostitutes repented when John preached – not when Jesus preached. John was ascetic; Jesus ate and drank. And Jesus was a friend of tax collectors and sinners – not of former tax collectors and sinners, which is what Zacchaeus was after he met Jesus, but of tax collectors and sinners. Jesus, I think, was a good deal more radical than John. Jesus thought that John's call to repent should have been effective, but in fact it was only partially successful. His own style was in any case different; he did not repeat the Baptist's tactics. On the contrary, he ate and drank with the wicked and told them that God especially loved them, and that the kingdom was at hand. Did he hope that they would change their ways? Probably he did. But 'change now or be destroyed' was not his message, it was John's. Jesus' was, 'God loves you.'

We can see better the distinctiveness of Jesus' message and style if we consider the parable of the Lost Sheep. If a man had a hundred sheep, and one went astray, the man would leave the ninety-nine to fend for themselves and go in search of the one (Matt 18.12–14; Luke 15.3–7). According to Matthew's version, the moral is this: 'It is not the will of my Father who is in heaven that one of these little ones should perish.' Luke offers a statement that we noted above, 'There will be more joy in heaven over one sinner who repents than over ninety-nine righteous people who need no repentance.' The emphasis of Matthew's conclusion agrees with that of the parable proper: *the shepherd goes after the lost sheep.* Luke's is different: *the lost sheep must decide to come back.* This clashes with the whole thrust of the parable, and it is in the parable itself that we find Jesus' own view. The shepherd is God: at a good deal of risk to the flock (sheep do not fend for themselves very well) God goes after a single lost sheep. God wants the sinner to come back, to be sure, but the emphasis falls entirely on God's search, not on the sinner's repentance. This is a parable of good news about God; it is not an illustration of the value of repentance.

This good news about God is potentially a much more powerful message than a standard exhortation to give up wickedness and turn over a new leaf. In a world that believed in God and judgement, some people nevertheless lived as if there were no God. They must have had some anxiety about this in the dark watches in the night. The message that God loves them anyway might transform their lives. I must, however, hasten to add that I do not know that Jesus' message was effective in actually changing the outlook, and consequently the lives, of the wicked of Galilee. Like the women who followed Jesus to Jerusalem, watched him die and returned to anoint him, the wicked of the gospels disappear from sight. We do not know what happened even to Levi, the customs officer whom Jesus called. It is hard to find room for such people in the Jerusalem church, headed by James the Just (as tradition has called Jesus' brother, who was very law-abiding). Perhaps they lived out their lives in Galilee, hoping that the man who made them feel so special would be back.

This glance forward to the situation of the early church is very useful for understanding Jesus. Were he a reformer of society, he would have had to face the problem of integrating wicked people into a more righteous social group. Then there would have had to be explicit rules about the parameters of behaviour, and also some sort of policy on sources of income. None of this exists. Since he thought that God was about to change the circumstances of the world, Jesus did not have to deal with such problems. He was an absolutist. He required a few people, those who actually followed him, to give up everything. To others, he promised the kingdom without setting down a lot of stipulations and conditions. It was coming; God intended to include even the wicked. Jesus did not want the wicked to remain wicked in the interim, but he did not devise a programme that would enable tax collectors and prostitutes to make a living in less dubious ways.

With regard to the lack of specific plans for integrating the wicked into a more upright society, we should now note that there is no instance in which Jesus requires the wicked to do what the law stipulates in order to become righteous. We saw those requirements above: those who had benefited by wickedness should repay what they had taken, add a fifth of its value as a penalty, take a ram to the Temple as a guilt offering, confess the sin with one hand on the head of the ram, sacrifice the ram and thus be forgiven (e.g., Lev. 6.1–7). In Luke's story about Zacchaeus, the tax collector promised to repay fourfold what he had taken wrongly, which is more than the law required, but there is still no hint of taking a sacrifice and receiving forgiveness at the Temple.

There are two possible explanations of why this theme is missing. One is that Jesus, those who heard him, the disciples and the early Christians all simply presupposed the sacrificial system. The wicked people who decided to change their ways, such as Zacchaeus, knew that the law required sacrifice, and so when they next went to Jerusalem they sacrificed a guilt offering. The second possibility is that Jesus thought and said that the wicked who followed him, though they had not technically 'repented', and though they had not become righteous in the way required by the law, would be in the kingdom, and in fact would be 'ahead' of those who were righteous by the law. If this was the point of Jesus' call of wicked people, he would have constituted a threat to the common and obvious Jewish understanding of the Bible and the will of God. I regard this second possibility as more likely than the first, since Jesus' treatment of sinners drew criticism. Here we see how radical Jesus was: far more radical than someone who simply committed minor infringements of the sabbath and food laws. Both far more radical and far more arrogant, in the common view. He seems to have thought that those who followed him belonged to God's elect, even though they did not do what the Bible itself requires. We should recall the conclusion of one of Jesus' parables: the servants of the king 'went out into the streets and gathered all whom they found, both bad and good; so the wedding hall was filled with guests' (Matt. 22.10). The servants did not first require all the bad to become good: they brought them in anyway.

I believe that this explains why Jesus' association with wicked tax collectors was offensive. Since my proposal is not what most readers will expect, I shall repeat it briefly. According to the gospels, Jesus was criticized for associating with tax collectors, who were regarded as 'wicked' – people who systematically and routinely transgressed the law. Most interpreters of the New Testament assume that Luke's story of Zacchaeus reveals Jesus' aim: he wanted the tax collectors to repent, to repay what they had stolen, to add a further payment of 20 per cent as a penalty, and to give up their dishonest practice. I have proposed that this is not right. First, only Luke presents Jesus as a reformer. Secondly, no one would have objected if Jesus persuaded tax collectors to leave the ranks of the wicked: everybody else would have benefited. If he were a successful reformer of dishonest tax collectors, Jesus would not have drawn criticism. But in fact he was criticized for associating with tax collectors. This is hard to explain, and I have offered a hypothesis that accounts for the criticism: Jesus told the tax collectors that God loved them, and he told other people that the tax collectors would enter the kingdom of God before righteous people did. That is, he seems to have said, in effect, that if they accepted him and his message, God would include them in the kingdom – even though they had not repented and reformed in the way the law requires (repayment, 20 per cent fine, guilt offering). This would have been offensive on two counts: Jesus did not try to enforce the commandments of the Jewish law that stipulate how one changes from being wicked to being upright; Jesus regarded himself as having the right to say who would be in the kingdom.

The assertion of the significance of his own mission and authority was probably the more serious offence. Jesus' self-assertion was not, strictly speaking, against the law. He did not tell people *not* to sacrifice; on the contrary, in two passages noted above he approved of sacrifice (the leper, Mark 1.40–45; first be reconciled to your neighbour, Matt. 5.23f.). Although he did not oppose the law, he did indicate that what was most important was accepting him and following him. This could eventually lead to the view that the law was unnecessary, but it appears that Jesus himself did not draw this conclusion, nor does this seem to have been an accusation against him. What stands out in the passages about the sinners is his presumption about the importance of his mission.

We see here the same self-conception that is evident in the miracles. Through him, Jesus held, God was acting directly and immediately, bypassing the agreed, biblically sanctioned ordinances, reaching out to the lost sheep of the house of Israel with no more mediation than the words and deeds of one man – himself. This, at least, is the most obvious inference to draw from the passages about the wicked. This view of himself and of the vital importance of his mission was offensive in a general sense – not because he opposed obedience to the law, but because he regarded his own mission as what really counted. If the most important thing that people could do was to accept him, the importance of other demands was reduced, even though Jesus did not say that those demands were invalid.

15. JESUS' VIEW OF
HIS ROLE IN GOD'S PLAN

We have just seen the clearest and possibly the most important point that can be made about Jesus' view of himself and, in particular, of his own place in God's plan for Israel and the world. He regarded himself as having full authority to speak and act on behalf of God. Sinners who followed him, but who may or may not have returned to the Mosaic law, would have a place in God's kingdom. From the point of view of those who were not persuaded, he was arrogant and attributed to himself a degree of authority that was most inappropriate. From the point of view of his followers and sympathizers he offered an immediate and direct route to God's love and mercy, establishing a relationship that would culminate when the kingdom fully came. Jesus was a *charismatic and autonomous prophet*; that is, his authority (in his own view and that of his followers) was not mediated by any human organization, not even by scripture. A rabbi, or a teacher of the law, derived authority from studying and interpreting the Bible. Jesus doubtless did both, but it was not scriptural interpretation that gave him a claim on other people. He did not say to potential followers, 'Study with me six hours each week, and within six years I shall teach you the true interpretation of the law.' He said, in effect, 'Give up everything you have and follow me, because I am God's agent.'

There are two aspects to Jesus' self-claim. One is the assertion of his own authority, which we have just noted, and which can further be seen in all the 'follow me' passages, especially those indicating that following him is done at high personal cost. I give a bare list of major instances:

Some followers gave up everything to follow him: Matt. 19.27–9.

Would-be followers should bear in mind that he had no place to
  lay his head, Matt. 8.19f.
The man whose father was dead should 'let the dead bury the
  dead' and follow Jesus, Matt. 8.21f.
Followers would lose family and even their own lives, Matt.
  10.34–8; cf. Matt. 16.24–8.
The rich man should sell all he possessed and follow Jesus, Matt.
  19.16–22.

We shall pay special attention to Matthew 19.27–9: Peter asked
what Jesus' followers, who had given up everything, would receive.
Jesus replied that they would receive a hundredfold, that they
would inherit eternal life and that the Twelve would judge the
twelve tribes of Israel. Here he was not only claiming authority in
the sense of knowing God's will and being empowered to call
people to follow him no matter what the present cost, but also in
another and more common sense: in the kingdom his followers
would be the judges. This makes him, presumably, viceroy: at the
head of the judges of Israel, subordinate only to God himself.

The second aspect of Jesus' self-assertion is the claim of an
immediate relationship to God, in the strict sense of 'unmediated'.
He regarded his relationship with God as especially intimate. As
Geza Vermes pointed out, other charismatic prophets besides Jesus
felt that they had a very intimate relationship with God, and we
should not overemphasize Jesus' view of himself in this regard.
There may have been numerous people who felt as close to God as
Jesus did. But we may be certain about him: he thought that he had
been especially commissioned to speak for God, and this conviction
was based on a feeling of personal intimacy with the deity.

Titles

We know substantially what Jesus thought of himself. We shall
now ask whether or not he gave himself a title. The authors of the
New Testament were interested in titles, and modern Christians
have followed their lead. Few topics of research have generated as
much scholarly publication. We all think that if we know the right
word for something we understand it better, but in this particular

case such a view is probably incorrect. The quest for the right title – the word that encapsulates Jesus' view of himself, as well as the first disciples' view – supposes that titles had fixed definitions and that we need only discover the definition of each. If title *a* meant *x*, and if Jesus used *a* of himself, we know that he thought of himself as being *x*. I think that the basic assumption, that titles had standard definitions, is in error.

We shall start with the title that has been most widely used of Jesus since his own time: 'Messiah' or 'Christ'. For convenience, I shall repeat the derivation of these words. The English word 'Messiah' is an approximate transliteration of the Hebrew *meshiah* or the Aramaic *mashiha*, words that mean 'anointed'. In Greek the translation of *meshiah* is *christos*, from which we derive the English word 'Christ'. Thus 'Messiah' and 'Christ' are the same. Most New Testament authors, who wrote in Greek, used *christos*, but sometimes they wrote *messias*, thus showing knowledge of the underlying Semitic word.[1] At least as early as the letters of Paul, *christos* began to be used as if it were not a title but part of Jesus' name: 'Jesus Christ'. Our present concern is with the title 'Messiah' in Jesus' own culture. What did it mean to first-century Palestinian Jews?

In the Hebrew Bible three classes of people were anointed: prophets, priests and kings. The Christian tradition early fixed on the third of these as giving a clue to Jesus' identity: he was descended from King David and was the Davidic Messiah – David's physical descendant, chosen by God (spiritually 'anointed') to perform a David-like task. New Testament scholars have accepted the definition of 'Messiah' as referring to a kingly Messiah, a second David. This definition should lead people who accept it to think that Jesus intended to raise an army and drive out the enemies of Israel. Since he did nothing of the sort, scholars then have to puzzle over why his disciples called him 'Messiah'. But is the definition of the Davidic Messiah as a warrior–king correct? We saw above that two Jewish sources that are unquestionably pre-Christian are relevant to understanding 'Messiah', especially 'Davidic Messiah' (pp. 89f.). I shall briefly repeat the point. In *Psalms of Solomon* 17, a son of David is depicted as purging Jerusalem of Gentiles and evil Jews. He rides a horse, and thus he sounds like a military leader. Yet it is not his troops that accomplish the task but rather God himself. Here we have a son of David who acts in some respects like David.

Nevertheless the conception has changed: there will not be any real fighting.

The second source that sheds light on the title 'Messiah' is the library found near the shores of the Dead Sea. In some of these documents there are *two* Messiahs, one a son of David and one a son of Aaron, the first high priest. The second, the priestly Messiah, is in charge. The other Messiah does nothing. There will be a great war (according to one scroll), but the Messiahs play no part in it.[2]

We cannot read these texts and then say that we know what 'Messiah' meant and consequently what the early Christians thought when they called Jesus 'Messiah' or 'Christ'. Even 'son of David' remains a little non-specific. Perhaps it points more clearly towards a military and political leader than does 'Messiah', but the Dead Sea Scrolls show that it does not require that definition. All we can really know, when we see the word 'Messiah', is that the person of whom it was used was considered to be the 'anointed' of God, anointed for *some* special task.

The authors of the gospels, and other Christians both before and after them, thought that Jesus was the Messiah – that is, that he was *some sort* of Messiah. The passages in the synoptics, however, make it doubtful that Jesus used this term of himself. At Caesarea Phillipi, in response to Jesus' question, 'Who do men say I am?', the disciples answered: 'John the Baptist; and others say, Elijah; and others one of the prophets.' Jesus pressed: 'But who do you say that I am?', and Peter answered, 'You are the Messiah' (Greek *christos*). Jesus 'charged them to tell no one' (Mark 8.27–30), possibly to avoid trouble, or possibly because he did not fully agree that the title was correct. He then proceeded to speak of himself as the Son of Man (8.31).

When Jesus entered Jerusalem for his last Passover, riding on an ass, some cried out, 'Hosanna! Blessed is he who comes in the name of the Lord! Blessed is the kingdom of our father David that is coming!' (Mark 11.9f.). According to Matthew, the crowd hailed Jesus as 'son of David' (21.9), according to Luke as 'the king' (19.38). This passage does not give enough evidence to say what the crowd thought, nor can we know how Jesus regarded these acclamations. If, however, Jesus deliberately decided to ride a donkey into Jerusalem in order to create a 'fulfilment' of Zechariah 9.9 ('your king comes to you . . . riding on an ass'), we know that he thought that 'king' was not entirely inappropriate.[3] But the word does not have to trigger the whole set of characteristics that scholars imagine are implied by the terms 'Messiah' and 'son of David'. On the contrary, a lot of Jews did not want a militaristic sort of king (above, p. 42). It is by no means inconceivable that Jesus' ride was a deliberate signal: '"king" yes, of a sort; military conqueror no'.

When Jesus was tried before the high priest, he was charged: 'Tell us if you are the Messiah [*christos*], the Son of the Blessed' (Mark 14.61 & parr.). According to Mark he answered 'yes', according to Luke he evaded the question, while according to Matthew he said, in effect, 'no' (Mark 14.62; Luke 22.67f.; Matt. 26.64).[4] Again he immediately referred to the Son of Man (Mark 14.62 & parr.).

There is thus no certainty that Jesus thought of himself as bearer of the title 'Messiah'. On the contrary, it is unlikely that he did so: all the gospel writers so regarded him, but they could cite little direct evidence; only Mark has 'yes' in response to a direct question about the title. Peter, perhaps thinking more in worldly Messianic terms than Jesus himself, received this rebuke: 'Get behind me, Satan!' (Mark 8.33). Jesus had known the temptation of worldly success (Matt. 4.1–11), but he rejected Satan's offer that time as well.

Jesus' actual claim may have been in fact higher: not only spokesman for, but viceroy of, God; and not just in a political kingdom but in the kingdom of God. We know this by inference from the implicit self-claim that we discussed above, and not because he gave himself an explicit title.

Since the question of the significance of the term 'Messiah' when applied to Jesus is a complex one, I shall enumerate the principal points as a summary. (1) Jewish literature that is earlier than Jesus, or contemporary with him, does not offer a single definition of the word 'Messiah'. (2) Jesus probably did not view 'Messiah' as the best title to describe who he was. (3) After his death and resurrection, however, Jesus' disciples decided that this title, which was one of the highest honorific titles they could think of, belonged to him. (4) In a very general sense it corresponded to his own view of himself: he would be the leader in the coming kingdom. (5) The disciples could also remember, however, that he rejected Peter's ambition for him, and that afterwards three of them (Peter, James and John) had a vision in which they saw him in glory with Moses and Elijah (Mark

9.2–13). According to the Bible, Elijah was taken bodily to heaven, and Jewish tradition often accorded the same honour to Moses. Jesus' presence with them in the disciples' vision testifies to high status indeed – again, not precisely 'son of David' or 'Messiah'. Both Elijah and Moses were 'prophets'. (6) In the end the early Christians kept the title 'Messiah' but redefined it to accord with their own experience: Jesus became for them a new kind of Messiah, one who had acted as a miracle-worker and prophet during his lifetime, but who was also the heavenly Lord who would return at the end. This definition of Messiah – prophet, miracle-worker and heavenly Lord – is *post factum*: the early Christians viewed him in this way and also called him 'Messiah'. As far as we know, the term 'Messiah' had not been defined in such a way in advance.

The title 'Son of God' is even vaguer than 'Messiah'. Because of the birth narratives in Matthew and Luke, modern readers often think that 'Son of God' meant 'a male conceived in the absence of human semen' or even 'a male half human and half divine, produced when God fertilized a human ovum without semen'. In discussing miracles (pp. 160–62 above), we observed that this notion would be at home in the Greek-speaking world. Such a story was told of Alexander the Great: he was the Son of Zeus; his mother was hit by a thunderbolt before she and Philip of Macedonia consummated their marriage, and so Alexander was a hybrid son.[5] No ancient Jew, to our knowledge, used 'Son of God' in such a crudely literal sense. The common Jewish use was generic: all Jews were 'Sons of God' (the masculine in this case included females). The use of the singular 'Son of God' to refer to a specific person would be surprising, but it would not make the hearer think of unnatural modes of conception and of a hybrid offspring. As we noted in ch. 10, the title would imply special standing before God and an unusual power to accomplish good.

It is difficult to say precisely what New Testament authors meant by the title 'Son of God', though we have their writings and can study them. Matthew and Luke, who have stories of Mary's conceiving by the holy spirit (Matt. 1.20; Luke 1.34), also trace Jesus' lineage through Joseph, Mary's husband (Matt. 1.16; Luke 3.23). The gospels have other ways of defining Jesus as Son of God, apart from the stories of his conception and birth. In the story of Jesus' baptism, a dove descends and a voice from heaven addresses Jesus: 'You are my beloved Son' (Mark 1.11 // Luke 3.22).[6] This is a quotation of Psalm 2.7, where 'Son of God' is applied to the king of Israel – who was an ordinary human being. It appears that in Mark 'you are my Son' is intended as a statement of adoption; God gave Jesus special status *when he was baptized*. According to one passage in Paul's letters, Jesus was 'designated' or 'declared' 'Son of God in power' *by his resurrection*, not at the time of his conception (Rom. 1.4). That 'Son of God' did not, to Paul, refer to the way in which Jesus was conceived is also indicated in those passages where he speaks of Christians becoming children or Sons of God.

For all who are led by the Spirit of God are Sons[7] of God. For you did not receive a spirit of slavery . . . , but you have received a spirit of adoption. When we cry, 'Abba! Father!' it is that very spirit bearing witness . . . that we are Children of God, and if Children, then heirs, both heirs of God and co-heirs with Christ, provided that we suffer with him so that we may also be glorified with him. (Rom. 8.14–17; cf. Gal. 4.4–7)

This is another passage that shows the definition of sonship as adoption. Paul did not write that Christians were sired by a divine substitute for semen, but rather that they were adopted, and in that way became siblings of Christ, and thereby co-heirs with him – and he had been declared Son, not literally sired by God. In another passage Paul wrote that people who have faith are Sons of God (Gal. 3.26). In the surviving correspondence Paul does not call anyone 'Son of God' in the singular except Jesus, but there is no hint in his letters that he thinks that the title, when applied to Jesus, meant that he was only half human. Nor does the title require a story of miraculous conception. Jesus was the Son of God, but others could become Sons (children) of God. Jesus himself thought that people could become God's children: he told his followers that if they loved their enemies they would be 'Sons of God'.

The early Christians, then, used 'Son of God' of Jesus, but they did not think that he was a hybrid, half God and half human. They regarded 'Son of God' as a *high* designation, but we cannot go much beyond that. When Gentile converts started entering the new movement, they may have understood the title in light of the stories about Alexander the Great, or of their own mythology: Zeus took the form of a swan, had intercourse with Leda, and sired Helen and Polydeuces. The first followers of Jesus, however, when they started calling him 'Son of God', would have meant something much vaguer: a person standing in a special relationship to God, who chose him to accomplish a task of great importance.

I have spent this many words on the idea that Jesus was hybrid because that is what a lot of people – both Christian and non-Christian – think Christians believe. Matthew and Luke, in their birth narratives, do sow the seeds of this view, but even these accounts do not systematically suppose that God directly sired Jesus, since the genealogies trace Jesus' descent from David through Joseph (Matt. 1.2–16; Luke 3.23–38). In any case, the birth narratives did not shape the early Christian conception of Jesus as 'Son of God'; in the rest of early Christian literature – including the other material in Matthew and Luke – the title is less crudely literal. Jesus is a special 'Son of God', living in a nation of 'Sons of God'. I should also remind the reader of a point made above (pp. 133–5): the Christian creeds, once the fathers of the church got around to defining 'Son of God', are 100 per cent against the definition 'half and half'. In creedal terms, that is heresy.

The synoptic gospels use 'Son of God' of Jesus in a few main contexts besides the birth narratives. Some of these we have already noted, but for convenience and clarity I shall collect all the principal passages here: (1) the voice from heaven calls Jesus 'Son' at his baptism (Mark 1.11 & parr.), a declaration that is repeated in the story of the transfiguration (Mark 9.7 & parr.); (2) demons call him 'Son of God' (Mark 3.11; Luke 4.41 and elsewhere); (3) in the temptation stories in Matthew and Luke the devil addresses Jesus as the possible Son of God ('if you are the Son of God': Matt. 4.3–7 // Luke 4.3–9); (4) at Jesus' trial the high priest asks if he is Son of God (Mark 14.61 & parr.); (5) the centurion who saw Jesus die confesses that he was Son of God (Mark 15.39 // Matt. 27.54). The only passage that might have a 'metaphysical' meaning – Jesus was something other than merely human – is the question at the trial, since the high priest follows the question by shouting 'blasphemy' when Jesus does not deny the title. We shall return to this passage in the next chapter. With regard to the other contexts, we see that the title means that Jesus had special status and the power to exorcize; it does not mean that he was not fully human. Moreover, we can only ask what *others* may have meant when they used it, since Jesus does not call himself 'Son of God' (except in the Markan trial scene, discussed in the next chapter).

The third principal title in the synoptics is Son of Man. In Jewish scripture this phrase has various meanings. In Ezekiel 'Son of Man' is simply the prophet's designation for himself: God speaks to him as 'Son of Man', which the NRSV translates, quite appropriately, 'mortal' (e.g., Ezek. 12.2). In Daniel the phrase 'one like a Son of Man' refers to the nation of Israel, or perhaps to its angelic representative. In the visions of this part of Daniel the other kingdoms of the world are represented by fantastic beasts; Israel, by contrast, is represented by a human-like figure (Dan. 7.1–14). In one of the parts that make up the pseudepigraphical work *I Enoch* the Son of Man is a heavenly figure who judges the world (e.g., *I Enoch* chs. 46, 48 and 69.26–9). This part of *I Enoch*, however, is the one section that cannot be proved to be pre-Christian.[8] Thus we cannot say that Jewish eschatology had already established the idea that a heavenly figure called 'the Son of Man' would judge humanity at the end of normal history, though this is possible.

'Son of Man' is used in the gospels in three major ways:

(1) It is sometimes a circumlocution for 'a person' or for the speaker, 'I': 'The sabbath was made for humans, not humans for the sabbath; so the Son of Man is lord even of the sabbath' (Mark 2.28). Here the phrase could mean 'I myself', but more likely it is simply parallel to 'humans' preceding, and thus means 'a human being is lord of the sabbath'. In other cases, however, 'Son of Man' certainly means Jesus himself: Jesus said to a would-be follower, 'Foxes have holes, and birds of the air have nests; but the Son of Man has nowhere to lay his head' (Matt. 8.20 // Luke 9.58). This is a warning of the hardship involved in following Jesus.

(2) In predicting his own death Jesus spoke of 'the Son of Man': 'He began to teach them that the Son of Man must suffer many things' (Mark 8.31). In these passages the phrase also means 'I'.

(3) The one who would come from heaven and usher in the kingdom of God is called 'Son of Man'. We saw above that Paul expected 'the Lord' to descend from heaven 'with a cry of

command, with the archangel's call, and with the sound of the
trumpet of God' (I Thess. 4.16). He calls this prediction 'the
word of the Lord' (4.15). The synoptics attribute similar sayings
to Jesus, but instead of 'the Lord' they speak of 'the Son of
Man'. The clearest parallels to Paul's saying are in Matthew:[9]
'the Son of Man is to come with his angels in the glory of his
Father' (16.27); the 'sign of the Son of Man' will appear in
heaven, and people will see 'the Son of Man coming on the
clouds of heaven with power and great glory; and he will send
out his angels with a loud trumpet call' (24.30f.). Like Paul,
Jesus expected this to happen soon: 'Truly, I say to you, there
are some standing here who will not taste death before they see
the Son of Man coming in his kingdom' (Matt. 16.28 // Mark
8.38 // Luke 9.26). It appears here that a saying by Jesus, 'the Son
of Man will come from heaven', has become for Paul 'the Lord
will come from heaven'. By 'Lord' Paul means Jesus: this is a
prediction of 'the second coming', when the resurrected Lord
returns. It is less certain, however, what Jesus meant when he
predicted the coming of the 'Son of Man'.

Let us accept all three main groups as being authentic words of
Jesus.[10] What is not certain is whether or not Jesus meant himself in
speaking of the future Son of Man. It is to be noted that no two of
the meanings ever occur together. We do not find, 'The Son of
Man must suffer and die *and* return', and it is not clear that we
should combine (2) and (3). Further, at his trial, Jesus seems to have
distinguished himself from the future Son of Man.

And the high priest said to him, 'I adjure you by the living God, tell us if
you are the Christ, the Son of God.' Jesus said to him, 'You have said so.
But I tell you, hereafter you will see the Son of Man seated at the right
hand of Power, and coming on the clouds of heaven.' (Matt. 26.63f.)

The word 'but' (Greek *plēn*) is adversative: 'But on the other hand',
and thus, according to Matthew, Jesus claimed to be expecting a
heavenly figure, not his own return. Mark combines the titles: Jesus
accepted the designations Messiah and Son of God, and added that
the Son of Man will come on clouds (Mark 14.61f.).
It is not possible to come to a firm conclusion about Jesus' use of

the phrase 'Son of Man'. He used it; sometimes he used it of himself; he expected the Son of Man to come from heaven; but it is not certain that he identified himself as that future Son of Man.

Because of the interest that has always attached to titles, I have wanted to offer a sketch of various possible meanings and their use in the synoptic gospels. I wish to return, however, to the main point. We do not learn precisely what Jesus thought of himself and his relationship to God by studying titles. There are three reasons for this. The first is that there were no hard definitions of 'Messiah', 'Son of God' or 'Son of Man' in the Judaism of Jesus' day. Even if he had constantly called himself by all three titles, we could learn what he thought of himself only by studying him – not by studying the titles in other sources. The second is that we do not know that he gave himself titles. The evidence is that he rejected the title 'Messiah'. As far as we know, he did not call himself 'Son of God'. He did refer to himself as 'Son of Man', but we do not know in what sense. In particular, we do not know if he thought that he would be the future Son of Man who would come on clouds.

The third reason that the study of titles does not tell us what Jesus thought of himself is that we have better information. Jesus thought that the twelve disciples represented the tribes of Israel, but also that they would judge them. Jesus was clearly above the disciples; a person who is above the judges of Israel is very high indeed. We also know that he considered his mission as being of absolutely paramount importance, and he thought that how people responded to his message was more important than other important duties. He thought that God was about to bring in his kingdom, and that he, Jesus, was God's last emissary. He thought therefore that he was in some sense 'king'. He rode into Jerusalem on an ass, recalling a prophecy about the king riding on an ass, and he was executed for claiming to be 'king of the Jews' (see the next chapter). There was no title in the history of Judaism that fully communicated all this, and Jesus seems to have been quite reluctant to adopt a title for himself. I think that even 'king' is not precisely correct, since Jesus regarded God as king. My own favourite term for his conception of himself is 'viceroy'. God was king, but Jesus represented him and would represent him in the coming kingdom.

16. JESUS' LAST WEEK

About the year 30 CE Jesus, his disciples and other followers went to Jerusalem for Passover. Technically, there were two separate feasts: Passover, which lasted only one day, and Unleavened Bread, which lasted the next seven days. Passover falls on the fourteenth day of the Jewish month Nisan, Unleavened Bread runs from the fifteenth of Nisan through the twenty-first. For all practical purposes, this was one long festival, and Jews often spoke of the entire eight-day period as being either 'Passover' or 'Unleavened Bread'.[1] Passover (as I shall call it) is a 'pilgrimage festival', one of the three that all male Jews were supposed to attend each year.[2] The spread of the Jewish population, both inside and outside of Palestine, meant that this was no longer possible, but nevertheless a lot of people attended each of the major festivals, and Passover was the most popular. Although the Bible requires only males to attend, men brought their wives and children (*Antiq.* 11.109). This was the big holiday of the year. Whole towns emptied as people streamed to Jerusalem.[3]

Josephus refers to fantastically large numbers of people. He relates that the priests counted lambs at one Passover and found that 255,600 had been slain. If one lamb served ten people (Josephus' calculation), there were more than two and a half million people in attendance. Discussing another Passover, he estimated that three million were present.[4] Everyone agrees that these numbers are too large. My own calculation is that the city and the Temple area could accommodate about 300,000 to 400,000 pilgrims, which is a more reasonable figure.[5] Some of the pilgrims lodged with householders in Jerusalem, and some stayed in nearby villages (Mark 11.12), but many of them pitched tents outside the city walls (*Antiq.* 17.217). The large crowds meant that the festivals were sometimes the occasion of civil unrest. As a consequence, the prefect came to

Jerusalem, with extra troops. Roman soldiers patrolled the roofs of the porticoes of the Temple, so that they could be on the look-out for trouble.[6]

Most pilgrims had to come a week early. The Bible forbids anyone with corpse impurity to celebrate Passover (Num. 9.9f.), and most people acquired corpse impurity in the course of a year. It was incurred by being in a room with a corpse, by touching it or by walking over a grave. Funeral processions and burials were occasions on which not only family and friends, but also more distant acquaintances and sometimes even strangers mourned with the bereaved family. Taking care of the dead and comforting those who had lost loved ones was a religious duty, and one that very few people would evade. In a village or small town, a death probably meant that most residents acquired corpse impurity. The removal of this impurity required a week (Num. 19). On the third day and the seventh day of the purification period, the impure person was sprinkled with a mixture of water and the ashes of a red heifer. After the second sprinkling, the impure person would bathe and wash his or her clothes, and then be pure. It is possible that priests took some of the special mixture to towns and villages in the immediate vicinity of Jerusalem, but most pilgrims had to be purified in Jerusalem, and this required them to come a week before the festival began. Philo discussed the religious value of this vigil, which he apparently had experienced,[7] and Josephus refers to the fact that pilgrims assembled for the feast of the Unleavened Bread on the eighth day of Nisan.[8]

The pilgrims, then, waited for a week near the Temple and prepared themselves spiritually while their bodies were being purified. On the afternoon of the fourteenth one member of every party took a lamb[9] to the Temple. There it was sacrificed, flayed and partially eviscerated. The owner brought it back, and it was roasted whole. That evening was the Passover meal. Since the Jewish day changes at sunset, the meal was held on the fifteenth, the first day of Unleavened Bread. In the year Jesus died, the lambs were slain on Thursday the fourteenth, and the meal was that evening, by the Jewish reckoning the next day, Friday.[10]

On the eighth of Nisan, Jesus and his followers, along with a vast multitude, entered Jerusalem.[11] Let us first note what is not in the gospels: they do not say that Jesus and his followers performed the basic religious acts that marked preparation for Passover: being sprinkled on the tenth and fourteenth of Nisan, bathing, and taking a lamb to the Temple on the fourteenth. The gospels remark that, on the first day of the festival, the lambs were slaughtered (Mark 14.12 & parr.), but they say nothing about Jesus or one of his followers joining the crowd and sacrificing a lamb. They have, instead, a curious story of preparation for the meal: Jesus told the disciples to go to Jerusalem, where they would meet a man carrying a jar of water. They were to follow the man and see what house he entered. They should then tell the householder that 'the teacher' would use the upper room for his Passover meal. Then, the gospels relate, the disciples 'prepared the Passover' (Mark 14.12–16 & parr.). Perhaps 'they prepared' means 'they bought a lamb, had it slaughtered at the Temple and put it on a spit to roast'. Similarly, when, during the days between the eighth and the fourteenth, Jesus is depicted as teaching near the Temple, we could imagine that he and the disciples were also sprinkled with the purifying mixture. But there is no explicit reference to purification, any more than to the sacrifice.

We cannot be sure just what this silence means. I think that it is highly likely that Jesus and his followers were purified, and that one of the disciples took a lamb to be slaughtered in the Temple. The readers of the gospels knew that animals were sacrificed at festivals, and they also knew that festivals and sacrifices involved purification. This was part and parcel of ancient life: Jews, Greeks, Syrians, Romans and the other inhabitants of the Roman empire all participated in such rites. Only the details were different. Thus failure to say that Jesus and his followers did what everyone else did is probably not significant. Had they not observed the laws and traditions, that would have been remarkable, but observance would cause no comment. Josephus, for example, who confirms that Jews came to Jerusalem a week before Passover, does not say what they did during those days (*War* 6.290). It did not matter for the purposes of his narrative just what they did; everybody knew well enough. Other sources, beginning with Numbers 19, and including Philo and rabbinic literature, reveal the specifics of the rites of purification.

With regard to Jesus' being purified, we should once more recall that the gospels refer to one purity law: leprosy. After Jesus healed the leper, he told the man to show himself to a priest and to do what Moses commanded (Mark 1.44 & parr.). We add to this the fact that the synoptics reveal no instance in which Jesus actually transgressed the law or counselled others to transgress.[12] This all makes it overwhelmingly likely that Jesus and his followers were purified, and that they ate a lamb that had been sacrificed in the Temple.

We shall now consider what the gospels positively tell us about Jesus' last week. I shall pass quickly over a lot of the material in the last chapters of the synoptics. The authors place in Jerusalem a fair amount of teaching material, and on the whole it is quite appropriate. Here we meet a question about paying taxes to Caesar (Mark 12.13–17 & parr.), a topic much more appropriate to Jerusalem than to Galilee, since in Judaea money and goods went directly into Roman hands, while in Galilee taxes were paid to Antipas, who in turn paid tribute to Rome. Direct taxation was more distasteful than was indirect tribute. Similarly it is in these chapters that we meet the Sadducees (Mark 12.18–27 & parr.). The Sadducean party was aristocratic, and few if any Sadducees would be found in Galilean villages. I pass over this teaching material, not because I regard it as unreliable, but in order to get to the heart of the matter: what Jesus did that led to his crucifixion.

The five main scenes that compose the drama of Jesus' last week are these:

(1) Jesus entered Jerusalem on a donkey; people welcomed him by shouting, 'Hosanna! Blessed is he who comes in the name of the Lord! Blessed is the kingdom of our father David that is coming' (Mark 11.9f.). According to Matthew and Luke, they explicitly called him 'son of David' or 'king' (Matt. 21.9; Luke 19.38).

(2) He went to the Temple, where he turned over the tables of money-changers and the seats of those who sold pigeons (Mark 11.15–19 & parr.).

(3) He shared a last supper with his disciples, saying that he would not drink wine again 'until that day when I drink it new in the kingdom of God' (Mark 14.22–5 & parr.).

(4) The high priest's guards arrested him and took him before the high priest and his council. Witnesses accused him of having threatened to destroy the Temple, but he was not convicted.

According to Mark (but not Matthew and Luke), he admitted to the high priest that he was both 'Christ' ('Messiah') and 'Son of God', and he was convicted of blasphemy (Mark 14.43–64; cf. parr.).

(5) His captors sent him to Pilate, who interrogated him and then ordered that he be crucified for claiming to be 'king of the Jews' (Mark 15.1–5, 15, 18, 26 & parr.).

These five incidents pose four central questions. What was the meaning of Jesus' actions (1–3)? Why did the high priest arrest Jesus (4)? Why did he send him to Pilate (5)? Why did Pilate execute him (5)?

Jesus' Actions

What was the meaning of Jesus' actions? They were probably all symbolic. Symbolic actions were part of a prophet's vocabulary. They simultaneously drew attention and conveyed information. Some examples from the Hebrew Bible: Isaiah walked 'naked and barefoot for three years as a sign and a portent against Egypt and Ethiopia' (Isa. 20.3); God commanded Jeremiah to break a pot and proclaim that the Temple would be destroyed (Jer. 19.1–13); Jeremiah also wore a yoke to indicate that Judah should submit to Babylon (chs. 27–8). Ezekiel performed much more complicated actions, which required a good deal of explanation, such as lying for long periods of time first on one side and then on the other (Ezek. chs. 4–5; 12.1–16; 24.15–24). All of these signs would be difficult to understand without verbal interpretation. Wearing a yoke symbolizes submission, but to whom? Breaking a pot symbolizes destruction, but of what? Going naked and barefoot is certainly striking, and everyone would know that the prophet was protesting against something, but they would have to ask him what it was to be sure.

Jesus also used symbolic actions, as we have already seen: his use of the number twelve when speaking of his disciples almost certainly conveyed his intention to call all Israel, which had at one time been divided into twelve tribes; Jesus and possibly others saw his miracles, especially the exorcisms, as symbolizing the conquest of evil and the near arrival of the kingdom of God. The three actions in Jerusalem are equally symbolic, though in some cases the symbolism is hard to read.

The first of these three acts is straightforward: Jesus rode into Jerusalem on an ass, thus fulfilling a prophecy in Zechariah, which is cited by Matthew, but which would have been apparent to many:

> Rejoice greatly, O daughter of Zion!
>> Shout aloud, O daughter of Jerusalem!
> Lo, your king comes to you;
>> triumphant and victorious is he,
> humble and riding on a donkey,
>> on a colt, the foal of a donkey. (Zech. 9.9)

It is possible to think either that the prophecy created the event or that the prophecy created the story and that the event never occurred. This is one of a sizeable number of cases in which we cannot be absolutely sure whether Jesus himself acted out a prophecy, or the Christian tradition depicted him as doing so. I incline to the view that it was Jesus himself who read the prophecy and decided to fulfil it: that here he implicitly declared himself to be 'king'. His followers understood and agreed: they hailed the coming kingdom (Mark 11.10) or even Jesus himself as king (Matt. 21.9; Luke 19.38).

Matthew and Luke refer to 'crowds' or 'the multitude', while Mark says that 'many' participated in hailing Jesus. If there was actually a large crowd, however, we must explain how it is that Jesus lived for another week. A public demonstration, accompanied by shouts of 'king' or even 'kingdom', would have been highly inflammatory. Passover was a prime time for trouble-makers to incite the crowd, and both the high priest and the Roman prefect were alert to the danger. I can only suggest that Jesus' demonstration was quite modest: he performed a symbolic gesture for insiders, for those who had eyes to see.

The second action is more difficult to interpret. Jesus turned over 'the tables of the money-changers and the seats of those who sold pigeons' (Mark 11.15 & parr.). He commented, '"My house shall be called a house of prayer", but you have made it "a den of robbers"' (Mark 11.17 & parr.). This statement brings together phrases from

Isaiah ('house of prayer', Isa. 56.7) and Jeremiah ('den of robbers', Jer. 7.11). Jesus also made, however, a second and possibly a third statement about the Temple. The authors of the synoptics attribute to him a *prediction* that the Temple would be destroyed (Mark 13.1f. & parr.), and they attribute to his accusers at his trial the testimony that he *threatened* to destroy the Temple (Mark 14.58 // Matt. 26.61). The threat comes up again, during the crucifixion scene; as he hung on the cross, onlookers taunted him: 'Aha! You who would destroy the Temple . . . , save yourself, and come down from the cross!' (Mark 15.29f. // Matt. 27.40). Later Stephen, an early Christian, was accused of saying that 'Jesus of Nazareth will destroy this place', that is, the Temple (Acts 6.14). These various statements make it difficult to say just what it was that Jesus' action in the Temple symbolized. Was it cleansing or destruction? If destruction, was it a prediction or a threat?

There is no way of eliminating any of these possibilities. It is conceivable that Jesus thought that the trade in the Temple area was dishonest and that he foresaw that his nation would one day revolt against Rome, which would lead to the destruction of the Temple; moral reform and foresight are both possible. We shall consider first reform, which is the implication of the quotation from Jeremiah 7.11: the Temple is a 'den of robbers'. There is no hint in other sources that the sacred money was being misappropriated by being used for purposes other than support of the Temple and its sacrifices;[13] but because of the general principle that reform and improvement are always possible, we may grant in advance that Jesus could have sought to amend 'the system'. What is lacking is any other indication that he wanted to reform the large and complex Temple system. Support of the Temple and its ministers was a major aspect of Jewish life: Temple tax, agricultural tithes, minor agricultural offerings ('first fruits'), redemption of first-born sons and animals, sin and guilt offerings, festivals, offerings of animals to provide food for banquets and festivities – Temple worship, in one way or another, affected every area of life. Had Jesus thought that the entire system was corrupt, that the priests were criminals, that sacrifices were wrong and should be done away with – or anything of the sort – we should have more material pointing in that direction. The Temple was central to Palestinian Judaism and important to all Jews everywhere. To be against it would be to oppose Judaism as a religion. It would also be an attack on the main unifying symbol of the Jewish people. If Jesus really assailed this central institution, we would have some evidence of this apart from the incident of the money-changers' tables. Moreover, we would learn of Jesus' opposition not only from the gospels, but also from Acts and the letters of Paul. In the gospels there are 'woes' against Galilean villages, though not against the Temple. Jesus seems to criticize rich landowners in parables, but not the aristocratic priests. He upheld the principal purity law that is mentioned in the gospels (leprosy, discussed above). He paid the Temple tax, even if he was a little reluctant to do so (Matt. 17.24–7). The few passages in the synoptics that deal with the Temple and priestly prerogatives are favourable, and no material represents him as a reformer of cult and taxes – except, possibly, this passage. If this was a singular flash of anger, it tells us little about him and his mission.

What about the second tradition, the prediction that the Temple would be destroyed (Mark 13.1f. & parr.)? Was this merely a sagacious political prognostication? Again, there are virtually no other traditions of this sort. For example, Jesus could have warned Antipas that his passion for Herodias would cost him his position (it did). Jeremiah's prophecies dealt largely with political and military matters, but not the sayings of Jesus, except for one in Luke: 'When you see Jerusalem surrounded by armies, then know that its desolation has come near' (Luke 21.20). Scholars generally maintain that this is Luke's own revision of a saying in Matthew and Mark, which he brings 'up to date'. This seems to me to be correct. Luke, that is, wrote after the Roman armies had in fact surrounded and destroyed Jerusalem, and his knowledge of what happened in the year 70 influenced his revision of Mark.[14] If this is so, there is no tradition of political or military predictions in the gospels – unless we interpret the prediction of the destruction of the Temple in this way.

Because of the general impossibility of proving negatives in historical research ('Jesus never thought . . . '), we cannot completely rule out either political sagacity or moral indignation, but we can say that Jesus did not otherwise (as far as we can tell) spend his time making political predictions and attacking the commerce that was necessary to the functioning of the Temple. He did, however, have quite a lot to say about a looming dramatic change to be wrought by God. This inclines me to think that the action of overturning symbolized destruction rather than cleansing as an act of moral reform. We shall look a little more closely at the sayings, first the prediction and then the threat.

This is the prediction:

And as he came out of the Temple, one of his disciples said to him, 'Look, Teacher, what wonderful stones and what wonderful buildings!' And Jesus said to him, 'Do you see these great buildings? There will not be left here one stone upon another, that will not be thrown down.' (Mark 13.1f.)

According to Matthew, Jesus said this to 'the disciples', not just to one (Matt. 24.1f.), and Luke has him address 'some people' (21.5f.). The principal thing to note is that the prediction was not precisely fulfilled. When the Romans took the city in 70 CE, they left much of the Temple wall standing; indeed, much of it is still there, supporting the present Muslim holy area. Most of the stones in the surviving wall weigh between two and five tons, but some, especially those on the corners, are much larger. One is 12 metres (c. 39 ft.) long and weighs almost 400 tons.[15] Jesus said that not one would be left on another.

When 'prophecies' are written after the event – that is, when a later writer composes a bogus prophecy – the prophecy and the event are usually in perfect agreement. Had the prediction of Mark 13.1f. & parr. been written after 70, we would expect it to say that the Temple would be destroyed by fire, not that the stone walls would be completely torn down. This prophecy, then, is probably pre-70, and it may be Jesus' own.

What about the threat? The authors of the gospels are at pains to assure us that Jesus did not really threaten to destroy the Temple.

And some stood up and bore false witness against him, saying, 'We heard him say, "I will destroy this Temple that is made with hands, and in three days I will build another, not made with hands."' Yet not even so did their testimony agree. (Mark 14.57–9)

Matthew has substantially the same tradition, but he does not have the phrases 'made with hands' and 'not made with hands'. The accusations against Jesus while he was on the cross do not quote him directly: ' "You who would destroy the Temple and build it in three days" ' (Mark 15.29 // Matt. 27.40).

While Matthew and Mark attribute this accusation to 'false witnesses', Luke leaves it out entirely. This is an extreme form of denying that Jesus said it. The early Christians did not want Jesus to look like a rebel or even a trouble-maker. Christianity, they wished to maintain, produced good and loyal citizens; the rulers of the cities and provinces of Syria, Asia Minor, Greece, Macedonia and Italy had nothing to fear. The author of Luke had this as a central concern, as may be seen in Acts, where he repeatedly blames everyone except the Christian apostles for the fact that wherever they went there was a certain amount of civil tumult. This concern probably explains why Luke does not have the threat at all, and a similar concern explains why Matthew and Mark maintain so vigorously that Jesus did not threaten the Temple.

They protest too much. It is probable that he made some kind of threat. We shall see this most clearly if we consider the possibility that Jesus really only *predicted* that sometime or other the Temple would be destroyed. This would mean that, as the gospels maintain, his enemies decided to say that he *threatened* it. They conspired to testify falsely against him, but they neglected to agree on what their testimony would be, and so the accusation was thrown out of court. This sort of mismanaged plot does not carry conviction. It is more likely that Jesus said and did something that onlookers believed to be a threat and that genuinely alarmed them. They reported it to the authorities. But when they were examined in court, they – like other eyewitnesses – gave slightly different accounts. We cannot know precisely what Jesus said. I shall assume that he *threateningly predicted* the destruction of the Temple; that is, he predicted destruction in such a way as to make some people think that he was threatening it.

It is perfectly reasonable to put together Jesus' action against the money-changers and his statement about the destruction of the Temple. The authors of the gospels wished to keep those two elements separate: on one occasion he cleansed the Temple, on another he predicted its destruction. There was probably a connection between the two. That, at least, is the way his action and words appeared to others. If they connected a saying about destruction with his symbolic action of overturning tables, we can understand why he appeared to be threatening the Temple. This created deep offence, which surfaced when he was on trial for his life, while he hung on the cross, and later when Stephen was tried. We cannot attribute this persistent tradition of a threat against the Temple to the authors of the gospels; they wished it would go away.

If Jesus threatened the Temple, or predicted its destruction shortly after he overturned tables in its commercial area (which would amount to the same thing), he did not think that he and his small band could knock down the walls, so that not one stone was left on another. He thought that God would destroy it. As a good Jewish prophet, he could have thought that God would employ a foreign army for this destruction; but, as a radical first-century eschatologist, he probably thought that God would do it directly.

Ancient people did not think that the destruction or preservation of a Temple was decided entirely by the relative strength of two armies. Truly secular political prognostication is not really an option for understanding Jesus. If the Persians damaged the temple of Athena in Athens, it was because Athena had decided to let them do it, or because the goddess herself was weaker than the Persian deities and was not able to defend her abode. Josephus reveals the depth of this thinking in the ordinary pious Jew. He describes numerous portents of the coming destruction of the Temple. At the feast of Weeks, for example, the priests heard first 'a commotion and a din', then 'a voice as of a host, "We are departing hence."'[16] This departure permitted the destruction of the Temple. Jesus also thought that God was in some sense in the Temple.[17] According to Matthew 23.21, he said that the person 'who swears by the Temple, swears by it and by him who dwells in it'. If Jesus thought that God dwelt in the Temple, he could hardly have thought that the Romans could destroy it against God's own intention. They might be his instruments, but they could not impose their will on him.

If Jesus said *anything at all* about the coming destruction of the Temple, he meant that God would destroy it, or have it destroyed by his agents. This, coupled by a hostile gesture, would be a *threat*. But no one – neither Jesus, nor those who heard and saw him, nor the high priest, nor Pilate – thought that he could actually tear the Temple walls down. If, however, he only said what God was going to do, why arrest him? Since God would do whatever he willed, why could not the high priest and others simply have disagreed that

Jesus knew? People were always afraid of prophets, at least a little. Antipas (or both Antipas and Herodias) feared John the Baptist.[18] Antipas had enough troops to quell an angry crowd, if it came to that; and he and his family had often been criticized. But he decided to silence John rather than let him continue preaching. At an earlier date one group of Jews wanted the prophet Honi to curse another group of Jews. He would not. They all thought that his curse would be effective, and when he refused to utter it he was killed.[19] Prophets were dangerous. They might arouse a crowd, which could easily get out of hand (especially at Passover). At another level they were dangerous because God listened to them or might listen to them.

I conclude that Jesus' symbolic action of overthrowing tables in the Temple was understood in connection with a saying about destruction, and that the action and the saying, in the view of the authorities, constituted a prophetic threat. Moreover, I think it highly probable that Jesus himself intended the action to predict the destruction of the Temple, rather than to symbolize its need of purification. It is impossible, however, to prove that the statement about a 'den of robbers' was not actually said by Jesus, or that what he said was 'I will destroy the Temple.' I must confess that I doubt the authenticity of the 'den of robbers' statement. It looks to me like an easy phrase for the evangelists to lift from Jeremiah to make Jesus appear politically innocuous to Greek-speaking Gentile readers. Many people then as now believed that periodic reform of the system was a good thing. Apollonius of Tyana became quite famous as a reformer of cultic practice. A real reformer, however, should have more of a programme of reform than Jesus seems to have had. If people could not buy sacrifical doves in the commercial area of the Temple, how could they get them? If they carried them from their dovecotes at home, the birds might become blemished. And the money-changers offered a mere convenience for pilgrims. The Temple required payment of the Temple tax in a reliable coinage, one that was not subject to adulteration by the admixture of too much base metal (a method often used by governments that were short of cash). People could acquire this reliable Tyrian coinage anywhere, as far as the Temple was concerned, but apparently many preferred to bring their own currency and change it at the Temple. So what would Jesus substitute if he eliminated these two trades? Jesus the thoughtful social and economic planner, who has again become popular, simply cannot be found in the gospels. He could have said 'den of robbers', but one saying would not make him a reformer.

He was a prophet, and an eschatological prophet. He thought that God was about to destroy the Temple. And then what? The saying continues, according to his accusers, 'in three days I will build another', and Mark adds 'not made with hands' (Mark 14.58 // Matt. 26.61). Jesus probably thought that in the new age, when the twelve tribes of Israel were again assembled, there would be a new and perfect Temple, built by God himself. That was standard eschatological or new-age thinking. The Christian Book of Revelation says that, when the new Jerusalem comes down from heaven, there will be no Temple, but the explanation is Christological: 'its Temple is the Lord God the Almighty and the Lamb' (Rev. 21.22). When the Book of Revelation was written, Christians believed that the age of the Temple was over, and that the ideal world would dispense with animal sacrifice, since the true Lamb had been sacrificed, but that is not what non-Christian Jews thought. Following the biblical prophets, they hoped for a new and glorious Temple: 'The glory of Lebanon shall come to you, the cypress, the plane and the pine, to beautify the place of my sanctuary; and I will glorify where my feet rest' (Isa. 60.13). The author of one of the sections of *I Enoch* reported on a vision:

And I stood up to see till they folded up that old house; and carried off all the pillars, and all the beams and ornaments of the house were at the same time folded up with it, and they carried it off . . . And I saw till the Lord . . . brought a new house greater and loftier than that first [one], and set it in the place of the first . . . : and its pillars were new, and its ornaments were new and larger than those of the first . . . (*I Enoch* 90.28f.)

These quotations exemplify both the expectation of a new or better Temple and also an important development in Jewish thought. In general, as the years went on, people thought that God would do more in connection with the new age: their expectations became more grandiose and more supernatural. In the classical period of Israelite prophecy (the eighth to the fifth centuries BCE), prophets thought that, for the most part, God worked in history by using human rulers and armies. This idea did not entirely vanish, but many Jews began looking back to more dramatic times as the model of how God would act in the future. God had once parted the sea, had produced manna in the wilderness, had caused the sun to stand still, had brought down the walls of Jericho. In the future he would do such great deeds and even greater. In the decades after Jesus, Theudas thought that God would part the water of the Jordan River, and the Egyptian expected him to cause the walls of Jerusalem to fall down. One of the authors of *I Enoch*, as we just saw, expected God to bring down a new and greater Temple, and the author of the *Temple Scroll* had the same hope.[20] I have more than once cited evidence that is pertinent to this issue.[21] To repeat briefly: the author of the Qumran *War Scroll* expected angels, led by Michael, to fight on behalf of the Jewish armies, but the final blows to be struck by God himself. The author of *Psalms of Solomon* expected the Davidic Messiah neither to 'rely on horse and rider and bow', nor to 'collect gold and silver for war', nor to 'build up hope in a multitude for a day of war'; he would, instead, rely on God (*Psalms of Solomon* 17.33f.).

This is what I mean by saying that Jesus was a 'radical eschatologist'. He expected God to act in a decisive way, so as to change things fundamentally. Jesus, like virtually all other first-century Jews, assumed that there would still be a Temple. On this as on other points, however, he did not give details.

This discussion of the sayings about the Temple has been lengthy. Some readers may think that I have made too much of the issue. I think that it is almost impossible to make too much of the Temple in first-century Jewish Palestine. Modern people so readily think of religion without sacrifice that they fail to see how novel that idea is. Judaism eventually had to give up the idea of returning to the sacrifical worship of God, and Christianity eventually came to see Jesus' death as the complete replacement of the Temple cult. But in Jesus' day these ideas lay in the future. Jesus had either to accept the Temple, oppose it or reform it. He seems to have accepted it, but to have thought that it would be replaced in the new age. After his death and resurrection, his followers continued to worship in the Temple. In Acts, Paul was arrested for trying to take a Gentile into the Temple.[22] Such activities are compatible with Jesus' view as I reconstruct it.

Now we turn to the third symbolic gesture of Jesus' final week: the last supper. The passage in general has the strongest possible support, putting it on a par with the saying on divorce in terms of certainty: there are two slightly different forms, which have reached us through two independent channels, the synoptic tradition and the letters of Paul.[23] I shall quote three versions so that the reader may compare them.

Mark 14.22–5	Luke 22.17–20	I Corinthians 11.24–6
And as they were eating, he took bread, and blessed, and broke it, and gave it to them, and said, 'Take; this is my body.' And he took a cup, and when he had given thanks he gave it to them, and they all drank of it. And he said to them, 'This is my blood of the covenant, which is poured out for many. Truly, I say to you, I shall not drink again of the fruit of the vine until that day when I drink it new in the kingdom of God.	And he took a cup, and when he had given thanks he said, 'Take this, and divide it among yourselves; for I tell you that from now on I shall not drink of the fruit of the vine until the kingdom of God comes.' And he took bread, and when he had given thanks he broke it and gave it to them, saying, 'This is my body which is given for you. Do this in remembrance of me.' And likewise the cup after supper, saying, 'This cup which is poured out for you is the new covenant in my blood.'	And when he had given thanks, he broke [the bread] and said, 'This is my body that is for you. Do this in remembrance of me.' In the same way he took the cup also, after supper, saying, 'This cup is the new covenant in my blood. Do this, as often as you drink it, in remembrance of me.' For as often as you eat this bread and drink the cup, you proclaim the Lord's death until he comes.

As is the case with the divorce pericope, we cannot completely reconcile the versions with one another. Jesus said something about the cup, the bread, his body and his blood. According to Matthew and Mark, when he passed a cup of wine he said 'this is my blood said 'this is my blood of the covenant' (Matt. 26.28 // Mark 14.24). Luke has 'this cup . . . is the new covenant in my blood' (22.20), and Paul has the same wording (1 Cor. 11.25). For present purposes I do not need to try to decide precisely what Jesus said about his blood and the cup. Without knowing this, we can see that he regarded the meal as symbolic and as pointing to the future kingdom. 'I shall not drink again of the fruit of the vine until that day when I drink it new in the kingdom of God' (Mark 14.25 // Matt. 26.29). Luke has, 'I shall not drink of the fruit of the vine until the kingdom of God comes' (22.18). Paul instructed his readers that when they ate the bread and drank from the cup, they were proclaiming 'the Lord's death until he comes' (1 Cor. 11.26). The meal pointed forward, to the new age. Jesus' eating and drinking with sinners (Matt. 11.18f.) probably pointed in the same direction. As one of the parables put it, the kingdom of God is like a wedding feast (Matt. 22.1–14).

As we noted above, we cannot know how literally Jesus thought about drinking wine in the kingdom. The entire theme could well be metaphorical. Nevertheless, this was his last symbolic gesture, and almost his last words to his closest followers. He solemnly proclaimed, in effect, that the kingdom was at hand and that he would share in it.

The saying makes it highly probable that Jesus knew that he was a marked man. Conceivably he thought that God would intervene before he was arrested and executed. In any case he did not flee. He went to the Mount of Olives to pray and to wait – to wait for the reaction of the authorities and possibly the intervention of God. According to the gospels, he prayed to be spared, but he did so completely privately (Mark 14.32–42 & parr.). The prayer that they attribute to Jesus, however, is perfectly reasonable. He hoped that he would not die, but he resigned himself to the will of God.

The three symbolic acts, then, all point to the coming kingdom and Jesus' own role. He will feast with his disciples, there will be a new or improved Temple, and he will be 'king'.

Jesus' Arrest

We turn now to our second main question: why did the high priest arrest Jesus? We have already substantially answered it: most immediately, the cause of Jesus' arrest was his prophetic demonstration at the Temple. At least some people thought that he threatened it. If the high priest Caiaphas and his advisers knew that Jesus had been hailed as 'king' when he entered Jerusalem, they would have already worried about him. The Temple action sealed his fate. The Markan trial scene seems to presuppose the high priest's knowledge of both events. Jesus was first accused of threatening the Temple. The witnesses, however, did not agree. Then Caiaphas asked Jesus if he were 'the Messiah, the son of the Blessed' (Mark 14.61). In the previous chapter we briefly discussed the different versions of his answer. According to Mark, he answered, 'Yes'; according to Luke, he replied only 'You say that I am'; and, according to Matthew, he said, 'You have said so; *but* [on the other hand] I say that you will see the Son of Man . . . '[24] Whatever Jesus' answer, however, we note that the question implies some knowledge of Jesus' pretensions or (more probably) knowledge of the cries of his followers when he entered the city. Jesus had also been teaching about 'the kingdom' while in Jerusalem, and this would have added to the negative impression. The high priest wanted him dead for the same reason Antipas wanted John dead: he might cause trouble.

We saw above (pp. 25–7) that the high priest was responsible for good order in Judaea in general, and in Jerusalem in particular. Caiaphas served longer than any other high priest during the periods of direct Roman rule, and this is good evidence that he was capable. If the high priest did not preserve order, the Roman prefect would intervene militarily, and the situation might get out of hand. As long as the Temple guards, acting as the high priest's police, carried out arrests, and as long as the high priest was involved in judging cases (though he could not execute anyone), there was relatively little possibility of a direct clash between Jews and Roman troops. To keep his job, he had to remain in control, but any decent high priest – and Caiaphas was pretty decent – also cared about the Jewish populace. The high priest had other obligations to the populace than just the need to prevent clashes with

Roman troops. He should also represent their views to the prefect, and he should stand up for Jewish customs and traditions. He was the man in the middle. This second responsibility was important, but it plays no role in our story.

The high priest, together with his counsellors, both formal and informal, often had the task of preventing trouble and stopping trouble-makers. I wish to illustrate this major fact of political life by giving very brief summaries from Josephus of three separate events.

(1) About the year 50 CE, during a clash between Samaritans and Galilean pilgrims passing through Samaria, one of the pilgrims was killed. A crowd came from Galilee, bent on revenge, but 'the best-known' men went to the Roman procurator, Cumanus, to urge him to send troops and punish the murderers, thus putting an end to the matter. He refused to do so. News reached Jerusalem, and many of the people there rushed to Samaria, though 'the magistrates' or 'rulers' tried to restrain them. The magistrates, however, did not give up; clad in sackcloth, and with ashes on their heads (two signs of mourning), they went after the hotheads and tried to persuade them not to do anything rash, since a battle would surely lead Rome to intervene with a heavy hand. This appeal was effective, and the Jewish mob dispersed (though some smaller bands stayed on for pillage). 'The powerful' Samaritans went to Syria to lay their case before the Roman legate, and 'the best-known' Jews, including the high priest, did the same. The legate went to Caesarea and Lydda, in each place ordering executions of some of the guilty parties. He sent others to Rome to be tried by Claudius: two men of the 'highest power', namely, the chief priest Jonathan and the serving high priest Ananias, as well as Ananias' son, other 'best-known' Jews and 'the most distinguished' Samaritans (*War* 2.232–44).[25]

This event took place during a festival, and it required action in Samaria. It is doubtful, in these circumstances, that the high priest was one of the leading Jews who went to Samaria to stop the mob. But we see, even here, that Rome regarded him as responsible: he went to Syria to see the Roman legate, and he had to go to Rome to be tried. He had nothing to do with the trouble in Samaria, but nevertheless he was responsible for good order. We also see that the high priest was only 'first among equals'. Responsibility to prevent trouble fell, to some degree, on all the leading citizens.[26]

(2) In 62 CE, during a brief period when no Roman procurator was resident in Palestine, the Sadducean high priest Ananus convened 'a council [*synedrion*] of judges'[27] and had James the brother of Jesus and probably others executed. Certain fair-minded, lenient citizens, those most precise about the laws, objected, but the execution took place. Many scholars think that the objectors were Pharisees, and this seems to me likely. In any case the protest was partially successful: Ananus was deposed (*Antiq.* 20.199–203), since he had transgressed the Roman rule that, in an equestrian province, only the highest Roman official could execute.[28]

(3) Jesus' arrest is closer to the third case, which concerns another Jesus, the son of Ananias, about thirty years after the execution of Jesus of Nazareth. At the Feast of Booths (Tabernacles), in a period that was otherwise peaceful, Jesus son of Ananias went to the Temple, where he cried, 'A voice from the east, a voice from the west, a voice from the four winds; a voice against Jerusalem and the sanctuary, a voice against the bridegroom and the bride, a voice against all the people.' This prediction of destruction – that it was such is clear from the reference to the bridegroom and the bride, taken from Jeremiah 7.34 – led to his being interrogated and flogged, first by the Jewish authorities, then by the Romans. He answered questions by 'unceasingly reiterat[ing] his dirge over the city' and was finally released as a maniac. He kept up his cries for seven years, especially at the festivals, but otherwise did not address the populace. Finally, a stone from a Roman catapult killed him (*War* 6.300–309).[29]

If we use this case as a guide, we can understand why Jesus of Nazareth was executed rather than merely flogged. Our Jesus' offence was worse than that of Jesus son of Ananias. Jesus of Nazareth had a following, perhaps not very large, but nevertheless a following. He had taught about the kingdom for some time. He had taken physical action in the Temple. He was not a madman. Thus he was potentially dangerous. Conceivably he could have talked his way out of execution had he promised to take his disciples, return to Galilee and keep his mouth shut. He seems not to have tried.

Collectively, the three stories illustrate how Judaea was governed when it was a province of Rome, formally administered by a Roman. I described this governmental system above (pp. 23–7), but I shall here repeat it. The Roman prefect or procurator had to maintain domestic tranquillity and collect tribute. Both tasks he turned over to Jewish aristocrats, especially the priestly aristocrats, headed by the high priest. Rome's choice of the high priest respected Jewish tradition. Judaea had been ruled by high priests for several centuries. When Herod became king he brought this system to an end, and Rome simply reinstated it when Herod's heir in Judaea (Archelaus) proved unable to rule successfully. When Caiaphas ordered Jesus to be arrested, he was carrying out his duties, one of the chief of which was to prevent uprisings.

I shall mention only briefly two other theories of why Jesus was arrested. One is that he was misunderstood. Caiaphas and Pilate thought that he had in mind a kingdom of this world, and that his followers were about to attack the Roman army; they mistakenly executed him as a rebel. This view basically derives from John 18.33–8, a long discussion about what kind of 'king' Jesus claimed to be. It is, however, most unlikely that Caiaphas and Pilate thought that Jesus led an armed force and planned a military take-over. Had they thought this, Caiaphas would have had Jesus' lieutenants arrested too, and his followers would have been executed – as were the followers of other prophets in later years, who made the mistake of marching about in large groups.[30] The solitary execution of the leader shows that they feared that Jesus could rouse the mob, not that he had created a secret army. In other words, they understood Jesus and his followers very well.

The second view has been that Jesus was arrested because of theological differences with the mass of Jews, led by the Pharisees. He believed in love and compassion, ideas that the Pharisees abomin-ated, and he disagreed with petty legalism and ritualism, which they favoured; for these reasons they conspired to have him killed. Scholars who hold this view do not explain the mechanics of how the Pharisees got Jesus arrested, but are content to maintain that Pharisaic opposition played a role. I shall not here repeat my numerous efforts to get Christians to see the Pharisees in a truer light, but only comment that such imagined disagreements explain nothing historically. Jews sometimes killed each other, but not because of these sorts of disagreements. The range of legal dispute between Jesus and others was well within the parameters of normal debate, and there is no reason at all to think that they were in conflict about love, mercy and grace. Conceivably Jesus opposed Pharisaic views about what produce counted as foodstuff and should be tithed (Matt. 23.23), but such criticisms as these were not matters of life and death. Moreover, the Pharisees are almost entirely absent from the last chapters of the gospels, and completely absent from the stories of the arrest and trial. According to the evidence, they had nothing to do with these events. The synoptic descriptions of the high priest and his council agree 100 per cent with Josephus' descriptions of how Jerusalem was governed when it was part of a Roman province. The high priest and the chief priests are the primary actors, and the Pharisees play no role at all.

The theory advanced here – that Caiaphas had Jesus arrested because of his responsibility to put down trouble-makers, especially during festivals – corresponds perfectly with all the evidence. Jesus had alarmed some people by his attack on the Temple and his statement about its destruction, because they feared that he might actually influence God. It is highly probable, however, that Caiaphas was primarily or exclusively concerned with the possibility that Jesus would incite a riot. He sent armed guards to arrest Jesus, he gave him a hearing, and he recommended execution to Pilate, who promptly complied. That is the way the gospels describe the events, and that is the way things really happened, as the numerous stories in Josephus prove.

The Recommendation to Execute

Can we say any more about *why* Caiaphas and his advisers sent Jesus to Pilate to be executed? The trial scenes in the gospels afford the only possible evidence. I have already briefly discussed them, but now we shall look at them more closely. I think that they are accurate enough for general purposes, but there are problems in detail. In this discussion I shall assume that both Matthew and Luke based their accounts of the Jewish trial on Mark.[31] I do not think that we can rely on Mark's description of the trial in a very precise way, as if it were a court-recorder's transcript, but it will form the basis of our examination.

In Mark and Matthew there are two accounts of Jesus' trial, one a bare report, the other a longer description. These accounts are now in Mark and Matthew as if they referred to separate trials: the short form is in Mark 15.1 // Matt. 27.1f.: 'And as soon as it was morning the chief priests, with the elders and scribes, and the whole council held a consultation; and they bound Jesus and led him away and delivered him to Pilate.' The second trial narrative describes an interrogation. We have previously discussed two of its major parts. False witnesses testified against Jesus because he threatened the Temple, but their testimony did not agree. Then the high priest asked Jesus, 'Are you the Christ, the son of the Blessed?' Jesus replied, 'Yes' (Mark) or 'You have said so; [but on the other hand] I say . . . ' (Matthew). In Mark and Matthew, after Jesus' answer to the high priest's question, he predicted that the Son of Man would soon come. The high priest then rent his garments (a sign of mourning) and said that they needed no witnesses, since they had heard blasphemy (Mark 14.55–65 // Matt. 26.59–68).

Luke offers a slightly different account. There was only one trial. It opened with the interrogators asking Jesus if he was the Christ. He offered an evasive answer, and added that 'from now on the Son of Man shall be seated at the right hand of the power of God'. Only then did the interrogators ask if he was the Son of God, which drew the reply, 'You say that I am' (Luke 22.66–71). The assembled judges said that they did not need more testimony. They had heard 'it' from his own lips. Luke does not use the word 'blasphemy'.

Mark's view is that Jesus was convicted for claiming titles for himself, and that these claims constituted blasphemy in the eyes of other Jews – or at least one, Caiaphas. In the decades following Jesus' death and resurrection Christians would give Jesus both titles (Messiah and Son of God) and interpret them in ways that some Jews considered blasphemous. 'Son of God' in particular would come to mean that Jesus was not a mere mortal. We saw in ch. 15 that on their own these titles have no such meaning. Mark's question, 'Are you the Christ, the Son of the Blessed?', supposes that these two titles go together and interpret one another. But that is a Christian achievement. The mere combination is suspicious, and the statement that the two titles, when combined, constitute blasphemy also looks like Christian creativity. Some early Christians wanted to attribute his death to confessing the christology of the church. Christology separated the new movement from its mother, and naturally they wanted their own distinctive views to go back to

Jesus. Titles, however, play such a minor part in the synoptic gospels that we must doubt that they were the real issue at the trial.

If, however, we back off from Christianity's preoccupation with titles that supposedly define the person of Jesus and look at Mark's trial scene with fresh eyes, we find that it is perfectly reasonable. If it were a transcript, if these exchanges between Caiaphas and Jesus took place precisely as Mark wrote them, we would still have to conclude that titles were not the real issue. What the passage says is this: Jesus threatened the Temple and gave himself airs. The high priest had him arrested because of his action against the Temple, and that was the charge against him. The testimony was thrown out of court because the witnesses did not say the same things. The high priest, however, *had decided that Jesus had to die*, and so he was not willing to drop the case. He asked Jesus to say something about himself, and then he cried 'blasphemy', rending his garments. The rest of the court went along. That is, as the story reads, the high priest did not want to try Jesus on the basis of claiming titles, but because of the Temple. He fell back on titles, and declared that Jesus' answer was blasphemy – no matter what he said. We do not have to decide whether Jesus answered 'yes' or 'maybe'. The high priest had already made up his mind.

Tearing one's garments was a powerful sign of mourning, and showing the signs of mourning had persuasive power. We saw above that the 'magistrates' or 'rulers' from Jerusalem put ashes on their heads and wore sackcloth (other signs of mourning) when trying to prevent mob violence in Samaria. For the high priest to tear his clothing was the most extreme sign of mourning, since the Bible forbids him to tear his garments, or even to dishevel his hair (Lev. 21.10). Caiaphas' transgression of the law showed horror. Few Jews would have denied him what he wanted, and certainly not his own counsellors. Jesus was sent to Pilate.

I am proposing two ways of reading Mark. One is Mark's own view. During his public ministry Jesus had not claimed titles for himself and had tried to silence others who called him 'Messiah' or 'Son of God'. Therefore the titles, according to Mark's Gospel, do not explain the decision to arrest. Caiaphas had Jesus arrested because he held the mistaken view that Jesus had threatened the Temple. Jesus had not done so, and his trial exonerated him of this charge. The high priest, however, asked a leading question about titles. Jesus accepted the two terms 'Messiah' and 'Son of the Blessed (God)' as applying to himself, and the high priest charged him with blasphemy. The second reading is a critical interpretation of Mark. It arises in part from the observation that Mark attaches to 'Messiah' and 'Son of God' a significance that they did not have prior to the development of the church's christology. Because of this, we may offer a better historical interpretation of Jesus' trial and execution *even if* we accept Mark's narrative. (1) During his teaching and healing ministry, Jesus did not give himself titles; when directly asked he declined to say who he was. (2) Jesus was arrested because he threatened the Temple. (3) When the witnesses failed to agree about Jesus' threat to the Temple, Caiaphas did not have him flogged and then released. He decided, instead, to try again. This shows that he had intended execution from the outset. (4) He then asked Jesus if he was Messiah and Son of God. (5) Jesus said that he was. (6) These titles did not, in and of themselves, constitute blasphemy. (7) The high priest decided to call them blasphemy because he had already decided on execution. (8) Instead of conducting a further inquiry into what the terms meant to Jesus, Caiaphas made an extravagant display of mourning and thereby persuaded his counsellors to join him in condemning the Galilean. An historical construal of Mark's trial scene *as written* is that the titles were an expedient and that the threat to the Temple was the immediate cause of execution.

I wish to distinguish my own view from the previous eight points, which offer a reconstruction of what Mark's account would mean if it gave a verbatim report of a trial. I think that Mark's trial scene is not a transcript and that we must assess the motives of the various actors on more general grounds. When we consider the way in which high priests discharged their civic responsibilities under the Roman prefects and procurators, we should conclude that Caiaphas was carrying out his duties as prescribed: Jesus was dangerous because he might cause a riot, which Roman troops would put down with great loss of life. The author of John attributed to Caiaphas an entirely appropriate statement: 'it is expedient for you that one man should die for the people, and that the whole nation should not perish' (John 11.50).[32] Although it was the Temple scene that decided the issue, other factors were probably contributing causes: Jesus' entry to Jerusalem and his teaching about the kingdom.

We do not know how much Caiaphas knew about these other matters, but it would be reasonable to think that, after he learned of Jesus' assault on the pigeon-sellers and money-changers, and before he ordered his arrest, he had sought and attained further information about him. As we shall see immediately below, he probably passed on to Pilate the fact that Jesus thought that he was 'king'. This self-claim is implicit in Jesus' entry into Jerusalem, especially when that symbolic act is combined with Jesus' teaching. While I doubt the Markan combination of 'Messiah', 'Son of God' and 'blasphemy', I do not doubt that Caiaphas and his counsellors knew that Jesus taught about the kingdom and claimed for himself a significant role in it.

I propose, then, that Caiaphas made only one decision: to arrest *and* execute Jesus. If so, he did not act because of theological disagreement, but because of his principal political and moral responsibility: to preserve the peace and to prevent riots and bloodshed. It was Jesus' self-assertion, especially in the Temple, but also in his teaching and in his entry to the city, that motivated the high priest to act.

Pilate's Decision

Why did Pilate order Jesus' execution? Because the high priest recommended it and gave him a telling charge: Jesus thought that he was king of the Jews. Pilate understood that Jesus was a would-be king without an army, and therefore he made no effort to run down and execute Jesus' followers. He probably regarded him as a religious fanatic whose fanaticism had become so extreme that it posed a threat to law and order.

The gospels, especially Matthew and John, want Jesus to have been condemned by the Jewish mob, against Pilate's better judgement. Pilate worried, he was advised by his wife to do nothing, he consulted the crowd, he pleaded on Jesus' behalf; finally, weakling that he was, he could not withstand the clamour of the crowd, and so he had Jesus executed (Matt. 27.11–26; John 18.28–19.16). These elements of the story of Jesus' last hours derive from the desire of the Christians to get along with Rome and to depict Jews as their real opponents. In all probability Pilate received Caiaphas' charge, had Jesus flogged and briefly interrogated, and, when the answers were not completely satisfactory, sent him to the cross with not a second thought. Philo, who was Pilate's contemporary, wrote an appeal to the emperor Gaius (Caligula), which included a description of Pilate. Philo wrote of 'the briberies, the insults, the robberies, the outrages and wanton injuries, the executions without trial constantly repeated, the ceaseless and supremely grievous cruelty' that marked Pilate's rule (*Embassy to Gaius* 302). Moreover, Pilate was eventually dismissed from office because of large-scale and ill-judged executions (*Antiq.* 18.88f.). This evidence agrees precisely with the sequence of events that the gospels narrate: Jesus appeared before Pilate and was executed almost immediately, with no further witnesses and with no trial procedure. The stories of Pilate's reluctance and weakness of will are best explained as Christian propaganda; they are a kind of excuse for Pilate's action which reduces the conflict between the Christian movement and Roman authority.

The Execution

Early on Friday, 15 Nisan, Jesus and two others were taken outside the city walls, nailed to crosses and left to die. Only a few brave followers watched. Jesus died before nightfall on Friday, and thus just before the sabbath began. A distant admirer, Joseph of Arimathea, donated a grave, and Jesus was buried. A few of his women followers watched. His disciples, afraid that they would be next, were in hiding.

The accounts of Jesus' crucifixion are full of quotations from, and allusions to, Psalm 22: 'they divided his clothes, casting lots for them' (Mark 1.24) is a quotation from Psalms 22.18; 'wagging their heads' (Mark 15.29) is from Psalms 22.7; Jesus' cry, 'My God, my God, why have you forsaken me' (Mark 15.34) is from Psalms 22.1. As usual in these circumstances, we do not know which elements really took place. My guess is that Jesus' cry was his own reminiscence of the psalm, not just a motif inserted by the early Christians. It is possible that, when Jesus drank his last cup of wine and predicted that he would drink it again in the kingdom, he thought that the kingdom would arrive immediately. After he had been on the cross for a few hours, he despaired, and cried out that he had been forsaken. This speculation is only one possible explanation. We do not know what he thought as he hung in agony on the cross. After a relatively short period of suffering he died, and some of his followers and sympathizers hastily buried him.

17. EPILOGUE:
THE RESURRECTION

===

Jesus thought that the kingdom of God was at hand, and his disciples had accepted his message. As I just suggested, he may have died disappointed. His disciples, reasonably thinking that they would be next, hid. Some of his women followers – who were safer than the men and possibly braver – watched him die and saw Josephus of Arimathea bury his body. I assume that, besides being afraid that Caiaphas and Pilate would turn on them next, all his followers were disappointed. The coming kingdom had sounded so marvellous! The last would be first, the meek would inherit the earth. These expectations were not fulfilled, at least not in any obvious way. What did happen was a surprise.

According to Matthew and Mark, when the women returned to the tomb a day and a half later to care for Jesus' body (he died on Friday and was buried; they returned Sunday morning), they found that the tomb was empty. According to Matthew (hinted at also in Mark), Jesus appeared to the women and then later to the disciples in Galilee.[1] The result of this was that the disciples gathered in Jerusalem to wait for his return, which they expected soon. That is, *they did not give up his idea that the kingdom would come*; they now expected him to return from heaven to establish it.

The resurrection is not, strictly speaking, part of the story of the historical Jesus, but rather belongs to the aftermath of his life. A few words about the different resurrection accounts may nevertheless be useful. According to Matthew and Mark, the disciples went to Galilee and saw Jesus there; according to Luke, they did not leave the environs of Jerusalem. The story of Jesus' ascension into heaven is different in Luke 24.50–53 and Acts 1.6–11, though both accounts were written by the same author. Equally striking are the divergences between the stories of Jesus' appearances. In Matthew he appears only twice, once to Mary Magdalene and the other Mary (28.9f.), once to the surviving eleven disciples (28.16–20; Judas had committed suicide). In Luke he does not appear to the women (see Luke 24.8–11), but first of all to two unnamed disciples (Luke 24.11–35), then to all the disciples, before whom he ate (Luke 24.36–49). According to Acts, he was with the disciples for forty days, appearing off and on (Acts 1.3f.).

The earliest evidence, however, is not in the gospels but in one of Paul's letters. He offers, as part of what had been 'handed down' to him, a list of appearances of the risen Lord: he appeared first to Cephas (Peter), then to the Twelve (not the Eleven!), then to more than 500, then to James (Jesus' brother), then to 'all the apostles' (apparently not just the Twelve), then to Paul himself (I Cor. 15.3–8).

Before commenting on the problems raised by these divergent accounts, let us first consider how our sources describe the risen Jesus: what he was like. According to Luke, he was not immediately recognizable; the first two disciples to whom he appeared walked and talked with him for some time without knowing who he was; he was made known 'in the breaking of the bread', when they ate together (Luke 24.35).[2] Although he could appear and disappear, he was not a ghost. Luke is very insistent about that. The risen Lord could be touched, and he could eat (24.39–43).

When Paul was engaged in a debate with his Corinthian converts about whether or not dead Christians would be raised, body and all, he tried to describe what the coming resurrection would be like. His answer is presumably based on his own first-hand experience of seeing the risen Lord ('Have I not seen Jesus our Lord?' [I Cor. 9.1]; God 'reveal[ed] his Son to me' [Gal. 1.16]).[3] In the resurrection, Paul explained, each individual will have a body, but it will be transformed: not a physical body but a spiritual body. One fact is clear: flesh and blood cannot inherit the kingdom of God; resurrected bodies will be spiritual, not fleshly. Paul then applied this to Jesus: 'Just as we have borne the image of the man of dust, we shall also bear the image of the man of heaven' (I Cor. 15.42–50). Paul repeated: everyone will be changed; when they are like the 'man of heaven', they will no longer have their perishable bodies, but rather imperishable ones (I Cor. 15.51–4).

In the first century people knew about two phenomena that are similar to resurrection: ghosts and resuscitated corpses. A ghost then was what a ghost is now, or what a ghost was to Shakespeare:[4] a phantasm, especially one that appears late at night.[5] Sophisticated ancients, like their modern counterparts, dismissed ghosts as creatures of dreams, figments of the imagination. The less sophisticated, naturally, were credulous. Both Paul and Luke opposed the idea that the risen Lord was a ghost, Luke explicitly ('a ghost has not flesh and bones as you see that I have', 24.40), Paul by implication: what is raised is a spiritual *body*. Yet they equally opposed the idea that Jesus was a resuscitated corpse. These were better known then than now, because embalming is so widespread. It is, however, possible for a person to be dead to all appearances, and later to 'regain' life. There are several such stories in ancient literature, some in the Bible and some elsewhere.[6] Paul and Luke, however, denied that the risen Lord was simply resuscitated. In Paul's view he had been transformed, changed from a 'physical' or 'natural' body to a 'spiritual body'. Luke thought that he had flesh and could eat, but also that he had been changed. He was not obviously recognizable to people who saw him, and he could appear and disappear.

Both authors were trying to describe – Paul at first hand, Luke at second or third hand – an experience that does not fit a known category. What they deny is much clearer than what they affirm.

Faced with accounts of this nature – sharply diverging stories of where and to whom Jesus appeared, lack of agreement and clarity on what he was like (except agreement on negatives) – we cannot reconstruct what really happened. Throughout this book I have offered suggestions about what lies behind passages in the gospels. On the present topic, however, I do not see how to improve on the evidence, or how to get behind it. I have views about parts of it, such as the movement of the disciples: they fled to Galilee and then returned to Jerusalem. Luke's view, that they never left the environs of Jerusalem, is explained by the 'Jerusalemo-centric' character of his two-volume work, Luke–Acts. But I do not pretend to know *what* they saw or just who saw it. The reader who thinks that it is all perfectly clear – the physical, historical Jesus got up and walked around – should study Luke and Paul more carefully. The disciples could not recognize him; he was not 'flesh and blood' but a 'spiritual body'. He was not a ghost, or a resuscitated corpse, or a badly wounded man limping around for a few more hours: so said Luke and Paul, and John (20.14f.) agrees.

The lists of the people who saw the resurrected Lord are in some ways even more puzzling.

Matthew	Luke	John 20	Acts	I Corinthians 15
Jerusalem	*Jerusalem and near by*	*Jerusalem*	*Jerusalem*	*No geographical information*
Two Marys	Two disciples	Mary Magdalene		Cephas (= Peter)
	The Eleven and others (same day)	The disciples The disciples (one week later)	The apostles during forty days	The Twelve 500 James
				All the apostles
		John 21		Paul
Galilee		*Galilee*		
The Eleven		Seven disciples		

Some of these divergences are not difficult to explain. The author of Luke–Acts was an artistic writer, and he thought that repeating himself was not good style.[7] Therefore, the risen Lord was with the disciples for only a few hours in Luke, and for forty days in Acts. The second account provides variety and also seeks to assure the reader that the disciples knew precisely what Jesus wanted: he talked it over with them extensively. John 21 is an appendix, probably by a later author who wanted to handle the troublesome problem created by the fact that, by the time he wrote, all the disciples had died (see above, pp. 179f.). A more general explanation of all the gospels is that their authors had to give narrative accounts. Paul produced a list, but they needed stories. In telling these stories, each author went his own way.

But despite these and other reasonable explanations of the variations, we are left with an intractable problem. The followers of Jesus were sure that he was raised from the dead, but they did not agree on who had seen him.

I do not regard deliberate fraud as a worthwhile explanation. Many of the people in these lists were to spend the rest of their lives proclaiming that they had seen the risen Lord, and several of them would die for their cause. Moreover, a calculated deception should have produced greater unanimity. Instead, there seem to have been *competitors*: 'I saw him first!' 'No! I did.' Paul's tradition that 500 people saw Jesus at the same time has led some people to suggest that Jesus' followers suffered mass hysteria. But mass hysteria does not explain the other traditions.

To many, Paul's evidence seems most suggestive. He does not distinguish the Lord's appearance to him from that of the other appearances *in kind*. If he had a vision, maybe they also had visions. But then why does Paul insist that he saw a 'spiritual body'? He could have said 'spirit'.

That Jesus' followers (and later Paul) had resurrection experiences is, in my judgement, a fact. What the reality was that gave rise to the experiences I do not know.

Much about the historical Jesus will remain a mystery. Nothing is more mysterious than the stories of his resurrection, which attempt to portray an experience that the authors could not themselves comprehend. But in the midst of mystery and uncertainty, we should remember that we know a lot about Jesus. We know that he started under John the Baptist, that he had disciples, that he expected the 'kingdom', that he went from Galilee to Jerusalem, that he did something hostile against the Temple, that he was tried and cruci- fied. Finally we know that after his death his followers experienced what they described as the 'resurrection': the appearance of a living but transformed person who had actually died. They believed this, they lived it, and they died for it. In the process they created a movement, a movement that in many ways went far beyond Jesus' message. Their movement grew and spread geographically. Twenty-five or more years later Paul – a convert, not an original disciple – still expected Jesus to return within his own lifetime. But the Lord tarried.

The 'delay' led to creative and stimulating theological reflection, seen especially in the Gospel of John; but the synoptic material was by no means immune from theological development. Meanwhile, the man behind it all became remote. The consequence is that it takes patient spadework to dig through the layers of Christian devotion and to recover the historical core. Historical reconstruction is never absolutely certain, and in the case of Jesus it is sometimes highly uncertain. Despite this, we have a good idea of the main lines of his ministry and his message. We know who he was, what he did, what he taught, and why he died. Perhaps most important, we know how much he inspired his followers, who sometimes themselves did not understand him, but who were so loyal to him that they changed history.

APPENDIX I.
CHRONOLOGY

Fixing the date of ancient events is a very difficult business, partly because the ancient Mediterranean world did not have a universally accepted calendar. Most ancient authors also worked without the benefit of archives, and frequently on the basis of hearsay evidence. Today we know more about the sequence of events in Palestine than did Luke (for example). We can compare Josephus with Roman sources and sometimes with inscriptional evidence. Luke may have had Josephus (this is a disputed point), but he could not do the kind of cross-checking that modern scholars can. We saw above that he puts the events of the first part of his gospel during the reign of Herod (Luke 1.5), but that he also dates Jesus' birth at the time of a census conducted by Quirinius ten years after Herod's death (the dates are 4 BCE and 6 CE respectively). This simply shows the limitations of his sources.

In this appendix, however, I wish to discuss another point, the year of Jesus' death. According to Luke 3.1, John the Baptist began his mission in the fifteenth year of Tiberius, and Jesus began his work shortly afterward. Tiberius succeeded Augustus in the year 14 CE; thus Luke puts the beginning of Jesus' ministry about the year 30. This is, however, only an estimate. Luke did not write that Jesus started precisely one year after John. Moreover, we do not know just how long Jesus' ministry lasted. Consequently, Luke's information cannot tell us when Jesus died. Matthew and John name Caiaphas as the high priest who condemned Jesus (Matt. 26.3; John 11.49; 18.13f.), and all four gospels and Acts agree that Pilate was the Roman governor of Judaea (e.g., Matt. 27.2 & parr.; John 18.29; Acts 3.13). This gives us only a broad range of dates: Caiaphas was high priest from about 18 to 36, Pilate was prefect from 26 to 36.

The dates of Paul's career, about which we have information in

Paul's own letters and in Acts, are also relevant to the question of when Jesus died. Paul's chronology is itself a complicated and difficult question, which I shall not try to explain. The general conclusion of numerous studies, however, is that we make the best sense of Paul's career, especially the chronological references in his letter to the Galatians, if we date Jesus' death very late in the 20s or early in the 30s CE. If we choose the earliest or the latest possible dates during Pilate's prefecture (27 and 36), the evidence about Paul's career does not fit in very easily.

Taking into account Luke's dating of the beginning of John the Baptist's ministry, the period of Pilate's administration and the evidence derived from the chronology of Paul, most scholars have been content to say that Jesus was executed sometime between 29 and 33 CE.

It is possible, however, that astronomy can give us a more precise date. The gospels indicate the day of the week and month when Jesus was executed. According to the synoptic gospels, the execution took place on a Friday that was the fifteenth day of the Jewish month Nisan (the day after Passover). According to John, he was executed when 14 Nisan (Passover) fell on Friday.[1] This is analogous to saying that something happened when either Christmas Eve, 24 December, or Christmas Day, 25 December, fell on a Thursday. In recent years that happened in 1987, 1992 (24 December) and 1986 (25 December). In what years did 14 Nisan or 15 Nisan fall on a Friday?

Unfortunately, numerous studies have failed to decide the issue to the satisfaction of everyone. To demonstrate where the problem lies, I shall have to explain the Jewish calendar. It was (and still is) luni-solar. The year was divided into months, and months were reckoned strictly according to the phases of the moon. A lunar month begins with the new moon and lasts about $29\frac{1}{2}$ days; therefore months were either 29 or 30 days long. Twelve such months produce a lunar year of about 354 days, $11\frac{1}{4}$ days too short for a solar (seasonal) year, which is determined by the position of the earth relative to the sun. In a strictly lunar year the months back up. Every year, each month comes about 11 days earlier than the year before. The consequence is that springtime festivals soon start arriving in the winter. In order to keep months in the right season, Jews 'intercalated' a thirteenth month every two or three years.

Thus while most years were 354 days, some were 383 or 384 days. Over a nineteen-year cycle, the total number of days comes out about right in terms of the solar calendar. This is why we say that the Jewish calendar is luni-solar: the months are lunar, but the number of months is adjusted in order to bring the calender into agreement with the solar year.

It will give us perspective to consider the present western calendar. We ignore phases of the moon. We have months, but the months do not start with the new moon, except coincidentally. On average our months are about 30½ days long, rather than 29½. Twelve months 30½ days long (that is, six months of 30 days and 6 of 31 days) yield a year that is slightly too long in terms of the seasonal year. Therefore one month, February, is shortened. But every four years we must intercalate a day to keep the months in the right season. If we did not do this, Christmas would eventually start arriving in the autumn. (If it were not for leap year, every 120 years each of our months would come 30 days earlier in the seasonal year.)

To determine just when a day occurred *astronomically* (decided by the tilt of the earth on its axis and the phase of the moon), we now have to know which years were leap years. We can retroject our own calendar into the past, taking account of leap years, and thus give absolute dates to ancient events (that is, dates in strict accord with the modern western calendar). In theory we can also retroject the Jewish calendar and then relate it to our calendar. In order to retroject the Jewish calendar, and determine when 14 or 15 Nisan fell on a Friday, we need to know which months had 29 days, which had 30 days, and which years were leap years (13 months long). Today, astronomers can determine which months *should* have had 29 days, which should have had 30 days, and which years should have been leap years. The Jewish calendar, however, was based not on astronomical calculation, but on *observation*. The Jewish observers had to look for 'the first faintly glowing lunar crescent following conjunction with the sun', since the new moon is, by definition, not visible.[2] We cannot know anything about local atmospheric conditions 2,000 years ago, and those helped determine the calendar. Ancient Jews knew when to start looking; the arrival of a new moon did not ever surprise anyone, but still, if observers had to see it, they had to see it. This introduces some

uncertainty. I shall quote from a classic treatment by J. K. Fotheringham, who preferred Friday, 14 Nisan, 33 CE, as the date of Jesus'
execution. He was commenting on scholarly efforts to follow the
synoptics and date the crucifixion on Friday, 15 Nisan, 30 CE.
Fotheringham accepted John, and so he believed this endeavour to
be pointless. He sarcastically suggested 31 instead, but in doing so he
made clear the range of uncertainty:

In the year 31, 14 Nisan should have fallen on Tuesday, March 27. We can
shift it to a Thursday by supposing that Nisan fell a month late and that the
appearance of the moon was delayed one day by cloudy weather . . .
Eclipse observers know that you can never count on an absence of clouds.
If anyone wants to find a year that will suit the synoptist's date, I should
certainly advise him to place Nisan one month late and the appearance of
its crescent one day late in AD 31 rather than with Gerhardt to place the
appearance of the crescent one day early in 30.[3]

This gives an idea of the problem. When dates are fixed by
observation, there is a range of possibilities, some more likely than
others.

When the ancient authorities fixed the date of Passover, they had
to consider not only the visibility of the moon, but also the season
as determined by temperature and the growth of crops. Passover
had to fall in the spring. In particular, during the festival of
Unleavened Bread that followed Passover the first fruits of barley
were offered in the Temple.[4] The priests would have intercalated an
additional month if unseasonably cold temperatures meant that
barley could not be presented during the festival.

If ancient Jews had fixed the months and years by astronomical
calculation, and if we had to choose between John's chronology and
the synoptic chronology on the basis of our own astronomical
computations, we would choose John. Given the two possibilities
for the day of the month (Friday, 14 Nisan, and Friday, 15 Nisan),
and given the general range of years established by literary evidence
(29–33 CE), the best choice astronomically is Friday, 14 Nisan, 33 CE
(which would be 3 April in our calendar).[5] But in fact we cannot
be sure that modern astronomical retrojection of the Jewish calendar
agrees with the actual calculation of dates in the first century. The
synoptic chronology cannot be confirmed by astronomy, but neither

can it be disproved. Most scholars continue to accept it because the Fourth Gospel's chronology agrees so strongly with its Christology: Christ was the Passover lamb. This leads to the suspicion that it was John who changed the day of the execution.

We shall now consider another way of reading some of the literary evidence, which has led some scholars to choose a late date for Jesus' execution, either 35 or 36. This theory, which had some currency in previous decades, has recently been revived by Nikos Kokkinos.[6] The evidence concerns the date of John the Baptist. According to Mark 6.14–29 (partially paralleled in Matthew and Luke), Antipas thought that Jesus might be John the Baptist, raised from the dead. Antipas, the passage explains, had executed John because John had criticized his marriage to Herodias. Mark 1.14 // Matt. 4.12 puts the beginning of Jesus' public ministry immediately after (Mark) or at about the time of (Matthew) John's arrest. Thus according to the gospels the sequence was this: John baptized Jesus; John was arrested; Jesus began his ministry; John was executed; Jesus was executed.

The scholars who date Jesus' execution in 36 note that Josephus narrates Antipas' marriage to Herodias after the story of the death of Philip, Antipas' brother, which was late in 33 or early in 34. This marriage led to Aretas' invasion of Galilee and the defeat of Antipas' army. Vitellius, the Roman legate of Syria, led a punitive expedition against Aretas. Vitellius' expedition took place in 37, since it was interrupted by Tiberius' death in that year.[7] According to the gospels, John's criticism of Antipas' marriage led to his execution. If Antipas married Herodias after 34 CE, obviously John was executed after that date. This leads to the conclusion that Jesus was active in the mid-30s and was executed in 36, shortly before Pilate was recalled to Rome. According to this theory, both John and Jesus must be fitted into the period between the death of Philip, which was in 33 or 34, and Vitellius' expedition, which was in 37.

The problem with this is that, in this section of Josephus' *Antiquities*, many of the stories are not in chronological order. They are prefaced by such phrases as 'about this time', 'about the same time' and 'meanwhile'. We shall look at the sequence in which Josephus mentions the people and events that concern us, as well as a few other events that can be firmly dated. I have put in brackets dates for which the chronological evidence is very strong.

1. the appointment of Pilate, *Antiq.* 18.35   (26 CE)
2. the death of Germanicus, 18.54   (19 CE)
3. the life of Jesus, 18.63 [8]
4. a scandal in Rome about the Isis cult, and another
   scandal involving Jews, also in Rome, 18.65–85   (19 CE)
5. the dismissal of Pilate, 18.89, giving a specific
   date: by the time Pilate reached Rome, Tiberius
   had died   (37 CE)
6. the dismissal of Caiaphas, 18.95
7. a letter from Tiberius to Vitellius 18.96
8. the death of Philip, 18.106   (33/34 CE)
9. Antipas' agreement to marry Herodias, 18.110
10. the trip of Aretas' daughter to her father,
    18.111–13
11. Aretas' invasion, 18.114
12. the death of John the Baptist, 18.116–119
13. the punitive expedition against Aretas, during
    which Tiberius died, 18.120–26   (37 CE).

In Josephus' account the life of Jesus comes between two events that took place in 19 CE, and John's execution falls between events dated in 33 and 37 CE. The proposal that Jesus' active career ran from about 34 to 36 requires us to believe that Josephus put the death of John the Baptist in its proper place, but not the life of Jesus. For the life of Jesus, we must, instead, accept the gospels' connection of John and Jesus. Since we 'know' the date of John's death, Jesus' career must be shifted later.

It is not surprising that some scholars take the opposite tack: we know the date of Germanicus' death: 19 CE. Other events in this section of the *Antiquities* also can be securely dated to the period 15–19 CE. Pilate's appointment precedes this event in Josephus' narrative; therefore he was appointed before 19 CE. Consequently, Jesus was active much earlier than 26–36. Actually, he was crucified in 21 CE.[9]

Both these theories assume that a section of Book 18 of Josephus' *Antiquities* places events in their actual sequence, but they disagree about which section it is.[10] In either case, the tail wags the dog. One fixed point gives a precise date to the neighbouring stories, and then the rest of the evidence is forced to fit. According to the theory that Jesus died shortly before 37, Josephus refers to his life too early. According to the theory that he died in 21, Josephus refers to John the Baptist too late. According to both theories, he was completely correct with regard to one event, and completely wrong with regard to the other.

Instead of allowing one supposedly fixed point to date everything else, we should back off and look at the evidence more generally. In this section of his work, Josephus is not narrating events in their precise chronological order. Tiberius dies, then writes a letter, and then dies (see 5, 7, and 13). Part of the arrangement is, as far as I can tell, random (except that everything relates to the period of Tiberius' rule), but part is topical. Item 4 above appears where it does because it concludes with a Roman attempt to force Jews to serve in the army, which was against the sabbath law (18.84). This is faintly connected to one of Pilate's affronts to the Jewish law, which Josephus relates in 18.60–62. Thus an event from the year 19 (scandals in Rome) appears to come between 26 and 36 (Pilate's prefecture in Judaea). The scandals of 19 CE, however, are too firmly fixed by Roman evidence to allow Josephus' placement of them to deceive biblical scholars. Jesus and John the Baptist, of course, cannot be precisely dated by Roman evidence, since their immediate impact was so slight, and consequently they can be moved around if one supposes that Josephus' sequence in some section or other was precise.

I shall comment just a little more on the theory of Nikos Kokkinos, which has been recently accepted by the eminent historian, Robin Lane Fox.[11] Kokkinos' basic argument, as we have seen, is that in the *Antiquities* the story about John the Baptist comes after the death of Philip and before the expedition against Aretas, both of which can be firmly dated: 33/4 and 37 respectively. It is beyond doubt that the punitive expedition against Aretas was connected to the fact that Antipas had decided to marry Herodias. The sequence must have been this: Antipas planned to bring Herodias to Galilee; his first wife, Aretas' daughter, fled to her father; Aretas invaded Galilee; the Roman troops in Syria launched a punitive expedition against Aretas. It is reasonable to think that Antipas' domestic rearrangement occurred *immediately* before Aretas' invasion. If John the Baptist criticized the new marriage, and *if* Aretas responded promptly when his daughter was replaced, then

John was alive very near the year 37. Kokkinos, following this line
of reasoning, writes, 'as soon as the alliance between the two kings
[Antipas and Aretas] was broken [by the divorce], Aretas exploited
the pretext of a border dispute and proclaimed war on Antipas'.[12]
This is plausible speculation with regard to the divorce and Aretas'
retaliation. But it is a speculation. We do not know 'as soon as': that
is the question, not necessarily the answer. Josephus wrote that
Aretas's daughter 'reached her father and told him what Herod
[Antipas] planned to do. Aretas made this the beginning of hostility
over boundaries in the district of Gamala.'[13] 'Made this the beginning of' is not necessarily 'as soon as'; on the contrary, one supposes
that some time elapsed between the divorce and the war. Kokkinos'
second defence of his theory is that the Jews considered Antipas'
defeat to be just retribution because he had executed John. 'To
argue that the Jews felt God's revenge did not occur immediately
after the deed is deceptive. Circumstances in the recent rather than
the distant past would be more likely to make the Jews attribute
divine punishments.'[14] This is partly sheer supposition and partly a
weak argument. It is not deceptive to say that Jews thought that
God's revenge tarried if that is what they thought. Kokkinos seems
to imagine that they had a choice and decided in favour of speedy
rather than delayed retribution. But since John was widely revered,
and since his execution was extremely unpopular, those who resented Antipas' action would have waited for some really serious
blow to him before declaring that God had vindicated John. An
immediate blow would have been desirable, from this point of
view, but John's many admirers had to take what they could get. If
the worst thing that happened to Antipas during the next five years
was that he strained his ankle while getting out of the bath, the
populace would have waited for something worse. When Aretas
defeated Antipas' army, those who had been waiting – how long
we do not know – proclaimed that God had exacted retribution.

It is best to think that the story of Antipas, Herodias and the
execution of John is a 'flashback', out of its historical sequence.[15]
The story of John's execution, in fact, is quite obviously a flashback:
Josephus refers to it after the event that it is said to have caused. In
this entire section (9–13) Josephus arranged the materially topically;
this explains why the stories about Herodias, Aretas' invasion and
the execution of John come so close together. Their proximity in

Josephus' narrative by no means proves that they actually occurred in rapid sequence. Looking back at the list above, we see that the dateable events are 8 and 13. 9–12 appear where they do because they are related in subject matter to 13. We do not know that all these events were squeezed into the period between 8 and 13.[16] Consequently, we do not know when Antipas met Herodias, when his former wife fled to her father, and when John was executed.

I am not attempting either to prove or disprove one date or another. I have, instead, wanted to give the reader a 'feel' of the historical difficulties that our sources present, and to illustrate how people can seize upon one point and try to make everything else fit in. We are better off if we accept the accuracy of the sources in a more general way. This allows not only one of them, but even all of them to be fuzzy or wrong on some details. Chronology provides the best example. The range of dates does not really matter for our understanding of the life of Jesus, as long as we place his death during the period when Pilate was prefect (26–36 CE). The precise date is actually more important when one studies the early church, including the life of Paul, since we need to know how long to allow for the development of early Christianity. For the sake of having a convenient round number, then, and granting that we cannot be certain, I shall accept 30 CE as being approximately the year of Jesus' death.

APPENDIX II.
JESUS' DISCIPLES

═══

This total list of names, divided according to attestation, is this:

All four gospels and Acts:
  Simon (called Peter; in Paul's letters often called Cephas)
  Andrew, his brother
  James ⎫ the sons of Zebedee; the Fourth Gospel does not use their
  John ⎭ names, but refers to them only as 'sons of Zebedee'
  Philip
  Thomas
  Judas Iscariot

Matthew, Mark, Luke and Acts:
  Bartholomew
  Matthew
  James the son of Alphaeus
  Simon the Cananaean or the Zealot

Matthew and Mark:
  Thaddaeus

Luke, Acts and John:
  Judas the son of James (so Luke and Acts; John has 'Judas, not Iscariot')

John:
  Nathanael

This gives fourteen names. Further, Mark and Luke name Levi as a tax collector who followed Jesus.

NOTES

===

1. Introduction

1. Besides the comprehensive volumes of Jefferson's correspondence and other papers, there are several useful handbooks, such as Adrienne Koch and William Peden, eds., *The Life and Selected Writings of Thomas Jefferson*, 1944, 1972.

2. See Randolph Churchill's spirited account, in which he berated 'propagandists' who created a 'socialist demonology' about his father: *Winston S. Churchill 1901–1914: Young Statesman*, 1967 pp. 359–72. More recently, see William Manchester, *The Last Lion. Winston Spencer Churchill. Visions of Glory 1874–1932*, 1983, pp. 417f.; Martin Gilbert, *Churchill: A Life*, 1991, pp. 219–21, 231–3.

3. On these marriages, see Robin Lane Fox, *Alexander the Great*, 1973 (Penguin ed. 1987), pp. 417–19.

4. See Robin Lane Fox, *Alexander the Great.*, pp. 409f.

5. On tests for 'authenticity', see for example pp. 94, 182, 199f., 263 below.

6. See pp. 57–9 below.

7. See Albert Schweitzer, *The Quest of the Historical Jesus*, English translation 1910 (German original 1906), pp. 13–26.

8. E. Forrester Church, 'Introduction', *The Jefferson Bible*, 1989, p. 7.

9. Ibid. p. 9.

10. Charles Dickens, *Hard Times*, ch. 6.

11. Charles Dickens, *Little Dorrit*, ch. 3.

12. Charles Dickens, *Hard Times*, ch. 12.

13. John Colville, quoted by Martin Gilbert in *Finest Hour. Winston S. Churchill 1939–1941*, 1983, p. 995.

14. Martin Gilbert, *Never Despair. Winston S. Churchill 1945–1965*, 1988, p. 730.

2. An Outline of Jesus' Life

1. The best succinct explanation of Dionysius' error that I have found is Hermann von Soden's contribution to the article 'Chronology' in T. K. Cheyne and J. S. Black, eds., *Encyclopaedia Biblica*, 1899, vol. 1, § 51 and § 57 (columns 805, 807).

2. The Gospel of John places a good percentage of Jesus' work in Judaea. See pp. 66f. below.

3. Tiberias is mentioned only in John 6.1 and 21.1, 'the Sea of Tiberias' (= the Sea of Galilee); 6.23, 'boats from Tiberias'. The gospels do not refer to the other Galilean cities at all.

4. On Josephus, see p. 15f. below.

5. I regard this event as being slightly less certain than the other items covered in this chapter. See below, p. 254.

3. Political Setting

1. For the Hasmonean revolt, we also have I Macc., which was Josephus' main source for this period. This and other overlaps allow scholars to examine how he used his sources. For the details of Josephus' career, see *Life* and *War* 2.569–646; 3.132–408 and elsewhere. See also Tessa Rajak, *Josephus: The Historian and His Society*, 1983.

2. Alexander and the generals who divided up his empire after his death were Macedonians, but their culture was largely Greek. It is customary to refer to the period between Alexander and the Roman conquest of the eastern Mediterranean as 'Hellenistic', as distinct from 'Hellenic' – that is, as 'Greekish' rather than 'Greek'.

3. In a brief summary of British government in India, Kate L. Mitchell referred to British use of 'Indian members of the army and civil service, the large landowners who hold their titles from the State, and the Indian Princes, whose power, privileges, and security against internal rebellion are guaranteed by the British Crown' ('The Mechanism of British Rule' in

Martin D. Lewis, ed., *The British in India. Imperialism or Trusteeship?*, 1962, p. 72. For the use of an Indian class of middlemen who served as revenue officers in parts of India, see W. H. Moreland and Atul Chandra Chatterjee, *A Short History of India*, 4th ed., 1957, p. 285 298–300, 317f., 335. During the long period of imperial rule, in some areas of life the use of Indians was increased (see Mitchell), while in others, such as the criminal justice system, it declined (Moreland and Chatterjee, p. 316).

4. For this history, see I Macc. and Josephus, *Antiq.* 12.234–13.218.

5. Josephus, *Antiq.* 14.

6. One example of Rome's use of a client ruler: Augustus gave Herod Trachonitis 'to prevent it from again being used by the brigands as a base for raids upon Damascus' (*War* 1.399).

7. On this saying, see E. P. Sanders, *Judaism: Practice and Belief 63* BCE – 66 CE (hereafter *P&B*), 1992, p. 519, n. 7.

8. Herod the Great: Matt. 2.1–22; Luke 1.5
   Antipas (the tetrarch of Galilee, Herod's son): Matt. 14.1–6; Mark 6.14–22; 8.15; Luke 3.1, 19; 8.3; 9.7, 9; 13.31; 23.7–15; Acts 4.27; 13.1
   Agrippa I (Herod's grandson): Acts 12.1–21
   Agrippa II (Herod's great-grandson): Acts 23.35
   Archelaus (the ethnarch of Judaea, Herod's son) is called by his own name in Matt. 2.22

9. In Scythopolis, which had a very large Gentile population, there were of course Gentile officials and institutions. Scythopolis is in geographical Galilee, but politically it was not under Antipas' jurisdiction. It was an independent city, as it had been since Pompey liberated it from Jewish control in 64 BCE. See Emil Schürer, *The History of the Jewish People in the Age of Jesus Christ*, revised by Geza Vermes and Fergus Millar (hereafter *HJP*), vol. 2, 1979, pp. 142–5.

10. Josephus, *Life* 65f.

11. See the list of prohibited marriages in Lev. 18.6–18. The Essenes, however, wished to prohibit a man from marrying his niece, on analogy with the prohibition against marrying an aunt.

12. Tiberius died during the campaign, and the Roman legate, Vitellius, recalled the troops; Aretas thus escaped unharmed (*Antiq.* 18.120–26).

13. Josephus, *Antiq.* 18.109–119.

14. See *HJP*, vol. 1, 1973, p. 357.

15. See *HJP*, vol. 1, p. 358. The inscription actually names Pilate as the prefect. Josephus uses the title 'procurator' for the first Roman governor of Judaea (*War* 2.117), but this is probably a retrojection from the later period. Moreover, Josephus and others who wrote in Greek did not always give precise translations of Latin titles. During the period 41–4, Judaea was governed not by a Roman administrator but by one of Herod's grandsons, Agrippa I.

16. See Thackeray's note to *War* 2.500 (Loeb Classical Library).

17. Booths (Tabernacles), during the reign of Alexander Jannaeus (103–76 BCE): *War* 1.88f. (Josephus remarks that 'it is on these festive occasions that sedition is most apt to break out'); Weeks (Pentecost), *c.* 40 BCE: *War* 1.253; Passover, 4 BCE: *War* 2.10–13; Weeks (Pentecost), 4 BCE: *War* 2.42–54. After Jesus' execution, see *War* 2.224.

18. On the prefect's right to execute, see *War* 2.117; 6.126. In 66, just before the revolt, Florus scourged and then crucified 3,600 people, including 'men of equestrian rank, men who, if Jews by birth, were at least invested with that Roman dignity' (*War* 2.306–8). The number of people executed, and the rank of some of them, shocked Josephus, not the fact that the procurator carried out exemplary executions. With regard to the warning inscription in the Temple, see most recently Peretz Segal, 'The Penalty of the Warning Inscription from the Temple of Jerusalem', *Israel Exploration Journal* 39, 1989, pp. 79–84. For the normal rules that governed equestrian provinces, see Adrian Sherwin-White, *Roman Society and Roman Law in the New Testament*, 1963.

19. For a narrative example of aspects of this procedure, see p. 266 below.

20. See *P&B*, ch. 21.

21. *War* 2.407.

22. *War* 4.313; cf. 4.206, 6,000. Not all these men were Temple guards during times of peace. There probably were, however, several thousand guards in all, who ordinarily served in rotation, as did the priests.

23. I deal more fully with some of these topics, especially the question of Graeco-Roman institutions, in my forthcoming paper 'Jesus in Historical Context', *Theology Today*, Oct. 1993 or Jan. 1994.

24. See further ch. 8 below.

25. *War* 2.169–74.

26. *War* 2.184–205; Philo, *Embassy* 159, 192–215.

27. John's message is discussed below, pp. 92f.

28. *War* 2.258–63; *Antiq.* 20.97–9, 167–72. Both Theudas and the Egyptian are mentioned in Acts: 5.36; 21.38.

29. *War* 2.499–555. In retrospect, Josephus thought that God had caused these events because he had decided to desert his sanctuary and permit its destruction (§539). That is, Cestius' defeat emboldened the Jews, who decided on full-scale war; this, in turn, brought about their destruction. At the time, however, the Jewish victory must have been regarded as a sign from God that the Jews would win.

30. See below, pp. 89f.

31. On eschatology, see below, pp. 93, 183f.

32. On the range of various hopes for the future, see *P&B*, ch. 14.

33. *War* 2.175–7. This incident shows that Pilate could be quite clever. He foresaw that the crowd would protest and planned a relatively gentle means of disciplining it, as American police sometimes use high-pressure water hoses against rioters, or as British troops often use rubber bullets against crowds in Northern Ireland. The cudgels killed some Jews, but had Pilate's soldiers drawn their swords, the chances of a large riot or even an insurrection would have been greater.

34. *War* 1.88–98.

4. *Judaism as a Religion*

1. All the topics in this chapter are discussed in detail in *P&B*.

2. In the surrounding cultures, there were both female and male gods, but in the Jewish conception God was very definitely male. This is a historical work, and it would misrepresent the sources to refer to God as 'she'.

3. Wisd. 13.1; Rom. 1.20.

4. On the sequence transgression – sickness as God's chastisement – forgiveness, see for example I. Cor. 11.27–32.

5. *Apion* 2.146; Philo, *Special Laws* 4.97; and elsewhere.

6. Tobit 4.15; *Shabbat* 31a; Philo, *Hypothetica* 7.6. On summaries of the law, and epigrams based on Lev. 19.18, see E. P. Sanders, *Jewish Law from Jesus to the Mishnah* (hereafter *JLJM*), 1990, pp. 69–71; *P&B*, pp. 192–4, 257–60.

7. This paragraph is quoted from *P&B*, pp. 248f.

8. Herod observed a super-strict purity rule in building the Temple: priests were trained as masons so that laymen would not enter the most sacred areas (*Antiq.* 15.390). Domestically, Herod provided himself, his family and his staff with religious immersion pools. (See *P&B*, pp. 225–7; in more detail, *JLJM*, pp. 219–21). Herod did not put objectionable images on his coins, such as his own portrait or that of Augustus. Only two of his actions, as far as we know, led pious Jews to question him. See the stories of his theatre and of the golden eagle above the gate of the Temple: *Antiq.* 15.268–75; *War* 1.648–50. He clearly calculated whether or not his public buildings, and his love of the theatre and games, would give so much offence that public uprisings would ensue. I find the most impressive fact to be that he built *gymnasia* for Gentile cities outside his realm, but not a single *gymnasion* inside his kingdom, not even in Caesarea. He doubtless had read or been taught the lessons of the revolt against Antiochus IV Epiphanes (above, p. 17). On Herod's policy, see further my essay 'Jesus in Historical Context'.

9. For fuller discussion, see *P&B*, chs. 10, 15, 18 (especially pp. 388–404), 21.

10. For an example of an ordinary priest who was a Pharisee, see *Life* 197, cited above. For the connection between Sadducees and aristocrats, see n. 20 below.

11. For the anti-monarchical tendency, see I Sam. 8.10–18. Deut. 17.14–20 shows the attempt to restrain the power of the king. Moreover (as we noted), Moses handed the law to the priests to administer (Deut. 31.9). For the preference of priestly rule to kingly rule, see *Antiq.* 14.41. Josephus, who was himself a priest, was perhaps prejudiced, but it is a fact that in his day priests had governed Israel for as many years as had kings, and they had done so fairly successfully. For Josephus' own view, that, if there had to be kings, they should be ruled by priests and a council, see *Antiq.* 4.186, 214–24, 304; 12.138–42; 13.166. The Dead Sea sectarians shared this view. They thought that in the last days there would be a Messiah who was a son of David, but they also expected a priestly Messiah, a Messiah of Aaron, who would actually be in charge. Moreover, the *Community Rule* depicts priests as being the principal leaders and instructors of the sect. See *P&B*, p. 297.

12. Biblical law assumes that virtually all males were farmers or herdsmen, except the priests and Levites (the lesser clergy).

13. Josephus' principal descriptions of the Pharisees are in *War* 2.162–6; *Antiq.* 18.12–15. See further *P&B*, chs. 18 and 19.

14. The history of handwashing is extremely complicated. See *JLJM*, pp. 228–31, 262f.

15. *War* 2.120–61; *Antiq.* 18.18–22; Philo, *Every Good Man is Free* 75–91; *Hypothetica* 11.1–18.

16. Philo, *Every Good Man is Free* 75; Josephus, *Antiq.* 18.20.

17. Geza Vermes, *The Dead Sea Scrolls: Qumran in Perspective*, 1977; *The Dead Sea Scrolls in English*, tr. Geza Vermes, 3rd ed., 1987; Michael Knibb, *The Qumran Community*, 1987; Philip R. Davies, *Behind the Essenes: History and Ideology in the Dead Sea Scrolls*, 1987. My own most recent account of the Essenes is *P&B*, chs. 16 and 17.

18. Josephus, *War* 2.162; *Life* 191 and elsewhere. So also Acts 26.5; cf. 22.3.

19. *Antiq.* 20.199.

20. They are mentioned with no description in Matt. 3.7 and 16.1–12. The passage about the resurrection is Matt. 22.23–33 // Mark 12.18–27 // Luke 20.27–40. For the same point, see also Acts 23.6–8. Acts 5.17 closely connects the high priest and the Sadducees, and their public responsibility for good order is implied in Acts 4.1.

5. External Sources

1. Suetonius, 'The Deified Claudius' in *The Lives of the Twelve Caesars*.

2. Tacitus, *Annals* 15.44.

3. I shall quote the text as we now have it, bracketing the most obvious additions by Christian scribes. Some non-bracketed phrases are also dubious, and we cannot be sure that the scribes only added phrases; they may have eliminated some of what Josephus wrote. The translation is that of L. H. Feldman in the Loeb Classical Library.

About this time there lived Jesus, a wise man, [if indeed one ought to call him a man]. For he was one who wrought surprising feats and was a teacher of such people as accept the truth gladly. He won over many Jews and many of the Greeks. [He was the Messiah.] When Pilate, upon hearing him accused by men of the highest standing amongst us, had condemned him to be crucified, those who had in the first place come to love him did not give up their affection for him. [On the third day he appeared to them restored to life, for the prophets of God had prophesied these and countless other marvellous things about him.] And the tribe of the Christians, so called after him, has still to this day not disappeared.

4. Tacitus, *Annals* 15.44, cited above.

5. Josephus, *Antiq.* 18.55–62; *War* 2.169–77; Philo, *Embassy* 299–305.

6. Julius Caesar had revised the Roman calendar in a very useful way, so that it agreed very closely with a solar or seasonal year, as does the modern western calendar. As the quotations from Luke and Josephus reveal, however, the Roman calendar was not universally adopted throughout the empire. An author writing for a restricted audience could use a calendar that his readers would understand. Had Josephus, for example, written in Hebrew or Aramaic for a Jewish audience, he could have given dates in a much more straightforward way. On calendars in the ancient world, and the problems involved in transferring ancient dates to our system, see E. J. Bickerman, *Chronology of the Ancient World*, revised ed., 1980.

7. *HJP*, vol. 1, pp. 284–6.

8. *War* 6.250. Josephus shared this tendency with others; see, for example, Mishnah *Ta'anit* 4.6.

9. On Varus and Quirinius, *HJP*, vol. 1, pp. 257–9, 399–427.

10. We shall discuss some of these topics in the next chapter.

6. The Problems of the Primary Sources

1. E. P. Sanders and Margaret Davies, *Studying the Synoptic Gospels* (hereafter *SSG*), 1989.

2. On dates, see *SSG*, pp. 5–21.

3. See *SSG*, ch. 9.

4. Paul's letters were composed in the fifties and possibly early sixties. The first gospel is probably post-70.

5. Matthew: Mark 3.18, Matt. 9.9 and elsewhere; John: Mark 3.17, Gal. 2.9 and elsewhere; Mark: Col. 4.10, I Peter 5.13 and elsewhere; Luke: Philem. 24 and elsewhere.

6. *SSG*, pp. 7–15, 21–4.

7. The fullest English translation of New Testament apocrypha is Edgar Hennecke, *New Testament Apocrypha*, ed. Wilhelm Schneemelcher, English translation ed. R. McL. Wilson, 2 vols., 1963, 1965.

8. On this problem, see p. 53 above and Appendix I.

9. So Billy Graham on TV, 5 September 1991; this is a common explanation of Judas.

7. *Two Contexts*

1. Compare the 'covenant-establishing acts' discussed in ch. 4 above (p. 34).

2. Paul's own mission: Rom. 11.13–16; 15.14–21. He quotes passages from the Hebrew Bible about the inclusion of Gentiles earlier in ch. 15. See E. P. Sanders, *Paul*, 1991, pp. 1–7.

3. In Mark the identification is only implicit; note also the Baptist's clothing, which recalls Elijah: Matt. 3.4; Mark 1.6; II Kgs 1.8.

4. See Margaret Davies' discussions in *SSG*, chs. 17, 18, 19.

5. The Protestant Bible does not include the Old Testament apocrypha, though some translations now print these works as a third section, in addition to the Old Testament and New Testament. The Catholic Bible includes the apocrypha as part of the Old Testament. I and II Macc., Judith and other works give some information about the Persian and Hellenistic periods, but there is no history of the Persian period, and a very partial history of the Hellenistic period.

6. *Typos* in I Cor. 10.6, 11 is usually translated as 'example' or 'warning', which conveys the correct sense but obscures the terminology.

7. See *HJP*, vol. 1, pp. 259, 399–427.

8. Joseph Fitzmyer, *The Gospel according to Luke I–IX*, 1981, pp. 404f., who cites the distinguished Roman historian, Ronald Syme. Syme pointed out that the similarities between 4 BCE and 6 CE easily led to confusion and still sometimes do: W. W. Tarn, a well-known Hellenistic historian, once wrote that Herod died in 6 CE.

9. On prophecies and portents, see Josephus, *War* 3.351–3; 6.291; 6.288–315.

10. On anti-monarchical views in the Hebrew Bible and Josephus, see p. 42 and n. 11 (p. 297) above.

11. For example, Philo, *Who is the Heir of Divine Things* 168–72; Josephus, *Antiq.* 15.375. I have given a substantial list in 'The Question of Uniqueness in the Teaching of Jesus', Ethel M. Wood Lecture 1990, University of London, pp. 28f.

12. See the entire section John 1.19–37.

8. The Setting and Method of Jesus' Ministry

1. Called: Mark 1.16–20; near Capernaum, Mark 1.21; according to John 1.44, however, Peter, Andrew and Philip were from Bethsaida.

2. Most passages in Mark are paralleled by passages in Matthew or Luke or both. I shall occasionally give full references (Mark 2.1–12 // Matt. 9.1–8 // Luke 5.17–26), but this is very burdensome and is often uninformative. I shall sometimes cite a passage as Mark 2.1 & parr., meaning Mark and both the other two synoptics. Mark 2.1 par. Luke means that the passage is in Mark and Luke, but not Matthew (similarly Matt. par. Luke, etc.). Sometimes, however, I shall regard it as unnecessary to indicate whether or not a passage is paralleled. Most English translations have cross-references, and the interested reader can find the parallels even when I do not cite them. The most convenient way of studying parallels is to obtain a synopsis, such as *Gospel Parallels*, ed. Burton H. Throckmorton, or *New Gospel Parallels*, ed. Robert W. Funk.

3. On first-century synagogues, see *JLJM*, pp. 73f., 77–81, 340–3 (especially n. 29); *P&B*, pp. 197–202.

4. On prayer in first-century Judaism, see *JLJM*, pp. 72–7; *P&B*, pp. 196f., 260–62.

5. Two further questions are usually asked about synagogue services. One is whether or not the Bible was read in Hebrew and then translated informally into Aramaic. If people in attendance could not understand Hebrew when it was read, then there would have been a translation, but we do not know how many people could understand Hebrew. The second question is whether or not women attended synagogues. There is no direct evidence, but my guess is that they did. They could attend the Temple services, and synagogues were much less restrictive than the Temple.

6. These passages on the call of the disciples are discussed below, pp.118–20.

7. Vassilios Tzaferis, *Excavations at Capernaum I: 1978–1982*, 1989, p. 216.

8. Michael Avi-Yonah, 'Beth-saida'. *The Interpreter's Dictionary of the Bible*; James F. Strange, 'Beth-saida', *The Anchor Bible Dictionary*; there are difficulties in identifying Bethsaida.

9. As far as we can tell, Jews generally accepted the rule that people should not travel on the sabbath, since Exod. 16.29 explicitly commands them to

remain in their places on the sabbath. This was understood to mean that they should not travel far. The rabbis, who probably continued the view of the Pharisees, limited a sabbath's day journey to 2,000 cubits (about 1,000 yards or metres). The Essenes were stricter: 1,000 cubits (about 500 yards or metres). Both of these distances were based on a biblical passage (Num. 35.4f.). (See *P&B*, p. 367.) My guess is that most people accepted the Pharisees' view, or possibly one that was a little more lenient.

10. I have discussed some of these topics in 'Jesus in Historical Context'.

11. The term 'Decapolis' was used by various writers, but it was not a numerically precise term. 'Ten Cities More or Less' would be more accurate. See Jean-Paul Rey-Coquais, 'Decapolis', *The Anchor Bible Dictionary*. Scythopolis, which is discussed below, was west of the Jordan. Two cities mentioned in the synoptics, Gerasa (Mark 5.1) and Gadara (Matt. 8.28), belonged to this group of cities.

12. Mark 5.1–20 & parr. (Gerasa was one of the cities of the Decapolis); 7.31. The second passage seems to put the Decapolis between the Sea of Galilee, and Tyre and Sidon to the west. Mark's geography is confused.

13. My colleague Eric Meyers informs me that archaeology has not yet found evidence of general destruction. He and others are still actively engaged in excavations at Sepphoris.

14. Antipas forcibly settled Tiberias, recruiting for this purpose 'a promiscuous rabble', but also some people of distinction (*Antiq.* 18.36–8).

15. The Greek word is *prostatis*. 'Helper' in the RSV, 'deacon' in the NRSV and 'a great help' in the NIV are too vague; 'good friend' in the NEB is totally off; 'has looked after' in the JB is close. Translators obviously do not like to say that Paul had a patroness.

16. We noted above that 'his house' in Mark 2.15 could be Jesus' house, but more likely it is Levi's.

17. *Antiq.* 17.41f.; cf. *War* 1.110f. on Salome Alexandra's support of the Pharisees.

18. These figures are approximate. See. R. B. Y. Scott, 'Palestine, Climate', *The Interpreter's Dictionary of the Bible*; Frank S. Frick, 'Palestine, Climate', *The Anchor Bible Dictionary*.

9. *The Beginning of Jesus' Ministry*

1. On fasting in Hebrew law, Jewish tradition and the gospels, see *JLJM*, pp. 81–4. Individuals sometimes fasted, there were sometimes emergency

community fasts (especially during times of drought), and probably the anniversary of the destruction of the first Temple was observed as a fast. There may have been other community fasts as well.

2. H. J. Rose, 'Mythology', *The Oxford Classical Dictionary*, 2nd ed., reprinted 1987, p. 718.

3. Luke lists Andrew in 6.14, but does not narrate his call.

4. On James the brother of Jesus, see Acts 15.13; 21.18; Gal. 1.19; 2.1–12. It appears from I Cor. 15.7 that James had a separate resurrection experience, and presumably this accounts for his commitment to the early Christian movement. According to I Cor. 9.5, Jesus' brothers (plural) were missionaries. Later Christian tradition named Judas, one of the brothers mentioned in Mark 6.1–6, as a leading member of the Christian movement. It attributed to him the epistle of Jude in the New Testament. (In Greek the author of the epistle is named 'Judas', the name borne both by one of Jesus' brothers and by Jesus' betrayer. English translations attribute the epistle to 'Jude' in an attempt to prevent confusion.) The fourth-century historian Eusebius quotes a story from Hegesippus (second century) to the effect that grandsons of Judas, Jesus' brother, were believers and were interrogated by Domitian near the end of the first century (Eusebius, *Ecclesiastical History* 3.20).

5. In this passage it is simplest to think that John used Luke. There are, however, other possibilities, including common dependence on prior sources.

6. The leprosy laws cover two chapters, Lev. 13–14. The ancients could not determine clinical leprosy readily; consequently many diseases of the skin were called 'leprosy', and the 'leper' was segregated from society until free of signs for a substantial period, during which elaborate rules were observed. 'Uncleanness' or 'impurity' in general in biblical law is not a matter of sanitation or health, but rather of taboo. In the case of the leper, however, there was clearly fear of contagion in the medical sense. Nevertheless, leprosy was dealt with as a matter of *religious* impurity. A priest had to conduct an examination; the leper remained in isolation for a week, he shaved his beard, eyebrows and hair; he washed his clothes and bathed; he made sacrifices; and he was clean. It was the priest, not a physician, who could say, 'He is clean.' It was a society in which disease, contagion, moral transgression and the *rites de passage* were all governed by ritual laws. They were not segregated: this person to the physician, this one to the bathtub, this one to the priest. All the cases were at least in part ritual. They involved the immersion pool, sacrifice, and the Temple and priesthood.

7. On proto-gospels, see p. 60 above.

10. Miracles

1. 'Messiah' and 'Son of God' will be discussed more fully below, pp. 160–62, 240–46.

2. See Emma J. Edelstein and Ludwig Edelstein, *Asclepius: A Collection and Interpretation of the Testimonies*, 2 vols., 1945.

3. Morton Smith, *Jesus the Magician*, 1978, p. 9.

4. On Hanina and Honi, and their significance for understanding Jesus, see Geza Vermes, *Jesus the Jew*, 1973, pp. 69–82.

5. Geza Vermes, *Jesus the Jew*, p. 75; Babylonian Talmud, *Berakot* 34b; cf. Mishnah *Berakot* 5.5.

6. See for example Mishnah *Ta'anit* 3.9.

7. Geza Vermes, *Jesus the Jew*, pp. 69f.; Mishnah *Ta'anit* 3.8.

8. *War* 2.261–3; *Antiq.* 20.97f., 167–72.

9. Some ancient intellectuals, such as the Stoics, saw the difficulty of attributing intervention to a deity, but many Gentile philosophers were prepared to grant that the gods could act in the natural world. Socrates' last words were a request to one of his followers to take a promised sacrifice to the god of healing, Asclepius, presumably for bestowing some sort of favour on the philosopher.

10. See above, p. 138, on a similar healing attributed to Hanina.

11. As we noted earlier, there are no exorcisms in John. The Fourth Gospel, however, does reveal the assumption that demons could possess people. According to John, some people thought that Jesus was possessed by a demon. For demons in the Fourth Gospel, see John 7.20; 8.48–52; 10.20f. In this catalogue I omit the longer ending of Mark (16.9–20), which most scholars regard as a later addition.

12. The ancient manuscripts disagree on the number.

13. Morton Smith, *Jesus the Magician*.

14. Matthew here as elsewhere multiplies by two: two demoniacs; cf. 9.27 and 20.31 (two blind people).

15. Some of the stories in the apocryphal gospels of the second century and later may be implicitly heretical according to the Chalcedonian Definition – 'implicitly' because they do not actually say that Jesus was superhuman.

Possibly the authors, if challenged, could have maintained that they depict Jesus as being able to persuade God to do things, rather than being able to do them himself.

16. See the helpful comments of Joseph Fitzmyer, *The Gospel according to Luke I–IX*, pp. 734f.

17. The Gerasene demoniac (Mark 5.7 // Matt. 8.29 // Luke 8.28) and various demons according to the summary in Mark 3.11 // Luke 4.41.

18. 'Sons' in Hebrew was sometimes used generically to mean 'sons and daughters'.

19. For a related motif in Hebrew scripture, see Gen. 6.1–4.

20. As Geza Vermes proposed twenty years ago: see n. 4 above.

21. Above, p. 30.

11. *The Coming of the Kingdom*

1. Matthew's term, literally, is 'kingdom of the heavens'. 'Heavens' is a Jewish circumlocution for 'God' (one may compare the English phrase 'Merciful heavens!'), and Matthew's term may be closer to Jesus' own. In the present discussion, however, I shall use the more direct phrase 'kingdom of God'.

2. Christians who are philosophically inclined might well wish not to think of 'God's kingdom' as being physically and temporally defined at all. It appears to me, however, that first-century Jews, including Jesus, thought in these terms.

3. See above, pp. 31, 33.

4. Johannes Weiss, *Jesus' Proclamation of the Kingdom of God*, English translation 1971 (German original 1892); Albert Schweitzer, *The Quest of the Historical Jesus*, English translation 1910 (German original 1906).

5. Rudolph Bultmann, *Jesus and the Word*, English translation 1934, Scribner pb., p. 51 (German original 1926).

6. C. H. Dodd, *The Parables of the Kingdom*, revised 1961, pp. 29f. (1st ed. 1935).

7. Norman Perrin, *The Kingdom of God in the Teaching of Jesus,* 1963.

8. Two of the most prominent recent books in this camp are Marcus Borg,

Jesus: A New Vision, 1987, and Richard Horsley, *Jesus and the Spiral of Violence*, 1987. For the point that Luke 17.21 determines the issue, see Horsley, p. 167.

9. For example, where Mark and Matthew have Jesus predict during his trial that his judges will *see* the Son of Man *coming*, Luke has 'from now on the Son of Man shall be seated at the right hand . . . of God' (Mark 14.62 // Matt. 26.64 // Luke 22.68).

10. On 'has come upon' (Greek *ephthasen epi*), see my *Jesus and Judaism*, 1985 (hereafter *J&J*), p. 134.

11. Paul's own view of where the kingdom would be is difficult to establish with certainty. See *SSG*, pp. 337f. and nn. 3 and 4 (p. 353).

12. On this independence of sources, see p. 4 above.

13. I have given a catalogue of Jewish hopes for the future in *P&B*, ch. 14.

14. *The Scroll of the War of the Sons of Light against the Sons of Darkness* 2.2, 7–8; 3.13; 5.1; cf. 57.5f.).

15. Scholars often cite many other passages as proving that banqueting was a standing symbol of the new age, but this is the only one that actually makes the connection.

16. For this banquet, see the *Messianic Rule*. The significance of the meal in the Qumran *Community Rule*, column 6, however, is not as clear as many scholars think. For discussion of one of the problems, see *P&B*, pp. 352–7. Of course the sectarians thought that there would be festivals in the new age, since they would have charge of the Temple, but I am not persuaded that they saw eating as a pointer to, or symbol of, the future ideal time. With regard to the two Messiahs, see p. 241 and n. 2 (p. 308).

17. Irenaeus, *Against Heresies* 5.30–33. See *SSG*, p. 338 and n. 5 (p. 353).

12. *The Kingdom: Israel, Gentiles and Individuals*

1. For the assumption that Peter was the leading disciple, see for example Gal. 2.6–10.

2. See Mishnah *Sanhedrin* 10.

3. For Jewish hopes that in the last days Gentiles would convert, see *J&J*, pp. 82–5, 212–18; *P&B*, p. 295.

4. I assume that the Gerasene demoniac (Mark 5.1–20 & parr.) was a Gentile, but ethnic origin is not mentioned.

5. Cf. Luke 13.28f.

13. The Kingdom: Reversal of Values and Ethical Perfectionism

1. 'The kingdom of heaven is like a farmer': strictly speaking, a kingdom cannot be like a man, but this wording is typical of the parables in the gospels. It means, 'The kingdom of heaven is like the following case: a farmer . . .'

2. *Covenant of Damascus* 4.21–5.6.

3. Ben Sira 7.9; 34.18f.; 35.12; Philo, *Special Laws* 1.235–7.

14. Contention and Opposition in Galilee

1. *JLJM*, ch. 1.

2. Palestinian Talmud, *Hagigah* 77b (2.1).

3. Mishnah *Shabbat* 14.4. For this and similar cases, see *JLJM*, p. 13.

4. *Antiq.* 12.185–9.

5. Mishnah *'Eruvin* 6.2.

6. On showing consideration to enemies even in war, see Josephus, *Apion* 2.212; *Joseph and Aseneth* 29.3f. (in James H. Charlesworth, ed., *Old Testament Pseudepigrapha*, vol. 2, 1985, p. 246).

7. See Josephus, *Life* 279; *JLJM*, p. 13.

8. Philo, *Hypothetica* 7.18; Josephus, *Apion* 2.213.

9. I discussed these briefly in *JLJM*, p. 22.

10. On the Pharisees' debates about handwashing, see *JLJM*, pp. 228–31.

11. The quotation is from the *Letter of Aristeas* 234; for sacrifices, see 170f. (in James H. Charlesworth, ed., *Old Testament Pseudepigrapha*, vol. 2, pp. 28, 24). This and other examples are in *JLJM*, p. 28.

12. The prohibited foods are listed in Lev. 11 and Deut. 14, and the lists are both thorough and explicit.

13. See, e.g., Philo, *Special Laws* 1.299f., 324.

14. See Tobit 4.15; Philo, *Hypothetica* 7.6; Hillel according to Babylonian

Talmud, *Shabbat* 31a. On epigrammatic summaries of the law, see *P&B*, pp. 257–60.

15. Sophocles' play *Antigone* pivots around the desperate efforts of the heroine to bury her dead brother despite Creon's decree that he could not be buried. For both Jewish and Gentile views of burying the dead, see Martin Hengel, *The Charismatic Leader and His Followers*, English translation 1981.

16. In the Septuagint, the enumeration of chapters and verses is different. For Psalm 10, see LXX Psalm 9.22–39.

17. *J&J*, pp. 203–5.

15. Jesus' View of His Role in God's Plan

1. John 1.41; 4.25.

2. In this discussion, I am assuming that the 'Messiah of Israel' in the *Community Rule* is to be equated with the 'Branch of David' in the *Midrash on the Last Days*, though possibly these are two separate figures. For references to the Dead Sea Scrolls, see *P&B*, pp. 295–8.

3. See further below, p. 254.

4. On this exchange, see below, pp. 247, 270.

5. For the thunderbolt, see Robin Lane Fox, *Alexander the Great*, p. 214. On 'Son of God', see pp. 210–18.

6. In Matt. 3.17 the voice speaks in the third person: 'this is my . . . Son'.

7. 'Sons' here is generic; I alter the translation to 'children' in the next verses. Some translations use children here, since that is certainly Paul's meaning.

8. *I Enoch* is a composite work, made up of five main sections. Texts from each section, except the Similitudes (chs. 37–71), have been found at Qumran, which establishes these four parts as being pre-70. Scholars divide over the question of the date of the Similitudes. In my own view, the Similitudes show the work of Christian revisers.

9. See the parallel passages printed above, p. 181.

10. I doubt the authenticity of the second group, the predictions that the Son of Man must suffer, since these predictions agree precisely with later Christian theology. For our purposes, however, we do not need to decide.

16. Jesus' Last Week

1. Josephus, *Antiq.* 18.19: 'the Festival of Unleavened Bread, which we call Passover . . .' Similarly Luke 22.1: 'the feast of Unleavened Bread, which is called the Passover'; Mark 14.1: 'two days before the Passover and the feast of Unleavened Bread'; Mark 14.12 // Luke 22.7: the lamb was sacrificed on the first day of Unleavened Bread. For further passages in Josephus, see *P&B*, p. 511, n. 39.

2. Three pilgrimage festivals each year: Exod. 23.14; 34.23; Deut. 16.16.

3. In *War* 2.515 Josephus states that Lydda, a town fairly near Jerusalem, had emptied for the festival of Booths (Tabernacles). Passover was probably attended by more people than Booths.

4. *War* 6.420–27; 2.280.

5. *P&B*, pp. 125–8.

6. See p. 295 n. 17 above.

7. Philo, *Special Laws* 1.261–72.

8. Josephus, *War* 6.290. He calls the month by its Macedonian name, Xanthicus.

9. Lambs were the most common Passover sacrifice, but the Bible allows kids and even calves. See *P&B*, p. 511, n. 38.

10. I am following the synoptic chronology. According to John, in the year that Jesus died the fourteenth of Nisan fell on Friday, and Jesus was executed that day. See p. 53 above and Appendix I.

11. Since the fifth century, Christians have celebrated Jesus' entry to Jerusalem on the Sunday before Easter, that is, seven days before the resurrection rather than seven days before Passover: I assume that Jesus actually entered Jerusalem when everyone else did: Friday, 8 Nisan.

12. See ch. 14.

13. In Babylonia, in the fourth century BCE, the priests spent sacred money on themselves, rather than keeping the temples in repair (see *P&B*, p. 188). The Jerusalem priesthood seems to have been dedicated to the Temple service, and there is no hint that they neglected the physical fabric of the Temple or the sacrifices in favour of their own pockets. On the priests' piety, see *P&B*, pp. 91f., pp. 182–9.

14. Where Luke has 'Jerusalem surrounded by armies', Matthew and Mark have 'when you see the abomination of desolation set up where it ought not to be' (Mark 13.14 // Matt. 24.15). This probably refers to the threat by Gaius (Caligula) to have a statue erected in the Temple. If so, it comes from about the year 40 or 41. That is, in Matthew and Mark the introduction to this part of Jesus' teaching has already been influenced by things that occurred after Jesus' death. Luke moved the date another thirty years later.

15. *P&B* p. 58.

16. *War* 6.300. See also 2.539; 5.19; 5.412; *Antiq.* 20.166.

17. In the first century all Jews, as far as we know, regarded their God as God of the universe and thus as omnipresent. They could pray to him and receive his response anywhere, anytime. Nevertheless, they still regarded the Temple as the place where God was *especially* present. See further *P&B*, pp. 70f.

18. See above, pp. 13, 92f.

19. Above, p. 139.

20. *11 QTemple* 29.8–10.

21. Above, pp. 89, 240f.; cf. 184f.

22. Acts 2.46 and elsewhere (the earliest period); 21.28 (the accusation against Paul). It is possible that Paul was arrested for some other reason. In general, however, he wanted to dispense with the parts of the law that separate Jew from Gentile, and it is not inconceivable that he took a Gentile into the Temple.

23. Luke agrees in important respects with Paul rather than with Matthew and Mark.

24. As I explained above (p. 247), the adversative 'but' in Greek (*plēn*) probably signifies a negative; for this reason I have added [on the other hand].

25. Some details are different in *Antiq.* 20.118–36.

26. Quoted from *P&B*, pp. 329f., with a few alterations.

27. Not '*the* judges of *the* Sanhedrin', which is the Loeb Classical Library's translation.

28. Abbreviated from *P&B*, p. 469. Who had the right to execute is a contentious point of long standing, but I think that it should not be. Roman historians whom I have consulted think that Sherwin-White (*Roman*

Society and Roman Law in the New Testament) was correct in arguing that in equestrian provinces (like Judaea) only the prefect or procurator had the power of life and death. The argument is supported by *War* 2.117. A speech that Josephus attributes to Titus supplies interesting evidence. Trying to persuade the defenders of Jerusalem to surrender, he asked, 'And did we not permit you to put to death any who passed [the balustrade in the Temple], even if he were a Roman?' (*War* 6.126). The precise wording seems to imply that permission to execute anyone who trespassed the barrier was a special benefit, though the weight falls on the clause 'even a Roman'. Execution by mob violence, of course, was another matter (as in Acts 7.57f.). If no harm (i.e., disruption) came of it, it might be overlooked.

29. Abbreviated from *P&B*, pp. 140f.

30. Above, p. 30.

31. Many scholars think that Luke had an independent source for the Jewish trial. In my own view, Luke's principal differences from Mark are best explained as editorial changes.

32. In John's Gospel, of course, this has a double meaning: Jesus died in order to save people in another sense.

17. Epilogue: The Resurrection

1. The best manuscripts of Mark end at 16.8, just after the women find the empty tomb, and there is no resurrection account. Earlier in Mark, however, Jesus predicts that he will meet his followers in Galilee (14.28), and the young man at the tomb repeats this prediction (15.7). This implies a resurrection story like Matthew's.

2. See also John 20.14f.: Mary Magdalene thought that he was the gardener.

3. The author of Acts was of the view that Paul saw a bright light (Acts 9.3; 22.6; 26.13), but Paul's view was that he had seen the Lord.

4. In *Macbeth* Banquo's ghost and the ghostly dagger, 'a dagger of the mind'; in *Hamlet*, his father's ghost.

5. See, e.g., Plutarch, *Brutus* 36.

6. I Kgs 17.8–14; II Kgs 4.18–36; Mark 5.21–43 (//Matthew 9.18–26; Luke 8.40–56); Luke 7.11–17; Acts 9.36–43; John 11.5–44; Philostratus, *Life of Apollonius of Tyana* 4.45; Pliny, *Natural History* 26.13; Apuleius, *Florida* 19.

7. That the author of Luke–Acts avoided precise repetition is clear in his

three acounts of Paul's conversion. For example, in one story (Acts 22.17–21), after the Lord first appeared to Paul, Paul went to Damascus and then to Jerusalem, where Jesus again appeared to him. It was at this second appearance that the Lord commissioned Paul to be apostle to the Gentiles. In Acts 9, however, the statement that the Lord appointed Paul to go to the Gentiles comes in Damascus (Acts 9.15) The author of Luke–Acts was not stupid; he doubtless knew that his stories varied. He could have told the same story in the same way, but that would not have been as good a narrative. Like many other authors, both ancient and modern, he disliked repetition; like other ancient authors, he would change events in order to avoid it.

Appendix I. Chronology

1. Many modern Christian scholars think that 'Passover' technically applies to the meal on 15 Nisan, and thus that 14 Nisan is the day before Passover (one example among many: Karl Donfried, 'Chonology', *The Anchor Bible Dictionary*, vol. 1, p. 1015). This is anachronistic and completely contrary to ancient evidence, beginning with the Bible, which states that Passover is on the fourteenth (Exod. 12.6; Lev. 23.5). In pre-70 Judaism 'the Passover' was technically the animal, and the day of Passover was the day on which the animal was sacrificed (e.g., Josephus, *Antiq.* 3.248f.; Philo, *Special Laws* 2.148–55; see further *P&B*, pp. 132f. and notes). The meal was held on the first day of Unleavened Bread, 15 Nisan. Since the destruction of the Temple, however, Passover in Jewish usage has come to refer to the meal, and this post-70 Jewish development explains the anachronistic dates given by modern scholars.

One of the sources of modern confusion is John 19.14, which says that Jesus was executed on 'the day of preparation for the Passover'. John may already have made the same mistake as modern Christian scholars: he seems to think that 'the Passover' was the meal and that the 'day of preparation' was the day of the sacrifice. In any case, John parallels Jesus' execution with the slaughter of the Passover lambs: 'none of his bones shall be broken', in John 19.36, is a quotation from Exod. 12.46 and other passages in the Hebrew Bible, all referring to the Passover lamb. It is the importance of this parallel that leads modern scholars to the view that, according to John, Jesus was executed on Passover day, 14 Nisan, when the lambs were sacrificed, rather than the next day, after the meal. John confusingly called the day of sacrifice the 'day of preparation'. John and the synoptics agree, however, that Jesus was executed on Friday, the day before the sabbath (for John, see 19.31).

2. Colin J. Humphreys and W. G. Waddington, 'Astronomy and the Date of the Crucifixion' in *Chronos, Kairos, Christos: Nativity and Chronological Studies Presented to Jack Finegan*, eds., Jerry Vardaman and Edwin M. Yamauchi, 1989, pp. 165–81, here p. 167. Humphreys and Waddington are Oxford scientists.

3. J. K. Fotheringham, 'The Evidence of Astronomy and Technical Chronology for the Date of the Crucifixion', *Journal of Theological Studies* 35, 1934, pp. 146–62, here pp. 159f.

4. Lev. 23.9–14, as explained by Josephus, *Antiq.* 3.251; see *P&B*, pp. 152f.

5. See the studies by Fotheringham and by Humphreys and Waddington.

6. Nikos Kokkinos, 'Crucifixion in AD 36: The Keystone for Dating the Birth of Jesus', *Chronos, Kairos, Christos* (n. 2), pp. 133–63. He correctly cites the earlier study by T. Keim (p. 134, n. 3), whose work was translated into English in 1883. One can add other names: see the discussion in Harold W. Hoehner, *Herod Antipas*, 1972, pp. 124–31.

7. For this sequence, see Josephus, *Antiq.* 18.106–25.

8. On this passage, which was revised by Christian scribes, see above, p. 298 n. 3. I assume, however, that the scribe who revised the account did not move it. If a Christian scribe had rearranged Josephus he would have put Jesus and John the Baptist together.

9. Jerry Vardaman, 'Jesus' Life: A New Chronology', *Chronos, Kairos, Christos* (n. 2), pp. 55–82. Vardaman does not cite his predecessor, R. Eisler, who proposed this view in 1929. Eisler thought that Jesus was executed in 21 and John in 35. See the discussion in Harold W. Hoehner, *Herod Antipas*, pp. 126–8. Vardaman, however, pushes John's activity and death early, to agree with Jesus' execution in 21.

10. Eisler thought that both sections were chronologically correct, and this led him to place John's death fourteen years after Jesus' (see the previous note). Of the scholars being considered here, Vardaman dates both John and Jesus early, while Kokkinos dates them both late.

11. Robin Lane Fox, *The Unauthorized Version*, 1991, pp. 33f. and note on p. 423.

12. Nikos Kokkinos, 'Crucifixion in AD 36', p. 134.

13. I give a literal translation. Kokkinos proposed '[Aretas] made this the start of a quarrel: a dispute about boundaries . . .' (p. 134). In his translation, the dispute over boundaries had already arisen; that was 'the start of [the]

quarrel', and the divorce triggered an immediate invasion. But this is not what Josephus wrote.

14. Nikos Kokkinos, 'Crucifixion in AD 36', p. 135. Kokkinos is criticizing Hoehner.

15. So Harold W. Hoehner, *Herod Antipas*, pp. 125–31.

16. It seems to me that the most probable reconstruction is that Aretas' invasion did not follow hard on the heels of Antipas' dismissal of his daughter. There were border disputes between Aretas and Antipas (*Antiq.* 18.113), and border disputes typically last for some time before there is direct military action. Thus the dispute between Antipas and his father-in-law may have simmered for a few years before Aretas invaded. See above, n. 13.

INDEX OF PASSAGES

315

POST-BIBLICAL JEWISH LITERATURE

Josephus

Apocrypha and Pseudepigrapha

Philo of Alexandria

INDEX OF NAMES AND
SUBJECTS